ONE G(

MW00789633

Graeco-Roman religion in its classic form was polytheistic; on the other hand, monotheistic ideas enjoyed wide currency in ancient philosophy. This contradiction provides a challenge for our understanding of ancient pagan religion. Certain forms of cult activity, including acclamations of 'one god' and the worship of Theos Hypsistos, the highest god, have sometimes been interpreted as evidence for pagan monotheism. This book discusses pagan monotheism in its philosophical and intellectual context, traces the evolution of new religious ideas in the time of the Roman Empire, and evaluates the usefulness of the term 'monotheism' as a way of understanding these developments in later antiquity outside the context of Judaism and Christianity. In doing so, it establishes a new framework for understanding the relationship between polytheistic and monotheistic religious cultures between the first and fourth centuries AD.

STEPHEN MITCHELL is Leverhulme Professor of Hellenistic Culture at the University of Exeter and a Fellow of the British Academy. His previous books include *A History of the Later Roman Empire AD 284–641* (2007).

PETER VAN NUFFELEN is Research Professor of Ancient History at the University of Ghent. He has published numerous articles on aspects of the ancient and medieval worlds, and has recently edited *Faces of Hellenism* (2009), and co-edited (with Stephen Mitchell) *Monotheism Between Christians and Pagans in Late Antiquity* (2009).

ONE GOD

Pagan monotheism in the Roman Empire

EDITED BY

STEPHEN MITCHELL and PETER VAN NUFFELEN

CAMBRIDGE
UNIVERSITY PRESS

CAMBRIDGE
UNIVERSITY PRESS

University Printing House, Cambridge CB2 8BS, United Kingdom

One Liberty Plaza, 20th Floor, New York, NY 10006, USA

477 Williamstown Road, Port Melbourne, VIC 3207, Australia

314-321, 3rd Floor, Plot 3, Splendor Forum, Jasola District Centre, New Delhi - 110025, India

79 Anson Road, #06-04/06, Singapore 079906

Cambridge University Press is part of the University of Cambridge.

It furthers the University's mission by disseminating knowledge in the pursuit of
education, learning and research at the highest international levels of excellence.

www.cambridge.org
Information on this title: www.cambridge.org/9781108984966

© Cambridge University Press 2010

First published 2010
First paperback edition 2021

A catalogue record for this publication is available from the British Library

Library of Congress Cataloging in Publication data
One god : pagan monotheism in the Roman Empire / edited by StephenMitchell,
Peter van Nuffelen.
p. cm.
Includes bibliographical references and index.
ISBN 978-0-521-19416-7 (hardback)
1. Monotheism – History. 2. Paganism – History. 3. Rome – Religion.
I. Mitchell, Stephen,
1948– II. Van Nuffelen, Peter. III. Title.
bl221.o54   2010
211´34 – dc22   2010000129

ISBN 978-0-521-19416-7 Hardback
ISBN 978-1-108-98496-6 Paperback

Contents

Preface and acknowledgements   *page* vii
List of abbreviations   ix

1 Introduction: the debate about pagan monotheism   1
   Stephen Mitchell and Peter Van Nuffelen

2 Pagan monotheism as a religious phenomenon   16
   Peter Van Nuffelen

3 Pagan ritual and monotheism   34
   John North

4 The case for pagan monotheism in Greek and
   Graeco-Roman antiquity   53
   Michael Frede

5 Monotheism between cult and politics: the themes of the
   ancient debate between pagan and Christian monotheism   82
   Alfons Fürst

6 The price of monotheism: some new observations on a current
   debate about late antiquity   100
   Christoph Markschies

7 Megatheism: the search for the almighty god and the
   competition of cults   112
   Angelos Chaniotis

8 *Deus deum . . . summorum maximus* (Apuleius): ritual
   expressions of distinction in the divine world in the
   imperial period   141
   Nicole Belayche

v

9   Further thoughts on the cult of Theos Hypsistos   167
    Stephen Mitchell

Bibliography   209
General index   231
Index of authors, works and citations   233

Preface and acknowledgements

This volume has its origins in a research project on the intellectual background to pagan monotheism, financed by the Arts and Humanities Research Council, and directed at the University of Exeter by Stephen Mitchell from 2004 to 2007. The funding provided for a post-doctoral research fellowship, taken by Dr Peter Van Nuffelen, and a PhD studentship, awarded to Anna Collar. Within the framework of the project they have respectively completed a monograph on philosophy and religion in the Roman Empire, from the first century BC to the second century AD, provisionally entitled 'Philosophical readings of religion in the post-Hellenistic period', which has focused on the evidence of major writers from Varro to Numenius, and a thesis on networks and the diffusion of religious innovation in the Roman Empire, based on a theorised approach to the documentary evidence for three forms of worship, the cult of Iuppiter Dolichenus, Diaspora Judaism, and the cult of Theos Hypsistos. As a focal point, we organised an international conference on pagan monotheism in the Roman world, held at Exeter in July 2006, which included more than thirty papers. These have formed the basis for two publications, a collection of essays entitled *Monotheism between Christians and Pagans in Late Antiquity*, edited by Stephen Mitchell and Peter Van Nuffelen and published by Peeters, Leuven (2009), and the present volume.

This addresses two related issues that were at the heart of our research. First, what was pagan monotheism? How should the term be defined, and how useful is it as a concept for understanding religious developments in the first four centuries AD? Second, is it possible to classify significant aspects of pagan cultic activity during this period as monotheistic? The introduction that follows presents the Exeter monotheism project in the context of other recent work on monotheism in antiquity, and indicates the different approaches to these questions by the contributors.

The British Academy supplemented AHRC financing with a conference grant. Kerensa Pearson, of the Exeter Classics Department, expedited many of the practical arrangements, as she has done on many similar occasions. Anna Collar designed the web-site: www.huss.ex.ac.uk/classics/ conferences/pagan_monotheism/home.html, which remains accessible as a record of the proceedings. The papers by Fürst and Belayche in this volume have been translated from their original German and French versions by Stephen Mitchell. We are especially indebted to Professor Hasan Malay of Izmir who provided the photograph of the much discussed inscription for a priest of the 'one and only god' which is reproduced on the book's dust-jacket and on p. 154 below. Peter Van Nuffelen not only organised the conference, but also, critically, set out its intellectual agenda with a version of the paper that is published in this volume. All the participants, not only those who offered papers, contributed enormously to lively discussions, which have left a perceptible mark in the subsequent publications. It is necessary to single out Michael Frede among these. He himself, by his role as contributor and co-editor with Polymnia Athanassiadi of the 1999 volume *Pagan Monotheism in Late Antiquity*, can reasonably claim to be the modern father of this subject. His own interventions at the Exeter meeting gave a decisive steer to many sessions. The developed version of his own lecture, which was sent to us in July 2007, was perhaps the last major piece of scholarly work that he completed before his untimely death. We would like to dedicate this volume, in sadness and gratitude, to his memory.

Stephen Mitchell and Peter Van Nuffelen

 Arts & Humanities
Research Council

Abbreviations

Periodical titles are abbreviated according to the conventions of *L'Année Philologique*, and short titles of other collections and ancient works follow the practice of the *Oxford Classical Dictionary*. Note in addition that inscriptions from particular sites are often cited in the form *I.* + ancient city name. Many are published in the series Inschriften Griechischer Städte aus Kleinasien.

AE	*L'Année Epigraphique*
Bull. ép.	*Bulletin épigraphique*, published in *Revue des études grecques*
CIG	*Corpus inscriptionum Graecarum*
CIRB	*Corpus inscriptionum regni Bosporani*
CMRDM	E. N. Lane, *Corpus monumentorum religionis dei Menis*, 4 vols., Leiden, 1971–8
CIMRM	M. J. Vermaseren, *Corpus inscriptionum et monumentorum religionis mithriacae*, 2 vols., The Hague, 1956, 1960
IGLS	*Inscriptions grecques et latines de Syrie*
IGUR	*Inscriptiones Graecae urbis Romae*
IJO	*Inscriptiones Judaicae Orientis*
IOSPE	*Inscriptiones orae septentrionalis Ponti Euxini*
JIWE	*Jewish Inscriptions of Western Europe*
PTS	*Patristische Texte und Studien*
RECAM	*Regional Epigraphic Catalogues of Asia Minor*
RICIS	L. Bricault, *Recueil des inscriptions concernant les cultes isiaques*, 3 vols., Paris, 2005
SBAU	*Sammelbuch griechischer Urkunden aus Ägypten*
SGO	*Steinepigramme aus dem Griechischen Osten*

CHAPTER I

Introduction: the debate about pagan monotheism

Stephen Mitchell and Peter Van Nuffelen

Within the largely stable social and political structures of the Roman Empire, the most far-reaching change was the religious revolution by which the polytheistic environment of the age of Augustus gave way to the overwhelming predominance of monotheism in the age of St Augustine. The study of monotheism is not easy for students of classical antiquity. This transformation in religious ideas and behaviour had profound consequences for individuals, for social organisation, for the exercise of political authority, and, above all, for the way in which men and women understood their place in the world. The prevalence of monotheism now marks one of the largest differences between the modern world and classical antiquity. Precisely for this reason the differences between Graeco-Roman polytheism and the Jewish, Christian or Islamic monotheisms, which have dominated our own religious and cultural experience since the end of antiquity, pose a serious challenge to our understanding of the past. We view ancient religion through a filter of assumptions, experiences and prejudice. Monotheism contains its own internalised value judgements about polytheistic paganism, and these have always influenced, and sometimes distorted, the academic study of ancient religion.

Monotheism today seems not only to have triumphed historically but also to be morally superior to polytheism. This is one of the reasons why the study of paganism is often segregated from historical work on early Christianity or Judaism.[1] Monotheism itself, in the strong and restrictive sense of believing in and worshipping only one god, is generally regarded as the defining element of post-classical religious systems. It is tempting therefore to treat the contrast between belief in one and belief in many gods as being the central issue at stake. However, the focus on the unity or singularity of the divinity has certainly diverted attention from other

---

[1] The most important modern exception to this rule is R. Lane Fox's magisterial historical study, *Pagans and Christians in the Mediterranean World from the Second Century* AD *to the Conversion of Constantine* (Lane Fox (1986)).

aspects of the transformation of ancient religion that have a fair claim to be more important than the bald fact of the triumph of monotheism. The emergence of post-classical religion in many forms brought with it changes in ritual, in social and political organisation, and in moral understanding, which require as much reflection and analysis as the fundamental shift in the perception that there was now only one god in place of many.

Monotheism has also become a central moral and political topic for the modern world.[2] The restrictions on belief and action demanded by strict monotheism entail a level of religious intolerance unknown in ancient paganism. Monotheism has thus become associated with religious fundamentalism. The political dangers of fundamentalism have accordingly led to serious theological reflection on the nature and effects of monotheism in contemporary societies. These preoccupations have encouraged a new attention to the phenomenon of belief in one god in its full historical context. Scholarly research has been concentrated on two periods in particular, the emergence of the worship of a single God in early Israel, set in its neighbouring Levantine and Egyptian environment,[3] and the growing prevalence of monotheism in later classical antiquity, which is the subject of this volume. The relationship between Jewish and early Christian monotheism and the paganism of the Graeco-Roman world of the Mediterranean and the Near East is of particular importance, because it was in this context that changes within religion and society won over most of the inhabitants of the ancient world to belief in a single God. We need to understand the essence of monotheism's appeal. We also, even more critically, need to define what monotheism is and was.

The papers in this volume derive from a conference held in July 2006 at the University of Exeter about pagan monotheism in the Roman Empire. This conference itself was part of a three-year research project concerned with pagan monotheism and its intellectual background, which ran from 2004 to 2007 under the direction of Stephen Mitchell and with funding from the Arts and Humanities Research Council. This project identified a series of research questions, which were also part of the explicit agenda of the conference. The first group of questions was conceptual. How should pagan monotheism be defined? In what ways should it be distinguished conceptually from other types of monotheism, in particular from

---

[2] The discussion has been particularly intense in Germany since the 1980s. The key work is Jan Assmann, *Die Mosaische Unterscheidung oder der Preis des Monotheismus* (Assmann (2003)), discussed below in Christoph Markschies' contribution to this volume. For a survey of the debate see Manemann (2002).

[3] Useful surveys are provided by Stolz (1996); Gnuse (1997) and (1999).

Christianity and Judaism? Were these differences fundamental or should all forms of monotheism be treated as essentially similar in nature? The second group of questions was concerned with the religious and intellectual context of pagan monotheism, and formed a particular focus for the work of the post-doctoral researcher on the project, Peter Van Nuffelen. What features of the intellectual climate of the Roman imperial period favoured the development of monotheistic beliefs and practices? In particular how and why did monotheistic ideas, which had been commonplace in mainstream Greek philosophy since the classical period, at this period begin to exercise a substantial influence on religious beliefs and cult practices, so that by the mid and later third century AD monotheistic ideas also seemed to emerge as part of the religious mainstream? What common ground and reciprocal influences can be identified between Greek philosophy in this period and the emerging monotheism of Jews and Christians? How had pagan religion itself developed in this environment?

Pagan monotheism has enjoyed particular currency in discussions of ancient religion since the publication in 1999 of the volume *Pagan Monotheism in Late Antiquity.*[4] Together the six papers in that collection suggested that pagan monotheism developed independently within Graeco-Roman culture to become a major force in the religious environment of late antiquity. The argument gained plausibility from the undisputed fact that Greek philosophers from sixth century BC until the end of antiquity had argued, with varying degrees of emphasis, that a single divine power lay behind the existence of the universe and our understanding of it, and that conceptually these views appeared to cohere with and indeed strongly influenced the viewpoint of Christian monotheism. What was less obvious was that this intellectual and philosophical insight had any significant religious consequences. Pragmatically, pagan polytheism continued to provide the standard framework for religious behaviour under the Roman Empire until the third century AD, much as it had done in the age of classical Greece. Outside Judaism and Christianity, monotheistic cult proved to be a much more elusive quarry than monotheistic thought.

So, around the apparently simple issue of whether belief in a single god came to replace the belief in many gods within Greek religious traditions, it has become necessary to pose a further series of questions designed to clarify the nature of this complex historical enquiry. For what is at stake here is not a superficial development, the discarding of one style of religion for another, as one might exchange a suit of clothes, but something that affects

---

[4] Athanassiadi and Frede (1999).

our understanding of society at large. It is necessary to define monotheism not simply as an intellectual construct but as a religious phenomenon. This in turn raises the question of defining what religion is, and assessing the role that it played in ancient society. There is, of course, no fixed answer to this question, as religion itself evolved and changed according to its social and historical context. Post-classical religion, in the form of the contemporary world's three great monotheisms, imposes significantly different forms of social and political organisation from those generated or shaped by pagan polytheism. This is particularly true when religion itself is linked to powerful secular political institutions.[5] Assmann has argued in numerous influential studies that monotheism introduced a basic moral transformation in social thinking. By introducing the distinction between true and false gods, it required men not only to choose truth, but also to reject falsehood. According to this analysis, the distinction provided a major spur to religious intolerance, something which is hardly perceptible within polytheism, and increased the potential for religiously inspired violence. This sweeping and generalised interpretation of the moral transformation which may supposedly be ascribed to monotheism is placed under direct and indirect scrutiny in this volume.

We need also to ask whether the religious transformation of later antiquity is due to the development of monotheism as such, or to the concomitant aspects of religious change which are subsumed within monotheism. These include the replacement of an indefinite mass of written and unwritten traditions by a fixed body of religious texts; the prevalence of exclusive belief in one God rather than the inclusive acceptance of the existence of many gods; the capacity of monotheism to be used as an instrument for social and political control at a supra-national level; and the emergence of religious identities as a key element in social organisation.[6] This book has taken shape as a series of essays that both pose and attempt to answer these questions. The problems that need to be addressed are closely related to wider religious, social and political issues, and the papers offer a variety of approaches to the phenomenon, and develop approaches to its many facets. In doing so they also put the spotlight on the effectiveness and functionality of the terms used to describe these religious changes. Is the term monotheism, or any of the other modern coinages that have been used to denote belief in one god, or at least belief in a supreme god, adequate to

[5] See Fowden (1993), an important and wide-ranging essay covering the period from Constantine to early Islam.
[6] Most of these issues are raised in John North's paper in this volume and the importance of the political context is stressed by Alfons Fürst's contribution.

describe not only the narrow phenomenon, but also the sum of the changes that it brought about? More specifically is pagan monotheism a concept that would have been intelligible to inhabitants of the ancient world, and one that they might have used to describe their own religious beliefs, or should it be seen rather as a heuristic tool, which may help to classify or categorise those beliefs from a modern viewpoint?

The 1999 papers edited by Athanassiadi and Frede were concerned with pagan monotheism in later antiquity, especially the period from the third to the sixth century AD, when Christianity had already become a major force. Thematically many of the contributions, led by the editors themselves, placed a strong emphasis on the philosophical background to monotheistic ideas, and on the contrasts and interplay between Christian and Platonic monotheism, which provide the backdrop for much high-level theological discussion in the later Roman world. Since the protagonists on both sides of this debate claimed to be monotheists, the term seemed to efface many important differences between Christians and Platonists and to create a homogeneous group of people who fundamentally had the same ideas about God but labelled themselves differently. This debate, especially among intellectuals, occupied a prominent place in the religious history of the fourth century and attracted considerable attention at the Exeter conference. Accordingly we have assembled a second collection of papers from the conference, entitled *Monotheism between Pagans and Christians in Late Antiquity*, which discusses these issues from various viewpoints and in relation to specific writers and their works.[7]

The contributors to *Pagan Monotheism in Late Antiquity* took over the framework of this ancient discussion, in particular by assuming the validity of the term 'monotheism' to describe the phenomena it discussed. Critics of this approach have questioned whether the single term can usefully be applied to the doctrinal forms of Christian monotheism and the much less specific and prescriptive forms of monotheistic belief to be found in the pagan philosophical tradition.[8] Thus various and different phenomena were subsumed under a single heading. Furthermore, only one of the papers in *Pagan Monotheism in Late Antiquity*, Mitchell's study of the worship of Theos Hypsistos, dealt explicitly with the question of pagan monotheistic cult, and this too has invited radical criticism, that it represents a fundamentally polytheistic phenomenon in misleading monotheist terms.

The papers in the current collection differ in important respects from those of the 1999 volume. On the one hand they have deliberately shifted

---

[7] Mitchell and Van Nuffelen (2009).   [8] *In primis* Edwards (2004).

the emphasis of the enquiry to the pre-Constantinian period of the Roman Empire, before Christianity became the prevailing religious norm, and before the later fourth-century debates between Platonists and Christians, although these cannot be left out of account as they colour much of our written source material. On the other they take a broader view of the documentary information, which provides the contextual framework for possible monotheistic cults. Pagan monotheism itself is not assumed to have objective status as a religious phenomenon, but is treated as a concept or a heuristic device to ask further questions about the development of religion in the Roman world, which between the first and fourth centuries evolved in other fundamental ways, not necessarily connected to monotheism. Thematically the papers fall into two groups. The first group deals with conceptual issues concerning the definition and evaluation of pagan monotheism, both as an object of study and as an analytical way of studying the religious culture of the Roman Empire. Less emphasis is placed on philosophy than in the 1999 volume, and more on the analysis of monotheism as a religious phenomenon in its social context. The second group of papers is largely concerned with documentary evidence for cults and ritual, which illustrate specific types of religious activity and illuminate the religious mentality of worshippers during this period. These papers highlight the particular difficulties of identifying and defining cultic forms of pagan monotheism.

The question of whether worship should be addressed to one or many gods is the most obvious way to frame an investigation of religious change between the first and fourth centuries. However, we are confronted at once by questions of definition. What constitutes monotheism? Many thinkers and writers of classical times, above all the Greek philosophers, could make statements about the unity of god, but only in a few cases, discussed in Frede's contribution to this volume, should they be defined in a rigorous sense as monotheists. Indeed, as John North's paper points out, for the most part writers about pagan religion simply did not make propositions about one or many gods that led to the creation of two opposed types of belief. From the pagan point of view monotheism, in a religious sense, was neither a meaningful category nor a contentious issue in the classical or Hellenistic Greek city states.

Forms of belief and practice, which at least bear some resemblance to monotheism, nevertheless began to emerge within pagan religious contexts from the late Hellenistic period. These owe their origin, in varying degrees and among other factors, to competition between cults, to intellectual speculation and the invention of new gods, to the fusion of smaller, localised cults into larger and more widespread patterns of worship, and to the influence of Jewish monotheism. However, it is open to debate how far the products of these developments can properly be called monotheistic. In most cases they did not require their followers to renounce other forms of religion. They were not exclusive and accordingly lacked many of the defining characteristics of the Christian and Islamic monotheisms of the post-classical world.

Alternative terms have been used to describe various forms of 'one god' belief, most notably henotheism, which enjoys wide currency in contemporary scholarship.[9] It nevertheless remains questionable whether the coining of henotheism as a new analytical category is a helpful tool in the debate, however practical it may be to differentiate between various styles of 'monotheism' in their historical contexts. Peter Van Nuffelen takes a critical look at the terminological issues, as well as suggesting that the most important methodological problem in current interpretations of ancient religion is the gap that has opened up between approaches that focus on ritual, and those that take philosophical conceptions as their starting point. He draws attention to a new approach to questions of religious truth which is evident in the work of philosophers and philosophically minded thinkers in the later Hellenistic world and in republican Rome, who attempted to reconcile religion and philosophy, and who also identified new ideas about religious truth.[10] Religious knowledge was thereafter integrated into philosophical argument. The claims about the unity of the divine, which had been commonplace in earlier philosophy, now acquire religious as well as intellectual significance, thus laying the foundations for pagan monotheism to become established as a meaningful concept within intellectual speculation and an active element in religious developments.

An alternative approach to religious change in this period is to move attention away from the question of monotheism to the nature of religion itself. If monotheism, at least in the form of pagan monotheism, was not recognised as a significant religious development by the inhabitants of the ancient world, but was never more than a subsidiary phenomenon identifiable in some of their cults, we need to pay attention to other changes in religious thought and behaviour and assess their role in the transformations between the first and fourth centuries. John North points to a variety of changes which affected beliefs, ritual and group dynamics, and presents important sociological arguments for shifting the terms of the debate in

---

[9] Especially since the appearance of Versnel (1990).
[10] See especially Van Nuffelen, forthcoming (a) and forthcoming (b).

this way. Thus it was not monotheism as such, but the growing expectation that believers would commit themselves to membership of religious groups, by expressing their allegiance to an explicit set of propositions about the cult and its gods, that was the main impetus to new forms of religious behaviour and, above all, to the formation of new forms of religious identity in late antiquity.[11] When this was combined with renunciation of other deities, it propelled collective religious experience firmly in the direction of monotheism. It remains, of course, a matter of contention whether the expression of new religious identities in monotheistic guise was widespread outside the classic formats of Judaism and Christianity.

Michael Frede's philosophical discussion highlights the conceptual differences between polytheistic gods and a monotheistic god, and his conclusions imply that in general the two categories of polytheism and monotheism, when simply taken to mean the belief and worship of many gods or one god respectively, are too crude, and contain too many ambiguities, to serve as tools for classifying the full complexity and spectrum of belief to be found in ancient Greek religion. He argues, nevertheless, that some ancient thinkers – Antisthenes, Chrysippus and Galen – developed a conception of a single transcendent god, which at least approximates to the criteria for the belief in one god that was established by later doctrinal monotheisms. Alfons Fürst's paper draws attention to the fact that Augustine in the *City of God* made a similar distinction between the God of the Christians and the gods of the pagans, which was more concerned with the quality and concept of divinity than with the numerical question of whether divinity was singular or plural.

Focusing on two paradigmatic debates between Christian and pagan apologists – between Augustine and the Platonists, and between Origen and Celsus – Fürst argues that it is also necessary to examine the relationship of religion to society in a political perspective. The matter of contention between Augustine and the Platonists, which can be seen as a prime case of the debate between pagan and Christian monotheists of the fourth century explored at greater length in the companion volume to this one, was not whether there was one or many gods, but what should be the object of religious worship. For protagonists on both sides of the argument this was not the confrontation of polytheism and monotheism, for each could agree on the existence of a single supreme divine being, but the question of religious authority. In a polytheistic environment the divine world is generally seen as a source of support and legitimation for society at

---

[11] For an important discussion of these emerging new forms of religious identity see Lieu (2002).

large, rather than as an independent source of absolute moral authority. In polytheism, if one god did not serve a society's purpose, another could be called upon to do so. The will of the gods for mankind, therefore, was not absolute but relative, and was adaptable to the needs and circumstances of a particular society. This was true even within the henotheistic but not exclusive religious systems favoured by later Platonists. Christian monotheism, in contrast, prescribed and required worship of one God. Other forms of religion were simply shams, and could not be called upon to justify any sort of political or social behaviour, according to the convenience of rulers or society's members. In the earlier debate between Celsus and Origen, Fürst argued that the debate between them essentially concerned the place of religion within a political environment. The pagan Celsus, although he accepted the current Platonic view that a single god should be regarded as the guiding force of the universe, and was thus in a philosophical sense a pagan monotheist, also took it to be axiomatic that the order of the world depended on a multiplicity of diverse cults, particular to each race and group. Origen insisted by contrast that God's moral law was a source of absolute divine authority, which overrode the relativism that characterised conventional religion.

Origen's theoretical statement of the Christian position anticipated the developments of the later Roman Empire, as Christian monotheism became coordinated, although never completely, with the secular authority of the Christian Roman state.[12] The alignment of secular and religious power, which was to a large extent made possible by the increasing dominance of monotheist religious notions, was a development of late antiquity which has foreshadowed many aspects of the modern world. The imposition of belief that is implicit in strict monotheism can readily be transformed into an instrument of coercion in a political sense. Monotheism restricted behavioural choice. Hence the dangers of monotheism have been identified at the sharp edge of the contemporary debate concerning fundamentalism, intolerance and extreme political behaviour, especially as these are harnessed to the coercive potential of modern states.

The political consequences of monotheism, and in particular its potential to underwrite and justify hate and violence based on religious intolerance, have been the most controversial features of Assmann's theological work on monotheism. Christoph Markschies calls the central premises of this argument into question on two grounds. First, he argues that the

---

[12] This alignment became much more prominent in Roman policy and propaganda in the time of Justinian; see Meier (2003) and especially Meier (2004).

antinomy between polytheism and monotheism was by no means sharp and schematic, especially at the level of ordinary religious practice. Second, he draws attention to the theoretical nature of Assmann's work and the extent to which it can be contradicted by specific historical examples. To make the argument he provides an interpretation of the 'one god' inscriptions, which were a feature of all the major religious traditions in the Near East in later antiquity: pagan, Jewish, Samaritan and Christian.[13] The affirmation of the powers of one god in the superlative, not the exclusive sense, was not a statement of strict monotheism, but acknowledged, while it also devalued, those of other divinities. Contextually interpreted these 'one god' acclamations are neither a monotheistic credo, nor evidence for a fundamental moral revolution within religious thought, but one technique by which groups of different religious persuasions expressed their identities, and the superiority of their god, within a still largely tolerant social environment. Nicole Belayche's study of these acclamations in pagan cult provides the historical background of the wider phenomenon, thus giving further weight to the continuities between the polytheisms and monotheisms of the later Roman Empire.

The papers of Markschies and Belayche on *heis theos* provide a bridge between the conceptual approach to the study of ancient monotheism and the search for cultic activity that might be regarded as monotheist. Their discussions highlight the point that the documentation itself, primarily from inscriptions, far from being clear-cut has led to a wide divergence of views in modern scholarship about how the evidence for specific cults should be interpreted. Pagan monotheism, in so far as it was a meaningful category, developed in the transition from a world of fluid and diverse polytheistic cults to that of the more unified dogmas of Judaism and Christianity. Historians of religion have often noted the emergence of monotheistic features in cults under the Roman Empire, which in some cases may have been the result of direct influence from Judaism and Christianity.[14] However, there is much room for argument about how these developments should be interpreted. From the perspective of Graeco-Roman paganism, the emergence of major unitary cults, such as the worship of the Egyptian gods Sarapis and Isis, of 'oriental' divinities – notably Mithras, Iuppiter Dolichenus or the Dea Syria – or the worship of the Sun god, was perfectly compatible with traditional polytheism. The readiness to fuse these divine

---

[13] See Peterson (1926); a new, supplemented, edition is in preparation by C. Markschies.
[14] Notably Nilsson (1950), 569–78.

figures by a process of syncretism did not generally lead to monotheism. There was much religious competition, but the promoters of successful cults had no interest in annihilating or denying the existence of other gods; it served their interests much better to prove the superiority of their own. Polytheism was alive and well in the second and third centuries AD, a period which witnessed a late flowering of paganism, closely related to the economic prosperity and social stability of the high imperial period.[15]

However, it is also undeniable that there were monotheistic traits detectable within contemporary religion. This partly derived from a growth in pagan theological literature which can be traced in a main stream running from Plutarch and Aelius Aristides to the emperor Julian. Peter Van Nuffelen argues in detail in a forthcoming monograph that the origins of this can be traced to the new status that religious truth acquired in intellectual discourse around the beginning of the Roman Empire. This may have encouraged intellectual speculation about the nature of the gods within the religious rather than the philosophical tradition. Some of this was certainly a deliberate response and reaction to Christian or Jewish writing, and it gave increasing weight to a hierarchical understanding of the cosmos, controlled by a supreme ruling divinity. Some of this religious–philosophical literature emanated precisely from the major oracular shrines of the Roman Empire, at Claros and Didyma in Asia Minor and at Delphi in Greece. These had a vital role to play in disseminating new ideas through theological oracles, which no longer dealt narrowly with specific aspects of cult practice, but with wider matters of religious belief. Probably before the end of the second century such oracles dealt with the question of whether there was one or many gods.[16] So, another approach to the documentary evidence of cult activity in the high Roman Empire has been to look for the influence of such ideas and to find evidence of monotheism within pagan cult, encouraged by the notion that this was a period when the polytheistic and monotheistic systems appear to overlap.[17]

Two of the papers in this collection argue strongly for the view that most of the documentary evidence for pagan cult should be interpreted firmly from a polytheistic viewpoint. They contend that monotheistic readings of this material, which includes votive inscriptions and specialised religious genres such as acclamations, are anachronistic and do not take

[15] The period of 'second paganism' in the terminology of Veyne (2005), 419–543.
[16] See most recently Busine (2005).
[17] This is the general model presupposed by Mitchell (1993), especially 11–51.

account of the social and psychological realities of a predominantly poly-theist society. Angelos Chaniotis argues that the increased tendency of worshippers to designate their god as the 'greatest' should be seen both in the context of competition between cities and communities, and as increasingly personalised ways of expressing religious experience. These transformed the style in which cult and religious beliefs were presented and communicated. Affective language and superlatives became increas-ingly common as a means to convey the feelings and emotions of wor-shippers, and thus stated the nature of their relationship to the divine world. Such affirmations rarely or never expressed exclusive monotheistic sentiments or promoted monotheistic concepts of divinity. Nicole Belay-che argues for a similar position in the overall debate about monotheism, by focusing on the *heis theos* inscriptions. Such acclamations to 'one god' were not monotheistic but conveyed the worshippers' enthusiasm for the unique powers and properties of their favoured divinity. The interpretative context of these affirmations of belief should be their local settings and surroundings, including the epigraphic habits of the local communities. They stemmed from the matrix of polytheism and the documentation must be interpreted in this context. It is a fallacy bred of historical hind-sight to assume that the spread of monotheism was the most important feature of late paganism. Even the tendency towards the 'megatheism' analysed in Chaniotis' paper remains embedded in local contexts and did not have substantial theological consequences or undermine the nature of polytheism.

Stephen Mitchell proposes a radically different interpretation of the worship of Theos Hypsistos, arguing that the inscriptions for this specific cult should be interpreted as giving a different perspective on religious experience in the eastern Roman world. Whether or not the worship of Theos Hypsistos should be classed as monotheistic in the narrow sense is less important than the characteristics which distinguished it from other cults: the worship of an anonymous supreme god who was associated with light and cosmic fire but never represented in human form, and who never received human sacrifice. There is much at stake in the different inter-pretations of this particular cult. On Mitchell's view it presents evidence for a widespread form of worship with monotheistic features that is to be found across the Near East and the eastern Mediterranean between the first century BC and the fourth century AD. The cult emphasised the humility of its followers in the face of god's supreme power and it is thus not surprising that its followers, as interpreted in this way, should have interacted closely with Jewish Diaspora communities and become some of the early converts to Christianity. For critics, there is no such thing as a unified cult of Theos Hypsistos, as the supposed evidence cannot be treated as a unity, and the term should simply be interpreted as a manner of addressing the various divinities of polytheism. On Mitchell's view Hypsistos worship provides a striking contemporary parallel to emergent Christianity, while the alternative is to accommodate the evidence fully within the range of polytheistic religious experience of later paganism.

This volume as a whole concentrates on the central issue of the observable transformation of Roman religion from polytheism to monotheism between the first and fourth centuries. Beside the central challenge for historians, to find approaches to the study of Graeco-Roman religion that are not compromised by the prejudice of modern monotheism against ancient polytheism, there are many specific problems of method that make the task difficult, but correspondingly rewarding. How can the different types of evidence, the epigraphy and the literary/philosophical sources, be combined to produce a valid analytical framework? Within the development of ancient paganism how is a balance to be struck between the internal forces for change and external impulses from Judaism and Christianity? How should we reconcile a universalising approach to the study of religion in the Roman Empire with the local diversity displayed in the myriad of cults and religious movements that it contained? What was the impact of changed social and political conditions of the Empire on religious beliefs and practices? The attempt to identify monotheistic elements in what is traditionally described as a polytheistic religious system also invites us to revisit that characterisation of Graeco-Roman religion and to develop more subtle ways of analysing it. Such a view opens up the possibility of locating the interaction of Christianity and Judaism with Graeco-Roman religion not just on the level of social interaction and shared places of cult, for example, but also on the level of how people thought about the divine, and about the importance of such concepts for social and political systems.

It would be inappropriate for the editors of this volume to draw general conclusions from these debates, in so far as a general synthesis inevitably blunts the sharper edges of the diverse arguments of the contributors. We hope that the variety of interpretations, which is particularly evident in the analysis of the cultic evidence, will prove a valuable tool in constructing a comprehensive narrative and interpretation of an epoque of fundamental religious change.

However, we would offer some final observations of our own. The study of pagan religion in classical antiquity has traditionally been dominated by a repertoire of familiar topics: the institutions and material culture of *polis* religion; religion that is based on ritual and cult acts in contrast to religions of belief; contractual religion as an agreement with the gods built on the principle of *do ut des*; religion, especially at Rome, as an explicit instrument of politics and the exercise of power. For better or worse these issues are not at the forefront of this volume. Instead, it is clear to us that, by confronting us with questions about definition and about the types of evidence that throw light on monotheism in a religious sense, pagan monotheism has proved its worth in conceptual terms as a tool for intellectual enquiry.

With historical hindsight it is seductively easy to posit monotheism and polytheism as complementary opposites, offering the inhabitants of the early Roman Empire a choice of contrasted religious experiences. In practice this was not the case. For pagans before the fourth century AD the notion of choosing to worship one or many gods was rarely meaningful or relevant to any significant part of their lives. In this important respect they were naturally different from Christians, whose beliefs demanded that they renounce all other gods. Only when Christianity became the dominant system in the fourth century did pagans begin to develop new ideas about their god (or gods), and thus became, in a much stricter sense, rivals to the Christians. It is only then that pagan monotheism can be identified as a distinctive religious movement.

However, pagan polytheism was not entirely unprepared for this development. Since the first century BC, there had been a notable growth in discussion and dialogue about religious matters, conducted by philosophers, priests and members of the intellectual elite. The conditions of the Roman Empire were hugely favourable to the exchange and spread of new ideas, and there is no doubt that the fertile mixture of the local with the cosmopolitan enriched religious life and widened the range of religious experience open to individuals and communities. This is as evident from the abundant religious literature as it is from the huge epigraphic documentation of the second and third centuries AD, the era of the 'second paganism'. These phenomena produced not only a quantitative but also a qualitative transformation in religious activity. People at all levels of society began to think about and express their relationship to the gods in different ways. The conventional categories for studying ancient religion – the cults of the *polis*, ritual actions, political religion with a largely functional purpose – no longer map on to the complex reality that can be charted on the ground through the inscriptions and other evidence. The Roman Empire was the most fertile period of religious innovation in antiquity, perhaps even in any period of history. Pagan polytheists did not individually become monotheists, but through philosophy and the comparing of religious ideas, by adopting and inventing new cults and learning how to individualise and express religious experience, they transformed ancient religion into a terrain of human experience where much, including monotheism, was possible.

CHAPTER 2

Pagan monotheism as a religious phenomenon

Peter Van Nuffelen

'Pagan monotheism' appears to be a paradox. Whereas paganism is intuitively seen as essentially polytheistic[1], the term 'monotheism' directs one's mind immediately to Christianity, Judaism and Islam, and not to the religions of Greece and Rome. The tension arising from the yoking of what seem to be two mutually exclusive terms expresses itself in three closely related problems. First, monotheism can be an ideologically loaded term, conveying the superiority of the Judaeo-Christian tradition for which it was coined. Consequently its application to Graeco-Roman religion may seriously hamper our understanding of this different religious tradition. Second, 'pagan monotheism' focuses on ideas about the godhead. It thus implies a theological and philosophical approach that may not be suited for the religions of antiquity, as these are often seen as essentially ritualistic. Third, as 'pagan monotheism' runs counter to our intuitive understanding of Greek and Roman religion, it raises the issue of the change that 'paganism' underwent in order to be able to accommodate monotheistic ideas.

The publication of the collection of essays on pagan monotheism in late antiquity by M. Frede and P. Athanassiadi in 1999 provided new impetus to the discussions about paganism and monotheism.[2] Many of them end in a stalemate, with the critics of pagan monotheism dismissing the concept as inadequate while its supporters emphasise its importance. In this paper, which will discuss the three problems indicated, I hope to contribute to a fuller awareness of the issues involved when using the term 'pagan monotheism', and, if possible, to overcome the deadlock between supporters and critics. Throughout my discussion of these topics, I shall suggest that we

---

[1] Polytheism is often proposed as the better alternative for paganism: Fowden (1991), 119; Maas (2000), 166.

[2] Earlier works include e.g. Zeller (1862); Cumont (1924); Nilsson (1950), 546–52 and (1963); Simon (1973); Teixidor (1977); Lehmann (1980); Moreschini (1983); Ramnoux (1984); Momigliano (1986); Versnel (1990); Kenney (1991); Fowden (1993).

should understand pagan monotheism as a religious phenomenon. We should not only consider it to be an intellectual, philosophical tendency, but also see it in relation to existing religions and religious practice. If understood in this way, 'pagan monotheism' can become a fruitful heuristic tool for studying how ancient philosophical conceptions of the divine came into contact with traditional religion, and for understanding some of the changes in the religious outlook of the Roman Empire.

THEORETICAL PROBLEMS: MONOTHEISM AS IDEOLOGY?

The current interest in pagan monotheism among classical scholars may look odd at a moment when biblical scholars and students of early Christianity are seriously questioning the propriety of this term for the religions they study.[3] The critique most commonly levelled against monotheism in these discussions is that it reflects the modern tendency to classify religions on their propositional content: how do they represent, divide and subdivide the divine? For pre-modern religions, these questions may be inadequate, for example because of a stress on orthopraxis rather than orthodoxy. In this way, the term seems fraught with ideological bias, as it implicitly assumes the superiority of the tradition that coined the term.[4] In consequence, the radical solution to do away with 'monotheism' seems attractive to many.[5]

One cannot deny that monotheism can be a strongly valued term, both positively and negatively. For example, expressions like 'true monotheism'[6], 'absolute monotheism'[7], 'radical monotheism'[8] have been used to indicate a higher (and better) degree of monotheism. On the other hand, monotheism is also the object of intense criticism, as is illustrated by the sweeping generalisation that monotheism and violence are essentially linked.[9] Whatever the degree of truth one recognises in this, the fascination for the ideologically tainted origins of monotheism is not very rewarding. (It may be, for that matter, an ideological concern in itself.) Behind it seems to lurk the illusion that we can create a perfectly neutral scholarly apparatus and thus obtain a perfect description of reality. Many, if not all, scholarly terms originate in a specific historical context and consequently reflect the interests of that period. Ideological origins and unintended connotations are the rule, not the exception. The idea that we can get rid of these in order to construct an objective terminology has a naïve ring to it, as deconstructivism and the (post-)modern critique of ideology should have taught

[3] E.g. Hayman (1991); Skarsaune (1997); Moberly (2004). [4] Price (1999), 11.
[5] Ahn (1993); MacDonald (2004); Moltmann (2002). [6] Cassirer (1946), 73.
[7] Stark (2001), 24–7. [8] Niebuhr (1943). [9] Fürst (2004a) surveys the debate.

us by now. Even the deliberate creation of new terms to replace older ones immediately entangles the former into the ideological web of the latter. The point is not how to escape this heritage, but how to negotiate it.

A similar reply to the critique of the ideology present in modern terminology comes from a different philosophical direction. The hermeunetical tradition has taught us that, when trying to understand ancient realities, we are eminently concerned with translating them into modern concepts, which have their own history. In every translation knowledge is gained, as the translated becomes accessible to a modern audience. To use an example from our field: using modern terms and theories we acquire some understanding of ancient tragedy. On the other hand, there is always a loss. We lose out on precision and accuracy as we cannot grasp the past on its own terms. Our understanding of Athenian tragedy is never that of an ancient spectator or playwright. Consequently, there is an alternative to abandoning monotheism. We should try to gain a precise appreciation of its meaning and the way it directs our understanding of a religion. This awareness may then help us to use the term with insight and acumen. In this way the current debate about 'monotheism' becomes useful, as it points to the difficulties and dangers of the concept.

I will pursue this line of inquiry here, by briefly discussing the alternatives created to avoid or qualify monotheism. Three options seem to have been chosen: the use of different terms already current in religious studies (e.g. henotheism), the creation of neologisms (e.g. megatheism), and the use of 'monotheism' with some qualification (e.g. inclusive monotheism). This survey will result in an informed justification of 'monotheism'.

The field of religious studies is rich in terms that transcend the simple opposition polytheism–monotheism. Biblical scholars have developed a wide array of terms for specific phenomena, and scholars have already called for its extension to classical antiquity.[10] 'Henotheism' in particular has acquired some popularity among scholars, exemplified in and also enhanced by the work of H. Versnel (1990). Its currency does, however, cause some confusion, as it is hard to find a single and universally accepted definition of henotheism. Versnel ranked three phenomena as henotheism: the exaltation of one god above the others, the *reductio ad unum* of many divinities, and the assumption by a single god of the role of many others.[11] Making the first point the central one, a philosophical handbook defines the classical Greek pantheon, with Zeus as its king, as henotheism[12] – something no classical scholar is likely to accept. On the other hand, a major encyclopaedia of

---

[10] Wallraff (2003).   [11] Versnel (1990), 35–6.   [12] MacGregor (1968), 59.

religious studies defines henotheism as the temporary worship of a single god, and opposes it to 'monolatry', which is the continuous worship of a single god. To add to the confusion, the same work but in a different article treats henotheism and monolatry as entirely synonymous.[13] This list can be expanded indefinitely and related coinages added.[14] There is a common denominator to all this: henotheism is used to designate a focus on a single god within a polytheistic religious framework, be it by identification with other deities, by exaltation, or any other way. What phenomena precisely are henotheistic seems to vary from scholar to scholar.

Henotheism and similar terms cannot claim to be more objective alternatives to monotheism. They are rooted in early nineteenth-century idealist philosophy, which saw monotheism as the logical coronation of the development of the geist: 'henotheism' was coined by K. F. Müller, who was inspired by F. Schelling, whereas 'monolatry' probably goes back to F. Schleiermacher, the famous German Protestant theologian.[15] Moreover, the proponents of henotheism, like those of monotheism, assess religious phenomena on the basis of their view of the godhead.

Neither the imprecision in definition nor their ideological origins render henotheism and monolatry useless. On the contrary, they have already proven their utility in the study of the religions of the ancient world. Nonetheless, although these terms may perhaps allow for a more subtle appreciation of monotheistic tendencies within a polytheist religion, they function within the same perspective as monotheism, and do not offer a real alternative to it.

As a second option there is the creation of new terms. This has the distinct advantage of being able to designate a phenomenon with a specific term, but the disadvantage that very few of these neologisms survive or acquire wider validity.[16] Henotheism is the exception confirming the rule. Moreover, hardly any religious phenomenon is exactly like another, which may create doubts as to the appropriateness of general terms. Indeed, neologisms tend to reflect a desire to stress the differences between phenomena, which is indeed useful. However, importing this propensity into scholarly debate will lead to a confusing inflation of terms, and we will probably still need

---

[13] Lang (1993); cf. Van Selms (1973); Auffarth (1993).
[14] Gladigow (1993), 327 defines 'insular monotheism' (the regionally limited worship of a single god) as a form of henotheism. Assmann (2004), 23 defines henotheism as a philosophical perspective, monolatry as a monotheism of cult.
[15] Schleiermacher (1828); Schelling (1985, orig. 1842); Müller (1882), 266; Van den Bosch (2002), 347–9; Lang (1993), 150.
[16] E.g. menotheism (Cobb (1895), 36); theomonism (Corbin (1981), 14–23); panentheism (Müller, see van den Bosch (2002), 355).

general concepts to classify them. This does not mean that no positive impetus can come from this approach, as A. Chaniotis shows in his paper on 'megatheism', but they can hardly be substituted for terms with more currency.

A third option is to qualify monotheism. The couple exclusive/inclusive is the most common: in its former guise it excludes all other divinities. Inclusive monotheism can be reconciled with polytheism,[17] as it recognises a deeper unity behind the multiple manifestations of the divine. Henotheism and monolatry are sometimes called 'practical monotheism', as they stress the cultic worship of one god out of many, and some scholars distinguish relative and potential monotheism.[18] Many other distinctions have been made, often coined for a specific case. H. G. Theissen, for example, distinguishes between monotheism from below (Israel) and monotheism from above (Echnaton).[19] All these qualifications make clear that monotheism is no longer (if it ever has been) a rigid concept, but rather a flexible term which can cover traditional monotheisms, and also monotheistic tendencies within polytheist religions.

From this brief doxography a few conclusions can be drawn. Most of the concepts currently in use have been framed in modern Europe, and imply, at least originally, a valuation of the phenomena they designate, with monotheism as the top of the ladder. Doing away with this scholarly apparatus for these ideological origins would, however, be naïve and ideological in its own right, and may deprive us of a way to understand ancient realities. Moreover, monotheism has, at least among scholars, lost its rigidity as a strongly valued term, and has become a general category that needs specification when applied to a historical phenomenon.[20] In addition, the field of religious studies has a wide terminological variety on offer, which allows us to describe the phenomena with some degree of precision. As far as the exact definition of the terms is concerned, the study of monotheisms has only a relative chaos to offer. This may be experienced as a disadvantage and incite one to coin new concepts. Yet, even then we will continue to need a general terminology in order to be able to describe phenomena

---

[17] Kenney (1986), 271 and (1991), xxiv; Lang (1993), 150; Dillon (1999), who uses hard and soft monotheism. Other terms are 'pantheonaler Monotheismus' (Wischmeyer (2005), 153); 'cultural monotheism' and 'theoretical monotheism' (Wallraff (2003)).

[18] Lang (1993) is a very useful survey.

[19] Theissen (1985), 45–81. See also Kenney (1991), xxix, who defines 'mystical monotheism' as the idea that the divinity is 'an ultimate and inclusive unity transcendent of being and intellection and so beyond human knowledge as it is standardly understood'.

[20] In this sense, I can agree with scholars who dispute the validity of a strict polytheism–monotheism divide among the religions in antiquity: e.g. Borgeaud (2003); Stroumsa (2005).

and to communicate with other scholars. Here the term 'monotheism' can find its justification, understood as a common denominator for various phenomena.

When we apply this to antiquity, pagan monotheism can be applied as an overarching term for monotheistic tendencies within Greek and Roman religion, without claiming that it constitutes a single phenomenon with a single manifestation. It can be taken to include the henotheistic phenomena described by Versnel, but also cults born from the interaction between paganism, Christianity and Judaism. It will be a term designating a wide variety of phenomena within Graeco-Roman religion, not a single movement but rather a tendency expressed in different forms.

Before we can do so, however, an additional problem must be addressed. The fact that monotheism can be a useful term on a theoretical level does not yet validate the study of 'pagan monotheism'. Several scholars have indeed argued that its specific focus on theology and on the structure of the divine may not be adjusted to the reality of ancient religions, which have ritual as their centrepiece. It has also been pointed out that an exclusive focus on the conception of the godhead may lead to an infelicitous disregard of what distinguishes, for example, ancient philosophy from Christianity.[21] There is more to religion than just the way it represents the divine. These criticisms lead us to a new problem: is pagan monotheism an adequate way of studying the religions of antiquity?

METHOD OF INQUIRY: PAGAN MONOTHEISM AND
ANCIENT RELIGION

Especially, but not exclusively, in the Anglo-Saxon world, the study of Greek and Roman religion tends to focus on ritual and religious practice. This is justified by seeing ancient religions as essentially ritualistic, a view that entails that belief or theology hardly played a role in them. This judgement often implies a rebuttal of modern Christian attitudes, for which belief is supposedly central and which are usually traced back to Protestant theology (with F. Schleiermacher as the main target).[22] Questions about what people believed about their gods are consequently seen as simply the wrong kind of questions for pre-Christian antiquity.

---

[21] See the critique of Frede (1999) by patristic scholars like Edwards (2000) and (2004); Wallraff (2003); and Fürst (2006a), 518. See also Sfameni Gasparro (2003), 127.

[22] E.g. Phillips (1986), 2697–711; Smith (1990); Durand and Scheid (1994); Rothaus (1996); Beard, North and Price (1998); Feeney (1998), 115–36; Frankfurter (1998); Price (1999); Parker (2005).

Even though this approach has led to interesting studies of ancient religion, the argument itself is actually an attempt to reify what is essentially a
difference in method, which goes beyond the boundaries of our field. The
focus on beliefs and conceptions of the divine is a characteristic of contemporary philosophy of religion in general, in contrast to anthropological
approaches to religion in which ritual is central. (It must be remarked that
it is somewhat one-sided to shift all the blame to Protestant theology, as it is
an attitude rooted in post-Kantian philosophy. For example, the German
philosopher of Jewish descent Hermann Cohen (1842–1918) considered
cult to be a relic of idolatry.[23]) Often the two fields and approaches hardly
seem to interact. Whereas the philosophy of religion is little or not at all
concerned with ritual and religious practice, anthropologists tend to blend
out the notion of 'belief', seen as a cultural construct. A recent handbook of
the anthropology of religion simply omits any reference to belief, god(s), or
metaphysics, whereas an introduction to the philosophy of religion bears
the title 'Belief in God'.[24] Rather than thinking that there is an essential
rift between ancient religion and modern Christianity along the lines of
the supposed opposition between ritual and belief, we must be aware of
the fact that a methodological cleft seems to have opened up in the study
of religion, extending also to classical scholars.

The 'ritualist' position has not gone without criticism. Most of it has
been aimed at the claim that theological concepts did not play a role in the
mind of the ancient worshipper, and that questions of theology are senseless
for the ancient world. Such a unilateral position cannot be sustained, as
has recently been argued by different scholars, and there is no need to
rehearse their discussions here.[25] Questions of 'belief' and 'theology' did
play a role in Greek and Roman religion. This does not mean that belief
and ritual must have been articulated in the same way in Rome as they are
in Christianity. In a suggestive essay entitled *Quand croire c'est faire* (Paris,
2005) John Scheid has shown how Roman concepts and hierarchies of the
divine were expressed in ritual, which became the location of the discourse
on and classification of the gods. Even in ritual there was theology.[26] But in
other religious phenomena of the ancient world a cognitive content must
have played a central role, as in many of the so-called oriental religions and

---

[23] Cohen (1915), 4, 25, 32.   [24] Bowen (2002); Mawson (2005).
[25] Bendlin (2000) argues that this view is simply a positive interpretation of the nineteenth-century
dismissal of Roman religion (e.g. Hartung (1836) and Wissowa (1912)) as empty and ritualistic.
See also Bendlin (2001); King (2003); Rüpke (2004). See John North's paper in this volume for a
qualified restatement of that position.
[26] For a different approach with similar conclusions see Ando (2005).

mystery cults – a feature probably overstressed by early twentieth-century scholarship,[27] but nonetheless vital to our understanding of those cults.

Although the 'ritualist' position has received most extensive criticism, the other side of the divide is not without its problems, especially when there is a tendency to reduce religion to theology. Studies that address concepts and ideas about the divine tend to be strictly philosophical, and devoid of any reference to actual religion.[28] However, some of them seem to claim at least implicitly that they refer to a religious reality or a religious feeling. This fact is particularly true of many studies on pagan monotheism, which are rather studies of philosophical concepts. They usually have had little to do with religious practice or its cultural background.[29] For example, the suggestion that pagan monotheism was already a major force in early Greece will simply appear exaggerated to an historian of ancient Greece, who fails to see any influence of this monotheism in the development of classical Greek religion. Two elements can account for this lack of clarity. On the one hand, the term 'monotheism' always has the appearance of alluding to a religion, even when it is used as a philosophical term to assess a metaphysical construct. On the other, ancient theology was mainly a philosophical discipline. This fact tends to turn modern discussions of ancient theology into philosophical analyses. As a consequence, we need a sound understanding of the relation between religion and philosophy when discussing pagan monotheism. How do philosophical conceptions of the divine relate to religious practice?[30]

For all its infelicitous consequences, the rift between philosophy and the anthropology of religion does draw attention to some methodological problems, an awareness of which is essential for the study of pagan monotheism. I will only discuss two of them: the split in source material and the relation between religion and philosophy.

Studies of ancient religion on the one hand and of theology on the other tend to draw on very different types of sources. The former is mainly reconstructed from documentary evidence, dedications, cult objects and places, in addition to descriptions of rituals and practices in literary sources. It is well known that inscriptions tend to be formulaic and stereotypical: unoriginality is their nature. To understand ancient conceptions of the divine we draw mainly on philosophical and literary texts, which often

[27] E.g. Cumont (1924); Bianchi and Vermaseren (1981); Turcan (1989).
[28] E.g. Albert (1980); Van den Broek and others (1988); Gerson (1990); Laks (2002).
[29] West (1999); Frede and Athanassiadi (1999); Frede (1999).
[30] Although in essence a study of philosophical conceptions, Frede's paper in this volume also raises the possibility that we are dealing with genuine religious attitudes.

explore and question traditional concepts. We expect here a higher degree of original and personal intervention. These methodological contrasts in the study of ancient religion reflect, at least in part, different scholarly approaches to the study of ordinary people and of the elite in antiquity. Most literary texts aimed at the elite, who, refined through education, were able to appreciate the delicate balance between innovation and mimesis that characterises these texts. The same is true for philosophy. For sure, the elite did produce inscriptions, even in high numbers, but this kind of material at least allows us to have access to the interests of the lower classes. Especially when we study religious texts from rural regions, we are conscious of entering a different world, often characterised by bad Greek and clumsy craftwork. Admittedly, these oppositions are too schematic. There are inscriptions that record so-called theological oracles,[31] and a sound awareness of literary rules can allow us to use literary texts as sources for ritual practice. Nevertheless, it is clear that one will get a different view according to the material one concentrates on.

This remark is especially true in relation to pagan monotheism. The clearest evidence for monotheistic tendencies comes from literary and philosophical sources. The first book of Macrobius' *Saturnalia* is a clear, albeit late, example from the late fourth–early fifth century. They give the impression that pagan monotheism was an exclusively intellectual phenomenon, without any contact with traditional religion or the lower classes.[32] It is hard to find undisputable documentary evidence of pagan monotheistic cults in the Roman Empire.[33] Stephen Mitchell's attempt (1999) to identify a monotheistic cult on the basis of the Theos Hypsistos inscriptions gave rise to a wide-ranging debate, part of which centres on the question if it is legitimate to interpret the inscriptions in the light of developments that can be traced in philosophy and literary sources. Many would argue for restricting the interpretative framework to the epigraphic habit. In that case, *hypsistos* does not have to be more than a traditional epithet of exaltation, without any monotheistic connotation.[34] If one does so, there appears to be little that is new in these inscriptions.

---

[31] See now Busine (2005).

[32] This is already the critique of Christian apologists, who accepted that pagan philosophers were monotheistic, but denied any influence of them on traditional religion (see Eusebius, *Praep. evang.* 14.5; Augustine, *De civ. D.* 4.11–21, 6.8, 8.12).

[33] In Athanassiadi and Frede (1999), only the paper by Mitchell (1999) deals with cults. Liebeschuetz (1999) in the same volume concludes with the paradox that Praetextatus may have held monotheistic ideas but was initiated in many different mystery cults. Athanassiadi (1999) refers to some practices of Neoplatonic philosophers.

[34] Cf. Ustinova (1999); Marek (2000); Stein (2001); Bowersock (2002); Baker (2005); Belayche (2005a) and (2005b); Wischmeyer (2005). Mitchell revisits the debate in his contribution to this volume.

Although a more restricted interpretation cannot be a priori excluded, I think it important not to disconnect epigraphic evidence from wider social and cultural changes that are documented elsewhere. A distinct change in the type or quantity of dedications may very well indicate a shift in religious sentiments. A recent paper by Alain Cadotte, analysing the increased use of the formulae *Pantheus* and *Dii deaeque omnes* in second-century North Africa, can illustrate this point.[35] He concludes that these formulae serve to designate the supreme deity in all its different forms, something one could call henotheism or monotheism. This offers a clear parallel with what literary sources teach us about the beliefs of contemporary upper-class individuals. Admittedly, in this case, the divide between elite and ordinary people is quite important, as the dedications are mainly made by officials and 'foreigners', and not by indigenous Africans. The tendency towards monotheism accordingly seems to be a Roman phenomenon.

This example shows that the more promising way of interpretation seems to be to assume a holistic perspective in which disparate elements of evidence can be integrated with respect for their specific generic characteristics. In this way, different types of evidence can contribute to a broader picture of the religious development of the Roman Empire. On the other hand, one should never lose sight of the precise context in which the texts were created. A tactful balance will, as usual, be the sign of good scholarship.[36]

A final remark: the problem of discriminating between traditional elements and innovations is not specifically related to epigraphic evidence. For example, the propensity to stick to traditional formulae and the traditional pantheon is also found in authors like Plutarch or Aelius Aristides, who do not do away with the traditional pantheon but rather try to integrate it into their own perspective. Classical antiquity was a profoundly traditionalist society, where the new was clothed as the old. We must be aware of the danger that we may be overestimating change and ignoring the continuous existence of traditional elements in paganism. A recent example is offered by the late antique cult of the Sun. In his excellent study on the Sun in early Christianity, Martin Wallraff explained the rapid acceptance of sun imagery for Christ in early Christianity by reference to the monotheistic character of the Sun cult, which was favoured by the emperors from Aurelian onwards. In his recent book, Stephan Berrens has argued, however, that there is no evidence to suggest that the cult of the Sun as created by

---

[35] Cadotte (2002–3).   [36] Cf. Ando (2003), 142; Belayche (2006a).

Aurelian was monotheistic or henotheistic, and that it is rather in Neoplatonic texts that the sun acquires a monotheistic character.[37] We must be
aware of the fact that the monotheistic interpretation is not necessarily the
correct one.

The second methodological problem I want to discuss here is that of the
relation between religion and philosophy in antiquity. It is important to
realise that theology, understood as a theoretical reflection on the divine,
was not an integrated part of religion in antiquity, in the way that theology
became an integral part of Christianity. This is not to say that there was
no theology implicit in Graeco-Roman religion, but the discipline of theology itself was the crown of physics, one of the traditional three parts of
Hellenistic philosophy. Consequently, it was traditionally located outside
religion.

It is tempting to use the term 'monotheism' when discussing ancient
philosophical concepts of the divine. Ancient philosophers routinely saw
the highest principle(s) as divine. In assessing the structure of the divine,
the term 'monotheism' can be applied to most of ancient philosophy,
as it searches for what constitutes the fundamental unity of the cosmos.
This is true as much for the Presocratic *arche* as for the Neoplatonic
'One'. However, the religious connotations that are unavoidably attached
to the term 'monotheism' may create the impression that a discussion
of philosophical concepts tells us something about wider religious life,
whereas in reality it may only reflect the speculations of a very restricted
group of the upper class. As long as philosophy is relatively autonomous
of religion, philosophical conceptions may seem of little relevance for the
study of religion. Consequently it may be misleading to apply the term
'monotheism' to philosophical propositions in that it suggests that this
was a widespread religious attitude. However, the term becomes more
appropriate when philosophy takes an active interest in religion. As I will
argue in the third part of this paper, this happens especially at the end
of the Roman Republic, when we see the view develop that traditional
religions, with all their gods and rituals, are in effect repositories of the
same truth that philosophy is looking for. This view will lay the basis for
the heightened interest in traditional religions that can be found in Stoic
and Middle Platonic philosophy of the first two centuries AD. This does
not mean that one cannot detect monotheistic tendencies in earlier Greek
philosophy, sometimes even with a religious connotation, as M. Frede will
argue in his contribution to this volume. However, it is only in the Roman

---

[37] Wallraff (2002); Berrens (2004), 115, 236.

Empire that philosophers like Plutarch engage in a dialogue, for example, with the cult of Isis, and try to reinterpret traditional religion to make it fit with their philosophical conceptions. It seems that such an attitude, which found philosophical truth in traditional religion, was widely shared among intellectuals of this period. It is only at this period that 'pagan monotheism' becomes a truly religious phenomenon.

Thus, a sensitivity to the changing relationship between religion and philosophy in the ancient world is important if we want to understand pagan monotheism as a religious phenomenon. If we restrict 'monotheism' to an assessment of philosophical doctrines, there is no need to take this aspect into account. Monotheism is then a term of strictly philosophical usage. If, however, we are interested in tracing changes in the religious outlook of the Roman Empire, it becomes essential to see how philosophy interacts with religion, and to ask whether and how philosophical ideas may have spurred religious change.

In conclusion, it must be clear that it is essential for the study of pagan monotheism to overcome the rift between ritualism and theology. If the former excludes a priori theological questions and the latter ignores any traditional religious dimension, pagan monotheism cannot find ground to stand on. Pagan monotheism needs both dimensions, as it is an approach to ancient religion that focuses on ideas about god(s). Although we can under-stand 'monotheism' simply as a philosophical proposition, I have argued that we must try to grasp pagan monotheism as a religious phenomenon, in order to be able to situate it in the wider environment of ancient reli-gion. This is not without difficulties, as my discussion of the disparities in the source material and of the changing relationship between religion and philosophy has shown. Nevertheless, an exclusive focus on either side of the equation may seriously distort our understanding of ancient religion and the changes it underwent. I now turn to a brief assessment of these changes.

APPROACHES TO THE HISTORICAL PHENOMENON: CHANGE IN
GRAECO-ROMAN RELIGION

Even though one can trace the origins of pagan monotheism back to early Greek philosophy, it was clearly not a traditional religious phenomenon. Classical Greek and Roman religion was not monotheistic in any mean-ing of the word, even though one may want to point to monotheistic philosophers. Asserting that the term 'pagan monotheism' can be used to designate a group of religious phenomena consequently implies the assumption that 'classical' religion had been changed either by internal or by external forces. The correct identification and appreciation of these factors will provide possible explanations for the religious phenomena.[38] This implies going beyond the individual piece of evidence and its particular problems in order to develop a general view of religion in the Roman Empire. I do not have the space or the ambition to attempt anything like that in this paper,[39] but want to single out three factors that seem central and that will unavoidably come up in almost any discussion of the topic: philosophy, the new 'oriental cults', and Judaism and Christianity.

The prime internal factor is philosophy. From the Presocratics onwards, thinking about God and the gods had always been high on the agenda of the philosophers, who were keen to identify the highest principle(s) as divine. As I have indicated above, many of these conceptions can be termed monotheistic in the philosophical sense of the word. Their influence on religion, however, seems very limited. Indeed, such philosophical concepts were often developed in opposition to traditional religious ideas and practices, as can be illustrated by the examples of Heraclitus and Xenophanes. In later philosophy as well, this philosophical monotheism hardly interacts with traditional religious notions. From the side of the philosophers, the contention seems to be that truth is to be found exclusively or mainly in philosophical reflection. As Glenn Most has observed, in areas such as cosmology, eschatology and morality religion was found deficient by philosophers, who attempted either to supplement religion or to correct it.[40] Plato's *Euthyphron*, traditionally seen as his first dialogue, can be read as developing this theme: Socrates showed by philosophical *elenchus* how ill-founded and pernicious Euthyphron's traditionalist fidelity to accepted religious views and stories was. This is not to say that philosophy and religion did not interact, as Plato's own interest in mystery cults, Orphism and the religion of his ideal *polis* illustrates. But as far as the conceptions of the divine are concerned, philosophy was in competition rather than in dialogue with religion. Religion was not identified as an important source of metaphysical knowledge.

A first impetus to changing this attitude came from Stoicism. Stoic allegory identified the gods with the elements of nature, and turned the

---

[38] I omit a discussion of philosophical and sociological explanations for the evolution towards monotheism. Most of them consider it to be a natural and unavoidable development. The interest of these theories for antiquity and their applicability is fairly limited. See e.g. Cassirer (1946); Gnuse (1997), 73–128 and (1999); Luhmann (2000); Stark (2001).

[39] In his contribution to this book John North offers an additional analysis of how Graeco-Roman religion changed internally.

[40] Most (2003), 307–10.

traditional Homeric pantheon into an image of Stoic cosmology. Traditional religion becomes philosophically interesting, and a possible source of knowledge. It is hard to trace the precise development of these ideas in the Hellenistic period, but we witness a general turn towards religion in the early Roman Empire. In particular the Stoics and Platonists started to look at religion as a source of truth about the world. Although some philosophers like Seneca continued to see their philosophical truth in opposition to religion and in that sense retained a more traditional attitude, many of their colleagues showed a keen interest in religion. The important thing to note is that we witness not simply an increased interest in religion, but also a changed perception of religion. Religion was incorporated in a view of the past according to which primitive man had perceived basic truths about the cosmos and expressed these in poetry but also in religion.[41] With all its gods and rituals it was now identified as a repository of philosophical truth. Philosophers started to look at religion as a source for the truth that they tried to reconstruct through reasoning. Reason and religion thus become two parallel sources for philosophical knowledge. Elsewhere I have suggested that Antiochus of Ascalon (died 69/8 BC) was the first to have propounded this view, based on the observation that we can first grasp it in the *Antiquitates rerum divinarum* of his pupil Varro.[42] Be that as it may, this change inevitably implies that philosophers tried to reconcile their 'monotheistic' conceptions with the traditional representation of the gods in religion, as can be witnessed in Plutarch, Dio Chrysostom, Celsus and Numenius. From now on, active engagement with and interest in religion became a common feature of most philosophy, in contrast to the rejection of traditional gods and religion to be found in Antisthenes or Zeno. Philosophical monotheism acquired a religious dimension.

It is hard to gauge whether this change in philosophical attitude spurred the transformation of the general religious atmosphere of the Roman Empire or whether it was actually its product. As usual, it probably was a two-way process, religion and philosophy becoming closely entangled in some instances. Some philosophers, for example, worked in close relation with traditional cults. Plutarch was priest in Delphi and Numenius has been linked to the temple of Bel in Apamea. People at the heart of the traditional religious institutions clearly harboured philosophical ideas.[43] It certainly is no accident that theological discussions began in these institutions in the second century AD. We know of several 'theological' oracles

---

[41] Boys-Stones (2001). [42] Van Nuffelen, forthcoming (a).
[43] From a literary point of view, Goldhill (2006) and Bendlin (2006a) have argued that the interest in religion during the Second Sophistic is part of the intellectual 'identity discourse' of this period.

which explicitly address the issue of how the god(s) should be conceived, a question which used to be a strictly philosophical one.[44] The new philosophical interest in religion and the personal entanglement of philosophers in religion was probably a factor in this change.

Thus, philosophy and religion seem to have come on intimate terms with one another in the early Roman Empire, a development that prefigured the later Neoplatonic interest in religion, and even the self-definition of Neoplatonism as a religion itself, surpassing all traditional cults. Although many details of the process still remain obscure, it is clear that this was a crucial development, especially in the light of the interpretation I have proposed here of pagan monotheism as a religious phenomenon. With the introduction of philosophical ideas into religion, pagan monotheism becomes a valid term to describe these new tendencies in the religion of the Roman Empire.

Another major characteristic of the religious life of the Early Roman Empire is the rise and expansion of new, mainly oriental, cults. Franz Cumont thought that they illustrated a general trend of paganism. As the deities of these cults developed into syncretistic universal *pantheoi*, they acquired a monotheistic character. Even though Cumont did not exclude Jewish influence, he interpreted this as a general trend directed by 'la loi qui préside au développement du paganisme',[45] and attributed the success of these cults to the fact that they provided a new link between religion and philosophy, between ritual and doctrine.[46] Many of the ideas that underpin his theories are now outdated. The concept of 'oriental religions' as having their own specific characteristics, for example, has been questioned and has lost much of its sweeping force.[47] They are now rather seen as individual cults, interacting each in their own way with their environment. Indeed, the question must be asked to what extent the oriental cults do constitute an external factor contributing to the change of ancient religion. Whereas earlier scholarship tended to see them as bearers of oriental philosophical ideas, more recent emphasis has been placed on how they developed in response to the Graeco-Roman environment. Mithraism, for example, is now seen less as bringer of Mazdaic ideas to the Roman Empire, and more as an original development from an Iranian ferment in the Roman Empire.[48] If this is true, the importance of philosophically inspired doctrines in these cults can be related to the new alliance between religion and philosophy that I have sketched above, rather than to any of their original features. Whatever

---

[44] Busine (2005).   [45] Cumont (1924), 101, 207.   [46] Cumont (1924), 47–8.
[47] Kaizer (2006).   [48] Beck (2006).

option one chooses, Cumont's fundamental intuition, that the oriental religions of the Roman Empire were characterised by a new alliance between philosophy and religion, still seems valid. For Cumont most important was the incorporation into the cults of moral and cosmological doctrines which could satisfy the intelligent while the dreadful rituals would suit the vulgar.[49] There may be too much early twentieth-century liberal sentiment in this but it cannot be disputed that as an important feature of the imperial religious landscape the 'oriental cults' did indeed incorporate philosophical ideas into their doctrine. As such they are a phenomenon that runs parallel to the increased interest in philosophy.

One cannot avoid the topic of the relation of pagan monotheism to Judaism and Christianity. Did these two 'truly' monotheistic religions, widespread in the Mediterranean, cause the changes in Graeco-Roman religion that we have described as pagan monotheism? Or were they part of a general trend, in which pagan monotheism to a degree conditioned the rise of Christianity? Whatever our choice between the alternatives (if a choice must be made), it is clear that we will need to assess the interaction between Jews, Christians and pagans. There is indeed sufficient evidence to suggest a degree of osmosis at a local level. It may suffice to refer to the so-called Godfearers, pagan worshippers of the Jewish God, and the possibility that the cult of Theos Hypsistos had close relations to these groups. As far as the relation between Christianity and paganism is concerned, a recent study argues that many of the seemingly strange features of Montanism, with its stress on ecstatic prophecy and female leadership, may point to the impact of the Phrygian pagan environment on this early Christian heresy.[50] The Naassenes, a second-century gnostic sect which interpreted hymns on Attis and attended the mysteries of the Great Mother, is another case in point.[51] The same may be true of other early Christian heresies. There is no need to multiply the examples, as there surely was interaction.[52] Again, as with the two other factors mentioned earlier, this is a phenomenon that starts in the first century AD, at the same time as the rapid expansion of the Jewish diaspora and the spread of Christianity.

[49] Cumont (1924), 325. A similar stress on moralisation is apparent in the concept of 'second paganism', now defended especially by Veyne (2005), 419–543, but going back to earlier French scholarship (e.g. G. Boissier). He would situate a major change in the second century AD, when the gods seem to become moral beings and the relation of the devotee to the god one of submission. Increased moralism in religion is also a major line of interpretation in earlier accounts of Roman religion: e.g. Liebeschuetz (1979). Veyne's concept is not irreconcilable with the idea proposed here that the major changes in Roman religion start in the first century AD.

[50] Hirschmann (2005).   [51] Lancellotti (2000).

[52] Cf. Rutgers (1995) and (1998); Mitchell (2003b) and (2005).

However, it is hard to estimate the extent of mutual influence. This is partially due to lack of unequivocal evidence. Much depends on the interpretation of inscriptions and of often much later literary sources. Moreover, we must not fall into the trap of overestimating the similarities of the Judaeo-Christian tradition to the religions that surrounded it. Whatever degree of proselytism we ascribe to Judaism (a long-standing debate),[53] Jews remained a small minority in the Roman Empire, always seen as having a distinct religious identity. Christianity, on the other hand, defined itself in opposition to the religions that surrounded it, although with less resistance to the acceptable ideas of the philosophers than to the abominable traditional cults. It is worth stressing these differences here, as it is a point often neglected in discussion by both critics and supporters of pagan monotheism.[54] Even when we can detect similarities in the way Christians and pagans conceived the godhead, there were still many theological issues that separated them.

As often when witnessing change in a complex society, it is difficult to establish clear causal relationships. More research and debate are required for a precise calibration, but it must be evident that the new alliance of philosophy and religion, the expansion of new religions, and the apparently increased interaction between Judaism, Christianity and paganism, will play an important role in any narrative of pagan monotheism in the Roman Empire. Such a narrative will also have to attempt to link these changes to what we witness in the epigraphic evidence. As we have seen, there seems to be an increase in dedications to 'all the gods' in Roman Africa; A. Chaniotis argues in this volume that there is an increased tendency to exalt the divinity especially in Asia Minor; in a reassertion of his earlier views on Theos Hypsistos, S. Mitchell points to the spread of the cult under the Roman Empire. It will be the task of a future synthesis to establish a framework in which these phenomena can be related to social, political and philosophical changes in the Roman Empire. For the time being, they seem to warrant the conclusion that there is an increased tendency towards monotheism in the Roman Empire.

To conclude, what is pagan monotheism as proposed in this paper? As I see it, pagan monotheism is a possible interpretation of change in the

---

[53] Compare Feldman (1993); Goodman (1994); and the works by Rutgers referred to in the previous note.

[54] Frede and Athanassiadi (1999), 7; Frede (1999); Price (2003), 192. Intent on doing away with implicit Christian conceptions, they fall into the opposite trap and rehearse arguments already found in ancient anti-Christian polemic: Porphyry, *Contra Christianos* frg. 76 Harnack; Maximus of Madaura in Augustine, *Ep.* 16 *PL* 33.82.

religion of the Roman Empire from the first century onwards, for which the major element is a new way in which people started to conceive the godhead. It was not a uniform or sudden process: change was gradual and took many different forms and tendencies, which we can group under the heading of 'pagan monotheism'. Whereas the evidence for the first century seems predominantly literary and philosophical, from the second century epigraphical texts seem to testify to a wider acceptance of such ideas. There seems to be a continuous spread of pagan monotheism up to the end of paganism. Indeed, at the end of the fourth century a correspondent of St Augustine can claim that any serious person believes in a single god.[55] Such an approach implies a holistic and global view of religion in the Roman Empire, which attempts to detect changes of a wider nature in individual cults.[56] Because of its variegated nature, the focus of pagan monotheism will be on religious interaction, for example between religion and philosophy, between different cults, or between different religious traditions like paganism, Judaism and Christianity.

It must be stressed here that pagan monotheism is only one approach to ancient religion, which must be complemented by others in order to obtain a full appreciation of the changes that religion underwent in the Roman Empire.[57] It presents its specific problems and dangers, the most important of which have been highlighted above. There is no need to summarise them here, but from what I have said, the major difficulty will be to strike a balance, a balance between change and tradition, between the general and the specific, between theology and ritual. On the other hand, any history of ancient religion that neglects the changes in the conception of the divine will be the poorer for it.

---

[55] Augustine, *Ep.* 16 *PL* 33.82 (*c.* AD 390).
[56] Consequently, it stands in contrast with approaches that focus on structural elements of specific cults or religious systems, and on how they functioned in society: Parker (2005); Scheid (2005).
[57] For examples see Stroumsa (2005); Veyne (2005); and North in this volume.

CHAPTER 3

Pagan ritual and monotheism

John North

The Quarrels and Divisions of *Religion* were Evils unknown to the Heathen. The reason was because the Religion of the Heathen consisted rather in Rites and Ceremonies than in any constant belief. For you may imagine what kind of Faith theirs was when the chief Doctors and Fathers of their Church were the Poets.

Francis Bacon, 'Of Unity in Religion' (1622)

INTRODUCTION

Bacon is here making – in a characteristically short space – three separate points, all of them still much in contention today; his thought will provide the starting points for this paper. First, he is claiming that religious life in antiquity was not the site of specific conflicts. Others were later to turn this into one of the virtues of pagan religious life, its toleration of religious difference,[1] but in this passage (virtually an aside) it is hard to detect a tone of anything but detachment from what the 'heathens' did. No doubt, it was a benefit that there should have been no 'religious' wars, but he is surely not making a claim for toleration as such. Secondly, he is seeing a contrast between matters of belief, or at least constancy of belief, and the maintenance of ritual traditions; and seeking to explain the freedom from religious conflict as the result of greater concern with ritual than with belief. Conflict, he is assuming, arises from consciously expressed religious views. Thirdly, while not assuming that pagan religion was totally lacking in 'faith', he sees the discussion of faith as having taken place outside the 'religious' context, i.e. not in the area of priests and rituals, but rather in that of poetry and drama. What he raises here, as we would express it, is the problem of deciding what should count, and what should not count, as 'religion' in the context of an ancient city.

[1] See especially Hume (1956), 48–51 = Section IX; on whom, Williams (1963) = Williams (2006), 267–73; North (2005).

If we approach that problem in institutional terms, and confine religion to the area of the activities of priests, magistrates and official bodies, or even to those of families and social associations (*collegia*), then there can be no doubt that professions of belief and arguments about the nature and influence of gods and goddesses scarcely figure as a part of 'religion' at all. But we know very well, in the instances where we have information about other aspects of the cultural life of a Greek or Roman city, that the gods play their part in many forms of expression both public and private, in drama and poetry, in philosophy and oratory, in art and architecture, in waking and dreaming. To limit religion to the religion of institutions may be convenient for the modern interpreter, but it also creates a wholly inadequate picture of the part played in ancient life by gods, goddesses and thoughts and feelings about them. It makes no sense, in my view, to say that the ancients did not believe in their own gods; but, having accepted that they did, we still have to face the issue of how we are to discuss and analyse the concept of 'beliefs' in a context so different from those with which we are familiar today.

Bacon's sharp observations raise issues still very far from resolved, and much in the minds of those (including me) who have been arguing, with some success, that religion in some sense of that word was a central concern of ancient societies and that understanding their religious life requires us to make great efforts to detach ourselves from the assumptions prevalent in our own societies and in our intellectual traditions about the discussion of religion. The most acute problem to be faced is that of vocabulary: virtually all the terms we use ('religion' itself, 'ritual', 'belief', 'faith', 'pagan' and 'paganism', 'polytheism' and 'monotheism', even 'sacrifice', 'vow', 'prayer') are in effect modern tools of debate, whose history lies in the modern world of anthropology, of comparative religion and of rival theologies.[2] It is a tempting position to argue that the word 'religion' itself (just like 'belief' itself) raises such inappropriate expectations in the modern reader that it would be best avoided completely. But that is a counsel of despair, threatening to cut the historian of ancient religions off from any possibility of communication or comparison with contemporary debate. The better course must surely be to redefine and refine the relationship between the reality of Graeco-Roman life, in so far as we can reconstruct it, and modern assumptions about the social space that a religion might be expected to occupy. The difference between the senses of the word in ancient and in

---

[2] On which see particularly Asad (1993), 27–79.

modern usage is crucial to developing any historically accurate understanding of the role of religion in ancient life.

Following this line of thought, which is not too far from Bacon's, it has in recent years become quite an established view, though anything but a universally accepted one, that the pagan world in the centuries BC had a particular style of religiosity, in which ritual was of central importance to their religious experience while beliefs were far less so.[3] Beliefs, following this view, began to be a gradually more important element in the course of the early centuries AD, as competition developed between different religious groups, and as membership of such groups came to depend on the individual's willingness to avow certain beliefs.[4] The implication is not, of course, that from a certain date onwards all those who professed adherence to a particular religious group were doing so on the basis of a rational choice between alternatives, only that such rational choices had become a possibility, whereas earlier they were not. It took many decades to formulate explicit beliefs, debate the wording of creeds, establish a vocabulary to describe those whose views deviated from accepted positions and so on. During this period of transition, it is questionable whether the concept of 'religious doctrine' should be applied, even in the context of Christianity.[5] But the new element in religious life was there, the seed planted. Even those who do not accept this analysis would agree that many other elements of religious life were sites of profound change in the course of the period from Cicero's lifetime to that of Augustine. By Augustine's day a man or woman could be said to have a religious identity based on membership of a group; they could be asked to know and profess the beliefs appropriate to that group; the group might expect to have a say about their moral conduct in everyday life, their ideas on the nature of deity, but also

---

[3] The claim that 'religious belief' is an inappropriate, Christianising, term should not be confused with the quite different claim that the rituals were empty of meaning or individuals of commitment to their rituals: Price (1984), 7–11; Beard, North and Price (1998) 1, 42–3. For an attack on this view see King (2003). King seeks to redefine the word 'belief' so as to make it usable in a pagan context, and in technical terms his argument is perfectly sound; but the redefinition has to be so radical that the term will necessarily continue to confuse those without expert knowledge of the subject. Further essential discussion in Phillips (1986), 2697–711; for a fruitful reappraisal of the relation between ritual and text, Rüpke (2004), 23–44.

[4] North (1992).

[5] On the notion of doctrine and its problems, Beck (2006), 41–64. For further recent discussions of the notion of belief in relation to ritual see Smith (2002); Rives (2007), 47–50; Ando (2008), xvi–xvii; 13–18. Ando's position, if I understand him, is to replace the notion of 'belief' with the notion of an 'empiricist epistemology' to which the Romans 'subscribed'. If this implies claiming that we should say of the Greeks and Romans not that they *believed* their gods existed, but rather that they *knew* they existed, this seems to me to be an interesting move in the right direction. But, of course, it must raise new logical problems.

about the past and the present, and about past sin and future redemption.[6] To sum up, it was possible for the individual to profess or to change their religious identity as a result of the beliefs they adopted, or lost. The religious identity they accepted or proclaimed would be dependent on these beliefs.

This book is concerned with one particular set of terms, 'monotheism' and 'polytheism', whose use carries the same potential for confusion as 'religion' itself, but which, like 'religion' itself, faces us with terms that we cannot avoid and questions that need to be answered.[7] What I am discussing here is the use of these terms in the context of the transformation of religious life in the period, as defined above. There cannot be any doubt that from the fourth century AD onwards the predominant religious view came to be the direction of belief and worship towards a single deity, as the worshippers themselves strongly asserted. This was a radical change in the character of religious life over a relatively short period of time. Contemporaries clearly identified this change as a matter of the highest importance: the existence of large numbers of Roman and Greek gods became a regular theme of polemic against the pagans; and denial of the gods a countercharge against Jews and Christians.[8] Translated into our terms, therefore, there was certainly a battle between monotheism and polytheism, even if those particular words did not exist as such, and did not have the comparative implications that we now read into them. This chapter will argue that it is a delusion to think that this change must have been the most important element in the religious revolution of these centuries or (still more controversially) that the many other changes in the religious life of the Roman Empire were determined by this particular change. It may be the case rather that the issue of the nature of deity became a shorthand term in the polemics for a whole range of confrontations that we need to analyse in their own terms.

There is a further problem connected with the use of the term 'polytheist' to describe the pagan side of the dispute. From one point of view, it is of course no more than a simple fact: pagans did worship many gods and goddesses. It is, however, a mistake, as I have argued previously,[9] to impose the term 'polytheist' as a full and valid description of the religious position of the pagans in the centuries before the emergence of a ubiquitous monotheistic alternative. They would not have recognised the term

---

[6] For more on this topic see below, pp. 42–5.

[7] For a concise survey of the development of monotheism see Assmann (2004b). Further: Momigliano (1986); Fowden (1993); Porter (2000); Krebernik and Van Oorschot (2002).

[8] Christian attacks: Arnobius, *Adversus nationes* 3 & 4; Augustine *De civ. D.* 7. For accounts of pagan religion in earlier Christian apologetic see Rüpke (2006).

[9] North (2005).

as having any function in describing their own activities. As in all such dualisms, each term is dependent on its opposite for its meaning. At least until the point in time at which Jewish monotheism became a familiar theme of discussion, it was assumed to be more or less a universal characteristic of the world the ancients knew that all peoples, even quite primitive ones, accepted some gods and goddesses. There might be different names for the same gods in different places; or there could be gods known to particular peoples and unrecognised elsewhere. But there was no state of religiosity which could be contrasted with polytheism and the term, had it existed at all, would have had no substantial application.

In these circumstances, it is perhaps unsurprising that ancient writers, however committed to the plurality of the divine, that is, to recognising a multiplicity of gods and goddesses of all kinds, simultaneously found it unproblematic to speak of these supernatural beings as if they formed a unity.[10] For them the modern opposition of monotheism/polytheism did not exist, so they had no fear that, if they spoke of the divine or of nature as playing a creative role, they would be accused of being covert monotheists or pantheists. This is one area where the Christian critics of pagan deities cannot be useful guides: for them, a slip into the language of monotheism is a precious confession that the great writers of the classical past agreed with them all the time. In fact, however, throughout the classical period and far earlier in the Near East, monotheistic assumptions are quite commonly found, without apparently raising any fears of weakening polytheistic practice.[11] The closing discussion in Book 2 of Cicero's *De divinatione* will serve to illustrate the point clearly. Cicero writes:

For it is the part of the wise man to preserve ancestral traditions by retaining rituals and ceremonies; and, meanwhile, both the beauty of the world and the regularity of celestial phenomena force us to confess the existence of an all-powerful and eternal nature which must be sustained and worshipped by the race of humans. (Cicero, *Div.* 2.148–9)

The context in which these remarks were made is precisely a defence of the tradition of worship of the Roman gods and goddesses. Cicero's purpose is not to attack traditional polytheism, but to expel the elements of superstition from the traditional worship.[12] He can accept as quite unproblematic what we today perceive as a radical inconsistency between his defence of traditional polytheism and his advocacy of the monotheism

---

[10] West (1999).
[11] On the Near Eastern tradition see Keel (1980); West (1999); Porter (2000); Assmann (2004).
[12] So Malouf (1992).

that seems to be implicit in his talk of nature and his use of the argument from Design. It seems evident that he sees (a) belief in the plurality of gods, (b) acceptance of the concept of a single creative force and (c) a critical attitude towards practices that strike him as irrational as forming an unproblematic combination; indeed he is recommending precisely that combination as the way to save the contemporary aberrant young from their moral weaknesses.[13] There seems nothing unusual in Cicero's argument here: he is simply placing nature (as the Stoics did) in the role of creator power.

There is a seeming way out of this dilemma, one that scholars sometimes find particularly appealing, but which is, in my view, a dead end. It might be called the conspiracy theory of ancient religion. Appealingly to intellectuals, it is a conspiracy of the intellectuals. From Xenophanes[14] and the commentator in the Derveni papyrus onwards,[15] if not earlier still, we can trace at all periods of Greek and Roman thought a critical attitude towards the gods and goddesses of the civic and poetical traditions, which notes their inconsistencies and immoralities and seems to offer a more intellectually acceptable conception of deity. We can often classify the language in which this is expressed as monotheistic (or at least proto-monotheistic); we can also fairly think of it as highly critical of the cruder versions of divine action to be found in some literary texts, not least in Hesiod and Homer.

The conspiracy theorist's way out would be to regard elite members as having from this point onwards a separate religion of their own, based on their rejection of polytheism and on their own perception of the role of the divine in the order of the cosmos. It would follow that the masses had quite a different religious consciousness from members of the elites; and that the acceptance of polytheism by elite members was always a matter of conscious hypocrisy. It is of course true that the manipulation of popular credulousness does occur as an occasional theme in Greek and Roman authors.[16] But that is not the same as accepting that different orders or classes have different religious perceptions. The fact is that virtually all ancients, so far as we know, continued to accept the ritual life embedded in their societies; citizens, both great and small, no doubt had their criticisms and reservations; but an attempt to rebel against traditional rituals is very rare.

[13] Cicero, *Div.* 2.4–7.
[14] Xenophanes frgs. 11, 14, 15 16 DK; see Kirk, Raven and Schofield (1983), 168–72.
[15] For the Derveni commentator: Janko (2002–3).
[16] See, for a notorious example, Polybius 6.56.6–15.

Meanwhile the suggestion that different classes have different qualities of religious experiences, so that they can be treated as if they were separate populations, is a highly contentious one. In the context of bodies of complex information or of developed sets of arguments, elite members alone may have the education and power of access to understand what the key issues are; and no doubt the maintenance of their religious authority requires such elite members to use their superiority in the control of argument and doctrine. It is quite another matter whether religious experience depends on these specifically intellectual activities. The language of ritual offers a level of communication which is precisely not dependent on the control of doctrines or argument.[17]

There has long been a strong consensus that much of what is discussed in this paper is not seriously problematic at all. A century ago the view was widely held that the development of religious history could be seen as a series of stages of which polytheism was the stage of the ancient and classical periods, preceded by more primitive conceptions of supernatural power, and destined to be followed by the stage of monotheism. The triumph of monotheism, therefore, did not need any historical explanation; indeed, if there was a problem it was why the emergence of the new forms of religion took so long. Such staged evolutionary theories of human development are no longer so fashionable, but in this case there is a residual grand narrative which still impedes analysis. It is ultimately rooted in the assumption that monotheistic explanations of the cosmos are more rational and therefore that monotheism must win out in any competition. The victory of monotheism in some form was therefore always guaranteed by its stronger basis of plausibility. Since most of those who study these matters are either overt monotheists or at least live in a monotheistic culture, this proposition for them is close to being self-verifying and scarcely in need of examination.

RELIGIOSITY, PAGAN STYLE

There cannot be much doubt that, as seen by observers in late antiquity, the primary characteristic of the pagan religion against which early Christianity fought was its polytheism. We have no reason to doubt that the pagans themselves, even though they have a very muted voice in such parts of the

---

[17] See the discussion in Beck (2004), 96–8. For the cognitive approach he is using here see n. 28 below.

debate as survive today,[18] also accepted this characterisation. It did after all summarise neatly a sharp difference between traditional religion and at least some of the forms in competition with it. There is no doubt either that, as a matter of fact, the religion of the pagans was profoundly polytheistic in its regular ritual aspect. There is no way out of this conclusion through arguing that pagans worshipping particular deities thought of themselves as really worshipping an aspect of some higher single being, even if individuals occasionally did so. In Rome, it was of the highest importance, as we know well, to identify correctly the specific deity and specific ritual for a particular purpose or occasion. If you had no knowledge of the name or gender of the specific deity, you needed a precise formula to address the unknown power: *sive deus, sive dea in cuius tutela hic lucus locusve est* ('whether it be a god or a goddess under whose protection this grove or place is').[19] John Scheid has rightly emphasised how modern scholarship has often refused to face up to the real implications of the rituals of polytheism.[20]

In view of all this, it is not at all surprising that those historians who perceive relations between pagans and Christians in the imperial centuries in terms of convergence, rather than of competition or conflict, should search for signs that the key step was the modification of this seemingly essential characteristic. Pagans from the later imperial period, i.e. from the third century AD onwards, were – so the argument goes – slowly but surely weakening in their conviction about the plurality of deity and, in proportion as they did so, their religion ceased to be fundamentally different from Christianity.[21] Hence the view that the 'development of pagan monotheism' should be seen as a crucial stage in the process by which paganism moved towards Christianity. Support for this view comes traditionally – and rightly – from the philosophical writings of the period and these have been very much emphasised in recent discussions. However, there are two solid reasons why this should not be allowed to close the argument down completely: first, as I have argued already,[22] there is nothing new for the pagan tradition in discussing the deity as a single force or entity, while simultaneously maintaining a committed polytheism; secondly, religion is

---

[18] The only extended text that puts a pagan point of view on the character of early Christianity is provided by the fragments of Celsus, as quoted in the hostile account of Origen, *Contra Celsum*. Translation in Chadwick (1953).

[19] For the formula: Scheid (1998a), 264 (= 94.11.3 & 12); Scheid (2005), 78.

[20] Scheid (1988), 425–57.

[21] For a notably fair-minded introductory discussion see Frede and Athanassiadi (1999).

[22] Above, pp. 38–9.

not a by-product of philosophy, nor is it a delicate plant easily destroyed by philosophical criticisms, much though secular liberal intellectuals may sometimes wish that it were. The philosophic discussions are, of course, important in themselves and for understanding Christian–pagan relations at the time, but cannot settle the issues for the historian of religion in this period.

There is yet another objection to treating an alleged evolution towards monotheism as the single most crucial change in the nature of religion in the imperial period: it is in fact only one of a series of changes and there is no obvious reason why it should be privileged over many others. A better approach might be to identify a whole bundle of related elements that serve to differentiate pagan religion from what we normally think of as 'religions' today. The transformation that takes place in the course of the first four centuries AD has its impact on a series of related elements of religious life; they might be listed as:

(a) the number of gods, goddesses and other powers and the nature of their mutual relationships
(b) the boundaries of 'religion' within society[23]
(c) the role of ritual in religious life
(d) the role of beliefs in religious life
(e) the issue of religious identity, as separate from civic/political or tribal identity
(f) the relation of the individual to the religious group
(g) the issue of religious 'profession'
(h) the relation of cult to morality
(i) the implied conception of the past and future
(j) the type and extent of religious authority
(k) the association of different world-views with different religious groups.

This list could be extended still further, and of course the themes it covers are not at all independent of one another, but overlap and interrelate. They are primarily intended to provide a template of the areas of life to which the religious revolution extends and which it influences. Each of them might alternatively be constructed as an axis along which religious practices moved in the course of the period. The new religions are in some cases at the opposite pole of a particular axis; pagan practices may be seen as moving rather reluctantly in the same direction. Some but not all of these areas need to be expanded further.

---

[23] On which see especially Markus (1990), 1–17.

(i) On (c) and (d) – ritual and belief

It is much easier to suggest that the balance between these two elements varies between different religious situations than to specify any particular criterion for assessing how they should be balanced against one another or how the differences might be quantified. We can state it as a fact that classical texts of all kinds, while they offer innumerable references to rituals performed, omitted or discussed, very seldom comment on the beliefs implied by those rituals or the beliefs of the individual actors. From such reports we can legitimately infer that some individuals were far more inclined than others to take religious factors seriously. Past generations of scholars have been rather given to detecting sceptical attitudes in both historians and agents; today, the reasons for hesitating about such judgements are becoming ever stronger. It would obviously be oversimple to argue that the infrequency of references to 'beliefs' by itself implies that they were not important; it is quite possible that such language was rather regarded as crude and inappropriate: speaking of relationships with divine beings called for greater delicacy and reticence.[24]

We can at least say with confidence that evidence of ritual activity is frequent and sustained in all forms of the surviving record – literary, epigraphic, papyrological or archaeological. We can also say that the beliefs of individuals do not appear in the record as the focus of any conflict, as they do so frequently in later periods.

(ii) On (e), (f) and (g) – profession of commitment to a group

The professing of your religious views might be taken as the key notion here, at least as providing the link between these three areas. 'Professing' implies that there are acts of commitment which bind the individual to a particular religious position. It was, of course, possible for a pagan to be accused in some cities (though not apparently in all) of impious behaviour; if you were, it might well be necessary to clear your name of such accusations by asserting your commitment to acts of piety, your devotion to the gods and your rejection of alien or magical practices. Apuleius' *Apologia* (whether real or fictitious) would be an instance of this possibility.[25] But there has to be a strong link between 'professing' and asserting your membership of a specific religious group, and, if so, as groups developed linked by commitment to shared conceptions and ideas, profession will have become an increasingly meaningful conception. It is quite clearly what Christians

---

[24] Discussion in Davies (2004), 96–142.
[25] For a full account of the speech: Harrison (2000), 39–88. The value of the text as evidence for the religious context is not much affected by the question of whether the speech was delivered in a real case.

do in the accounts of their martyrdoms; by implication the judges in these proceedings ask them to profess acceptance of paganism by an action of ritual or speech. When in the third century AD the requirement to sacrifice is imposed on all for the first time, it becomes in effect an act of pagan profession, which can hardly have existed as a regular event until this point.[26] This emergence of 'profession' could well be taken as one index of the set of changes taking place.

(iii) On (k) – world-views

The profoundest changes of all may very well be related to the world-view embedded in the new religions as opposed to the old ones. Here the distinction of J. Z. Smith between locative religions and utopian religions becomes a valuable tool.[27] Locative religions essentially seek to invoke deities in order to maintain the established order of the cosmos, which is perceived as essentially benign to human beings; so they use ritual means to maintain a right relationship with powers that can ensure peace, fertility, productivity and the continuation of the past into the future. Religious festivals, as performed, typically invoke the past and are conceived as having taken place annually every year since the origin of the city order and as continuing every year into the indefinite future.[28]

Admittedly, to take the case of Rome, there are stories of the origins of rituals, set in mythical time and attributed to the second King, Numa Pompilius, and also of additions to the ritual programme in later periods. Thus the games at Rome were known to have been introduced at specific dates and in specific circumstances, the *ludi Apollinares*, for instance, as a result of an oracle; an established cult might be changed or supplemented, as the Greek cult of Ceres was added in the third century BC to the older Roman one; or again the occasional introduction of new cults from abroad and the divinisation of rulers in the imperial centuries both implied the addition of gods or goddesses at recorded dates.[29] Such adjustments to the cults or the ritual calendars show that the Romans had awareness of religious change over time without feeling threatened by it, though in practice such understandings are often elided or assisted at the time of introduction by

---

[26] Rives (1999).

[27] Smith (1990), 121–43 and (2004), 15–16. For these ideas see also Sfameni Gasparro (1986).

[28] A different dualism, based on a cognitive account of the development of religion, should also be considered in this context: see Whitehouse (2004); Tremlin (2006); for difficulties in applying the theory to Roman religion: Gragg (2004); more positively, in relation to Mithraism: Beck (2004) and (2006), 88–98.

[29] For recorded innovations: Beard, North and Price (1998) I, 61–72, 79–87, 196–210.

means of reinterpretations of myths or of past traditions.[30] But many of the central rituals are not affected by recorded changes, above all the ritual of sacrifice and such procedures as the rituals of war (under the *ius fetiale*), the dedication to the gods of sacred space or the rituals of lustration. It remains broadly true that the ritual order is conceived as endlessly repeated and that its purpose is the maintenance of a well-established relationship with deities who have the power to maintain or to disturb the normal functioning of everyday life.[31]

Utopian religions on the other hand, and especially Christianity and Manichaeism, bring with them the new conception, of seeing the everyday world as fallen and distorted by evil forces, so that the role of religion begins to create the option of defying or rebelling against the established order. So the past becomes the place where the hope of salvation was revealed and the future as the location of a redeemed and ideal order, whether for the individual or for society as a whole. There cannot be much doubt that this is the message that was preached in at least some Christian texts from the beginning of the religion; how great its impact was in the early centuries is a matter of judgement.

RITUAL AND RELIGIOSITY

If it is true, or true to a significant extent, that changes took place along the lines discussed above, affecting not just narrowly defined groups but all the inhabitants of the Empire, the question to be asked in this book is how far such changes can be said to have resulted ultimately from a change in the conception of deity. It will be helpful at this point to look in somewhat more detail at what can be said about the Roman pagan conception of deity and its place in their society.[32] This conception is known to us from four main sources, all of which are more specialised than we should ideally like: the first is our knowledge of rituals and calendars; the second antiquarian accounts and Christian polemic, which turns the antiquarian accounts against the pagan religion; the third is late republican and early imperial literature, prose and poetry; the fourth is the archaeology and art of Rome

---

[30] As for instance the introduction of Cybele in 204 BC was, at some point, linked with the myth of Trojan origins: Beard, North and Price (1998) 1, 97–8, 197–8.

[31] On the relationship of the ritual order with time see Bell (1992), 118–30; Rappaport (1999), 181–90, 216–35.

[32] What follows draws heavily on Scheid (2005). I use the case of Rome as the best-known example, which I take to be not untypical of Graeco-Roman cities in general. For the parallel case of classical Athens see Parker (2005), especially the discussion at 387–451.

and Roman colonies in Italy and the Empire. This tradition is rich enough in itself, but almost devoid of any general statements of the principles that underlie the actions we hear about.[33]

There is no conception that we can detect of a Pantheon as such, in the sense of a fixed or closed list. Iuppiter, Iuno and Minerva, the three gods of the Capitoline triad, may be the senior deities, but we have no indication of the relative status of other gods and these like the others reappear with an endless array of defining names and local invocations. We can make a distinction between, on the one hand, the major gods, such as Mars, Apollo, Diana, Ceres, Hercules, Mercury, and, on the other, many 'lesser' gods who appear only in one ritual context, or are worshipped in only one location, or have a shrine with altars, but no temple. There may be fragments of particular ritual sequences or liturgies to be detected: so, the three most ancient *flamines* (priests devoted to a single named deity) are named after Iuppiter, Mars and Quirinus in that order of importance,[34] while Vesta appeared as the last deity invoked in a list.[35] Meanwhile the records of the Arval Brethren, the key ritual source to survive from the imperial period, show that the order of invocation in a particular ritual context is of great importance.[36] But trying to arrange the Roman gods in any kind of authoritative overall sequence belongs to the efforts of modern scholarship, not to any ancient ritual order to which we can appeal.

At the same time, it is clear that the list of deities was never finally determined. They might be invoked in groups, or the members of a group might be distinguished or differentiated.[37] Endless lists of deities were recorded in the late republican antiquarians and provided huge entertainment for the late imperial Christian critics.[38] In older work on Roman religion, they were fitted into a scheme of primitive or even of pre-deistic powers, which were conceived as developing out of an animistic phase and preceding the development of true anthropomorphic deities of the Graeco-Roman type.[39] More recent work has shown quite clearly that this was a mistake, which led to belief in a period when religion became fossilised and unchanging and to a failure to identify the creativity of later cultic activity, based on

---

[33] For the Roman deities: Turcan (1998) and (2000b); Beard, North and Price (1998) II, 26–59; Scheid (1998b), 123–40; Rüpke (2001), 67–85; on the gods in Latin literature: Feeney (1998), 115–36; Cole (2001), 67–91.

[34] See especially Dumézil (1970), 141–280, who famously argued for the primacy of this triad on the basis of Indo-European parallels.

[35] According to Cicero, *Nat. d.* 2.27; Dumézil (1970), 322–3.

[36] Scheid (1999) and (2005), 75–80.   [37] Scheid (2005), 58–83.

[38] Arnobius, *Adversus nationes*, on which see North (2007).

[39] Warde Fowler (1912), 270–313; Latte (1960), 195–212.

the great wealth of knowledge about the divine inhabitants of the city held by priests, their assistants and the records they kept.

The same pattern of endless potential knowledge with which a person might be equipped to deal with the divine can be seen expressed in the ritual sphere. Animal sacrifice, which is one of the central ritual concerns of religious life, was in itself a highly complex and variable sequence of actions in which the killing of the victim was one moment, of course an essential one, but not necessarily the most important, and certainly not the only important one. There was endless complexity too in the rules that attended the ritual: the colour, age and sex of the victim had to be appropriate to the deity and the occasion. The ritual had to be performed accurately to rule or the consequences might be dangerous.[40]

How this knowledge was handed on is not clear to us. So far as the state cult was concerned, much of the conveying of the victims, the provision of the equipment, the killing, butchering and cooking must have been carried out by the slave or lower-class officials whom we see in representations of the ritual. Responsibility for supervising the conduct of the ritual and expert knowledge about them was the province of the colleges of priests.[41] Within a family, where the *pater familias* conducted the rituals, we can only assume that fathers handed knowledge on to their sons.[42] At whatever level, possessing the right knowledge and skill must have been crucial. We meet this parade of knowledge when there are disputes or debates about the correct procedures to be used or doubt as to whether the right ritual has taken place. Roman historians are as anxious as Roman priests or politicians or emperors to show that they have the expertise to debate and decide the finer points of the rules of ritual.[43]

RELIGIOSITY, NEW STYLE

This sketch of how Roman polytheism worked suggests that the issues at stake here must have been far more complicated than can be explained by any single factor. If the claim is nevertheless that the number of gods and goddesses to be worshipped is the key to understanding the situation, what would that claim imply? In its simplest form, that the choice of monotheism is prior and that the rest of the religious changes are automatic

---

[40] For sacrificial rituals: Beard, North and Price (1998) I, 148–65; Scheid (1998b), 71–93 and (2005); on the transformation of rituals: Stroumsa (2005), 105–44.
[41] On whom Beard, North and Price (1998); Scheid (1998b), 109–22; Rüpke (2005), 1405–71.
[42] For discussion see Momigliano (1984), 885–8 = (1987), 85–7; Bremmer (1995).
[43] On the historians see the important work of Davies (2004).

consequences of that initial change. That may be the simplest theory, but it is scarcely a necessary one: the revolution might have started through the formation of differentiated groups, or of rival religious ideas or views of the world, and the polarisation between monotheists and polytheists might have emerged from the interplay of their rival conceptions. On that view, the adoption of monotheism might be seen as chronologically just an incident in the rivalry, but it might still have played a crucial role in the way the conflict developed. If an argument along these lines is to be put forward, it would have to be based on the assertion that the sequence of changes could only have been the consequence of monotheism. No other kind of religious movement could generate ideas of sufficient force.[44]

If that is the argument, is it valid? What we might more obviously infer from the data is that some radical change in the social location of religion had to take place before this established order could be displaced by new religious forces. Older theories on this subject[45] did indeed begin from the premise that pagan religion in the whole imperial period was in a state of deep decline, that its practices were almost universally neglected and despised, that the scepticism started among the elite was now widespread. If there were any attempts to defend it, these came from small groups of disgruntled aristocrats, with a specific interest in defending the status quo. This theory does have the merit of explaining why the religious tradition of pagan cities should have collapsed over a relatively short time span and long before the Empire of which it had seemed to be an essential part. Recent work, however, has questioned the factual basis of the theory: there seems little reason to believe that the pagan life of the early Empire was radically different from that of earlier centuries. If this negative view of the alleged state of pagan religion is discounted, as it now increasingly has been, we lack any theory to explain the collapse of paganism.[46]

One alternative, as we have seen already, is even simpler and itself has a long and distinguished history. We can adopt the view that monotheism is a later and a superior stage of religious history.[47] What we see therefore is the inevitable triumph of a religious outlook that was bound to emerge from the process of evolution. This proposition can be put in a form less obviously committed a priori to the superiority of monotheism, by linking

---

[44] It is certainly arguable that the formation of specifically religious groups within the Empire was started, or at least accelerated, by the splitting of Christians from Jews, on which see Lieu (1998) = (2002).

[45] For discussion of the development of views; Scheid (1988).

[46] See, e.g., Lane Fox (1986), Part 1.

[47] For examples see, e.g., MacMullen (1977); Assmann (2004).

the simplification of the list of deities to the increasing complexity of society. In the formulation of Rodney Stark:[48] 'As societies become older, larger and more cosmopolitan they will worship fewer gods of greater scope.' The problem with this and similar propositions is that both the idea of monotheism and the increasing complexity of societies had been in existence for many centuries in the Mediterranean areas and in the Near and Middle East without having the effects the theory proposes. It is not at all obvious that the fourth century AD is qualitatively different in social or political organisation from many centuries that preceded it, during which polytheism and its rituals had been maintained unproblematically in a huge range of societies of very different types, many of great complexity. It is then difficult to see Stark's formulation as anything other than a restatement of the grand narrative of the evolution of monotheism. The word 'older' is a particular giveaway: why should a society have to be 'old', whatever that means, for its size and complexity to have the effect postulated? The word 'old' simply smuggles back the ideology of sequential stages. Wait long enough and Monotheism always wins through.

There does, however, seem to be one crucial new element, introduced by the proponents of the new religions. They seem by the third century AD to be putting forward statements expressing the relations between men and deities in verbal propositions. It seems extraordinarily difficult to do this in the context of the type of paganism that we have been discussing. It is not just that Christians quite soon produce a creed, where the pagans never had one; but that it is very difficult to imagine what a pagan creed could ever have been.[49] It thus becomes possible to ask for acts of commitment by members or potential members of a group, which take the form of assenting to a brief statement of belief in the group's doctrine. This may be seen as a reformulation of Stark's theory, but bringing the notion of simplification into direct contact with the development of group membership.

To put the argument into counterfactual terms:[50] suppose we were trying to construct a religious revolution which took place not between traditional paganism and newly emergent monotheistic or dualistic faiths, but between two or more rival versions of polytheism, we should virtually be obliged to perceive them as selecting from amongst the available pagan deities and prioritising selected individuals, to whom specific characteristics would

[48] Stark and Bainbridge (1987), 85–7 (proposition 61); Stark (1996), 201–3, (2001), 23–9. Stark's ingenuity and theoretical perspectives offer a good deal of profit to the discussion of all these issues, though I disagree with most of his conclusions about the religious history of the Roman Empire.
[49] For the development of Christian creeds see Kelly (1972).
[50] For the relationship between history and counterfactuals: Hawthorn (1991), 1–37.

need to be ascribed: it is here that the phenomenon usually now called henotheism comes into the picture. This is another modern term of debate, devised to describe a situation where one of the pagan deities is privileged over the others.[51] Characteristically, this seems not to have involved the denial of the other pagan deities, though in some cases the 'one' may be seen as absorbing many others, as in the case of Isis.[52] Even the cult of Hypsistos, who might seem to be a supreme deity, seems mostly still within the ambit of polytheism.[53] What is commonly found in autonomous cult-formations of this kind is the development of a circle of deities, as would be exemplified by the circle of Egyptian deities associated with Isis.[54] What these examples might suggest is not so much the emergence of single-deity formations as the association of individuals with groups having their own pattern of worship and commitment.

The most readily available model for this process would be the form of Bacchic worship suppressed by the Roman senate in the 180s BC.[55] Here it seems fairly clear that in a pre-Christian, pagan, context something approaching a separate religious identity was developed, or at least was in the process of development when the senate destroyed it. We have no reason to think that the Italian Bacchus-worshippers in question had rejected paganism or denied the divinity of the other pagan gods. But they did form separate religious groups with an authority structure of their own, funds of their own and religious practices of their own. The whole cultic activity was regarded as Bacchic, their sacred place was called a Bacanal and the women devotees were named as Bacchae; indeed commitment to the cult seems to have been described as 'going to the Bacchic women'.[56] Whatever the truth about the religious situation in the 180s BC, thinking beyond the point to which we can reconstruct it, it is not hard to imagine, in counterfactual mode, that this cult could have generated an exclusive devotion to Bacchus, or the deities of the Bacchic circle, of a henotheistic type.

A similar speculation could be based on the form of Mithras-worship found in the later Empire, at least according to some of its interpreters.

[51] See especially the work of Versnel (1990), esp. 1–38, and (2000), 79–163.
[52] For Isis' identification with many other deities see e.g. Apuleius, *Met.* 11.5.
[53] For discussion see Roberts, Skeat and Nock (1936) = Nock (1972), 414–43; Mitchell (1999); Belayche (2005a); and the contributions of Belayche and Mitchell to this volume. For the Jewish image of God at this time: Goodman (2003) = Goodman (2007), 205–17.
[54] Malaise (2005), 25–117.   [55] Gallini (1970), 5–52; North (1979); Gruen (1990).
[56] The details can all be derived from the senate's decree banning the cult, which is preserved on bronze: Degrassi, *ILLRP* 511. The phrase *Bacas vir nequis adiese velet...* (Let no man be minded to go to the Bacchic women...) seems clearly to stand as a formula for attending the group's rituals.

Following the thought of Roger Beck,[57] the cult combined a committed membership with a religious conception built from an intellectual theory about the relationship between human beings and the cosmos as revealed by astronomy and astrology. It had a central deity in Mithras, as the Unconquered Sun, but certainly recognised other powers as well.[58] Whether it could be said to have its own doctrine or creed, we do not know, but the formula DEUS INVICTUS SOL MITHRAS[59] could be said to constitute the kernel of a teaching. There is no reason to suppose that Mithraists rejected the other pagan deities or that their ideas or practices were seen as incompatible with the normal standards of life in the Roman world. Indeed it is still very arguable that the grade system at the heart of the Mithraic system of group organisation was essentially confirmatory of the social order of the Roman Empire.[60]

These counterfactual speculations serve the useful purpose of setting the limits of our argument. They suggest two working hypotheses: first, that monotheism in any strict sense is not a necessary condition for the religious transformations we are seeking to analyse; but, secondly, that some degree of simplification of the complexities of traditional pagan practice was a necessary but not sufficient condition for those transformations to take place. These two propositions, taken separately or together, suggest the lines along which it might be possible to analyse and to some extent explain what happens in the later centuries of the Roman Empire, without having to conjure up the ghost of a defunct grand narrative. A list of required adaptations might be:

1. An increased level of commitment to a specifically religious group
2. Required acts expressing commitment to the group
3. Clarified and consistent theological propositions
4. A verbal formulation of the beliefs of the group
5. A requirement to reject all deities other than those accepted by the group.

In fact, of course, all this was realised, not by the evolution of paganism or of groups within paganism, but through co-existence and competition with monotheistic rivals that were far better adapted to the new conditions.

This is not the place to attempt a causal explanation of the religious revolution of the Roman Empire, if such a thing could ever be possible. What is possible is to realise that the assumption that monotheism was the primary

---

[57] Beck (2006), for the fullest statement of his position.
[58] Though the relationship between the different divine personalities in the cult's iconography is not easy to decipher. See Turcan (2000a), 62–7.
[59] For the formula: Beck (2006), 4–6.   [60] So, convincingly, Gordon (2001).

cause is driven by religious commitment, not by rational argument, though of course it remains one of the range of theories to be considered. But it is equally possible to argue (for instance) that the original driving force could have been the emergence (for whatever reasons) in the cities of the Empire of competing religious groups of various kinds, some traditional, some ethnic, some driven by new ideas. Within this competition, the interest of the groups lay in attracting and retaining members. Both the requirement of higher commitment to the group and the need for clear criteria of membership will have encouraged the development of verbal formulations of belief to which the members were expected to adhere. In this radically new situation, groups with a radical message such as monotheism or dualism would have had a clear competitive advantage. On that view the popularity of monotheism should be seen as a consequence of the overall religious situation of the Roman Empire.

CHAPTER 4

The case for pagan monotheism in Greek and Graeco-Roman antiquity

Michael Frede

DEFINING MONOTHEISM

A fact of crucial importance for the history which many of us share is that in late antiquity a large part of the population of the Roman Empire, perhaps even the majority, but in any case the dominant part of the population, converted to Christianity, and Christianity became the official religion of the Empire. Part of becoming a Christian, put in modern terms, is to become a monotheist, that is, roughly speaking, a person who believes in just one god, namely in God with a capital 'G', unless, of course, one already was a monotheist. But at least the vast majority of the inhabitants of the Roman Empire had been, again in modern terms, polytheists, that is, again roughly speaking, persons who believe in a plurality of gods. Given the importance of the fact that Christianity within the relatively short time of a few centuries came to be the dominant religion within the Empire, replacing, and for the most part eliminating, the various forms of paganism, one would like to know how this came about. Obviously there are answers to this from a religious perspective. But, since we are dealing with a remarkable historical phenomenon, we might want to understand how this came about in purely historical terms. From this perspective the change is bound to present itself as a highly complex matter.

One possible factor in this matter, though, of particular relevance in the case of city dwellers, as opposed to the rural population of *pagani*, and especially in the case of the educated elite which dominated life in the city, may have been that their conversion was facilitated by the fact that their religious view already favoured some form of monotheism or other, rather than a polytheistic belief in the traditional gods. I am inclined to think that there were many educated pagans who, like Synesius of Cyrene, were monotheists before they became Christians. Whether or not this is so, is, though, a matter of controversy. But, if it is so, pagan monotheism in Greek or Graeco-Roman antiquity becomes a topic for the historians of

Greek religion or religion in the Roman Empire, quite independently of the further general historical question whether or not a general tendency towards monotheism facilitated the widespread acceptance of Christianity. It seems to me that there was not just a tendency towards monotheism in Greek religion and Greek religious thought, clearly observable for instance in the Derveni author of the fourth century BC, but that this tendency evolved into one or another form of monotheism, even if there is a question as to how widespread such forms of monotheism were. In any case, it is this topic in the history of ancient religion which I will be concerned with.

But, if one wants to talk about pagan monotheism in Greek or Graeco-Roman antiquity and the various forms it took, one first has to assure oneself that there actually was such a thing as pagan monotheism in antiquity for us to have something to talk about and to study. The need for this arises not so much because it is a topic which has been so neglected that one's audience might not be aware of the fact that there was such a thing as monotheism in antiquity and that it is worth studying. The need arises primarily because, for highly complex reasons which it is difficult to identify, since they are rarely spelled out in sufficient detail, eminent scholars have taken the view, either in discussing particular ancient authors, or in writing about Greek religion or Greek religious thought quite generally, that ancient pagan thought never reached a stage of development or evolution which we properly could call 'monotheistic'. Very, very roughly speaking, these scholars seem to have been guided by a vague general intuition, namely the thought that ancient pagans, however enlightened they may have been, never managed to entirely shed their polytheism; moreover, that even when in some sense they were to believe in one god, it was just not the right kind of god to qualify them as monotheists, namely the kind of god Christians believe in, but, for instance, some abstract theoretical or philosophical principle, which is not the appropriate object for one to have a religious attitude towards, let alone the kind of god a large population would be persuaded to worship as the sole appropriate object of religious veneration.

As a paradigm of such a scholar I will single out Martin Nilsson because of his authoritative status in matters of Greek religion. Nilsson quite generally rejects the suggestion that pagans ever on their own came to adopt a monotheistic position, and he discusses some apparent examples to the contrary, trying to show that these are not really examples of true monotheism, of monotheism properly speaking. In fact, in Volume II of his *Geschichte der griechischen Religion* (Munich 1962, 2nd edn) he devotes a whole section to the topic of monotheism (pp. 569–78). It is a rather curious text. For, on the one hand, Nilsson says that the monotheistic idea arose early in Greece, that there was a strong tendency towards monotheism in Greek religious thought which in late antiquity even became overwhelming, and that the spread of Christianity was greatly helped by this tendency towards monotheism. On the other hand, Nilsson says right from the beginning (p. 569) that 'the so-called monotheistic gods' of the pagans were just that, so-called monotheistic gods, and that paganism never managed to arrive at the espousal of a fully monotheistic god. He then, as I said, goes on to argue for this by discussing particular examples, prominently among them examples of Greek philosophers. I will return to this discussion of these examples later. For the moment I just want to point out that I find it very puzzling why, if there was such an ultimately even overwhelming tendency towards monotheism, among pagans it should never have issued in what we properly call 'monotheism'.

Thus, given how widespread the sort of position in which we find Nilsson is, we, to begin with, have to address the issue whether there is such a thing as pagan monotheism in antiquity. Now the problem obviously arises because, almost without exception, pagans in antiquity, however educated and enlightened, condoned, supported, tried to justify the public cult of a plurality of traditional gods, or even participated in it themselves. Often we do not know with what personal reservations they did so. But often enough, for instance in the case of late ancient Platonists who more or less demonstratively or even aggressively defended the cause of pagan Hellenism and the religious cult it involved, it is difficult to believe that their participation in traditional cult depended on a *reservatio mentalis*. So, on the face of it, the matter seems simple enough: Christians without equivocation believed in one God, pagans, even the most highly educated pagans, with perhaps an exception here or there, did believe in a plurality of gods or at least did not unequivocally affirm that there is just one god. Yet the matter seems to me to be more complicated. One can believe unequivocally that there is one sense of the word 'god', the most proper, strict, appropriate, enlightening sense of the word, in which there is just one god, but also believe that this one god manifests itself in many ways and that these different ways correspond to the different gods of traditional cult, and hence without reservation participate in their cult and support the maintenance of these cults arguing that ordinary citizens in this way do worship God, though they themselves do not understand this. This seems to me to be at least one of several possibilities in which one may support traditional public cult of polytheistic gods, though one only believes in one god. In fact, it seems to me to be a fairly realistic possibility, since it is not far removed from what Xenophon attributes to Socrates in *Memorabilia* 4.3, on Socrates' piety, but also from how Socrates, according to Xenophon, conceives of piety. We have been created by the demiurge, that is God, with great providence and hence should recognise this. But the way to do this, according to the Delphic oracle, is to follow the law of one's city, that is to say to follow the traditional cults of one's city. The question, then, is whether we should regard this, or something like it, as monotheism or as polytheism.

Now, which view one adopts on this of course crucially depends on what one means by 'monotheism'. And so, for a while, I want to turn to the issue of what one can reasonably, or perhaps even should, understand by 'monotheism', if one wants to apply this modern term to ancient religious thought of any kind, whether pagan, Christian, Jewish, or whatever else. This is a somewhat tedious topic, but without some clarification the discussion of pagan monotheism in antiquity will continue to be obstructed by misunderstanding. Most authors who use the term 'monotheism' seem to assume that it is sufficiently clear what is meant by the word and that, hence, its use does not require any further explanation. Perhaps they take it for granted that we all understand that to be a monotheist is to believe in only one god, namely in God with a capital 'G'. And in the context of the societies we live in it is supposed to be reasonably clear what that means, clear to such an extent that even an atheist understands it. He is thought of, and thinks of himself, as somebody who does not believe in God. In this context the god in question in the first instance is the God Christians believe in, but then perhaps also the god some non-Christians, for instance Jews, or even Muslims, believe in. Hence we might be tempted to say that to be a monotheist is to be a person who believes in any one god, namely the sort of god, or even the God, that Christians believe in.

If we start this way, we have to be very careful about the way we proceed further. The way Christians in modern terms conceive of God, at least those who write about such matters, is in a highly specific sort of god. If we make it part of the very notion of monotheism that to be a monotheist one has to believe in this specific sort of god, or even in this god thus conceived of, we run the risk that by definition only Christians, or perhaps even only Christians from a certain point onwards, will count as monotheists. For example modern Christians normally think of God as an incorporeal or perhaps even as a transcendent being. But if we think of Tertullian and the young Augustine before he became exposed to Platonism, we may wonder whether early Christians really conceived of the god they believed in as incorporeal and transcendent, and nevertheless we think of them as monotheists. Notoriously Tertullian thought that God was a body (cf. *Adversus Praxean* 7), and Augustine learned from the Platonists that there was an intelligible realm of things immaterial. Hence, if we say that to be a monotheist is to believe in one god, namely the sort of god the Christians believe in, we should understand the phrase 'the sort of god' not so narrowly as to tie the notion of monotheism to a belief in the specific sort of god modern Christians do, or at least are supposed to, believe in. For in doing so we face the risk of excluding many whom, for other reasons, we would want to call 'monotheists'. Hence it seems to me that we should try to isolate within the Christian conception of God a more general element, in virtue of which we count Christians as monotheists without thereby implying that only Christians, or even only Christians from a certain point onwards, can count as monotheists. To see how this might be done, let us approach the question about what is to count as monotheism in a somewhat different way.

Let us suppose that the descendants of some person called 'George' came to think that George not only had been a truly remarkable man, but persuaded themselves that George regularly appeared to them when they were in difficulty to unfailingly give them good, even if somewhat mysterious, advice which needed to be interpreted appropriately, which they sometimes did not manage to do. But this was not George's fault, as each time they could see in hindsight when they had misunderstood him. And hence they came to think that he must be immortal and, indeed, a god. They formed a George cult community which others could also join. Up to that point they had been hesitant, undogmatic atheists, not believing in any gods, let alone in God. But now they believed in George, even if not in God or in any other god. It seems to me to be clear that, though they only believe in one god, we would not call them 'monotheists'. And this is not just, or even primarily, because they do not believe in God. It rather is that even if George were a god, he would not be the right kind of god to qualify believers in him as monotheists. For the role George supposedly plays in the world, even on the Georgians' own view, is very limited: he, one does not quite know how, gives them good advice in difficult situations. But the way of the world in general, and the way it takes its course, seem to be almost entirely independent of George. By contrast, the way we think of a monotheistic god, is as a god without whom the world as a whole would not be the way it is, or perhaps would not even exist, or a god who rules the world in that he determines, at least in rough outline, if not in all detail, the course the world takes, or something along these lines. Once we take this step and think that monotheism is not just a matter of believing in only one god, but also a matter of believing in a certain kind of god, namely the sort of god who somehow runs the world as a whole, it is very tempting to take one further step, namely to take the view that monotheism is a matter of believing in the sort of god who plays such a pervasive role in determining what the world is like and what course it takes, and that there is no conceptual space left for any other god or other gods besides him, because the one god determines everything which one might think was divinely determined, and which one might think must be the work of a divine being. If one believed in this sort of god, there would be no point in believing in any other gods besides this god. What is wrong about the worshippers of George, apart from their factually being mistaken about George's miraculous posthumous powers, is that, even if George were a god, he would not be the right sort of god to qualify them as monotheists, but at the same time one would not understand why, on the Georgians' view, there could not, or should not, be any number of gods like George. There is something inherently incongruous and unstable about the Georgians' belief in just one god. Hence, if we are looking for what it might be about the sort of god the Christians believe in which qualifies their belief as monotheistic, but which itself is not a matter of specifically Christian belief, so as not to rule out the possibility that also non-Christians might be monotheists, the answer might be that this god is conceived of in such a way that there is no space left for any other gods besides him, for instance because he is conceived of as having all the power there is, or as providentially arranging everything.

But making this assumption about what is to count as monotheism comes with a price. For it now will no longer be the case that anybody who believes in any god at all will be either a monotheist or a polytheist. For, given the suggested understanding of 'monotheism', the Georgians will be neither. This, though, is a price we should be willing to pay, since the position of the Georgians is inherently unstable and incongruous, and since the religious phenomena we are interested in do not include something like the Georgians anyway. So we will say that anybody we are interested in, if he believes in any god at all, is either a monotheist or a polytheist. But, if we take a monotheist to be a person who not only believes in one god, but a god conceived of in such a way that there is no space for other gods, we should also assume that the polytheist is a person who not only believes in many gods, but also in gods none of which is conceived of in such a way as to be a monotheistic god. And this seems to fit our intuitions about polytheism as involving belief in a plurality of gods, all of which, though, have their obvious limitations, reasonably well.

But one can see how complications are bound to arise from this way of distinguishing between monotheism and polytheism. Monotheism, as we have been trying to capture the notion, presupposes a rather elevated conception of God. It more likely than not, at least in the Greek case, is the product of long reflection, reflection in good part on what a god would have to be like in order for one to believe in him as the worthy object of cult, rather than becoming an atheist or turning one's back on the gods of popular belief and public cult. We get a rather vivid view of the sorts of reflections apparently common in Athens in Plato's time in Plato's *Republic* 2.360e–367e, but in particular in the whole of his *Laws* 10. Now, given his elated conception of God, a monotheist not only is going to deny that any of the gods of the polytheist is God, he is likely to challenge the notion that any of the gods of the polytheist deserves to be called 'god'. What this suggests is that there is something problematic about saying that a monotheist believes in one god, whereas a polytheist believes in many gods. For this obscures the fact that their conceptions of a god, and to that extent the meaning of the word 'god', are not quite the same. If the polytheist conceived of his gods, say Zeus, in the way the monotheist does, he would not be a polytheist and believe in many gods. But differently, a polytheistic god is not a god in quite the same way and sense in which a monotheistic god is. But this, in principle, opens up the possibility for a monotheist to say that, strictly speaking, there is just one god, namely God, but that there are also beings which, given the way the word 'god' commonly is used and understood, would be called 'gods', and might well be called 'gods', as long as it is understood that this is a catachrestic use of the word. Thus in principle a monotheist could talk of many gods without thereby in the least compromising his monotheism, since the many gods would not be gods in quite the same sense as God.

But at this point it might be in order to turn at least briefly to the history of the word 'monotheism'. For it seems to me that if we follow our somewhat vague intuition about what monotheism is, and accordingly say that monotheism is not just a matter of believing in one god only, but also of believing in a certain kind of god, namely the sort of god whose existence rules out the possibility of there being other gods, we at least in part are influenced by a modern tradition of debates about monotheism. 'Monotheism', along with its cognates, is not an ancient or even medieval but a modern word. It seems to have been introduced first into English in the seventeenth century. It is used, for example, in H. More's *An Explanation of the Grand Mystery of Godliness* (London 1660, p. 62). It only gained wider currency around 1750 and then, later still, entered German, French and Italian. Nor is there an ancient word, or at least a phrase, that appropriately would be rendered by 'monotheism', given the way the word came to be used in modern times. Hence one may wonder whether the ancients had the concept of a monotheist in the sense we have been discussing, namely the sense in which a monotheist not only believes in just one god, but also the right sort of god, who by his nature leaves no space for the possibility of other gods. It may well be the case that what primarily concerned ancient Christians was whether one believed in one god or in many, as they supposed the pagans as a rule did. And it may have been understood or taken for granted that if our belief is in only one god, it would be the right sort of god, namely the God the Christians believed in. What primarily concerned educated pagans, especially pagans in late antiquity, was not so much whether one believed in one god or in many, but whether one believed in one god who was the right sort of god, not one god among many, but a super god, as it were. From at least the second century AD onwards pagans might compare this one god with the God of the Jews and the Christians. Numenius, for instance, writing in the second half of the second century, in his work *De bono*, that is on what he takes to be the first god, praises the ancient notions, among them that of the Jews, for having preserved the conception of this god as something incorporeal (frg. 1b Des Places = Origen, *Contra Celsum* 1.15). But Numenius also acknowledged other gods or divine beings entirely dependent on this first god. Hence it is far from clear whether the ancients, pagans or Christians, thought of things in terms of the modern notion of 'monotheism'.

That this notion is a modern notion does not mean, of course, that it is not perfectly adequate or even helpful in describing and explaining Greek religion or religion in Graeco-Roman times. If we look, though, at the use of the term 'monotheism' in modern times, it not only is clear that the term was not introduced to describe religion in Greek or in Graeco-Roman antiquity, but that it came to be used in discussions in which the finer details of the development of Greek religious thought did not seem to matter. What was at issue in the debates about monotheism were rather global questions in the philosophy of religion, in the history of religion, in comparative religion, and in cultural anthropology. A main issue was whether monotheism, or a form of monotheism, was the original religion of mankind, or at least of part of mankind, which then got corrupted into polytheism, or whether it was the other way round, namely that monotheism was the most advanced and highest form of human religiosity which had developed out of polytheism, but also, moreover, whether polytheism itself was preceded by a more primitive stage or a series of more primitive stages, which again raised the question of the ultimate origin of religion. In these debates, it seems, it was for the most part just taken for granted that monotheism is the most advanced or most enlightened form of religiosity, and that Christianity is the paradigm of this form of religiosity. And when one talked about Christianity, one thought of Christianity as understood in modern times. What matters for our purposes is that, as far as I can see, these debates do not provide us with any guidance as to how to deal with the more complicated cases we have to deal with, if we want to decide whether there was such a thing as monotheism in pagan antiquity and what forms it took, since they are not sensitive to these details. Hence, if we want to use the term 'monotheism' in discussing the details of the development of Greek religious thought, we will need some further reflection on how to understand the term when applied to ancient thought. It is telling that Ramsay MacMullen in his book *Paganism in the Roman Empire* in discussing the question of pagan monotheism shows considerable reservations towards the term. He says (1981: 88): 'We must first confront the very term "monotheism". Like most big words, and "-isms" worst of all, it is no friend of clear thought. It indicates acknowledgement of one god only. Very good. But it suggests no definition of "God".' This, indeed, is a major, if not the major, source of difficulty I have alluded to in the preceding discussion. To overcome it, we will have to take into account the various ways in which the ancients themselves conceived of a god or used the word 'god'.

Against this somewhat abstract background I now want to consider some actual concrete cases of what I take to be pagan monotheism in the hope of being able to show that there was such a thing as pagan monotheism in antiquity, but also of shedding some light on how we should understand the term 'monotheism' if we want to apply it to current religious thought. Since ancient philosophy seems to be the most likely place to find monotheism in antiquity, I have chosen three philosophers, Antisthenes, Chrysippus and Galen. I have chosen them because they represent different periods in Greek thought, but also are representative of some of the quite different forms monotheism can take in antiquity. Moreover I have chosen Antisthenes because I do not see any way in which one could deny that Antisthenes was a monotheist by any standard of what is to count as monotheism. Having thus minimally achieved the purpose of establishing that there was such a thing as pagan monotheism, I want to turn to the more complicated cases of Chrysippus and Galen in the hope of being able to shed some light on how to understand 'monotheism' and the various forms of monotheism we find in antiquity. Their case is more complicated because they try to accommodate belief in a plurality of divine beings, including the gods of traditional cult.

ANTISTHENES

Let us, then, begin with Antisthenes, a follower and companion of Socrates, active at the end of the fifth and in the first third of the fourth century BC. We have two sets of testimony concerning his views about God and the gods (frgs. 39a–e and 40a–d Decleva Caizzi). Within the first set we can distinguish two subgroups. There are, first, the testimonies of Philodemus (*De pietate* 7) and Cicero (*Nat. d.* 1.13.32), and, second, three further testimonies to the same effect as the testimonies by Philodemus and Cicero. I am inclined to think that the three further testimonies, one by Minucius Felix (19.7) and two by Lactantius (*Div. inst.* 1.5.18–19 and *De ira Dei* II.14), are derived from Cicero. They still are of interest in so far as their authors are Christian and as they reflect these Christians' understanding of Antisthenes' views as reported rather briefly in Cicero. But let us concentrate on Philodemus' and Cicero's testimonies. Philodemus says that Antisthenes in his work *Physicus* claims that by convention (κατὰ νόμον) there are many gods, but that by nature (κατὰ φύσιν) there is just one. Cicero presents the Epicurean Velleius as saying that according to Antisthenes the popular gods are many, but that by nature, in the nature of things, there is just one god. Velleius claims that Antisthenes in taking this position does away with the power and the reality of the gods. Antisthenes, then, seems to have said that in popular belief there are many gods, but that they are merely conventional, that they do not exist in reality; for in reality there is just one god. According to these testimonies Antisthenes does not seem to be saying that by convention there are many gods, but that just one of these conventional gods exists in reality. He seems to be saying that none of the gods of popular belief exists in reality. When according to Philodemus he says that the many gods only exist by convention, I take it that what he has in mind is this. People have been brought up to think and talk about things and to behave as is customary and right, for instance to honour one's parents and worship the traditional gods, to follow custom and law in thinking that there are many gods and participate in their cult, for instance in the cult of Apollo and of Zeus and many others, as piety requires, and so on. As we learn, for instance, from Aristotle's *Constitution of Athens* (55.15–17), Athenians in Antisthenes' day have been raised to think and say that they, through Ion who settled in Africa, are descendants of the god Apollo, and that they worship Zeus Herkeios as the protector of the household. If an

Athenian wants to stand for office, he is subjected to formal questioning to ascertain whether he qualifies as a candidate. Among other things he is asked whether he recognises Apollo as an ancestral god and Zeus as the protector of the household. According to Antisthenes, Apollo and Zeus Herkeios only exist κατὰ νόμον, by custom and convention, and this was partly anchored in written and unwritten law concerning piety, which laid down what one owes to one's parents, one's ancestors, one's elders and betters, and the gods.

Since this for our purposes is an important matter, I want to give some more attention to the claim that the many gods of popular belief only exist by convention by referring to Plato's *Laws* 10, a book entirely devoted to legislation against impiety in word and deed. Plato makes fifth-century enlightenment in Athens partly responsible for the impiety and the injustice associated with it (cf. 886a–b9; 886d3 ff.), for it leads to the view that the gods do not exist by nature but by art, namely the art of legislation. In the same way as what is just or not just is a matter not of the nature of things, but of what is deemed just or not by custom and law in a society, and this differs from society to society, so also the gods do not exist in the nature of things, but are the product of what is deemed to be a god by custom and law, and differ from place to place (889e–890a1). This sort of view was backed up by various theories as to how people came to believe in gods in the first place, but also by views about the social utility of making people believe in gods, for instance the view that this will make them abide by the law. It is in this sense, then, that Antisthenes thinks that the gods of popular belief and public cult are conventional. What distinguishes him, though, from the atheists attacked in the *Laws* is that he does believe that there is one god by nature.

Before we proceed, we should note that both Cicero's and Philodemus' testimonies clearly are drawn from one and the same source, a lost Epicurean text on piety in which a whole array of philosophers were criticised for their impious views, among them the Stoics and Antisthenes for his rejection of the traditional gods of civic cult. Given that the testimonies in Lactantius and Minucius Felix presumably are derived from Cicero, there is ultimately only one source for this set of five testimonies, and that is a hostile, namely Epicurean, source. The concern this may raise about the value of this information fortunately is more than balanced by the fact that it coheres perfectly with the other set of testimonies about Antisthenes' views about this god. We should also mention that Minucius Felix and Lactantius are not disinterested witnesses, either. They refer to Antisthenes' view in support of their claim that even some of the ancient philosophers already shared the Christian belief in one god. Though their testimony presumably does not have any evidential value in addition to that of Cicero's testimony, as far as Antisthenes' belief in one god is concerned, it does show that some ancient Christians had no difficulty in saying that some pagans did believe in one god, as the Christians do, and that Antisthenes was one of these. Surely Minucius Felix and Lactantius must have had some idea what, from the point of view of an ancient Christian, it meant to believe in one god, and we should not easily brush this aside, assuming either that we know better than they did what ancient Christians meant when they talked about belief in only one god, or better than what Christians generally mean when they talk about belief in only one God.

The second set of testimonies concerning Antisthenes' one god consists of four passages (frgs. 40a–d Decleva Caizzi), two from Clement of Alexandria (*Strom.* 5.14.108.4; *Protrep.* 6.71.1), one from Eusebius (*Praeparatio evangelica* 13.13.35) and one from Theodoret (*Graecarum affectionum curatio* 1.75). I take it that Theodoret depends on Eusebius, and Eusebius in turn on Clement. Clement, who in both cases finds it relevant to refer to the fact that Antisthenes was a follower of Socrates, reports that according to Antisthenes God is unlike anything else, and that therefore there is no point in resorting to images to find out through them what he is like. This, for a start, looks like a criticism of cult-statues, and hence fits the report that Antisthenes rejected the gods of popular belief and cult. We may also assume, on the basis of these testimonies, that Antisthenes rejected the popular gods because of the anthropomorphism involved, not to mention the widespread ancient belief that in some regards the gods as traditionally conceived were all too human and could be flattered and bribed by sacrifice and prayer or hymns.

But the claim that God is unlike anything else seems much more real. There are two directions in which we might pursue this further. The first is that we try the idea that according to Antisthenes God is not anthropomorphic because he is some basic physical entity which governs the course of the world, let us say air. We might be encouraged in this thought, since according to Philodemus he talked about his one god in a work called *Physicus.* But air, or anything like it, is not unlike anything else we know. Nor is there any evidence that Antisthenes was interested in what we would call a physical account of the natural world, just as Socrates was no longer interested in natural philosophy when Antisthenes, the 'late-learner' (Plato, *Sophist* 251b), joined him. Hence we should take the title *Physicus*, if it is an Antisthenes title at all, rather to refer to a different kind of account of the natural world, namely one whose very point is to explain the natural world as somehow being a creation of God and ruled by him.

Clement in both places in which he refers to Antisthenes' view of God thinks he should refer to the fact that Antisthenes was a follower of Socrates. It is rather hazardous to venture conjectures concerning Socrates' views about matters divine and their role in the world. But I now, like others, am inclined to think that Xenophon's *Memorabilia* 1.4 and 4.3 do reflect, however inadequately, Socrates' view. If this is correct, Socrates believed in a god who has created the world, but who is hidden and of whose existence we only become aware if we reflect on the providential arrangement of the world and on how well in particular human beings are provided for. But for our purposes what matters as much as what Socrates actually may have thought is what Clement may have had in mind in connecting Antisthenes' remark about God's otherness with Socrates.

Now Xenophon in later antiquity became a much read and admired author. Clement obviously knew the *Memorabilia*, for he refers to and quotes from them repeatedly. *Memorabilia* 4.3 was a text pagans and Christians took a particular interest in. As we will see, Galen also clearly refers to it in his *De propriis placitis* (Chapter 2 end; cf. below, p. 77). Clement twice quotes as by Xenophon a text so remarkably similar to *Mem.* 4.3.13–14 as to appear to be a variant version of it, a version which is also quoted by Stobaeus (*Ecl.* 2.1.33, p. 15, 6–10 Wachsmuth). I do not want to discuss the textual problem, since it does not affect our argument. What matters for our purposes is that Clement quotes a version of the text of *Mem.* 4.3.13–14 in *Strom.* 5.14.108.5 and *Protr.* 6.71.3, that is immediately after referring to Antisthenes' view about the otherness of God in these two texts. Clement claims that Xenophon says more or less the same thing as Antisthenes, namely that 'it is obvious that he [*sc.* God] moves and stabilises it, is great and powerful; but of what shape or form (μορφή) he is, is completely unclear. For not even the sun, which seems entirely conspicuous, appears to allow itself to be seen; rather, if somebody should shamelessly look at it, he loses his eyesight.' The text in our standard version says that the creator can be seen in his works, but remains himself invisible, just as the sun does not allow us to properly see it, but deprives those who try of their eyesight. In any case Clement ascribes to Antisthenes a view like the view Xenophon ascribes to Socrates, namely that we recognise God in his works, but do not know what he himself is like. Even if we are more cautious, it seems safe to say that Antisthenes was talking about a god governing the world, but being himself different from and unlike anything he brings about.

The two sets of testimonies which we have been considering at least also fit some further evidence which helps to give some more content to what Antisthenes' position may have been. Diogenes of Sinope, whether he was a student of Antisthenes or not, was heavily influenced by him. It is difficult to make out what he thought about the gods. But the number of anecdotes in which he is made to ridicule popular cult practices and religious beliefs is conspicuous. This makes sense if he followed Antisthenes in thinking that the gods of popular belief and cult are conventional, but also warns us against assuming that Crates was irreligious or an atheist. Zeno, the founder of the Stoic school, for some time was a student of the Cynic Crates, and thus at least indirectly influenced by Antisthenes. In an early work, the *Politeia*, an answer to Plato's *Republic*, he argued that in an ideal state in which all citizens are wise there will be no temples, and no cult statues (*Stoicorum veterum fragmenta* I, 264 = Clement, *Strom.* 5.12.76; Plutarch, *De Stoicorum repugnantiis* 1034b; *et aliter*). Thus, though we would like to have more evidence concerning Antisthenes' theology, the picture which emerges from these testimonies seems to be sufficiently clear and coherent to appear reliable.

We are now in a position to try to answer the question whether Antisthenes was a monotheist. If monotheism is just a matter of believing in one and only one god, Antisthenes should be called a monotheist. For he unequivocally says that in reality there is just one god. If more is demanded, namely that this one god is also the right kind of god, the answer also seems to be clear. Antisthenes' god is not like the George in our example. He is none of the gods of popular belief and cult. He is something more elevated. Though this is somewhat conjectural, he seems to be rather like the god who creates and rules the world which Xenophon ascribes to Socrates in *Mem.* 4.3. In any case, Lactantius thinks so (*Div. inst.* 1.5.18–19). And Minucius Felix, Lactantius and Clement think that he is the sort of god, if not the God, the Christians believe in. That Antisthenes thinks of him as a god who rules the world is suggested also by the fact that Philodemus and Cicero give as the ultimate source of their information Antisthenes' work *Physicus*. Given the title, it must be a work about the world we live in. Furthermore, given that Antisthenes does recognise only one god, it is not even the case that this god shares his rule with other gods. Obviously Antisthenes saw no need to postulate further gods, since the one god he does assume is conceived of by him in such a way that he by himself manages to do all the things for which one might appeal to a god.

Given all this, the question does not seem to be so much whether we should call Antisthenes a monotheist, but rather why we should not call him this way. The only scholar I know of who does address this question is Martin Nilsson in the section on monotheism in his *History of Greek Religion* which I have referred to above. In the short second paragraph of the section he first discusses Xenophon in three and a half lines, then Antisthenes in three lines, then briefly the Xenophontic Socrates we have been discussing above. The conclusion he draws from this discussion of the three philosophers at the beginning of the third paragraph is that 'it is hardly necessary to continue to talk of philosophy which identified its highest principle with God'. I will not take issue with Nilsson's comments on Xenophon and on the Xenophontic Socrates. But I will discuss in considerable detail his comments on Antisthenes, since I set out to try and show that Antisthenes was a monotheist and since, if even Antisthenes is not to count as a monotheist, it is difficult to see how any pagan in antiquity can count as such.

But, before I turn to Nilsson's comments on Antisthenes, some comment is needed on the conclusion he draws, namely that we do not have to consider the philosophers any further, since they just identify their first principle with God. For if we accept this reasoning, then all later philosophers whom we might consider to be monotheists will fail to count as such, since they do regard God as a first principle. Nilsson himself points out whom he has in mind, Aristotle with his unmoved mover, the Platonists with their transcendent, and the Stoics with their Immanent God. This conclusion also deserves comment, because it reflects a more widespread view, and because I will want to argue next that Chrysippus should be called a monotheist. I should begin by pointing out that Nilsson does not explain why he thinks that philosophers do not need to be further considered under the heading 'monotheists', since they identify their first principle with God, but also that I do not understand at all what Nilsson thinks and why he does so. I suspect that he thinks that a first principle of philosophy is a very abstract and highly theoretical item and as such not the appropriate object of a religious attitude, while to believe in a god, not to mention to believe in God, is a matter of taking a religious attitude towards what one believes in. Now one might assume that to believe in a god is not a purely theoretical matter, but involves taking a religious attitude to the god in question. But it does not at all follow from this that a philosopher, just because as a matter of theory he believes in a certain principle, cannot take the appropriate attitude towards this principle, namely in the case of God a religious attitude. And part of the reason for this is that a philosopher does not have to think of his principles as very abstract and in our sense highly theoretical items. For a Platonist the One is not an abstract item, and, though a principle, the ultimate principle, it clearly is an object of a religious attitude. One can see this, for instance, by looking at Plotinus' *Enneads* 6.8, in which Plotinus among other things tries to disabuse us of a blasphemous view about the One or God, namely that God does what he does of necessity, given his nature. We would not understand why Aristotle could talk about his first principle as an intellect, or even something beyond the intellect, in a writing entitled *On Prayer* (Simplicius, *De caelo*, p. 485, 19–22 = frg. 49 Rose), if he did not think that this first principle was the appropriate object of a religious attitude. What is more, we all know that according to Aristotle the unmoved mover moves things as an object of love, that is the love of God, a perfectly respectable religious attitude (*Met.* 1072b3). Nor would we understand why Cleanthes writes his famous *Hymn to Zeus* if the first principle of Stoicism, their Immanent God, was just an abstract, theoretical principle. And obviously on this assumption we will not understand a good deal of medieval philosophy, for instance Duns Scotus. But perhaps I do not understand Nilsson's point. Perhaps his point is a different one.

At the end of the first paragraph Nilsson had said that 'paganism had not produced a fully monotheistic god who would meet the demands of popular religion. Its so-called monotheistic gods were either a summation of all or of several gods, under one of these gods, or a philosophical or theological principle.' So perhaps the idea rather is that a philosophical or a theological principle does not serve the needs of popular religion, since it is not, or at least not sufficiently, accessible to a population in general. And this is true for Aristotle, the Platonists and the Stoics that Nilsson refers to. For according to these views, and especially those of the late ancient Platonists, belief in a monotheistic god not only demanded considerable intellectual effort, but also required a virtuous and pure life. They all depended on doctrines about the unity of virtue, which inseparably linked theoretical understanding with moral virtue. This must have contributed to the philosophers' willingness to condone or even support popular belief in, and worship of, anthropomorphic gods. Aristotle, who, apart from the first unmoved mover, the god, assumes a whole series of unmoved movers, immaterial intellects, explains (*Met.* 1074a38 ff.) that the truth behind the belief in the plurality of traditional gods is that there are a number of such divine immaterial beings, but that this truth has been transmitted in mythical form to persuade the many of the existence of gods, but also to be law-abiding. For this reason the gods are presented as having human, or sometimes animal, forms. It seems right, then, that for philosophers, if they believed that their first principle should be God, this God was not a suitable object of a religious attitude of the kind they thought appropriate, which was attainable for ordinary people without a radical change in their life. But granting this, it is difficult to follow the further step Nilsson seems to take, for he seems to assume that the god of the philosophers is not a fully monotheistic god, because he does not satisfy the demands popular religion makes on what can be an object of religious attitudes, like worship for a whole population. This may create problems if we try to explain how philosophers and their followers who shared their views of God facilitated the spread of Christianity. These problems can be dealt with, but we set this question aside at the outset to be able to focus on the more modest problem in the history of religion, whether there was such a thing as pagan monotheism. And the question whether there were philosophers and their followers who believed in a god of the sort we would call 'monotheistic' should not depend on the question whether the god they believed in and had a religious attitude towards could be sufficiently understood by, and hence appeal to, a large population.

But Nilsson in the sentences last quoted makes a further claim we have to address, namely that the so-called monotheistic gods were either philosophical or theological principles, or the result of the subsumption of all the gods, or a number of them under one of these gods. I take it that what he has in mind is a tendency we can observe, for Greek authors to speak of Zeus in such a way that, even if they also speak of other gods, it is clear that things ultimately are in the hands of Zeus and his will prevails. It seems to me to be right that we should draw a line between this sort of god and the god of monotheists, though in some cases it will be difficult to decide into which category and on what grounds a particular case falls.

But let us venture to Nilsson's reasons for denying that Antisthenes can be regarded as a monotheist. He says (vol. II, p. 569): 'This high god [*Hochgott, sc.* the god of Antisthenes] first had to work his way through the cover of the usual polytheism.' There seem to be two objections: (i) Antisthenes' god is a high god, rather than a monotheistic god; (ii) this high god, before it could become the object of fully monotheistic belief, would have to shed the traces of its polytheistic origins. I find it somewhat difficult to understand precisely Nilsson's objections, because it is not entirely clear what he means by a 'high god'. This is a term which emerged from the anthropological discussions concerning monotheism and the development of religion I referred to earlier. Nilsson discusses the notion and various conceptions of a high god in vol. I, pp. 60–3, in a way which suggests that he does not find this notion particularly useful. He does reject the idea that polytheism arose out of a primitive precursor of monotheism, in that a high god's functions were split up and distributed over a plurality of divine beings, but considers the possibility of the opposite development, that the functions or powers of a plurality of divine beings were bundled and transferred to one of these gods. So perhaps this is what Nilsson has in mind, especially given that he had said at the end of the first paragraph that one sort of god, which gets mistaken for a monotheistic god, is a traditional polytheistic god who has come to subsume under himself all or some of the traditional gods. But, given the evidence I have set out in considerable detail, I do not see on what basis Nilsson thinks that Antisthenes' god is a high god in any sense of this term. Nor do I see how Antisthenes' god can be a high god in the suggested sense of a traditional god who has come to acquire the functions and powers of at least some of the other gods or all of them.

For Antisthenes denies the reality of all the traditional gods, quite apart from the fact that he unequivocally denies any plurality of gods. I also have argued that presumably Antisthenes thinks of his god as having all the powers one might want to attribute severally and jointly to a god. I also do not see that Antisthenes' god still shows the traces of his polytheistic origin. For he seems to owe his origin to Antisthenes' thought that none of the gods as they are traditionally conceived of deserves to be regarded as a god and an appropriate object of worship, and that they all are the product of convention. Hence, unless one, on the basis of a modern conception of how we should think of a monotheistic god, for instance the God the Christians believe in, is willing to make further demands on what is to count as monotheism, demands which might threaten even the status of early Christians as monotheists, I do not see how one can deny that Antisthenes was a monotheist. I should emphasise that it is not my intention to say something about how one should conceive of a monotheistic god from the point of view of a theologian or a philosopher of religion; I am just trying to say something about how one should think about monotheism and polytheism if one wants to retain these terms as useful for the description and explanation of the complexities of ancient religion and religious thought.

CHRYSIPPUS

With this we can turn to the case of Chrysippus. The Stoics talk of gods in the plural. These are not the traditional gods of popular belief and cult. For the traditional gods and the traditional myths about them the Stoics offer physical allegorical interpretations, as we find for instance in Cornutus.

When they talk about their gods they mainly talk about such things as the stars, in particular the planets like the sun. For they take these to be wise, benevolent, rational living beings. Given that they talk of the gods in the plural it would seem obvious that they must be polytheists. Against this I want to suggest that, appearances to the contrary notwithstanding, we should think of them as monotheists. For they believe in a god who is monotheistic, and if they also call other beings 'gods', they are called 'gods' in a sense which does not compromise the Stoics' monotheism. The case for this is made more easily if we consider the standard Stoic doctrine of a periodic conflagration of the world, which was not accepted by all Stoics. It was accepted, though, by Chrysippus, and we are reasonably well informed about Chrysippus' view since Plutarch reports it in some detail in two places, in *De communibus notitiis* 31–6, and in *De Stoicorum repugnantiis* 38–41. These two texts also provide us with testimony as to how Chrysippus tried to avoid a difficulty faced by all those Stoics who believed in the total conflagration of the world but also assumed a plurality of gods, namely the difficulty that, when the whole world is consumed by fire, also the sun, the moon, the other planets and the stars pass away. But this seemed to be incompatible with the very basic assumption that what distinguishes gods from human beings is that we are mortal, whereas the gods are immortal. Chrysippus found a way of explaining how these astral gods can still be called 'immortal', though they pass away. This rather artificial explanation, to which we will turn later, gives us a first indication that according to Chrysippus these gods are second-class gods, as it were. They are not even immortal in the sense in which this is, and in antiquity was, ordinarily understood.

They are second-class gods, since there is another god presupposed by the doctrine of periodic total conflagration who is truly immortal in the sense that he never passes away or comes into being. He is the only being which survives the conflagration, in fact survives all conflagrations, and is eternal (cf. Plutarch, *Com. not.* 1075b, *De Stoicorum repugnantiis* 1051f–1052b; Diogenes Laertius 7.137). For obviously the Stoics cannot assume that the world in the total conflagration passes into nothing. There must be something which is left and which is able to recreate the world, if the conflagration is to be periodic. Accordingly the Stoics assume that what is left at the end is a certain kind of fire. This fire is an intelligent fire, in fact an intellect. It is constituted by the whole of qualitiless and shapeless, passive matter and an ἰδία ποιότης, a special quality which turns matter into the particular, individual thing, if a peculiarly qualified thing (ἰδίως ποιόν), just as a common quality turns something into a particular kind of thing, for instance a horse or a human being. This individual variously is called 'the God', 'the demiurge' or 'Zeus' (cf. Diogenes Laertius 7.135, 137). In the final state of conflagration it takes the form of a particular kind of fire.

This god, then, sets out to create the world anew not out of nothing, for that is impossible, but out of himself, since this is all that is there at this point (Diogenes Laertius 7.137 end). More precisely he turns the whole of matter from fire into air or airy stuff and then from airy stuff into wet or moist stuff. And out of this wet stuff he generates the four elements, earth, water, air and fire (Diogenes Laertius 7.142; Plutarch, *De Stoicorum repugnantiis* 1053a). Everything else is formed by mixture from these four elements: not only living beings on earth, including human beings who have a share in reason and thought, but also the stars and the planets, including the sun and the moon. The result is the best possible world, arranged in a providential way, a providence which extends to the smallest detail, but in particular makes provision for human beings, each and any of them. As this demiurge creates the visible world out of himself, he becomes the soul of the world, which hence is an intelligent living being, and this becomes the world, in so far as it is an intelligent living being (Plutarch, *De Stoicorum repugnantiis* 1053b). As the soul of the world this god is present everywhere in the world and governs what happens in it.

Now, if we just look at this part of the account and, for the moment, forget about the talk of astral gods, it would seem to be clear that this god, who creates and governs the world, who is a wise and good rational individual, who is optimally provident down to the smallest detail and thus obviously knows all and has power over everything, is a monotheistic god, in that there also are the astral gods. In order to see whether they actually stand in the way of calling Chrysippus a monotheist, we have to look more closely at the status of these astral gods. To begin with, we should note that they, like all other beings in the world, are God's creatures. God has created them in order that it be as good a world as it can be. The astral gods have an important providential role to play. This is particularly clear in the case of the sun, without which there would be no life on earth.

Important though they may be, the question is why the astral gods should be accorded such a special status as to be called 'gods'. Part of the answer no doubt is historical. There is the advance of astral theology, noticeable already in Plato's *Laws* and *Timaeus*, but also in Aristotle, but by no means restricted to philosophers. I also take it that the Stoics are very much influenced by Plato, in particular the *Timaeus*, and not implausibly identify the younger gods in the *Timaeus* with the planets. But, more importantly, there is a systematic answer to this. The stars play an important role in making the world the best possible world. That the world is the best possible world shows itself in the awesome rationality, insight and thoughtfulness it reveals. It does so in part in that it contains as a conspicuous element the stars, which are living beings of perfect rationality, themselves models of rationality, who unerringly, without wavering, will do with ease what they want to do, namely move in the way they do. They want to move this way, because they understand that this is what they are meant to do, for instance in order to maintain life on earth. But it is God who has created them in such a way that they unfailingly do what they are supposed to do. Hence they are created in such a way that by their nature they are wise and good and have great power. By nature they are far superior to human beings. For human beings at best can only acquire wisdom and goodness and a very limited power. Thus calling the stars 'divine' marks a real difference between them and human beings. And calling them this way seems to be justified at least in that in ordinary Greek living beings which have lived a life of bliss and are immortal (ἀθάνατος) are called 'god'. The stars have a blissful life. They unperturbedly with ease take their course, free of care, since nothing threatens their life or their well-being. And they are immortal, though according to Chrysippus this is so only in the sense that they will not die, even if in the conflagration they will pass away.

But the fact that there is a sense, the ordinary Greek sense of 'god' or something close to it, in which they can be called 'gods' does not obliterate the radical difference between them and God. These gods are not the gods of polytheism. The latter do have a power of their own, though only a limited one. In their sphere of power they can act and interfere on their own account. If Poseidon brings about a shipwreck, it unambiguously and unqualifiedly is Poseidon who does this. But things are quite different with Chrysippus' astral gods. They are creatures of God. They have been created in order to do certain things and have been given the powers to unfailingly do what they are meant to do, for instance to act in such a way as to maintain life on earth. But they do not have a power of their own. The power they have has been given to them by God. They do not act on their own account. If they do maintain life on earth, it is not unambiguously and unqualifiedly they who do this. It is God who maintains life on earth, hence Zeus is said to be the ultimate source of life of all living beings, including us. But he does this through the stars who are his agents. This is part of what he has created them for. So all the power is still his; but he delegates it, as it were, to agents he creates who will act in his name and on his authority. So the status of God as a monotheistic god is not in the least compromised by these minor gods. He still is an all-powerful, all-knowing god who rules over beings down to the smallest detail. It is just that he has created for himself agents to do the work for him who will execute his will without fail. And that this is so becomes clear if we see that the minor gods do pass out of existence, namely in the total conflagration, once they have done what they were meant to do. Polytheistic gods do not pass out of existence.

With this we can briefly come back to the argument by which Chrysippus manages to explain that the minor gods are immortal, but do pass away in the conflagration. As we saw, when God creates the world, he creates himself a body, the visible world, whose soul he becomes. In the conflagration we get the reverse; the soul of the world reabsorbs the body of the world into itself such that all that is left is the soul, now an intellect (cf. Plutarch, *De Stoicorum repugnantiis* 1052c; Diogenes Laertius 7.137 end; Philo, *De aeternitate mundi* 49). Chrysippus relies on the notion of death which we find already in Plato's *Phaedo* as the separation of body and soul (Plutarch, *De Stoicorum repugnantiis* 1052c). This allows him to agree that the living, that is the visible world, does pass away in the conflagration, but does not die, since the soul does not get separated from the body; it rather absorbs it into itself. Similarly in the conflagration the souls of the stars do not get separated from their bodies, but rather get absorbed into their souls and ultimately into the soul of the world. In this sense Zeus can be said to absorb all other gods (Plutarch, *Comm. not.* 1075b). And in this sense also the astral gods are immortal, just as the visible world is. Their soul never gets separated from their body.

For the reasons I have explained we cannot, or at least should not, call this position polytheistic. For the minor gods of Chrysippus are not polytheistic gods, and regarding them as polytheistic is incompatible with the belief in a monotheistic god which Chrysippus' demiurge clearly is, given the way we tried to elucidate the notion. Hence we should think of Chrysippus as a monotheist. This also would seem to fit best the spirit of his position, in spite of the fact that he talks of a plurality of gods. But nothing would have been lost if he had had another term to mark the difference between these divine beings and human beings. The obvious term readily available in ordinary Greek was 'god', and this was not misleading as long as it was clear that it was used to refer to God's agents or servants, his instruments in creating and maintaining the best possible world. This position intuitively does not at all fit our intuitions about polytheism. And this to me just seems to show that the simple distinction between monotheism and polytheism as a matter of belief in just one god or of belief in many gods is ill-suited to capture the different positions in Greek religious thought.

Finally I will, again briefly, turn to Galen. Galen too talks about a number of gods, yet at the same time seems to believe in a divine demiurge who has all the marks of a monotheistic god. But he seems to be more accommodating to the traditional gods than Chrysippus. He himself professes, for instance, to worship Asclepius. In *De libris propriis* 2 (*Scripta Minora* II, p. 99, 9–11 Mueller) Galen tells us how Marcus Aurelius asked him to accompany him on his campaign against the Marcomanni, but Galen persuaded the emperor to excuse him. He explained that Asclepius, the god of his forefathers (πάτριος θεός), had told him not to join the emperor on campaign, and that he had been devoted to the god ever since Asclepius had saved him from a life-threatening disease. It presumably is the disease referred to in *De curandi ratione per venae sectionem* 23 (11.314.18–315.7 Kuhn) which Galen, following two clear dreams sent by Asclepius, tried to cure by arteriotomy. Asclepius also otherwise played an important role in Galen's life. Galen's father, prompted by evident dreams, sent his son, who so far had been made to study philosophy, to study medicine. And, of course, by Galen's time Asclepius was one of the traditional gods, perhaps the most important one, in his native Pergamum. Galen then believed in Asclepius, a particular god among many, though particularly dear to him. This looks like a clear case of polytheism.

But Galen also believed in a demiurge who has given the world we live in the order it has and who maintains this order. He calls this god 'the demiurge', 'Zeus' or 'the God' (ὁ θεός). One of Galen's most important and most impressive treatises is the *De usu partium*. He characterises his work as a hymn on the demiurge (1.174.5–17 Helmreich). In this work Galen tries to show that the study of the function of the parts of the human body, especially if aided by anatomy, unequivocally reveals the wisdom, the power, the providence, but also the goodness and the justice of the demiurge. In one famous passage he talks as if he took the demiurge to be the same as the God of Moses (11.14 = 2.158.7 ff. Helmreich), except that Galen thinks that this god is misconceived by the Jews. If they think that God can turn anything into anything by an act of will, they overlook the enormous wisdom which is required for and revealed by, for instance, the construction of the eyelids. Galen, then, believes in Asclepius, but also in what looks like a monotheistic god, that is God. This raises the question what the relation between these two gods is supposed to be.

This becomes a tantalising question if we turn to another Galenic text, namely his *De propriis placitis*. Up till recently this text was only partially extant in Greek. For the part particularly relevant for our purposes we have had to rely on Latin and Hebrew versions, both translations from an Arabic version. The text was edited accordingly by V. Nutton in the *Corpus medicorum Graecorum* v.3.2 (Berlin 1999). But Pietrobelli meanwhile discovered in MS Vlatadon 14 a complete version of the Greek text, on the basis of which Boudon-Millot and Pietrobelli (2005) published a new edition of the Greek text. In this work as a whole Galen tries to present his views on particularly important, but controversial, questions. To some he thinks he has a definitive answer, to others at best a plausible answer, yet others he declares himself unable to answer. After a preparatory first chapter Galen in Chapter 2 begins with the questions whether the world at some point has been created or not, and whether there is something beyond the world or not. Galen has no answer to these questions. Correspondingly he also has no answer to the following two questions about the demiurge of all the things in this world, namely (i) what is he like, that is for instance whether he is incorporeal or corporeal, and (ii) where is he located. But, Galen goes on, he is not like Protagoras, who claims to have no knowledge of matters divine. At this point the Greek text has already diverged crucially from the Latin and Hebrew versions and continues to diverge, in that the latter talk both of powers of God and the power of God, while the former talks of gods and of Asclepius and his power. It is tempting to think that these divergences at least in part are due to Muslim monotheist piety. By accident this hardly effects our agreement. According to the version of the Latin and Hebrew translations, Galen thought that he owed the cure of the illness he had ascribed to Asclepius (see above, p. 75) to God and his power, and this would have meant that what was effected by Asclepius was the work of God. In this case we would have to try to understand how he can think this. But it also is the case that, according to the Greek version, one thing which Galen claims to know about the gods, unlike Protagoras, is that they do exist, as we can tell from their works (ἔργα), the observable effects they have on the world. Now one set of observable effects which Galen ascribes to the gods are the various kinds of signs they send us, but the other work which he ascribes to the gods is the constitution of animals. But, according to the *De usu partium*, we should have thought that that was the work of the demiurge. In fact, earlier in this chapter Galen himself had referred to the demiurge of all things in the world. So who is responsible for the constitution of animals? Presumably what Galen has in mind is that in Plato's *Timaeus* the demiurge creates or is responsible for the world as a whole, but leaves the actual formation of the bodies of living beings to the so-called younger gods. This might be compatible with some form of monotheism in that it is God who also is responsible for the constitution of living beings on earth, though the work is delegated to minor gods. And, if we followed the translations, it would also be God who cured Galen when he was cured by Asclepius. But, given the recently discovered Greek manuscript of the text, it was just Asclepius who cured Galen, and hence it would be hazardous to build an account on the assumption that the translations preserve the right text, though clearly also the Greek text of the manuscript is problematic in this chapter and elsewhere.

But the end of the chapter gives us a precious clue as to what Galen's view might be. There is a reference to a law which Galen follows and advice which Socrates gave in both the translations of the text and its Greek version (except that the Hebrew version does not refer to Socrates). The reference to a law guarantees that the implicit reference here is not to Xenophon's *Memorabilia* 1.1.11–16 or 1.4, but to *Memorabilia* 4.3. For only there, in Section 16, Xenophon lets Socrates talk about a law, namely the law of the city one lives in, when he is asked how one should worship the gods. Now the newly discovered Greek text in addition refers to the oracle in Delphi. And this makes our identification of Galen's reference certain. *Memorabilia* 4.3.16 indicates that, according to Socrates himself, it was the Delphic oracle which gave this advice that Socrates endorsed. We should note that this at first sight is somewhat curious advice, since different cities in their public cult worship different gods. But it does fit Galen's case in that Galen follows the advice and, being a Pergamene, worships Asclepius. Yet it also suggests that the Delphic oracle, Socrates according to Xenophon, Xenophon and, following them, Galen are not particularly worried, when it comes to true piety, about the difference between the different gods in different cities.

If we try to think, though, about how Galen understands this worship of Asclepius following the advice of the oracle endorsed by Socrates, we have to take into account that Xenophon must report this and Galen must understand it in the light of what precedes Paragraph 16 in *Memorabilia* 4.3. What we are told there is how wonderfully and how providentially the world is ordered by the gods, how they care for us human beings, and that we should not wait to express our respect and gratefulness to them until we have set our eyes on their actual shape and form, but worship and honour them anyway. The gods themselves suggest this. For the gods other than the god who orders and keeps the world together do not show themselves in providing us with their gifts, and the cosmic god who administers the world remains invisible to us. We are reminded that even the sun does not allow us to look at it. So we do not really know anything about the gods except that they are the source of all these blessings and that there is one god who rules the whole world. It is in this ignorance that all we can do to honour these gods is to worship, each in our city, the gods worshipped in this city, for instance Asclepius in Pergamum.

This corresponds well enough with what Galen says here in Chapter 2, but also elsewhere (cf. *De placitis Hippocratis et Platonis* 9.7.12–14, p. 588, 20–6 De Lacy). Here he says that he does not know at all what the demiurge is like, whether he is corporeal or incorporeal, whether he transcends the world or is immanent and where in this case he would be located, but also that he has no idea of the οὐσία of the gods quite generally, that is what, or of what nature, they are, and that it does not do human beings any harm not to know this. All that we need to know is that they do exist and are provident and have power. And so it seems reasonable to infer that Galen's cult of Asclepius is not understood by him as worship of a particular god he can identify, but as a way to worship the demiurge and the other gods. There is no doubt that Galen does distinguish between the demiurge and the other gods, but also that the demiurge, especially in the *De usu partium*, does have the traits of a monotheistic god. Hence the question is how Galen thinks of the other gods who clearly have a subordinate function, corresponding to the younger gods in the *Timaeus*. The question is how they are subordinated.

Before a Greek text of the whole of the *De propriis placitis* was discovered, Chapter 2 seemed to make various references to both the power and the powers of the demiurge. There is a reference to the power of Asclepius or, more precisely, to that of the god worshipped by Galen in Pergamum, and to the power of the Dioscuri only in the Greek text. The editors of the Greek text (Boudon-Millot and Pietrobelli (2005), 191 n. 8) note that before the sentence about Protagoras the scribe might have omitted a passage of text to be found in the translations, which refers to the power of the demiurge, identified with the powers whose operations and effects we perceive in this world, effects which we would not be able to understand unless we assumed that they were the workings of the demiurge. But, even if *De propriis placitis* 2 does not say anything about the power or the powers of the demiurge, the *De usu partium* constantly does speak of this power, revealed for instance by the construction of our body and its parts. We easily speak of the power of God, as some of the ancients did, for instance the author of [Aristotle] *De mundo* 397b23. It is true that God is supposed to be enormously powerful, to have all the power, to be omnipotent. But what is the power he actually has? As I will explain, Galen must have had thoughts about this.

There was a widespread view in antiquity that a certain kind of substance (οὐσία), depending on the kind of substance it is, has a certain power (δύναμις), and that under the appropriate circumstances this power (ἐνέργεια) will be exercised and produce an effect (ἔργον). Thus fire has a certain power and brought into contact with the appropriate material will inflame and burn it. This is the way fire works or operates. Now one might think that one can look at how something works, at what effect it has on something, infer from this what the power involved in bringing about this effect must be, and hence infer of what nature the thing must be to have this power. But as we can see even from his *De propriis placitis*, Galen is surprisingly sceptical about our ability to identify what the power of something really is, given its observable effect, and hence is willing to resort to the expedient of just calling the power after the effect, given that we cannot identify the power independently of, without reference to, the effect. Galen in *De propriis placitis* 14 explains that we see that scammony produces purging and medlar constipation. But we do not really know what scammony and medlar are, hence we do not really know how they produce this effect, what their powers are which allow them to produce this effect. And hence we have to resort to identifying the power of scammony as a purgative power and the power of medlar as constipating. Now Galen in *De propriis placitis* 14 uses these examples to explain how we identify the powers of the soul. He already in *De propriis placitis* 3 had said that he knows that the soul exists, since the soul is just that, whatever it is, in virtue of which we are alive and are able to do the things we do. But he claims to have no idea what the soul really is, of what nature it is, but hence also no idea of whether the soul is mortal or immortal. Hence we also do not know what the real nature of the power or powers is which it has. Hence we identify its powers by the observable effects it has on us. Thus, to return to *De propriis placitis* 14, we attribute to the vegetative soul, that is the aspect of the soul which accounts for how vegetative life functions, the power of attraction of nourishment, the power of expulsion of waste, the power of retaining what is needed, and the power of its transformations and assimilation. But we do this in ignorance of what the powers of the soul really are, since we do not know what the soul really is.

If with this and the background of the *De usu partium* we return to *De propriis placitis* 2, it is clear that Galen thinks that he has no idea of

what the power of the demiurge is, but also no idea of what the powers of
the gods are. It is just overwhelmingly clear to him from his observations
and his experiences that the world abounds in observable effects of divine
power. One such effect are certain cures. And so we attribute to a god the
power to cure. Traditionally the power to cure is associated with Asclepius.
Hence people worship Asclepius on the assumption that certain cures are
due to Asclepius. But it is clear that Galen must assume that if there is such
a god as Asclepius we do not know what his power is in virtue of which
he effects these cures. In fact we do not know anything about him except
that he effects certain cures. If somebody should ask how we know that
there is such a god, the answer should be in parallel to Galen's answer as to
how we know that there is a soul. We see that human beings move around
according to choice and that they perceive things by means of sense-organs,
and we call 'soul' that, whatever it is, which is the cause of what we know
human beings are doing in being alive. Similarly we will say that 'Asclepius'
is just the name we use for the divine being, whoever or whichever it is,
which causes certain observable cures.

Now, if one says this, one leaves open the possibility that the god in
question is none other than the demiurge himself. In this case Asclepius
would be none other than God or Zeus, in so far as we attribute to him
the power to heal, since we take him to be all-powerful. There is reason
to believe that some took this position and that Galen would be familiar
with it. In Galen's lifetime his compatriot Rufinus, a Roman senator, built
a grandiose new temple in Pergamum dedicated to Zeus Asklepios. Aelius
Aristides, a friend of Rufinus, tells us: 'The powers of Asclepius are great
and many; or rather all his powers are universal. And it is precisely because
of this that the people here [sc. in Pergamum] erected a temple for Zeus
Asklepios' (Or. 42.4). Given that all power is attributed to this god, it
appears that Asclepius is identified with a monotheistic god, in so far as
this god is all-powerful; and one to whom we can also attribute the power
of healing. Analogously we could explain all gods as this one god, in so
far as his power manifests itself in the different observable ways which we
ascribe to divine power, and to which we give the corresponding name
'Asclepius', in so far as his power is revealed in acts of healing. This would
be a straightforwardly monotheistic position.

But it does not seem to be Galen's position, because Galen does appear
to believe in a plurality of gods, as we see from De propriis placitis 2. Yet
it is also true that Galen here and elsewhere makes a clear distinction
between the demiurge and the other gods. What is more, in spite of his
agnosticism about the nature of the demiurge, he clearly wants to leave

open the possibility that this is a transcendent god by refusing to answer the initial questions about the world and the demiurge. That is he leaves no room for a god higher than the demiurge. *De usu partium* suggests that he is all-powerful. So he qualifies as a monotheistic god.

It also is clear that Galen's worship of Asclepius is at least not worship of a polytheistic god. It is worship of the demiurge and the other gods, following the advice of the Delphic oracle endorsed by Socrates. Asclepius is some divine being he does not know, whose power he does not know, but associated in particular with one kind of blessings we owe to the gods, certain cures. This at the very least is consistent with monotheism. For it leaves open the possibility that there are divine agents on whom the demiurge relies to maintain the order of the world and to exercise his providence. Galen in his agnosticism about matters divine deliberately may have left open this possibility, rather than identify Asclepius with God. Given the way he thinks about the demiurge it is highly unlikely that he would ascribe any independent power to Asclepius.

In conclusion I want to say that ancient religion is not just a matter of cult and ritual, but that ancient religious thought and writing are a crucial part of it, especially if these themselves are regarded as religious activities. And it seems to me that, if we want to understand ancient religious thought and the practice which accompanies it, the terms 'monotheism' and 'polytheism' will only do justice to the complexity of Greek or Graeco-Roman religious thought and religion if we appropriately reflect on and refine these notions. But, with or without refinement, I hope to have shown that Antisthenes was a monotheist and that hence there was such a thing as pagan monotheism.

CHAPTER 5

Monotheism between cult and politics: the themes of the ancient debate between pagan and Christian monotheism

Alfons Fürst

The debate about pagan monotheism, which was sparked by the publication of Athanassiadi and Frede's *Pagan Monotheism in Late Antiquity* and the critical response that it provoked, has run for several years, and has led to numerous related publications.[1] The span of these contributions is wide and extends from the ancient Near East and Egypt to ancient Israel and Hellenistic Judaism, and as far as classical Greece, the Hellenistic world and the Roman imperial period up to Christian late antiquity.[2]

This contribution does not aim to undertake another thematic approach but to pose the basic question of what the ancient discourse between pagan and Christian monotheists was in fact about. Monotheism was already a topic for discussion between Christians and non-Christians in the imperial Roman age, and this lent an explosive quality to the issue of what could be called monotheism in antiquity. Both types of monotheism were defined by rapprochements and confrontations, and these brought a series of issues to the surface. What were the basic themes of this discussion? What were the front lines that were established in this debate? How did the disputants conceive their respective positions, and what were the charges they brought against one another? I tackle these questions in the context of two controversies: those between Augustine and the Platonists and between Celsus and Origen. I begin by drawing attention to aspects of these debates which have been largely neglected, but which in my view are of central importance, so that these can be correctly related to broader aspects of the problem in the concluding section.

---

[1] Athanassiadi and Frede (1999); see too Spieckermann and Kratz (2006).
[2] See the collections of papers edited by Krebernik and Van Oorschot (2002) and Palmer (2007).

THE CONCEPT OF GOD AND THE WORSHIP OF GOD:
AUGUSTINE AND THE PLATONISTS

A characteristic feature of the debate between Christian theologians and pagan philosophers in later antiquity was their broad agreement on central aspects of the concept of God. Since both parties were philosophical Platonists, they shared the broad consensus of ancient philosophy about the unity of reality and so, theologically expressed, about the unity of God. This convergence in their points of view is not simply a discovery of modern research, fundamentally recognised since the nineteenth century,[3] but was also acknowledged and discussed by contemporary participants in the ancient debate.[4] Among other observations, Olympiodorus, the late Alexandrian Neoplatonist, commented on the call 'By Hera' in Plato's *Gorgias* with the remark: 'We also certainly know that the first principle is singular, namely God. There cannot be a plurality of first things.'[5] The emphatic 'we also' is aimed at Christian readers, since the 'we' are the non-Christian Platonists of late antiquity. One may readily imagine that Olympiodorus in the sixth century, the final phase of antiquity, wrote in these terms under the growing influence of Christianity. Yet even if that must have been the case in practice, the comment offers a classic formulation in theological form of the unitary thinking of ancient philosophy, the unitary nature of the first principle: the unique first principle is called 'God'. Olympiodorus was expressing a pagan–Christian consensus in this question. His Christian counterparts could have agreed with him on this point without discomfort and had in fact done so several centuries earlier. Athenagoras had already observed in the second half of the second century that 'we [i.e. in this case the Christians] are not the only ones who limit God to a single being',[6] since 'almost all those who have reason to speak about the principles of the world are unanimous, even if unwillingly so, that the divine is singular'.[7] Around the middle of the third century it was clear to someone with as deep a knowledge of ancient philosophy as Origen that Christians and non-Christians were broadly in agreement about the oneness of the creator God: 'many philosophers have written that there is

---

[3] Zeller (1862), (1875), 1–29; see Nilsson (1950), 546–52; Burkert (1977), 486; Fowden (1993), 37–79. A comprehensive depiction of pagan and Christian monotheism, which reproduces all the relevant sources, is also to be found in the long fourth chapter of *The True Intellectual System of the Universe* by Ralph Cudworth. See Cudworth (1678), 183–770.
[4] For the following and other passages see Fürst (2006a), 501–5; Fürst (2006b), 94–102.
[5] Olympiodorus, *Commentary on Plato, Gorgias* 4.3 (p. 32 Westerink), discussing Plato, *Gorgias* 449d5.
[6] Athenagoras, *Supplicatio* 6.2 (*PTS* 31, 32).   [7] Athenagoras, *Supplicatio* 7.1 (*PTS* 31, 34).

a single God who has created everything. In this they agree with God's law
[i.e. the Old Testament].'[8] Augustine was also aware that there was agreement between him and his philosophical adversaries, and that the idea of
God should be conceived as singular. He cited Varro, the most learned
of Romans, and Porphyry, the most learned of philosophers, as witnesses
to the one true God, the object of Christian confession.[9] Claims of this
sort were also especially used by pre-Constantinian apologists to construct
a consensus regarding a 'monotheistic' concept of god with the educated
pagans, who held Christianity in contempt, and to build bridges by which
these could cross over to Christianity. This consensus was not purely a
construct, but had foundations in reality. There was a high degree of convergence between Christian belief in one God and philosophical ideas of
unity, and there was a 'monotheistic' consensus in the matter of whether
God was singular or plural, in so far as this question addressed theoretical
principles and was deemed to be about the first principle of all reality.[10]
    The question to be asked at this point is: how far did this consensus
extend, or alternatively, where did disagreement begin? Michael Frede drew
the conclusion from these and similar observations that pagan philosophers, especially the Platonists, were monotheists in exactly the same sense
as the Christians and, consequently, found it curious that Christians portrayed the situation differently, insisting on their monotheism as a mark
of difference.[11] Frede cited Augustine as well as Justin as authorities for the
view that Christian theologians already perceived no differences between
the pagan and Christian positions.[12] Augustine's elaboration of the theme
is, in fact, extremely enlightening, although it leads, I would maintain, to
a different conclusion from that reached by Frede. We need to examine the
decisive passages more closely.[13]
    In De civitate Dei, Augustine assumed an astonishingly broad consensus
in late antiquity about the singularity of God. In the extensive exchange of
views in Books VIII to X concerning Platonic philosophy and theology, he
emphasises that the differences in the first instance were merely to do with
nomenclature. Platonists, who employed the notion of a hierarchy of gods
to reconcile their conviction about the unity of god, the first principle of
everything, with polytheism as it was practised, were obviously referring to
demons or angels when they spoke of gods. Augustine was even prepared to

---

[8] Origen, In Genesim homilia 14.3 (GCS Orig. 6, 123–4).
[9] Augustine, De civ. D. 19.22 (II, 392 Dombart/Kalb).
[10] For the example of Seneca see Fürst (2006b), 103–7.
[11] Frede (1999), 67; see the critical remarks of Wallraff (2003), 531–6.   [12] Frede (1999), 58ff.
[13] For the following see Fürst (2007), 273–6.

accept calling them gods, provided that the term was correctly understood: 'When the Platonists prefer to call demons (or alternatively angels) gods rather than demons and are prepared to count as gods those who are created by the highest God, about which their originator and teacher Plato has written in the *Timaeus*, let them express themselves in this way, as they wish, since there is no reason to have a dispute with them about words. In fact, when they call them immortal, in the sense that they have at all events been created by the highest God, and blessed, in the sense that they are blessed not in virtue of their own internal qualities but for the reason that they depend on their creator, then they are saying the same thing as we are, whatever terminology they use to express themselves.'[14] In Augustine's opinion, the terms used for describing the divine were irrelevant. What mattered was the underlying theological concept. The position of the one true God would be imperilled if immortality and blessedness were considered to be attributes of the so-called gods in the sense that could only be applied to the one true God. As long as this was not the case, it was immaterial what names were given to beings subordinate to the one true God. The background to this argument rests on the ancient notion that gods were distinguished from mankind by their immortality (contrasting with mortality) and their blessed state of being (contrasting with misfortune, suffering and error). Augustine allows that one may in this respect use the ancient manner of speech and call beings who are generally agreed to have these characteristics gods, provided that it is clear that they do not possess these characteristics by themselves, but derive them from a true God, the one original principle of all existence. In Augustine's view, in so far as the Platonic idea of god meets this criterion, simply talking about gods meant no distinction from Christian monotheism.

Augustine found the decisive difference at the level not of the concept, but of the worship of God. The Platonists might indeed have reached a correct understanding of God, but drew false conclusions from this for religious practice. They might 'for that reason be the most famous of all philosophers, because they had achieved the insight that the immortal soul of man, although endowed with rational sense and the capacity for understanding, can become fortunate only through sharing the enlightenment of that God by whom they and the rest of the world have been created. So they contest that no one may achieve what all men strive for, namely a happy life, if he does not attach himself in pure and chaste love to what is unique and best, that is the unchangeable God. They, too, stand up for

---

[14] Augustine, *De civ. D.* 9.23 (1, 398 Dombart/Kalb).

the worship of many gods or at least used to do so, and many of them even allowed divine honours to be paid to demons through festivals and sacrifice.'[15]

Augustine considered practice of this sort to be false, because it contradicted the concept of God. He used a soteriological argument: if the gods, demons or angels, or whatever these intermediate beings happened to be called, did not derive their immortality and blessedness from themselves, but from the one God, then they had no rational claim to cultic worship, for they would in themselves be no more capable than mankind of achieving a state of blessedness. In this respect, both were dependent on God, to whom alone worship should be due. 'Thus may this book end with the clear conclusion that the immortal and the blessed, who have come into being and been created, however one may choose to describe them, are not mediators able to lead wretched mortals to immortal blessedness, for they differ from them in both respects. The intermediate beings, however, who share the immortality of the higher being and the wretchedness of those below them, since they are rightly in a state of wretchedness by reason of their own wickedness, are more liable to deny us than to provide us with the blessedness that they do not possess themselves. Hence the friends of the demons can provide us with no valid reasons why we should worship them as helpers, since we should rather avoid them as deceivers.'[16]

Augustine claimed that he had demonstrated the error of polytheism in that he had shown the congruence of the Platonic and Christian concepts of God, and from this demonstrated that the cultic worship of gods was senseless. The difference in the debate between Augustine and the Platonists lay not in the idea of God, but in man's religious disposition towards the divine. With respect to the first principle of all reality, and in the context of the lack of division between philosophy and theology in the ancient world, there was really hardly any possibility of drawing a distinction between philosophical and theological monotheistic ideas. This, however, is a narrowing of the perspective, when one compares pagan and Christian 'monotheism' with one another. In the De civitate Dei, Augustine followed a rhetorical strategy to combat this.[17] On the pagan side, Augustine treated the Platonists as the only theological adversaries that needed to be taken seriously and as the most dangerous, because in his view they came very close to Christian concepts. However, this closeness, which Augustine developed in his idea of the concept of God in order to establish the

---

[15] Augustine, De civ. D. 10.1 (I, 401 Dombart/Kalb).
[16] Augustine, De civ. D. 9.23 (I, 400 Dombart/Kalb).
[17] Fuhrer (1997) has made this point specifically.

genuine identity which lay beneath simple terminological differences, is not only factually observable, but also deliberately manufactured and – this is the decisive point – consciously exaggerated. Augustine portrayed the consensus at this point as so close, and at the same time raised the Platonists to such a high level, in order to be able to destroy them with all the more decisive and lasting effect. For, although they had achieved a true notion of God, of his Oneness and of his other qualities, they now committed the worst of errors that a man could make in that they worshipped as God something that was unworthy of worship, because it was not the one God, but many gods.

Augustine's rhetorical strategy in his argument with the Platonists corresponded strictly to religious reality in later antiquity. The great slogan of ancient Christian propaganda – away with the many (false) gods; turn to the one (true) God – exactly matched religious practice. The women and men of the ancient world who had become Christians should play no more part in pagan religious festivals, cults or any public events in which pagan cult had a role to play, but participate only in the life of the Christian community and in worship of the Christian God. The decisive religious boundary was created by religious behaviour.[18] Educated pagans and Christians, who were all Platonists in the sense of the term that applies in later antiquity, stood at no great distance from one another in their theoretical reflections and pronouncements on the concept of God. The differences that mattered began with religious practice. The conflict between pagan and Christian monotheists was practical and concerned religious cult rather than theoretical and concerned with religious philosophy.

These observations lead to the following conclusion: the question in the debate about 'God' in late antiquity between Christians and non-Christians, at least at the highest level of discussion, did not concern the number of gods, that is whether there was one God or many, still less the concept of God in itself, but the question of the right way to worship God.

Like theologians, philosophers were monotheists. That is, they were convinced of the unity of reality and of the oneness of the original principle of all reality, God. They were not at one over the question of religious practice. Since Plato, who thus became the model for all his later followers, the philosophers had reconciled their monotheistic convictions with polytheistic religious practice.[19] The Christians criticised this with the argument

---

[18] For a thorough study of the pre-Constantinian situation see Mühlenkamp (2008).

[19] Moreover, Christian authors depicted Plato's behaviour as caused by fear that he might suffer the same fate as Socrates; so Ps.-Justin, *Cohortatio ad Graecos* 20.1 (*PTS* 32, 50), 22.1 (*PTS* 32, 53), 25.4 (*PTS* 32, 58).

advanced by Philo of Alexandria that one should not honour the servants in the place of the master and that one could not serve several masters at the same time.[20] These individual points are well known. An important inference for the current debate about pagan and Christian 'monotheism' needs to be drawn. The question of the number of gods was not at issue in the ancient debate. Its central concern was with religious practice. What should mankind worship?[21]

RELIGION AND POLITICS: ORIGEN AND CELSUS

A second observation can be closely linked to this first conclusion. In the ancient world, religious practice was not a private matter for individuals, but a matter of considerable social and political relevance, and did not exist outside the confines of the contemporary social and political system.[22] The cult of the gods in its various forms was a social and political phenomenon. It created a sense of community, staged and strengthened the feeling of belonging together, and communicated political options and structures through symbolic rituals. The high point of this political phenomenon was the imperial cult. Ancient religion was public religion with a polit-ical function, the staging and consolidation of rulership, and involved a demonstration of social conformity and political loyalty. Religion and pol-itics, which could not be divided or even distinguished from one another in antiquity, were expressed through socially embedded religious practice.

Hence, when the Christians called ancient religious practice into ques-tion, it inevitably had immediate political relevance. This can be studied paradigmatically in Origen's discussion with Celsus.[23] We encounter the same phenomenon concerning their respective concepts of God as we do in Augustine's arguments with the Platonists. Philosophically, Origen was as much a Platonist as Celsus, and on this basis they agreed with one another in the essential points about 'God'.[24] Both assumed the existence of a single god as the principle and origin of being, both took for granted the presence of intermediate beings between God and the world, or between God and mankind, and both, explicitly including Celsus, directed their souls' piety not towards these intermediate beings but towards the one God. 'When you shut down the perception of the senses and look upwards

---

[20] Philo, *De specialibus legibus* 1.31 (v, 8 Cohn/Wendland); *De decalogo* 61 (IV, 282 Cohn/Wendland); Origen, *Contra Celsum* 7.68 (*GCS* Orig. 2, 217), 8.2 (*GCS* Orig. 2, 221–2).
[21] For the wider philosophical context see Kobusch (1983).
[22] This point is continuously expressed in Bendlin (2006b), especially 287.
[23] Fürst (2007), 258–68. [24] This was first demonstrated by Miura-Stange (1926), 113–19.

with your spirit', replied Celsus to the Christians, 'when you turn your-
selves away from the flesh and open the eyes of the soul, only then will you
see God.'[25] There was no difference between this philosophical spirituality
and the piety of the Christian theologian Origen. Furthermore, it made no
great difference, as Augustine said, whether Celsus qualified these intermediate beings as demons and gods, or whether Origen viewed them as
demons or angels. The difference only became clear at the level of worship.
While the Platonic philosopher identified the traditional gods, who could
be worshipped unproblematically, as agents of the one god's world rulership, the Christian, whose view was focused on the tradition of the Bible,
saw such behaviour simply as idolatry, the worship of false gods in place
of the one true God.[26] Celsus and Origen, as they conceived the world,
agreed about its fundamental structure, in that there was a transcendent,
almighty power, which both called God (in the singular), but disagreed
on what value to give to the intermediate beings and on how men should
behave in respect to them.

Origen did not lay as much emphasis as Augustine on the identity of the
respective concepts of God and the difference in the matter of cult, and
the issue of cult practice was not at the centre of his argument with Celsus.
The latter, and Origen in reaction to him, were more concerned with
the implications of the contemporary concept of God and the associated
religious practice for the way men lived together with one another. We
can perhaps infer the reason for this emphasis from the fact that Celsus
had begun his attack against Christianity with a discussion of the social
and political consequences of Christian 'monotheism': 'The first main
criticism for Celsus', so Origen begins his defence, 'rests on the charge
that the Christians secretly create associations with one another against
the existing social order. For among associations, some are public, that
is all of them that conform to the laws, but others are secret, namely all
of them that come into being against the existing order.'[27] This charge is
not to be interpreted in a restricted legalistic sense, but in a more general
one, that Christian groups came into conflict with existing notions and
norms of social order.[28] In the first part of Book 1, Origen systematically

---

[25] Origen, *Contra Celsum* 7.36 (*GCS* Orig. 2, 186).
[26] Origen, *Contra Celsum* 7.69 (*GCS* Orig. 2, 218–19).
[27] Origen, *Contra Celsum* 1.1 (*GCS* Orig. 1, 56). It can hardly be resolved whether Origen is here citing
Celsus word for word or paraphrasing him. Wifstrand (1942), 395 considers the first sentence to
be Origen's paraphrased summary of the first main criticism in Celsus, and the second to be the
beginning of Celsus' work. The philological problems are not significant for the substantial issue.
[28] Speigl (1970), 186–8, followed by Pichler (1980), 122.

expounds the central charge advanced by Celsus.[29] If one assumes that he introduced the most important point first, then we may infer from this starting point that the dispute had developed around ideas of social and political order in the first instance. Celsus was not concerned with the monotheism of Christians as such or with their religious practice for its own sake. The socio-political implications of Christianity's theological and practical religious convictions were much more at the centre of the debate. These were connected with monotheism, but attention was focused on aspects which immediately affected how men lived together with one another.

Origen's riposte moved across the terrain that had been marked out by his adversary, and in any case linked questions about society to religious and ethical convictions: 'To this the following can be said: if someone were to find himself among the Scythians, who have godless laws, and were compelled to live among them because there was no possible way out, then he would probably act very sensibly if, in the name of the law of truth, which is certainly contrary to the law among the Scythians, he were to associate with like-minded persons even against the order that existed among those people. Exactly in this manner, before the seat of truth's judgement, the laws of the pagans, which rely on images of the gods and the godlessness of many gods, are laws of the Scythians and if possible even wickeder than these. It is therefore perfectly proper to create associations for the benefit of the truth against the existing order. Just as persons who act together in secret to drive out a tyrant who has seized power in a city for himself would be acting in an honorable way, so the Christians, under the tyrannical rule of the one whom they have called the devil and his deceits, create associations against the devil's established order, to act against him and to rescue others, who can perhaps be persuaded to extract themselves from the rule of law, that is, so to speak, from a law established by the Scythians and a tyrant.'[30]

Origen identified the existing order, on which Celsus depended, as 'the laws of the pagans, which rely on the images of the gods and the godlessness of many gods',[31] and so connected ideas of the social order with religious features. That was completely appropriate to the situation, for the two, as observed above, were never separate in the ancient world. By making this connection explicit, Origen found a way of arguing against pagan notions. He used Christian standards to condemn the 'established order',

[29] Origen, *Contra Celsum* 1.1–27 (*GCS* Orig. 1, 56–79).
[30] Origen, *Contra Celsum* 1.1 (*GCS* Orig. 1, 56).   [31] Pichler (1980), 238.

which Celsus had introduced into the argument against Christianity, by recourse to 'the seat of truth's judgement'. The Christian Origen insisted on the difference between true and false, neither in the notion of God nor in religious convictions and practices as such, but in the field of political and social order. Without undertaking a discussion of the wide-ranging implications of Origen's pronouncements at this point, notably his opinion about driving out a tyrant (we may note that this does not extend to his murder), and his formulation of the right to mount political resistance on ethical grounds, it is evident that he was engaged in a discussion with Celsus about fundamental questions of political order, and the criteria he established for deciding between true and false derived from his ethical and religious convictions. The number of the gods was of no importance.

When Celsus' text first mentions a single god, in a passage of polemic against Moses, Origen returns to speak afresh about notions of order. 'Following their leader Moses, the herders of sheep and goats fell for this clumsy deceit and believed that there was only a single God', wrote Celsus. In his counter-argument, a polemic against the world of the Greek gods, Origen indicated what the material issue in this question was: 'How much more effective and better than all these fantasies it is, when confronted with the visible truth, to become convinced of the good order of the world and to worship the one creator of the one world, which is completely in harmony with itself and accordingly cannot have been created by many creators'.[32] Apart from the facts that Origen could probably have come to an agreement with Celsus over this particular issue, and that this was a matter of ideas about the order of the cosmos not of state and society, it is clear once again that the question whether there was one or many gods was not a problem in itself, but became a matter of controversy when it was connected to ideas about order and harmony.

The contestants are to be found within the same defined area in another passage where these problems are discussed. For Celsus, the established order consisted in a multiplicity of religious and social laws and customs: 'Every people honours the tradition of its fathers, however this may once have been set up. This appears to result not only from the fact that different peoples have established different forms of social order as they are perceived to be necessary, and are obliged to follow decisions that are valid for the community, but also from the fact that different parts of the world have been allocated to different governors and divided into specific regions of government and are also administered accordingly. And so we may presume

---

[32] Origen, *Contra Celsum* 1.23 (*GCS* Orig. 1, 73).

that the customs of individual peoples, when they are acted on in this way, are followed in the correct manner, as it pleases their governors. It would not suit god's purpose to do away with the order that had been established from the beginning in each region.'[33]

Celsus was explaining the origin of the many types of social and religious organisation. Many historically contingent models of communal life had developed that corresponded to the many types of peoples. Celsus linked this theory to a theological explanation of the plurality of religion and customs. This was the outcome of god's will, specifically in the sense that it could be traced back to the individual gods who had been entrusted with administering the different parts of the world by the one highest god. The 'monotheistic' philosopher Celsus in this way conceived a pluralistic theory of society which was inseparably connected to a pluralistic theory of religion. He had no need either to discover the foundation stones of his system or to justify the many types of contemporary cult. They were the objects of experience. All he was doing was explaining the facts.[34]

Celsus had one more observation to make with regard to the Christians. He provided an answer to the question of the right and wrong forms of cult practice and to the requirements which such forms of social order expected of their participants. It was correct practice, Celsus said, for 'the customs of individual peoples to be followed in the way that pleased their governors'. That is a relative principle: each according to its governor. Concretely, correct behaviour depended on the region and the society where it belonged. Celsus treated this arrangement as binding. In respect to religious implications, it was not pleasing to god 'to do away with the order which had been established from the beginning in each region'. Celsus thereby referred to the charge which he had brought against the Christians at the beginning of his work, namely that they were making secret pacts among themselves against the established order. The reason why Celsus considered such behaviour to be godless emerges from the passage that has just been discussed.

Origen's reply followed the line of what he had already said at the beginning of his work. Again he returned to customs such as those of the Scythians who kill their fathers, or of the Persians who allow marriage with a man's mother or daughter, 'in order to cast doubt on the claim that the customs of individual peoples are practised in the correct way, to the extent that it pleases their governors'.[35] It is not of prime importance

[33] Origen, *Contra Celsum* 5.25 (*GCS* Orig. 2, 26); compare 5.34 (*GCS* Orig. 2, 36–8).
[34] Speigl (1970), 190ff.   [35] Origen, *Contra Celsum* 5.27 (*GCS* Orig. 2, 28).

that Origen here repeatedly cited examples from classical Greek literature, especially Herodotus.[36] The goal of his argument is decisive. Origen posed the question whether a rational choice between true and false could be made in Celsus' system. He did not use these terms, but implicitly assumed that this choice was necessary to decide whether actions could be judged as pleasing to God or godless: 'Celsus should tell us why it might not please God to do away with customs inherited from the ancestors which allow marriage with a mother or a daughter, or deem that those who have hanged themselves with a rope to end their lives are fortunate, or which declare those who have immolated themselves and finished their lives in the fire to be utterly pure! Why might it not please God, for example, to do away with the normal customs of the Tauri, who present strangers as sacrificial offerings to Artemis, or the normal custom of many Libyans to slaughter children for the god Kronos?'[37]

In Origen's view, Celsus' theory of society and religion introduced a relativism which provided no foundation for norms and values and disabled value judgements. 'If one follows Celsus, it becomes impossible to consider what is pleasing to God as something which is naturally godly, but which is based on an arbitrary arrangement. For one people regards it as pleasing to God to worship a crocodile and to eat the flesh of animals that are offered prayers by others, while another thinks that it pleases God to worship the calf, and another again considers the goat to be a God. In this manner, one and the same person may consider that doing the same thing pleases God according to some laws, but is godless according to others, which would be completely absurd . . . One must consider whether that does not indicate great confusion about what is right and pleasing to God and likewise what piety might mean, when it is not clearly defined and an independent absolute category, and would not define as pious those whose dealings it shapes. Should piety, pleasing God and justice really be classed as relative terms so that the same behaviour could be pleasing to God and godless at the same time according to circumstances and customs, then one ought to admit as a strict consequence that self-control should also belong to these relative terms, and likewise courage, intelligence, understanding and the other virtues – nothing could be more absurd.'[38]

Again, it is clear that Celsus and Origen were discussing the basis of men's ability to live together. For Origen, the issue was the choice between true and false in religion and society. Monotheism as such was not in dispute.

---

[36] See the notes in Chadwick (1965), 284 n. 3.   [37] Origen, *Contra Celsum* 5.27 (*GCS* Orig. 2, 28).
[38] Origen, *Contra Celsum* 5.27–8 (*GCS* Orig. 2, 28–9).

In general, the discussion was not dependent on the heading *theos*, but on
the complementary headings *logos* and *nomos*, whose meanings in an old
and honourable tradition of cultural and religious history overlapped one
another.[39] Since *nomos*, the organising principle of life, depended on *theos*,
the concept of God, the two could not be separated from one another,
and yet the disputants were not able to agree with one another concerning
nomos, the valid existing order. Celsus regarded Christian monotheism as
problematic above all in its implications for the political order: 'In fact,
whoever considers that only a single master is meant when he speaks
of God, is acting in a godless fashion, for he splits up the kingdom of
God and causes uproar, as though it contained a division into parties and
another god, an opponent'.[40] The refusal of the Christians to serve several
masters (gods) was 'the rebellious talk of those who close themselves off
and tear themselves apart from other men'.[41] Celsus judged that Christian
monotheism and the consequent anti-polytheistic religious practice which
it involved were a form of rebellion against the pluralistic religious and
social order which he was defending.[42]

The front line is well set out in a final passage to be discussed
here.[43] According to Origen, Celsus expressed a sort of wish towards the
end of his work: 'If only it were somehow possible, if all the inhabitants
of Asia, Europe and Libya, Greeks and barbarians alike, to the very ends
of the world, could unite around a single law'.[44] From the language it
is hard to decide whether Celsus here really expressed a wish, as Origen
understood the sentence, or simply posed a question – 'would it be possible
that...'[45] The interesting point is that in either case Celsus obviously had
no problems with monotheism as such. The difficulties of monotheism
began in his view with its implications for mankind living together. Even
in this case, according to whether the sentence is understood as a wish
or as a question, he seems to have been ready at least to contemplate 'a
single law' for all men. Admittedly, he discarded such a notion at once: his
remark 'whoever believes that knows nothing' interrupted his thoughts as

---

[39] Signposted in the study of Andresen (1955), 189–200.
[40] Origen, *Contra Celsum* 8.11 (*GCS* Orig. 2, 228).
[41] Origen, *Contra Celsum* 8.2 (*GCS* Orig. 2, 222).
[42] Andresen (1955), 221–3; see also Lona (2005), 432ff.   [43] See on this Fürst (2004a).
[44] Origen, *Contra Celsum* 8.72 (*GCS* Orig. 2, 288).
[45] The Greek construction εἰ γάρ with the optative introduces a wish that might be fulfilled. However,
since Celsus immediately thereafter declares that such an idea would be impossible and wholly
unrealistic, and furthermore the verb is missing, he had probably rather posed a question, which at
all events featured the wish of a third party. The sentence may thus be understood as an anacoluthon.
Lona (2005), 417 inferred from the context and from Tatian, *Oratio* 28.1 (*PTS* 43, 54) that Celsus
was probably here reproducing and rejecting a Christian contention.

soon as they had been expressed.[46] A single universal *nomos* would be the alternative vision to the plural reality of the many *nomoi* of the peoples, which Celsus defended against the Christians.

Origen's reply sketched exactly this vision of the unity of the race of mankind under a single *nomos*, precisely as a Utopia, whose complete realisation in every individual case might only be expected at the end of time: 'We say on the contrary that one day the *logos* will come to rule over all being that is endowed with reason, and every soul will be transformed in accordance with its accomplishment as soon as each individual simply makes use of his freedom, chooses what he intends to do, and stays by his choice. Although there are cases of bodily illnesses and injuries which defy all attempts by doctors to cure them, we consider it unlikely that among souls there is anything that has its origin in wickedness that cannot be healed by the sense that rules over everything and by God. For since the *logos* and the healing strength that lives within it are stronger than all the evil in the soul, it allows this strength to work on each individual according to the will of God, and the conclusion of the treatment is the abolition of evil.'[47]

One strand of Origen's detailed and complicated eschatological reflections is important for his discussion with Celsus of a shared order of life for all mankind.[48] Origen contemplated the 'whole being endowed with understanding' from the viewpoint of the individual. Correct order in society begins with the correct order of the individual or, as Origen expressed it, with the correct use of his freedom. While Celsus foregrounds the community, in which the individual must find his proper place, and demands precisely this from the Christians, Origen focuses on the individual, even against the community, as is shown at the beginning of his apologia by his insistence on the right to resist a perverted social and political order.[49] Origen shares this thoroughly modern emphasis on the freedom of the individual with Augustine, who also adopts the perspective of the individual in his concept of the right order in *De civitate Dei*. Proper order in a man is Augustine's prerequisite and starting point for proper order in state and society, and since this order had religious connotations in ancient understanding, the connection presupposes correct forms of worship on the part of the individual and of society: 'As the soul serves God, so it rules the body in the proper manner, and good sense, subordinate to the Lord God, prevails in the soul in the proper manner over

---

[46] Origen, *Contra Celsum* 8.72 (*GCS* Orig. 2, 288).   [47] Origen, *Contra Celsum* 8.72 (*GCS* 2, 288–9).
[48] For further discussion see Brox (1982); Fürst (2000).
[49] Origen, *Contra Celsum* 1.1 (*GCS* Orig. 1, 56).

desire and the other passions. When a man does not serve God in this manner, what sort of righteousness can there be in him? For when he does not serve God, the soul cannot rule the body and the soul cannot rule the passions in the correct manner. And when there is no sort of righteousness in such a man, then there can undoubtedly be none in a gathering of men, which consists of such men.'[50] Continuing from this fundamental point, Augustine, in analogous fashion to Origen, criticised the Roman state and its religious foundations. The moral qualities of a state depended on the moral quality of its members, in the religious sense defined by Augustine. The Roman state could not be said to be in proper order because of its erroneous relationship to God and religious practice. Given the presumption of such religious and moral foundations for a state, the Roman state could not even be treated as a state at all: 'Unless they are utterly stupid or unashamed troublemakers, how could all those who have followed me through the earlier books up to this point still be in doubt that the Romans have served wicked and impure demons? Yet I do not want to discuss what sort of beings they are that they worship with their sacrificial offerings; in the law of the true God it stands written: "whoever sacrifices to the gods and not to the Lord alone shall be destroyed". He who uttered such a fearful threat had no wish that sacrifice should be made to any god, whether good or evil.'[51] Accordingly, false cult practice was connected with the false ordering of state and society, and both in turn depended on the individual and his religious disposition.[52] This should be a sufficient indication of the importance of the individual in Augustine's and Origen's theories of social and state organisation.

The discussion between Celsus and Origen demonstrates that Celsus' theology and theory of society were designed to justify the existing pluralistic order.[53] At all events, Origen was not prepared to compromise on this. He would not accept that all possible forms of human activity could be pleasing to God in a relative sense, but sought to make a distinction between true and false, good and evil. He thus looked for a sense of order in the world that corresponded to the vision of mankind's religious unity that he had formulated.[54] Celsus argued for a conservative pluralism which was presented through cults and guaranteed at a metaphysical level. The

[50] Augustine, De civ. D. 19.21 (II, 391 Dombart/Kalb). For the sequence of the argument in the final chapter of Book 19 see the survey in O'Daly (1999), 206–10.

[51] Augustine, De civ. D. 19.21 (II, 391 Dombart/Kalb) with citation from Exodus 22:20. See Brown (1963), reprinted in Brown (1972), 44.

[52] Heyking (1999) overlooks this emphasis on individual conduct.

[53] See Frede (1997); Droge (2006), 241–3.

[54] For a fuller treatment see Peterson (1951), 86ff.; Ratzinger (1971), 41–68.

Christian vision of unity, which for him represented a rebellion against the established order, was for Origen the beginning of a new and better order.[55] For Origen, the Christian model was a way to do away with and to put a stop to conflict and war, while for Celsus it was a unique source of disturbance and violence. This role of religion in social and political conflicts is a topic of sharp contemporary relevance and was to my knowledge a matter for discussion for the first time in the argument between Celsus and Origen. That was the heart of their debate.

We can conclude from this discussion that in the intellectual debate between Christians and pagans about notions of God and cult practice, which was characterised by contemporary philosophical paradigms, the issue concerned not the number of gods, but the role of religion in states and societies with respect to religious practice, especially the potential of religion to produce peace or conflict, and ideas in general about social and political order, which were connected to specific types of religion. When we discuss pagan and Christian 'monotheism' in antiquity, we should accordingly follow the direction of the ancient debates. We should not only not neglect the social and political implications of their notions of God and cult practices, but should place these at the centre of our attention.

DIFFERENTIATION IN THE CONCEPT OF GOD: ETHICAL MONOTHEISM

By pressing the argument, I have tried in the two previous sections to direct attention to aspects of 'monotheism' which in my estimation have received too little notice in modern analyses of the ancient debate. These aspects are identified under the headwords 'cult' and 'politics'. This is the intended meaning of the title of this contribution: cult and politics delineated the terrain in which the ancient debate about God (as a singular term) was conducted. The decisive differences between pagan and Christian monotheism were to be identified in religious practice and its social and political implications. Admittedly, this does not mean that the contestants agreed with one another in every respect about the concept of God. For sure, they agreed in principle about the uniqueness of God as the first principle of all reality, because both of them, pagan philosopher and Christian theologian alike, were Platonists. Over and beyond this consensus, there were certainly differences in their more precise understanding of the concept of

[55] Baumeister (1978), 167, 170, 176.

God,[56] which should also not be overlooked, since these had consequences for the worship of God and the ideas of social and political order which depended on this. A final reference needs to be made to this aspect of the ancient debate between pagan and Christian monotheists.

If one looks at the theoretical principles underlying the concept of God in the philosopher-theologians of late antiquity, be they pagan or Christian, there is in fact hardly any difference observable between pagan and Christian monotheists. We can here speak of 'monotheism' in the sense of the oneness of this god of the philosophers. However, the perspective must be appreciably widened to grasp and describe the full breadth and complexity of this discourse from late antiquity, not only in relation to the aspects of cult and politics, which have been discussed above, but also in relation to the concept of God itself. Such a broad approach produces the following outcomes.

Even where the concept of God is formulated 'monotheistically' on theoretical principles, 'monotheism' does not always equate to 'monotheism'. Rather, we can identify differences between the pagan and Christian concepts, which on the Christian side can be marked with the headings 'incarnation', 'Christology' and 'Trinity'.[57] The connections that are thereby addressed delimit the specific contours of Christian monotheism, which distinguish it as much from Jewish as from pagan philosophical monotheism. I cannot here provide closer analysis of what that means in its particulars, but content myself with the observation that these specific details must be taken into account in the debate about pagan and Christian monotheism in antiquity.

A further characteristic of Christian monotheism, which Christians inherited from Judaism, is closely connected to their religious practice and their social and political conduct. Origen represented the case for an ethical monotheism which provided the foundation for the attacks that he formulated against Celsus. Origen insisted on the difference between true and false precisely in the concept of God, and deduced criteria from this for establishing true and false forms of worship and also ethical norms in the realm of society and politics.[58] The concept of God, the worship of God and the conduct of life are not separable in this respect, but have a reciprocal effect on one another. The differences between pagans and Christians in

---

[56] For the technical philosophical differences in this connection between Celsus and Origen see Dörrie (1967), reprinted in Dörrie (1976).
[57] This point has been made emphatically by Edwards (2004), 212–17.
[58] Assmann has called this the Mosaic distinction; see Assmann (1997), (1998), (2003), and the discussion by C. Markschies in this volume.

questions of worship and socio-political order are not intelligible without taking account of this difference in the concept of God.

Accordingly, the term 'monotheism' is suitable only to a limited degree and may even be inappropriate to account substantially for these ancient phenomena and the ancient debates that pertain to them. It suggests common ground between pagan and Christian notions of God, part of which, namely the oneness of God based on theoretical principles, was certainly a reality. But it conceals to an excessive degree the conceptual differences which were no less real, and, above all, their different consequences for individual, social and political conduct. These must be described with a sharper eye for differentiation, precisely by paying attention to and analysing the individual aspects and lines of argument used in the corresponding ancient discourse.

CHAPTER 6

The price of monotheism: some new observations on a current debate about late antiquity

Christoph Markschies

RECENT DEBATE AND THE SILENCE OF HISTORIANS

My title refers to *Die Mosaische Unterscheidung oder der Preis des Monotheismus*, the most prominent of Jan Assmann's publications, which have been at the centre of a debate about monotheism among contemporary theologians.[1] Assmann proposed a structural division between primary and secondary forms of religion which broadly conforms to the divide between polytheism and monotheism. The decisive factor in the emergence of secondary religious forms was not the decision to honour one rather than many gods, but to distinguish true from false doctrine. The choice of truth necessarily entailed the rejection of falsehood; thus the secondary religion was exclusive, not inclusive, and intolerant of error and religious deviation. The price for the identification and pursuit of religious truth was paid in hostility to and the repression of false gods, heresy and religious ideas that deviated from the true religion. Violence and hatred were therefore inevitable partners of secondary, monotheistic, religion. It is likely that widespread discussions of Assmann's thesis will continue, not without inevitable repetition of the ensuing arguments. This paper does not intend to side with Assmann's critics and praise monotheism for its integrative and peaceful characteristics, nor will it defend his views with new or old arguments. Rather, my reflections proceed from the comment recently made by a historian: 'the screaming muteness of the historians and scholars of the social sciences'.[2]

As an introduction I begin by asking a question that makes the historical and social dimension of the problem immediately apparent: if this is a discussion about monotheism, whose views are the subject of the debate? Or,

[1] Assmann (2003); cf. also Assmann (1999) and (2000), 62–80. This paper was prepared for the Religionswissenschaftliche Societät in the Forschungsstätte der Evangelischen Studiengemeinschaft e.V. (FEST) on 19 January 2004. Only the footnotes have been slightly augmented. I would like to thank Andreas Heiser for his assistance with the completion of the manuscript.
[2] Weichlein (2003).

to put it more clearly, who actually is a protagonist of the monotheism and the history of ideas that Jan Assmann has reconstructed, thereby initiating this heated discussion? What meaning does the concept of 'monotheism' have when it is considered on the level of 'religion as practised'? The collection of essays *Religion und kulturelles Gedächtnis*, edited by Assmann, contains a number of relevant critical statements. The remarks of Klaus Koch, Egyptologist and expert in the area of Old Testament studies, on the 'multifarious overlapping of poly- and monotheism' also seem to focus on the question I have raised, that is the question of religion as practised in concrete historical situations and social contexts. But he is also concerned with intellectual history, or the history of ideas, which he assigns to political, economical and social factors, and it comes as something of a surprise against this background when he suggests that Assmann's pursuit of a history of ideas is founded on thin air, in his words: 'Ideengeschichte gleichsam ohne Bodenhaftung'.[3] However, he himself is not far removed from this spectre, which looms over all recent historians and sociologists.

Of course Assmann is right first to reconstruct monotheism as a theoretical concept. But who would seriously consider that history is guided by ideas which are theoretical constructs in the first instance and are only represented in reality by the activities of a minority? His position takes for granted that this is 'no argument against the thesis of a Mosaic distinction, which finds no support in the history of religion in the sense that a strict monotheism existed neither in ancient Israel nor in early Judaism'; it takes for granted that very few advocates of this 'intellectual point of view' suffice to impose it; and it takes for granted that a few 'monotheistic elements' in polytheistic or syncretistic practice fulfil the requirements.[4] But it must remain the privilege of the historian to ask why such ideas that stem from minorities become generally established, and why this was especially the case with pressure groups who were without political power. Furthermore, and not least, the historian must ask in what form these ideas, albeit generally in a moderated form, were concretely established.

THE CONCEPT OF MONOTHEISM IN THE RECENT
DEBATE IN GERMANY

In order not to assume the seemingly positivistic superior position of the historian of religion and pursue the question in total hermeneutic naïvety,

---

[3] Koch (1999), reprinted in Assmann (2000), 234.
[4] Assmann (2003), 51 clarifies his thesis in this way.

it is, of course, necessary that I clarify a few points beforehand. With my introductory question of what is monotheism I am in fact searching for the monotheists. But what actually is monotheism? What concepts of monotheism have been assumed in the recent debate? Odo Marquard, in his somewhat mischievous and not totally serious pamphlet *Lob des Polytheismus*, linked monotheism with 'monomyth',[5] and formulated his well-known working hypothesis: 'the polymyth is digestible, the monomyth detrimental'.[6] The polymyth is fitted out with all kinds of notions which imply positive meanings. For example, leaving aside the culinary metaphor of 'digestibility', polymyth is also denoted as the more democratic form by reference to the key concept of 'division of power',[7] since it allows man to develop his individuality freely. The classical form of polymyth was polytheism, because many different fables were related within it,[8] while monotheism is the classical murderer of both polytheism and polymyth.

Comparably, Jan Assmann regards the decisive factor in monotheism not to be 'the differentiation between the one God and many gods...', but the distinction between 'the true God and the false gods', the so-called Mosaic distinction.[9] In his latest book this is explicitly linked with the 'Parmenidean distinction' between true and false knowledge. Assmann explains that both the followers of monotheism and those of Parmenides must be structurally intolerant towards a false god or false knowledge.[10] The 'enforcement of thought' in the Parmenidean distinction corresponds with the enforcing of belief in the Mosaic distinction, as Assmann put it in agreement with Werner Jaeger.[11] It becomes clear from this comparison that here, in the first place, strict theoretical consistency is involved.

Of course, the political vocabulary of enforcement and tolerance which dominates Marquard's and Assmann's terminology suggests swift conclusions about how theory may be put into practice in the religion and philosophy of everyday life. In another paper I somewhat impertinently ascribed the use of this political vocabulary in the context of polytheism and monotheism to a 'concerned old European democratic view', which

---

[5] Marquard (2000b), first published in 1981. Klaus Koch asserts rather disparagingly that the text gave the impression that the author was slightly inebriated whilst writing it.

[6] Marquard (2000b), 98.   [7] Marquard (2000b), 98.

[8] Marquard reduces religion as well as myth to this simple formula: Marquard (2000b), 93 and 100.

[9] Assmann (2003), 12; Assmann (1998), 250. The first to advocate the Mosaic distinction, however, was not Moses, but the Egyptian pharaoh Akhenaten, who formed the basis of his 'theoclasm' in opposition to traditional Egyptian pantheism.

[10] Assmann (2003), 23 and 26.   [11] Assmann (2003), 24, in agreement with Jaeger (1934) I, 237.

might be expected from the Giessen philosopher and the Heidelberg historian of religion. Naturally, at the time I did not seek to deny that there are always new grounds for expressing this concerned democratic view, and that it is perhaps not detrimental that such a perspective does play a role within historical research.[12] The consequences of the chosen imagery come as no surprise. The fact that the 'monotheistically inspired writings of the Bible' represented the establishment of the worship of Yahwe, the one God, 'as violent, even as a direct result of a series of massacres' is a matter which is concerned with 'the cultural semantics and not the history of events', as Assmann himself proclaims.[13] It is another question, however, whether one can describe these passages of the Old Testament as the 'anticipation of Auschwitz'.[14]

Against this theoretical background of a current debate I would now like to ask if one can really speak of 'monomyth' and of a definite distinction between the true God and false gods in the different forms of monotheism that are actually believed in – Hebrew, pagan and Christian. Can one really say that in piety as practised 'translatability is blocked'[15] by the 'hermeneutics of difference' which were characteristic of the primary religions that existed before the 'monotheistic transformation', as formulated by Assmann? When Assmann claims that 'the religions always had a mutual basis. Therefore, they could function as a medium of intercultural translatability', were the features that characterised pre-monotheistic religions brutally destroyed?[16] Or, to put it in a different way, can we observe in these ancient forms of monotheistic piety what Odo Marquard sees as their inevitable implication, that is, the 'liquidation' of polymyth and polytheism?

I want to note explicitly that I do not want simply to join the mass of Assmann's critics, because in Assmann's most recent publication one can naturally also read that, as a matter of course, Christianity insisted on the 'universalisation of the Mosaic distinction', which 'no longer applies only for the Jews, but for all mankind'.[17] Furthermore, one can find a memorable analysis which already observed this universalisation in Hellenistic Judaism.[18] I essentially want to query once again the efficiency of the category of 'monotheism' as well as the duality of 'monotheism' and 'polytheism' as ways of comprehending the social and religious history of antiquity. I would call into question the efficiency of conceptual forms

---

[12] Markschies (2006). [13] Assmann (2004a), 37.
[14] Assmann (2000), 72. The passages referred to are Deut. 28. [15] Assmann (2003), 38.
[16] Assmann (2003), 19. [17] Assmann (2003), 30.
[18] Assmann (2003), 44–7 (on Wisd. of Sol. 14:23–7).

'which stem from controversial theological debates of the 17th and 18th centuries and' – as Jan Assmann now states with surprising clarity – 'are totally unsuitable for the description of ancient religions'.[19]

One could attempt to answer the given questions using many examples stemming from the ancient history of religion, or analyse an endless number of texts written by Christian theologians of antiquity, or turn to the everyday Christian piety of the time, as well as Neoplatonic treatises or pagan magic papyri. But, in doing so, the extensive material of a yet-to-be-written monograph on the subject could only be presented in a very abbreviated form, and I will therefore concentrate on a single characteristic example of so-called ancient 'monotheism'. Because I am currently working on a much expanded new publication of an inventory of the inscriptions from antiquity which contain the 'one God' (εἷς θεός) formula,[20] I will take this formulation and its history as a paradigm, which will help answer both my questions, about what monotheism was, and who the monotheists were, and likewise support my attempt to make certain basic observations on the terminology of 'monotheism' or rather 'polytheism'.

OBSERVATIONS ON MONOTHEISM FROM LATE ANTIQUITY

Let us take a walk through a small village situated in the vicinity of Damascus in the province of Syria in the fifth century AD. The village is called El Dumeir or Hirbet Ed-Dumèr; its ancient name is unknown today. In antiquity this location would have much resembled the traditional, unchanged, small villages one finds today in the Hauran. The irregular unpaved streets that run through the village are lined, to a great extent, with windowless, one-storey, houses, built mostly of local basalt, sparingly divided into a few rooms, and with roofs made by spanning blocks of basalt supported by an arch or a central supporting column. Today one can still visit such houses, or rather their ruins, in the deserted villages of the Golan, occupied by the Israelis, and in the dead cities of North Jordan. Some have been used continually for almost 5,000 years, and the height of the floors and their low ceilings alone betray the fact that they have been lived in for such an extended period of time. The decoration of the buildings mostly comprises only an ornamented lintel over the door, often still preserved, or utilised in the vicinity for some other purpose. Walking through El Dumeir or Hirbet Ed-Dumèr we confront a basalt lintel and read the inscription εἷς ὁ θεὸς ὁ βοηθῶν, 'one God who helps'. Two names are included on the

[19] Assmann (2003), 49.   [20] Peterson (1926).

lintel under these lines, which ask us to remember the two persons who commissioned the inscription and – as one can easily assume – also paid for the whole house. On closer scrutiny it is very soon apparent that the inscriptions are of Jewish origin,[21] and that the εἶς θεός, the 'one God', who is called upon here, is the God of Abraham, Isaac and Jacob, that is, the God of Israel. Were a Jew of late antiquity to accompany us on our walk, it would have been immediately clear that the acclamation was naturally an abbreviated formula signifying Israel's fundamental profession of faith, the deuteronomistic *Sch^ema Jisrael*, in the Greek form ἄκουε Ἰσραὴλ κύριος ὁ θεὸς ὑμῶν κύριος ἐστίν. However, the biblical reference, as well as the formulation on the lintel ('one God who helps'), make it very clear that the existence of additional gods and divine powers was not denied. Rather, the fact that they also can be effective helpers and as such be addressed as 'Lord' at all was being contested. Analogously, knowledgeable specialists in the field interpret the intentions of many layers in the Old Testament as testifying to monotheism. However, if one is aware of these connections, which in my judgement can neither clearly be termed monotheistic nor polytheistic, and which scholars of religion accordingly categorise a little unfortunately as 'monolatry', then it is questionable if this Hebrew 'monotheism' is really appropriately described in Jan Assmann's convenient formulation of the 'Mosaic distinction'.

After these considerations we continue our walk through the village and come to realise that, if the archaeological evidence does not deceive, this is the only inscription of its kind to be found. We have encountered the inscription εἶς ὁ θεὸς ὁ βοηθῶν, 'the one God who helps', written over the entrance of this single Jewish house in the village. We pause for a moment and sit on one of the stones which line a small garden in the village centre, and try to interpret this discovery. It is obvious that the formula εἶς ὁ θεὸς ὁ βοηθῶν served to signify the identity of the two Jewish owners of the house, to differentiate them from the other dwellings, which were probably Christian and pagan. A Jewish fellow believer passing through the village in late antiquity would have known immediately whom he could turn to, where he could expect to be offered hospitality, and where not.

We continue our journey through Syria in late antiquity and travel roughly 250 kilometres from El Dumeir or Hirbet Ed-Dumèr, passing through Damascus and Apameia, to the middle of the Syrian Limestone

[21] Brünnow and Domaszewski (1909), no. 37. J.-B. Frey, *CIJ* ii, 89–90, no. 848 interprets the text as a Jewish inscription and corrects Peterson's readings again according to Brünnow; compare also Schwabe (1951) and the new edition by D. Noy and H. Bloedhorn, *IJO* iii (Syria and Cyprus), 63–5 Syr41.

Massif in the north-west of the province. On the high plateau of the
Gebel Barîha, we arrive at a somewhat larger ancient village named Dâr
Qita. This village, 25 kilometres south of the famous church of St Simeon
Stylites, is now forsaken and in ruins. It was a commercial centre on the
high plateau massif, from which olive oil and wine, the products grown
and produced by the landowners of the small and large estates of the area,
were formerly transported to the coast. Because we are interested in the
subject of monotheism, we will ignore the three basilicas of the village and
again study only the lintels over the entrances of the houses, which are
mostly larger complexes with residential buildings and stables surrounded
by walls, and sometimes also by shops and stores or small hostels. In doing
so, we make some remarkable discoveries. For, if we have correctly counted
and carefully studied each lintel that has been preserved over the years,
thirteen inscriptions prominently display the familiar formula εἷς θεός,
'one God'. Strangely enough, these inscriptions all appear to be exclusively
Christian: for example, one text dating back to AD 431 reads εἷς θεὸς καὶ
ὁ Χριστὸς αὐτοῦ καὶ τὸ ἅγιον πνεῦμα.[22] However, we also encounter
varied forms of our customary formula from El Dumeir or Hirbet Ed-
Dumèr: εἷς θεὸς καὶ ὁ Χριστὸς βοήθισον τοῦ κόσμου; this inscription
may date to AD 515/16.[23] Oddly enough, not only the formula with Christ's
name appears on Christian houses, but also the simple and very familiar εἷς
ὁ θεὸς ὁ βοηθῶν combined with the names of those who commissioned
the inscriptions.[24] A comprehensive study has shown that inscriptions
including the formula εἷς θεός were used especially by newly converted
Christians and hence serve as an index of the gradual Christianisation of
the North Syrian Limestone Massif in late antiquity.[25] Thus the formula
reading εἷς θεός in Dâr Qita and other villages in the Limestone Massif
served exactly the same purpose as it did in El Dumeir or Hirbet Ed-
Dumèr near Damascus. It marked out certain houses of a village by a
sort of 'house sign' in the very same way that one still finds the houses
of Christians today, indicated by a plaque depicting St George, and the
houses of Moslems, using a vignette displaying the Jerusalem Dome of the
Rock. Our South Syrian and North Syrian examples differ only in that in
the former case the house of a Jew was made to stand out amongst the
Christian residences, and in the latter thirteen houses of Christians were
singled out from an incomparably larger number of households inhabited

---

[22] *IGLS* II, 536.   [23] *IGLS* II, 537.   [24] *IGLS* II, 543 or 544: ὁ βοηθῶν ἡμᾶς.
[25] Trombley (1993–4) II, 260.

by people of pagan belief.[26] Therefore, there was no brutal 'liquidation' of polytheistic piety by monotheism, as formulated by Odo Marquard, in Dâr Qita, because the worshippers of gods, whose ability to provide help was doubted by both Christians and Jews alike, were still physically present in the neighbourhood, and they could, by ancient standards, still provide palpable experience of their own divine reality.

But we have not fully exhausted the possibilities of the formula εἷς θεός with these examples. One can find even more evidence for the said connection than has been found in the individual villages of the North Syrian Limestone Massif by investigating a single village in the Holy Land, which has been revealed through the large archaeological excavation of the Church of Mary Theotokos on Mount Gerizim above Nablus/Shechem. This excavation has been carried out for a number of years on the peak of the holy mountain of the Samaritans by the Department of Antiquities for Judea and Samaria, following work commissioned by the Görresgesellschaft that was begun by German archaeologists in the 1930s.[27] A single εἷς θεός inscription was published then, but it was not possible to estimate the real extent of the finds until recent years. An Israeli epigrapher has not only published three further εἷς θεός inscriptions in recent years, but also verbally confirmed the observation of every attentive visitor of the excavations, that one positively stumbles over εἷς θεός inscriptions, especially in the fortress-like buildings which encompass the Church of Mary Theotokos. Even though we still await the final publication of these inscriptions – one can estimate about seventy examples – we have here by far the greatest number of texts containing this formula found in a single location. In general the inscriptions are to be found on floor slabs of single rooms and in the central ambulatory outside the church. On closer scrutiny, it is evident that they are not texts that originally belonged to the still highly impressive Christian church building dating back to late antiquity, but are elements from a Samaritan sacred building, constructed during imperial times on Mount Gerizim and razed to the ground in AD 484 by order of the Byzantine emperor.

At this point I could – perhaps in the style of a travel journal – produce further examples of the use of the εἷς θεός formula, which have been

[26] Trombley (1993–4) II, 313–15, esp. 313 ('Appendix v: The "One God" inscriptions'): 'There can be little doubt that the Christian use of the "One God" formula in the inscription of the Limestone Massif and elsewhere is to be understood as a statement of monotheistic belief vis à vis the villagers' abandonment of polytheism'. Trombley counters the position argued by Jarry (1988).
[27] Schneider (1949/51), esp. 228, 230–1 with Plate 9; reprinted in Schneider (1998), esp. 200, 202; cf. also Di Segni (1990).

unearthed in Israel/Palestine especially in connection with Samaritan synagogues.[28] By doing so, I would reveal that the monotheistic acclamation εἷς θεός also served the Samaritans as a characteristic way of representing their specific identity, which differentiated them from other Jewish, Christian and pagan centres of cult worship in Palestine and in Nablus/Shechem. The invocation 'one God' therefore fulfilled precisely the function that it had at other locations in Syria for those very groups from which the Samaritans had sought to distance themselves for centuries.

My observations on the εἷς θεός inscriptions can be rounded off by a reference to the example of milestones in Palestine, which were erected in AD 361/2 under the rule of the Emperor Julian and which, as they bear the inscription of εἷς θεὸς νίκα Ἰουλιανέ, must also be counted as evidence of the fact that the apostate used precisely the εἷς θεός formula of the Christians as a form of propaganda against their religion.[29] Or I could point out a carved gemstone found in Egypt, which introduces an obviously pagan oracle with the words εἷς θεὸς λέγει.[30] However, it is not necessary to continue in detail as these examples are more than sufficient to answer both our questions, and lead us to a few final remarks on the usefulness of the category 'monotheism' and the dual terms 'monotheism' – 'polytheism' for a history of religion in antiquity.

THE USEFULNESS OF MONOTHEISM FOR THE HISTORY OF RELIGION

We have seen in our examples that at least everyday Jewish 'monotheism' in the South Syrian village of El Dumeir or Hirbet Ed-Dumèr, that of the Christians in Dâr Qita, and that of the Samaritans on Mount Gerizim near Nablus, served the purpose which Odo Marquard contested. It stabilised the individual identity of another distinctive religion within a continuing polytheistic–polymythical environment. We were unable to observe any sign of the tendency towards the intellectual or physical liquidation of polytheistic religions related to professing a monotheistic faith in one god who helps. Rather, the opposite tendency seemed to prevail. The inhabitants in the above-mentioned villages lived peacefully side by side, even after the 'Constantinian transformation'. One can hardly speak of 'liquidation', but at most discern that a certain religious group pointedly professed faith in one single helper, displaying a tendency to emasculate, subordinate and sublimate the gods worshipped by neighbours.

---

[28] Di Segni (1998), 55.   [29] Di Segni (1994), 104, no. 31; cf. SEG 41 (1991), 1544.
[30] Nock (1940), 313.

Correspondingly, the memorable formulation of the 'Mosaic distinction' coined by Jan Assmann does not in reality correspond to the contemporary circumstances. On the contrary, it is exactly the aspect which Assmann holds to be typical for polytheism, its ability to synthesise foreign gods within its own system of myths, which in fact characterises how Jews, Christians and Samaritans dealt with the gods of their pagan neighbours. They were regarded as ultimately helpless and weak divine powers, simply as demons, but their existence was by no means liquidated. What is more, Jews, Christians and Samaritans would of course have differentiated themselves more pointedly and perhaps more exactly than in pagan polytheism, but did every Thessalian farmer really worship all the gods of the Greek pantheon? Did a simple citizen who farmed land in the vicinity really visit Artemis one morning, Apollo of Claros the next, and go to the temple of the deified emperor Hadrian the day after? Does not the alleged clear-cut differentiation between 'monotheism' and 'polytheism' become more blurred as we adjust the optics and view the situation more precisely? On closer observation were not polytheists as well as monotheists sometimes violent and sometimes peaceable? Do not other factors, such as the polit-ical and economic circumstances of the times, play a much more decisive role when trying to explain the reasons behind the liquidation and rise of religions? As for the headword 'monolatry', the worship of only one god, while it still acknowledges the existence of other gods and demonic beings, are not all cats grey anyway?

The exemplary finds in the Near East of late antiquity should warn us not to overestimate the efficiency of the category 'monotheism' and its counterpart 'polytheism'. These paired terms have been in use since the seventeenth century, but since then have yet to play a dominant role in religious and theological history. It was probably Friedrich Schleiermacher in the introduction to the second edition of the *Glaubenslehre* (1830–1) who initially moulded the notion and matter of 'monotheism'[31] into a charac-teristic that identified Judaism, Christianity and Islam.[32] Incidentally, this explains his very critical position in relation to the Church's teachings on the Trinity, in which he detects the 'unconscious echo of the heathen'. Put in less genteel wording, the remaining stock of polytheism required 'new treatment' and 'remodelling', and this was to be found embryonically in

[31] Cf. two more recent definitions: Bloch (2000), 375: 'Glauben an die Existenz eines einzigen Gottes im Gegensatz zu Polytheismus und Henotheismus'; Schwöbel (1994), 257: '"Monotheismus" beze-ichnet im allgemeinen eine Interpretation des Göttlichen, die dieses als wesentlich eine, einzig und einheitliche, in genauer zu bestimmendem Sinn personhafte . . . Wirklichkeit darstellt, die auf das welthafte Seiende als deren Grund und Ziel bezogen ist.'

[32] Schleiermacher (1960), §8. It displayed, however, varying degrees in Judaism and Islam; cf. the observations made by Schwöbel (1994), 257.

the theology of the Trinity.[33] This view converges in a sense with that of Odo Marquard. So, if one critically reconsiders the function and efficiency of the dual terms 'monotheism' – 'polytheism',[34] the results would be in no way as crucial for reconstructing the history of religion in antiquity as has been concluded by certain researchers, even by whole generations of researchers, who have eagerly sought out evidence for polytheism as practised by monotheists in late antiquity.

The evidence of inscriptions found among ordinary Christians indicates that the confined limits of a clearly defined concept of monotheism, to which excessive attention has been paid in the widely inculcated tradition introduced by Schleiermacher, did not exist in late antiquity. The overall picture in later antiquity was varied and colourful. We may recall the problematical role played by the angels in monotheistic religions.[35] As early as the nineteenth century some scholars of religion believed that the intensive worship of angels in Judaism weakened monotheism and thereby, so to speak, provided suitable conditions for the Christian theology of the Trinity.[36] This view has also, of course, been strongly refuted since.[37] Inscriptions in particular reveal how popular the worship of angels was in the everyday life of ancient times amongst Jews and Christians alike,[38] but one could also demonstrate the commonplace 'polytheism' of the 'monotheists' by citing the many magic texts which were used by the Jews, Christians and Samaritans of antiquity as a matter of course. I will abstain from citing further evidence for the 'routine polytheism' of many ancient 'monotheists', because here too our examples are already enough to illustrate the basic thesis.[39] Additionally, theoretical reflection in the time of the Roman Empire was often not at all concerned with our modern questions about the singularity of God in opposition to 'polytheism', but, as many Middle Platonic and Neoplatonic texts suggest,[40] with the simpler question of what stands at the beginning of all things, a single principle, a final reason, or even a dualistic principle. The function of the dual categories of 'monotheism' – 'polytheism' should be reviewed, not

---

[33] Schleiermacher (1960), §172.

[34] According to Julian, *Contra Galilaeos* 72.20–1 cited by Cyril of Alexandria, *In Julianum* 9.306B, the question concerning monotheism and polytheism is 'a trivial matter'.

[35] Corbin (1981).   [36] Bousset (1926), 302–57; see, most recently, Koch (1994).

[37] Hurtado (2003), 24–7 and also 41: 'The "weakened monotheism" of post-biblical Judaism described by Bousset and others is an erroneous construct'; Hayman (1991).

[38] Leclercq (1924), 2144–53.   [39] For Egypt see Vinzent (1998), 43–6.

[40] For example, cf. the following passage from the sixth century: Olympiodorus, *In Platonis Gorgiam* 4.3 (p. 32.16–17 Westerink): καὶ γὰρ ἴσμεν καὶ ἡμεῖς ἐν τὸ πρῶτον αἴτιον τὸν θεὸν οὐδὲ γὰρ πολλὰ πρῶτα ('And we also know that the first cause of all things is one and that it is God. Therefore there cannot be many first causes').

only because they are relatively recent coinages, but also because of their limited explanatory power. This applies by no means only to the social history of religion, but also particularly to the history of religion and ideas in general.

My examples have shown that basing our understanding of the relationship between 'monotheism' and 'polytheism' as corresponding to a conflict between an open and a totalitarian society misses the truth at least in the case of the historical circumstances of antiquity. One may assume that the case was similar in the earlier eras of Israeli and Jewish religious history. I have also voiced considerable doubts about the efficiency of the terms 'monotheism' and 'polytheism' within history and religious studies. This result leads us to a final question. How could one construct such clearly demarcated patterns for religions?

It is my belief that imposition of such terminology, which fits the historical truth only under very limited conditions, is linked with the very one-sided orientation to be found in many studies of religious history which – to put it succinctly – impose a bias towards intellectual history. This is also the case with many works written by theologians and ecclesiastical historians, who approach the subject matter from the viewpoint of dogmatic and theological history. The sensitive subject of 'monotheism' – 'polytheism' is treated purely in the context of a certain social class of ancient society, against the background of views held by erudite teachers and highly educated cultic functionaries. The historical picture that is conveyed remains correspondingly tendentious.

Jan Assmann's extremely erudite monograph displays a similar bias, not so much in representing the history of ancient mentality, as implied by the subtitle, but rather in presenting a prehistory of a previous European mentality, and thus demonstrating the impressive self-enlightenment of a member of the German professorial class concerning the light and dark sides of his identification as a German and European academic. From this viewpoint, all the above-mentioned patterns are particularly relevant to intellectual history and to a mentality which is not to be underestimated, even though we have vehemently disputed their relevance for approaching the history of ancient religion. They are relevant in the present day, when, for example, the construction of clearly differentiated 'monotheism' and 'polytheism' is used to enlist support for religious and political tolerance and to preserve the basic principles of democracy based on the rule of law. It would not at all become a theologian to contradict such an argument.

CHAPTER 7

Megatheism: the search for the almighty god and the competition of cults

Angelos Chaniotis

A FEW THOUGHTS ON MONOGAMY AND MONOTHEISM[1]

If I avoid using the term monotheism in my paper in connection with religious trends in the Roman East, it is because I take the word to mean what it says – the exclusive worship of a single god – exactly as monogamy means the state of being married to a single person at a time. Admittedly, monogamy has never prevented humans from having sex with other partners as well, hoping that the one and only would not find out about it – a soft monogamy as it were. It is only with a similar tolerance towards human weakness that we might accept as monotheism the situation in which an individual accepts the existence of a single god, but nevertheless worships many others, either because he thinks it would do no harm, or 'just in case'. But I wonder whether it really helps us understand the religions of the Roman Empire if we modify the term monotheism beyond recognition through the addition of attributes, such as soft, pagan, inclusive, hierarchical, affective or whatever.

By saying this I do not deny the sporadic existence of genuine monotheistic ideas in intellectual circles. I also do not deny the existence of monotheistic tendencies. But I do find the term pagan monotheism misleading in as much as it reduces the quest for the divine in the imperial period to a question of quantity, whereas the textual evidence for this period shows that we are primarily dealing with a question of quality. What are the properties of the divine? What is the most effective way of communicating with the divine? What is the proper form of worship? Is there a hierarchy among the gods? These were the questions asked by both philosophers and

[1] This paper stems from two research projects I have directed in Heidelberg, both funded by the Deutsche Forschungsgemeinschaft: the project 'Ritual and communication in the civic communities of ancient Greece' (part of the collaborative research programme 'The dynamic of rituals', 2002–7); and the project 'The language of religious communication in the Roman East' (part of the priority programme 'Roman imperial religion and provincial religion', 2005–7). I completed this article in April 2007; I have added bibliography which appeared later only in a few exceptional cases.

worshippers. By highlighting the rather artificial opposition mono- versus poly-theism, we might neglect other oppositions that dominated the religious discourse of the imperial period: e.g. individual versus collective, ritualised versus internalised or spiritual, public versus private, traditional versus philosophical and so on. It is for these reasons that I have provocatively introduced the neologism 'megatheism', and not only in order to fulfil the dream of many a scholar to create a new word.

I use the term megatheism not as an alternative to monotheism or henotheism,[2] but as a designation of an expression of piety which was based on a personal experience of the presence of god, represented one particular god as somehow superior to others, and was expressed through oral performances (praise, acclamations, hymns) accompanying, but not replacing, ritual actions. That the existence of such a god was a concern in the imperial period is directly attested by an oracle quoted in the *Theosophia Tubingensis*, a response to someone who asked Apollo if there is another god with a superior power (εἰ ἔστιν ἕτερος θεὸς μείζονα παρ' αὐτὸν ἔχων ἐξουσίαν).[3]

My interest in 'megatheism' stems from my interest in the highly competitive context of the quest for the divine in the imperial period. There is no need to stress here that the imperial period was a period of competition in various forms: competition among the members of the civic elite, competition among the cities for privileges, titles and rank, competition among festivals for participants and audiences, competition among cults and cult centres. That these competitions could become violent confrontations is known from the many conflicts among the cities for the rank of metropolis and the privilege of *neokoreia*.[4] The field of religion was equally competitive and not at all peaceful. Pliny's letters concerning the Christians of Pontus and Bithynia and Lucian's narrative of the competition between Alexander of Abonou Teichos and the Christians[5] were until recently rather isolated

---

[2] 'Henotheism' is appropriate as a designation of a very specific religious concept, the idea of the unity of god (e.g. *Orphicorum fragmenta* 239 Kern: εἷς Ζεύς, εἷς Ἀΐδης, εἷς Ἥλιος, εἷς Διόνυσος, εἷς θεὸς ἐν πάντεσσι; Dio Chrys. *Or.* 31.11.8–10: πολλοὶ δὲ καὶ ἁπλῶ τοὺς θεοὺς πάντας εἰς μίαν τινὰ ἰσχὺν καὶ δύναμιν συνάγουσιν); cf. de Hoz (1997) and Belayche, in this volume. For a cautious assessment of this idea see Versnel (1990), 232–6. However, in that study, from which I have profited more than the footnotes reveal, Versnel uses the term 'henotheism' to describe the elevation of one above all others (cf. 'affective monotheism'); cf. Versnel (2000), esp. 85–8, and e.g. Belayche (2005c). It is for this phenomenon that I prefer the term 'megatheism'.

[3] *Theosophia Tubingensis* 39 (*Theosophorum Graecorum fragmenta* p. 26 Erbse). On this curiosity see Nock (1933), 99–116.

[4] See e.g. Roueché (1989b), 206–28; Dräger (1993), 107–200; Nollé (1993), 297–317; Collas-Heddeland (1995); Heller (2006), 179–341.

[5] Pliny, *Ep.* 10.96–7; Lucian, *Alexander* 25 and 38; cf. Victor (1997), 149–50.

pieces of evidence for religious confrontation in Asia Minor, but a new inscription from Kollyda in Lydia gives a fascinating if enigmatic narrative of an attack against a sanctuary of Mes Motylleites during the celebration of his festival (AD 197/8). A crowd gathered, armed with swords, sticks and stones, and attacked the sanctuary and the sacred slaves and destroyed the images of the gods. Unfortunately, neither the identity of the attackers nor their motivation is known.[6]

Ephesos provides a good example of how the local cult of Artemis was promoted in conscious competition with other cult centres.[7] As early as AD 22/3, when the inviolability of sanctuaries was under scrutiny by the Roman authorities, the Ephesians supported their claim to *asylia* by pointing out that Apollo and Artemis were born in their city; this claim explicitly excluded the birth of these gods on Delos.[8] One hundred and forty years later a prominent member of the local elite, C. Laverius Amoinos, took the lead in efforts to strengthen the cult by proposing to the assembly that the entire month Artemision should be dedicated to Artemis (*c.* AD 162–4).[9] His proposal repeatedly stressed the privileged relationship between Artemis and Ephesos: 'Artemis, the patron goddess of our city (ἡ προεστῶσα τῆς πόλεως), is honoured not only in her native city, a city which she has made more glorious than any other city with her divinity, but also among the Greeks and the barbarians, to the effect that in many places sanctuaries and sacred precincts have been dedicated to her, and temples, altars and statues have been established, on account of the clear manifestations of her power. And the greatest proof of the respect rendered to her is the fact that she has her eponymous month, which we call Artemision, while the Macedonians and the other Greek *ethne* and their cities call it Artemisios. . . . Because of all that, the demos regarded it appropriate that the entire month, which bears this divine name, should be sacred and dedicated to the goddess and has approved with this decree the establishment of the worship required

---

6 Herrmann and Malay (2007), 110–13 no. 84: Μηνὸς Μοτυλλείτου ἰορτῆς γενομένης, ἐρχομένου αὐτοῦ ἀπὸ τῆς ἰορτῆς, συνῆλθεν ὄχλος ἐπὶ τὴν βασιλικὴν ἔχοντες ξίφη καὶ ξύλα καὶ λίθους, συντρίψαντες τοὺς ἱεροδούλους καὶ τὰ ἀφιδρύσματα τῶν θεῶν καὶ μηδενὶ χρῶμα τηρηθῆναι, μήτε τοῖς θεοῖς μήτε τοῖς ἱεροδούλοις... ('when a festival of Mes Motylleites was celebrated and he was returning from the festival, a crowd gathered attacking the basilica with swords and sticks and stones, crushing the sacred slaves and the images of the gods, so that neither the dignity (?) of the gods nor that of the sacred slaves was preserved...').

7 On measures for the promotion of the Ephesian cult see e.g. Knibbe (2002), 49–62; Berns (2006), 273–308. Cf. Engelmann (2001), 33–44.

8 Tacitus, *Ann.* 3.61.1: *primi omnium Ephesii adiere, memorantes non, ut vulgus crederet, Dianam atque Apollinem Delo genitos: esse apud se Cenchreum amnem, lucum Ortygiam, ubi Latonam partu gravidam et oleae, quae tum etiam maneat, adnisam edidisse ea numina.*

9 *I.Ephesos* 24 = *LSAM* 31; Horsley (1992), 154–5; Chaniotis (2003), 184–6.

for this month . . . Thus, when the goddess is honoured in an even better fashion, our city will remain more glorious and prosperous for ever.' Only a few years earlier, the Ephesian goddess was declared in a public document to be, in direct comparison with the other Olympians, 'forever the greatest among all the gods'.[10]

It is in the context of competition that we should study the various forms of interaction among religious concepts, including the impact of monotheistic tendencies in philosophy and of mystery cults on traditional worship.[11] In this paper, I will attempt to sketch how the epigraphic evidence, primarily from the Roman East, reveals the interdependence of religious concepts, whose common denominator was a strong interest in a privileged relationship with an almighty god. Although one may observe a convergence in linguistic expression, I shall argue that this convergence is not always the result of a homogeneity of ideas but of emulation and competition among the followers of different conceptions of the divine.

DISSEMINATION OF RELIGIOUS IDEAS AND RELIGIOUS INTERTEXTUALITY

Sometime in the second century AD, a certain Sextus dedicated at Vasio Vocontiorum (Vaison-la-Romaine) an altar to Baal, the master of Fortune. He explained his motivation in the Greek version of the bilingual dedicatory inscription: 'because he remembered the oracles at Apameia' (τῶν ἐν Ἀπαμείᾳ μνησάμενος λογίων).[12] Did Sextus expect the readers of his inscription to know what these oracles were? In this case, we will probably never find out; but in other cases we may be certain that the words of the gods travelled a long distance. The dissemination of the Sibylline oracles is the best example.[13] Making known the oracles of Glykon, the New Asklepios, was part of the marketing strategy of Alexander of Abonou Teichos for the propagation of the new cult.[14] An oracular *lex sacra* from Lindos, stressing the priority of purity of mind over purity of body, provides an

---

[10] *SEG* 43 (1993), 756 (*c.* AD 128–61): ἥ τε πάτριος Ἐ[φεσίω]ν θεὸς Ἄρτεμις καὶ θεῶν πάντων πώποτε μεγίστη.

[11] On the complex subject of syncretism, interaction and competitions see more recently North (1992); Bonnet and Motte (1997); Engster (2003); Belayche (2003), 9–20; North (2003); Belayche (2006a) and in this volume. Cf. Osborne (2003).

[12] *IG* XIV, 2482; *IGR* I, 14; Decourt (2004), 111–12 no. 87, with summary of the interpretations of this text: *Belus Fortunae rector mentisque magister ara gaudebit quam dedit et voluit.* Εἰθυντῆρι Τύχης Βήλῳ Σέξστος θέτο βωμὸν τῶν ἐν Ἀπαμείᾳ μνησάμενος λογίων.

[13] Potter (1990), 95–140. On the role of sanctuaries in the collection and dissemination of oracles see Busine (2005), 53–4 and below, n. 16.

[14] Lucian, *Alexander* 24. Cf. Victor (1997), 23; Chaniotis (2002c), 74.

instructive case of religious intertextuality based on the dissemination of oracles. The first verse is taken from an older metrical oracle from Epidauros: 'You shall be pure inside the temple that smells of incense'; the second is part of an oracle of Sarapis preserved in a manuscript in Vienna: 'Come here with clean hands and with a pure mind and with a true tongue. Clean not through washing, but pure in mind.'[15]

Through their dissemination, oracular texts could easily become channels for the diffusion of religious concepts, the more so since in the imperial period oracles reflected contemporary theological and religious trends.[16] The theosophical oracle of Apollo Klarios, the best-known text of this kind, is of crucial significance for this subject: 'Born of itself, untaught, without a mother, unshakeable, not contained in a name, known by many names, dwelling in fire, this is god. We, his angels, are a small part of god. To you who ask this question about god, what his essential nature is, he has pronounced that aether is god who sees all. To him you should pray at dawn, gazing on him and looking towards the sunrise.'[17]

This oracle is known both from the inscription at Oinoanda and from literary sources.[18] Stephen Mitchell has plausibly associated it with the cult of Theos Hypsistos and the *theosebeis*,[19] and although it is far from certain that every single dedication to Theos Hypsistos is connected with this concept of the divine (see below), the wide distribution of the relevant testimonia supports the assumption that this oracle was widely known. What was its impact? Some of its readers, familiar with Orphic theogony and theology, must have recognised a familiar concept. The supreme Orphic god was born of himself (αὐτογενής in the Testament of Orpheus), he was associated with fire (ἀκαμάτου πυρὸς ὁρμή), seated on a fiery throne (θρόνῳ πυρόεντι); he was regarded as a god who cannot be seen but sees

---

[15] The Lindian text: *LSCG Suppl.* 108. Discussion: Chaniotis (1997), 163; Petrovic and Petrovic (2006), 157 no. 8. On the text from Epidauros (Clement of Alexandia, *Strom.* 5.1.13.3; Porphyry, *Abst.* 2.19.5) and its possible date see Chaniotis (1997), 152 (fourth century BC); Bremmer (2002b), 106–8 favours a later date; but see the comments in *SEG* 52 (2002), 343. The oracle in the Vienna manuscript: Totti (1985), 147 no. 61.

[16] Busine (2005), 154–224; cf. Robert (1968); Belayche (2007a).

[17] *SEG* 27 (1977), 933: αὐτοφυής, ἀδίδακτος, ἀμήτωρ, ἀστυφέλικτος, | οὔνομα μὴ χωρῶν, πολυώνυμος, ἐν πυρὶ ναίων, | τοῦτο θεός· μεικρὰ δὲ θεοῦ μερὶς ἄγγελοι ἡμεῖς. | τοῦτο πευθομένοισι θεοῦ πέρι ὅστις ὑπάρχει, | αἰθέρα πανδερκῆ θεὸν ἔννεπεν, εἰς ὃν ὁρῶντας | εὔχεσθ᾽ ἠώους πρὸς ἀντολίην ἐσορῶντας. Robert (1971); Hall (1978); Potter (1990), 351–5; Livrea (1998), 90–6 (comparison with other theosophical works); Mitchell (1999), 83–91, 98, 102, 143 no. 233; Merkelbach and Stauber (2002), 16–19; Petzl (2003), 99–100; Busine (2005), 35–40, 203–8, 423; Jones (2005), 294–5.

[18] *Theosophia Tubingensis* 13.105–8 (*Theosophorum Graecorum fragmenta* pp. 8–9 Erbse); Lactantius, *Div. inst.* 1.7.1.

[19] Mitchell (1998), 62–3 and (1999).

all, being served by much-labouring angels (πολύμοχθοι ἄγγελοι); and he was a polyonymous god.[20] But for many worshippers of traditional religion it must have been as shocking to learn from Apollo that the traditional gods were only messengers and a small part of a motherless polyonymous god as it was for Julian two centuries later to learn, again from Apollo, that his oracle was no more.[21]

Two new finds may be related to the theosophical oracle from Klaros or other oracles. The first text is a dedication to Theos Hypsistos from Amastris: 'upon the command of the god with the long hair, this altar [has been erected] in honour of the Highest God, who has power over everything, who cannot be seen, who sees to it that the dreadful bane can be driven away from the mortals'.[22] The nature of this supreme god is described in similar terms as in the theosophical oracle: the Highest God has power over everything, he cannot be seen, but observes everything. The oracle of Apollo ('the god with the long hair'), which gave instructions for the erection of this altar, may have been no other than the theosophical oracle of Klaros; but the βροτολοιγέα δείματα which Theos Hypsistos averts may be an allusion to the plague during the reign of Marcus Aurelius (cf. below), and in this case the oracle may have been one of the oracles of Apollo Klarios connected with this event. Despite these uncertainties, the similarity of this dedication to other religious texts (see n. 20) is striking.

We are confronted with similar uncertainties as regards the second text, an inscription from Pisidia, according to which a dedication was made to the gods and goddesses in accordance with the interpretation of an oracle of Apollo Klarios.[23] A Latin version of the text is known from ten inscriptions found in Dalmatia (Corinium), Italy (Cosa, Gabii and Marruvium), Sardinia (Nora), Numidia (Cuicul), Mauretania (Volubilis

---

[20] This similarity has already been observed by Robert (1971), 603. See the following Orphic fragments (now in *Poetae epici Graeci* II.I Bernabé): frg. 243 line 22 (hymn for Zeus): σῶμα δέ οἱ ... ἀστυφέλικτον; frg. 377 F lines 8–10: αὐτογενής ... οὐδέ τις αὐτὸν εἰσοράαι θνητῶν, αὐτὸς δέ γε πάντας ὁρᾶται; frg. 31 F line 5 Bernabé: ἀκαμάτου πυρὸς ὁρμή; *Orphicorum fragmenta* 248.9–10 Kern: σῶι δὲ θρόνωι πυρόεντι παρεστᾶσιν πολύμοχθοι ἄγγελοι. See Herrero de Jáuregui (2009). Cf. the use of similar attributes in the Orphic hymns: 10.10: αὐτοπάτωρ (Physis), 8.3 and 12.9: αὐτοφυής (Helios, Herakles), 12.13: ἀστυφέλικτος (Herakles). For πανδερκής see below, n. 98.
[21] Busine (2005), 427 with bibliography.
[22] Marek (2000), 135–7 (*SEG* 50 (2000), 1225, imperial period): θεῷ ὑψίστῳ ὀμφῇ ἀκερσεκόμου βωμὸν θεοῦ ὑψίστοιο, ὃς κατὰ πάντων ἔστι καὶ οὐ βλέπεται, εἰσορᾷα δὲ δείμαθ' ὅπως ἀπαλάκηται βροτολοιγέα θνητῶν. Marek has observed the similarity between the properties attributed to this deity and those described in contemporary texts and has suggested identifying this deity with Helios Theos Hypsistos.
[23] Mitchell (2003a), 151–5 no. 13 (*SEG* 53 (2003), 1587): [θ]εοῖς καὶ θεαῖς ἀπὸ ἐξηγήσεως χρησμοῦ Ἀπόλλωνος Κλαρίου.

and Banasa), Spain (La Coruña) and Britain (Vercovicium).[24] According
to Eric Birley, who knew only the Latin inscriptions, the wide diffusion
of the dedications required the intervention of a central authority; he suggested associating these dedications with an oracle given during Caracalla's
illness in AD 213.[25] Observing that most of the Latin texts were inscribed
on plaques, presumably designed to fit into walls and, therefore, to have
an apotropaic function, Christopher Jones has suggested that the interpretation concerned an oracle of Apollo Klarios recommending measures in
order to face the plague that began in AD 165;[26] from the uniformity of the
copies he inferred that they were set up on instructions from Rome and
disseminated through the Roman army. The oracle at Klaros is known to
have given recommendations concerning a plague (probably this plague),
and altars in Rome, set up *ex oraculo* to 'the gods that avert evil', 'Athena the
averter', Zeus Hypatos and Zeus Patrios, may indeed be related with this
event.[27] However, the copy from Cosa, depopulated in the second half of
the second century, may be later, and plaques were often used to cover the
front of altars. Furthermore, the occasions envisaged by Birley (illness of
Caracalla) and Jones (plague under Marcus Aurelius) explain the existence
of an oracle, but not why an interpretation (ἐξήγησις) recommending dedications to the gods and the goddesses was necessary. We should, therefore,
not exclude the possibility, recently suggested by Stephen Mitchell, that the
oracle which required an interpretation was no other than the theosophical
oracle of Apollo Klarios. The exegesis may have recommended the worship
of the traditional Olympian gods, although they ranked below the Highest God, thus reconciling traditional religion with the rising popularity of
monotheistic tendencies. It should be added that the exegesis of another
theological oracle of Apollo Klarios is attributed to a certain Cornelius
Labeo, author of a treatise *On the Oracle of the Clarian Apollo*.[28] Although
clarity on this matter is (still) not possible, it is not inconceivable that the
priests at Klaros took a lead in sending this message to the Latin-speaking
parts of the Empire,[29] exactly as Alexander of Abonou Teichos made sure
that the oracles of his new god became known.

---

[24] The Latin version reads: *diis deabusque secundum interpretationem oraculi Clarii Apollinis*. For the
references see Jones (2005), 293; Busine (2005), 184–5.
[25] Birley (1974). [26] Jones (2005); cf. Jones (2006).
[27] Jones (2005) 297–301, and (2006), 369 (*IGUR* 94–7).
[28] Macrobius, *Sat.* 1.18.18–20; see Mastandrea (1979); MacMullen (1981), 87. Jones (2005), 295 has
pointed out that the last lines of the theosophical inscription from Oinoanda may be an exegesis of
the theosophical oracle; for a different explanation see Potter (1990), 353–5.
[29] See Jones (2005) 301; Busine (2005), 189.

Even if not directly related to each other, these texts reflect the religious quest of the imperial period. Whom should we worship and how? Sometimes the quest was fundamental, sometimes it was triggered by a very specific critical situation. The answers were not only provided by intellectuals in philosophical schools or by the members of exclusive circles of theologians and initiates. They were also given by the cult personnel, which administered the traditional sanctuaries and was fully aware of contemporary trends.[30] When a treasurer at Didyma submitted an enquiry concerning the relocation of an altar of Tyche (*c.* AD 200), the oracle he received went beyond simply answering his question: 'you should honour and revere all the immortals' (πάντας χρὴ τειμᾶν μάκαρας πάντας τε σέβεσθαι).[31] At least indirectly, this text was in a dialogue with other theological texts circulating in the Empire. The numerous inscriptions of religious content – dedications, praises of the gods and records of acclamations, funerary imprecations, vows, oracles, cult regulations, confessions – are responses to the same questions: whom should we worship and how? Although they originate in different religious communities, they often share the same vocabulary, which often makes the attribution of a text to a particular community impossible.[32]

The different religious communities were not isolated but engaged in a dialogue. The shared vocabulary should not always and uncritically be taken as evidence for either homogeneous concepts or syncretisms. Already Erik Peterson, in his seminal study of the acclamatory phrase εἷς θεός ('one god'), had observed a diversity in the use of this formula.[33] Not every attestation of the formula *heis theos* refers to a *single* god; sometimes it designates a deity as *unique* within a polytheistic system.

---

[30] See Busine (2005), 202–8 on the convergence between the theological oracles of Apollo and contemporary trends.
[31] *SGO* 1, 84–5 no. 01/19/06; Busine (2005), 450 no. 32 (with further bibliography). Cf. Bernand (1969), 573–6 no. 165 = Totti (1985), 123 no. 47 (Talmis, second/third century AD): σέβου τὸ θεῖον, θύε πᾶσι τοῖς θεοῖς (but followed by the recommendation to honour in particular Isis and Sarapis).
[32] Many recent studies point to the ambiguities in the use of a shared religious vocabulary, already observed by Peterson (1926), Nock (1933) and others. See e.g. Di Segni (1994); Marek (2000), 133–4, 135–7, 141–6; Bowersock (2002) (on *hypsistos* and *theosebes*); Chaniotis (2002a), 224–6 and (2002b), 112–19 (on the convergence of the religious vocabulary of pagans, Jews and Christians in late antiquity); Markschies (2002), 209–14 (*heis theos*); Trebilco (2002) (the formula ἔσται αὐτῷ πρὸς τὸν θεόν); Petzl (2003) (on the convergence of religious ideas in Asia Minor); Foschia (2005); Chaniotis and Chiai (2007), 117–24. See also my remarks in the 'Epigraphic bulletin for Greek religion', *Kernos* 13 (2000), 128; 14 (2001), 147–8; 15 (2002), 334; 16 (2003), 250; 17 (2004), 190; 18 (2005), 425; 20 (2007), 243–4; 21 (2008), 224–5.
[33] Peterson (1926), 268–70. See also below, n. 62.

The same observation has been made recently by Nicole Belayche with regard to Theos Hypsistos.[34] The wide diffusion of dedications to Theos Hypsistos should not be taken as evidence for the existence of a single Theos Hypsistos stemming from a single and homogeneous religious concept.[35] The homogeneity of language sometimes conceals a diversity of concepts; the shared vocabulary may not be the result of a harmonious dialogue, but of competition or confrontation.

The cult of Thea Hypsiste provides an instructive example. This cult was already known through a dedication from Kula (Kollyda) in Lydia, included by Stephen Mitchell in his extremely useful collection of testimonia for the cult of Theos and Zeus Hypsistos.[36] That Thea Hypsiste was somehow related to Hypsistos is certain, but was she his female hypostasis, a consort, a competitor, or perhaps just a traditional goddess addressed with a new name under the influence of the worship of Theos Hypsistos? Is her cult evidence for the transfer of ideas, for syncretism, or for competition? A new epigraphic find brings us one step further in the quest for an answer. A second dedication to Thea Hypsiste was published a few years ago, again from Kollyda (imperial period). Luckily here Thea Hypsiste is accompanied by another epithet that clearly designates her as the patron (προκαθημένη) of a small community, whose name is only partly preserved ('to Thea Hypsiste, the patron of the Kla[–]tai'). We are dealing with a local goddess addressed with a trendy acclamatory epithet. In this case, the use of the female form of the epithet Hypsistos cannot be regarded as deriving from a homogeneous conception of the 'Highest God';[37] and of course, there is no certainty that the two inscriptions from Kollyda refer to the same goddess.

This example shows how cautious we should be when interpreting short fascinating texts, often isolated and found in unclear contexts. The convergence of language does not always reflect a convergence of ideas. The cult foundation of Alexander of Abonou Teichos exemplifies how a new cult adopted pre-existing cultic elements and religious concepts, but by

---

[34] Belayche (2005a); cf. Belayche (2005c), 268.

[35] This has been suggested by Mitchell (1998) and (1999), who has collected the relevant testimonia. For different views see Ustinova (1999); Stein (2001); Bowersock (2002); Wallraff (2003) 534–5; Ameling (2004), 13–20. Cf. already Lane (1976), 94–5.

[36] *TAM* v, 1.359; Mitchell (1999), 138 no. 167, updated by Mitchell, in this volume.

[37] *SEG* 49 (1999), 1588 (imperial period): Θ[ε]ᾷ Ὑ{σ}ψίστῃ Κλα[. . . . .]τῶν προκαθημέ[νῃ]. Belayche (2005a), 36–41 provides evidence for the use of *hypsistos* as an acclamatory epithet for several different deities; cf. Belayche (2005c), 261, 264–5, 268. For a different interpretation see Mitchell, in this volume. Already de Hoz (1991) identified *hypsistos* as an acclamatory name. For acclamatory epithets see below, nn. 72 and 80.

combining them in a unique way and introducing slight variations created a cult with a distinctive profile.[38]

SOME GODS ARE MORE DIVINE THAN OTHERS

A long funerary epigram for an anonymous woman in Kerkyra, set up and probably composed by her husband, Euhodos (second/third century AD), contains an exegesis about the nature of gods: 'Many daemons have their seat in Olympos, but their god is the great father, who has ordered the world and has commanded the Moon to follow the night and the Titan [*sc.* the Sun] to follow the grace of the day'.[39] This is followed by references to dualistic eschatological ideas. The woman asserts that her immortal, heavenly, soul (ψυχὴ οὐράνιος) dwells in the skies, while her body is covered by earth. The latter idea, connected with Orphic concepts, is often found in epitaphs.[40]

Euhodos' wife addresses the reader with the certainty of an eyewitness. She knows the origin and destiny of her soul. She does not reveal how she had acquired this knowledge – from the *hieroi logoi* of a mystery cult, from oracles, or from visions; but she implicitly distinguishes between true and false belief. She informs the person who stands in front of her grave that the monument is deceiving: the grave is not her dwelling; the truth is that she has gone to the stars. That she felt the need to communicate her knowledge about the gods to others presupposes the ignorance, the uncertainty or the different view of others; her knowledge competes with the false beliefs, the rival conceptions, or the weak faith of others.

The didactic nature of this epigram is evident. It not only gives advice concerning life and afterlife, it also explains the nature of divinities. The author distinguishes between the many gods (*daimones*) and a more powerful god, who is designated as their great father. The existence of a hierarchy among the gods is as old as Greek literature. That some gods were more powerful than others is implied e.g. by the expression τηλικοῦτος θεός ('so

---

[38] Sfameni Gasparro (1996) and (1999), 275–305; Chaniotis (2002c).

[39] *IG* XI².1, 1024: δαίμονες ἀθάνατοι πολλοὶ κατ' Ὀλύμπιον ἕδρην, | ἀλλὰ θεὸς τούτων ἐστὶ πατὴρ ὁ μέγας, ὃς κόσμον διέταξε, Σελήνην νυκτὶ κελεύσας | πείθεσθαι, Τειτᾶνα ἡμεριναῖς χάρισι. For a hierarchy of gods, cf. e.g. Drew-Bear, Thomas and Yildizturan (1999), 335 no. 541 (Phrygia): θεῶν ἄναξ... ἄριστε δαιμόνων, Ὀλύμπιε.

[40] For a relatively early example see *SEG* 28 (1978), 528 (Pherai, third century BC); Avagianou (2002): 'I, Lykophron, the son of Philiskos, seem sprung from the root of great Zeus, but in truth am from the immortal fire; and I live among the heavenly stars, raised up by my father; but the body born of my mother occupies mother-earth.' Recent discussions of this motif: Chaniotis (2000), 164 with n. 16; Le Bris (2001), 81–96; Peres (2003), 81–6, 110–13. Tybout (2003) rightly stresses the often contradictory ideas expressed in epitaphs. Cf. Bremmer (2002a), 7 n. 62.

powerful a god') used in connection with emperors.[41] The author of the Kerkyraian epigram describes important capacities of this central divine figure: he is a father figure, the creator of the regular course of night and day. The latter capacity associates this god with the most elementary of human experience: the observation of the rising and setting of the sun. This evokes the continual presence of god in the world of the mortal; the very coming of the day testifies the presence of the god. It is very unlikely that the author of this text did not know that the same capacity, control of the heavenly bodies, was attributed to Isis in the contemporary so-called 'aretalogies'.[42] Euhodos' concept of the almighty divine father, probably the conception of the divine accepted by the group to which he belonged, seems to be confronted with the rival conception of the divine of the worshippers of Isis. His text is another piece of evidence for the implicit 'religious intertextuality' of the imperial period.

Finally, the passer-by who stood in front of the grave and read the text aloud lent Euhodos' wife his voice and allowed her to speak from the grave – a well-known strategy of epigrammatic texts and graffiti.[43] The reader's voice transformed this text into a permanent eulogy of the great god, into an oral performance that could be repeated as long as people read the text.

This text was composed by an intellectual, as the metrical form and the content suggest – with possible allusions to an Orphic theogony. But analogous features can be found in textual evidence originating in a more humble milieu. Let us consider another text, this time not an epitaph but a dedication from a sanctuary of Mes somewhere in Lydia.[44] The text is a record of words said in a sanctuary in the presence of an audience, as we may infer from comparative iconographic and textual evidence, which I cannot present here.[45] The text begins with an acclamation ('Great is the Mother of Mes Axiottenos!'), followed by two other sets of acclamations

[41] E.g. Syll.³ 798 lines 5 and 9 (Caligula); F.Delphes III.4.304 lines 12–13 (Hadrian); SEG 53 (2003), 659A lines 20–1 (Claudius). For a hierarchy among gods see also nn. 3, 39, 54–5, 67 and 70.

[42] Totti (1985), 2 no. 1 lines 12–14 (= I.Kyme 41), 6 no. 2 lines 27–34 (= IG XII.5, 739), 13 no. 4 lines 16–17 (= SEG 9, 192). On these texts see Versnel (1990), 39–95.

[43] E.g. Rutherford (2000), 149–50; Chaniotis (forthcoming).

[44] Malay (2003), 13–18 (SEG 53 (2003), 1344; north of Ayazviran, AD 57): Μεγάλη Μήτηρ Μηνὸς Ἀξιοττηνοῦ. Μηνὶ Οὐρανίῳ, Μηνὶ Ἀρτεμι/δώρου Ἀξιοττα κατέχοντι Γλύκων Ἀπολλωνίου καὶ Μύρτιον Γλύκωνος εὐλογίαν ὑπὲρ τῆς ἑαυτῶν σωτηρίας καὶ τῶν ἰδίων τέκνων. Σὺ γάρ με, κύριε, αἰχμαλωτιζόμενον ἠλέησες. Μέγα σοι τὸ ὅσιον, μέγα σοι τὸ δίκαιον, μεγάλη νείκη, μεγάλαι σαὶ νεμέσεις, μέγα σοι τὸ δωδεκάθεον τὸ παρὰ σοὶ κατεκτισμένον. Ἠχμαλωτίσθην ὑπὸ ἀδελφοῦ τέκνου τοῦ Δημαινέτου. Ὅτι τὰ ἐμὰ προέλειψα καί σοι βοίθεαν ἔδωκα ὡς τέκνῳ. Σὺ δὲ ἐξέκλεισές με καὶ ἠχμαλώτισάς με οὐχ ὡς πάτρως, ἀλλὰ ὡς κακοῦργον. Μέγας οὖν ἐστι Μεὶς Ἀξιοττα κατέχων. Τὸ εἰκανόν μοι ἐποίησας. Εὐλογῶ ὑμεῖν. Ἔτους ρμβ´, μη(νὸς) Πανήμου β´. Discussion: Chaniotis (2009), 116–22.

[45] Chaniotis (2009), 118, 120, 123, 125, 140–2.

('Great is your holiness! Great is your justice! Great is your victory! Great your punishing power! Great is the Dodekatheon that has been established in your vicinity!'; and: 'Now, great is Mes, the ruler over Axiotta!'). Acclamations could occur spontaneously when humans experienced the power of god(s), but in most cases acclamations were part of ritual actions.[46] The technical terms are βοᾶν and its compounds (ἀναβοᾶν, ἐκβοᾶν, ἐπιβοᾶν), κράζειν/ἀνακράζειν, εὐλογεῖν/εὐλογία and εὐφημεῖν/εὐφημία ('use of good words').[47] The most likely context for the eulogia of Glykon is that of the erection of the stele itself.

The phrase 'for you, Lord, showed mercy when I was captured' is an expression of gratitude for divine assistance which the worshipper has experienced personally. In this regard, this text from Lydia is a 'thanksgiving offering' (εὐχαριστήριον, χαριστήριον). Its dedication involved some form of ritual action (e.g. a libation or a sacrifice) as well as an exaltation in the presence of an audience. This is directly attested, for instance, for the sanctuary of Asklepios on the Insula Tiberina in Rome. As we may infer from the healing miracles recorded in an inscription, after his rescue, the worshipper was expected to come to the sanctuary and express his gratitude to the god in public.[48] Presumably, the phrase 'for you, Lord, showed mercy when I was a captive' reflects what Glykon said aloud when he came to the sanctuary of Mes to set up his inscription.

---

[46] On religious acclamations, in general, see Peterson (1926), 141–240; Versnel (1990) 193–6, 243–4; Belayche (2005a and 2006a); on spontaneous acclamations, usually in connection with miracles, see Peterson (1926), 193–5, 213–22; on acclamations as ritual actions see Chaniotis (2008a) 81–4 and (2008b). See also the references in notes 47–8, 58–61, 63–5, 72–6, 80, 95–6.

[47] *Boan, krazein*, and their compounds: Peterson (1926), 191–3. *Eulogein/eulogia*: Robert (1964), 28–30; Pleket (1981), 183–9; Mitchell (1993), 36; de Hoz (1999), 119. *Euphemia* is usually understood as 'ritual silence', and at least some of the literary evidence supports this interpretation; but see Gödde (2003), 27–30; Stehle (2004) and (2005), 103 ('euphemia, which means "speech of good omen", prescribes the only kind of utterance that the gods should hear within the ritual space of opened divine-human communication'). The etymology of the word suggests the use of words of praise and not silence. For the imperial period, there is enough unequivocal literary and epigraphic evidence that *euphemein/euphemia* designated acclamations: e.g. *I.Ephesos* 1391 line 5: δεξιούμενοι μὲν εὐφ[ημίαις]; Josephus, *AJ* 16.14: ὑπατῶντος τε τοῦ δήμου παντὸς ἐν ἑορτώδει στολῇ καὶ δεχομένου τὸν ἄνδρα σὺν εὐφημίαις; Plutarch, *Brut.* 24.7: δεξαμένου δὲ τοῦ δήμου προθύμως αὐτὸν σὺν εὐφημίαις; Menander Rhetor 2.381.10–14: πάντες φιλοφρονούμενοι ταῖς εὐφημίαις, σωτῆρα καὶ τεῖχος, ἀστέρα φανότατον ὀνομάζοντες, οἱ δὲ παῖδες τροφέα μὲν ἑαυτῶν, σωτῆρα δὲ πατέρων; 2.417.27–30: καὶ εὐαγεῖς χοροὺς ἱστάτωσαν αἱ πόλεις, ἀδέτωσαν, εὐφημείτωσαν.

[48] *Syll.*³ 1173 = *IGUR* 148 lines 9–10: καὶ δημοσίᾳ ηὐχαρίστησεν τῷ θεῷ καὶ ὁ δῆμος συνεχάρη αὐτῷ...; lines 13–14: καὶ ἐλθὼν δημοσίᾳ ηὐχαρίστησεν ἔμπροσθεν τοῦ δήμου; line 18: καὶ ἐλήλυθεν καὶ ηὐχαρίστησεν δημοσίᾳ τῷ θεῷ; cf. lines 4–5: τοῦ δήμου παρεστῶτος καὶ συνχαιρομένου. Cf. Aelius Aristides, *Hieroi logoi* 2.7: 'there was also much shouting from those present and those coming up, shouting that celebrated phrase, "Great is Asklepios"'. Cf. Chaniotis (2006), 229–30.

After the motive for the dedication is explained, a second group of acclamations follows in which the worshipper characterises the various qualities of Mes: his holiness, his justice, his victory, his punishing power. The reference to the Twelve Gods ('Great is the Dodekatheon that has been established in your vicinity!') confirms that the acclamations took place in Mes's sanctuary, where the Iranian Moon-God was worshipped together with an Anatolian group of the Twelve Gods. The expression τὸ δωδεκάθεον τὸ παρά σοι κατεκτισμένον implies that images of the Twelve Gods (statues or reliefs) were set up in the sanctuary.[49] It was in the presence of images or symbols of the gods that Glykon performed his acclamations.

The next phrase ('for the son of my brother Demainetos made me his captive') contains Glykon's accusations against his nephew, whose name is not given. In the course of a family quarrel Glykon was obviously locked up by his nephew, until divine punishment (illness, accidents etc.) forced the nephew to set him free. After his liberation, Glykon came to the sanctuary, certainly accompanied by his nephew, who was present when Glykon not only praised the god, but also brought forth his accusations in a very emotional manner: 'For I had neglected my own affairs and helped you, as if you were my own son. But you locked me in and kept me captive, as if I were a criminal and not your paternal uncle!' Glykon uttered these phrases turning to his nephew and addressing him directly. We may suspect that Glykon's dedication and praise were accompanied by the nephew's propitiation of the god and request for forgiveness. The dedication ends with a final acclamation ('Now, great is Mes, the ruler over Axiotta!') and an address that reciprocated the worshipper's thanks to the deity: 'You have given me satisfaction. I praise you.'

Although we are dealing with a text of an entirely different nature from that of the epigram of Euhodos, we may observe a convergence in certain features. Glykon's piety is based on a very personal experience of the presence of god,[50] although – unlike in the case of Euhodos – Glykon made his piety dependent on the efficacy of god: 'You have given me satisfaction. I praise you.' A convergence exists in the fact that both Euhodos and Glykon communicated their experience of the divine to others; in the case

---

[49] Cf. Strubbe (1997), 46–7 no. 51: τὸν Ἀξιοττην[ὸν κε?] τὸ ἐκεῖ δωδεκάθην καθημ[– –].

[50] The importance of the personal experience of divine power for faith is demonstrated by an epigraphic find from Aizanoi, Lehmler and Wörrle (2006), 76–8 (second/third century AD). A certain Menophilos founded a cult of Great Zeus after a terrifying experience of the god's might: [κ]ατεπλήχθη δε[ινῶς καὶ] ἐκτίσθη Ζεὺς Μέγας Μηνοφίλου. See also Versnel (1981b), 35: 'the exalted and omnipotent god owed much of his inaccessible majesty to the fact that he lent an ear to lowly mortals'. More examples in notes 61, 67–8 and 85.

of Euhodos the reading of the stone resembles an oral performance, in the case of Glykon it re-enacts the ritual of exaltation. Finally, the acclamations in Glykon's text describe the god's most important properties: holiness, justice, victory (or success) and punishing power.

I have the impression that Glykon's text reflects a coherent theology, which was in part influenced by and in part opposed to competing religious conceptions of the divine. The reference to the Mother of Mes at the very beginning of the text, in the first acclamation, is more than a eulogy: it alludes to a theogony. The Mother of Mes is mentioned in other inscriptions from Lydia.[51] Of course, it is impossible to determine whether the 'motherless' (ἀμήτωρ) god of the Klarian theosophical oracle was meant to be a response to the worshippers of Mes or any other divinity, in whose cult and myths a mother figure was prominent;[52] or if, conversely, the worshippers of Mes opposed their god to the 'motherless' Highest God. However, the ostentatious reference to the Mother of Mes seems to fit the particular profile of this cult. Similarly, the epithet Ouranios in Mes's eulogy is an ostentatious allusion to the god's dwelling in heaven – again a property often shared by gods with a dominant position.[53] Mes's epithet (Axiottenos) alludes to the locality with which the cult is connected and records the name of the cult founder, a certain Artemidoros, who may have been as important a religious figure as Alexandros of Abonou Teichos. Finally, Glykon's text suggests the priority of Mes over other gods, designated here as the Dodekatheon.

What was the relation between Heavenly Mes and the Twelve Gods? An answer may be provided by two confession inscriptions which suggest that Mes was conceived as a god presiding over a council of gods. The first inscription, published recently,[54] explicitly refers to the senate

[51] Malay (2004), with further references; cf. Lane (1976), 81–3; Petzl (1994), 66–7; Belayche (2005c), 259–60. Μεγάλη Μήτηρ Μηνὸς Τεκοῦσα: *SEG* 39 (1989), 1278 (north of Kollyda, AD 160/1); Μηνὸς Τεκοῦσα: *SEG* 39 (1989), 1275; Lane (1975), 174 no. A8 (area of Manisa, AD 161/2). It is not certain whether the 'Mother of (the) God' mentioned in two other inscriptions is identical with the Mother of Mes. Μητρὶ Θεοῦ: *TAM* v.2, 1306 (Hyrkanis, third century AD); τὴν Μητέρα τοῦ Θεοῦ: Malay (2004) (unknown provenance).

[52] Μήτηρ Ἀπόλλωνος: Robert and Robert (1948), 24 n. 4; Μήτηρ Ἀναΐτιδος: *TAM* v.1, 450 and 575.

[53] For examples in the theosophical oracles of Apollo see Busine (2005), 207. For this idea among the Stoics see Diogenes Laertius 7.138: οὐρανὸς δέ ἐστιν ἡ ἐσχάτη περιφέρεια ἐν ᾗ πᾶν ἵδρυται τὸ θεῖον. For other deities see e.g. *SEG* 31 (1981), 361 (Zeus Ouranios, Sparta, second century AD); *SEG* 38 (1988), 1087 (Theios Angelos Ouranios, Stratonikeia, imperial period); *I.Sultan Daği* 509: τὸν οὐρ[άν]ιον θεόν; Graf (1985), 70–3 (Θεᾷ Κόρῃ ἐπήκοος ἀνείκητος οὐρανία, probably from Asia Minor, imperial period). For Mes/Men Ouranios see also *SEG* 39 (1989), 1278 and 42 (1992), 1280.

[54] Herrmann and Malay (2007), 113–16 no. 85 (Kollyda, AD 205/6): . . . Ἀμμιανὸς καὶ Ἑρμογένης Τρύφωνος πάρισιν ἐρωτῶντες τοὺς θεοὺς Μῆνα Μοτυλλίτην καὶ Δία Σαβάζιον καὶ Ἄρτεμιν

(συνᾶτος) and council of the gods (σύνκλητος τῶν θεῶν). A council of gods (σύνκλητος) is also mentioned in one of the longest and most intriguing confession inscriptions. This text presents Mes explaining why he had punished Theodoros, a lascivious sacred slave, with blindness and then forgave him upon the intervention of Zeus and an enquiry of the council of gods.[55] The fact that two texts explicitly call this council a *synkletos* or 'senate' suggests that Mes's position was assimilated to that of the emperor, that of the other gods to that of the senate – or whatever the Anatolian population may have imagined the Roman senate to be. Mes's priority over other gods seems to have been an essential feature of his worship in the sanctuaries where the aforementioned texts were found.

The priority of a local god over other gods is a prominent feature of a group of graffiti from the gymnasium at Delphi which record acclamations for Apollo and for victorious athletes during the Pythian festival in the late second and early third centuries AD.[56] I present a few examples: 'Good Fortune! One god! Great god! The greatest name of the god! Great Apollo Pythios! Great is the Fortune of the Delphians! This is the place of – – from Plataia, a boy long distance runner, winner at the Pythia.'[57] Another one: 'Good Fortune! Place of Marcus Aurelius Iuncus Aemilianus Onesimos, long distance runner, winner at the Pythia. God! Great is the Fortune of the Delphians! Great is Apollo Pythios! Good luck, Daidalos [a nick-name of the runner]'.[58] And another one: 'Good Fortune! One god! Great is Apollo Pythios! Great is the Fortune of the Delphians! Great is Artemis! Great is Hekate! Place of Sextius Primus.'[59] The rest of the texts attest

---

Ἀναεῖτιν καὶ μεγάλην συνᾶτος καὶ σύνκλητον τῶν θεῶν... ('Ammianos and Hermogenes, sons of Tryphon, appear [at the sanctuary] asking the gods Men Motyllites and Zeus Sabazios and Artemis Anaitis and the great senate and council of the gods').

[55] Petzl (1994), 7–11 no. 5 lines 22–6: ἔσχα παράκλητον τὸν Δείαν... – Ἡρωτημαίνος ὑπὸ τῆς συνκλήτου· εἵλεος εἶμαι ἀναστανομένης τῆς στήλλην μου, ᾗ ἡμέρᾳ ὥρισα. Ἀνύξαις τὴν φυλακήν, ἐξαφίω τὸν κατάδικον διὰ ἐνιαυτοῦ κὲ μηνῶν ι´ περιπατούντων ('I asked for Zeus' assistance'... – 'Asked by the council (I respond that) I am kindly disposed, if [or when] he sets up my stele, on the day I have ordered. You may open the prison. I set the convict free after one year and ten months'). For an analysis of this text with the earlier bibliography see Chaniotis (2004a), 27–9.

[56] Queyrel (2001), see SEG 51 (2001), 613–31; Chaniotis (2008a), 82 and (2008b), 202–3, 207–8, 215. Cf. the acclamation 'great is Artemis of Ephesos' in the theatre of Ephesos: Acts 19:28 and 19:34.

[57] SEG 51, 614: Ἀγα[θῆ Τύ]χη· [εἷς θ]εός· μέγ[ας] θεός· μ[έγιστ]ον ὄν[ομα τ]οῦ θε[οῦ· Πύθιος μέγ]ας Ἀπ[όλλων· μεγά[λη Τύχ[η Δελφῶν· τ]όπος [– – ο]υ Πλα[ταιέως? παιδὸς] δι[α]υλ[οδρόμου Πυθιονίκου – –]. On the expression μέγα/μέγιστον ὄνομα τοῦ θεοῦ see Peterson (1926), 206, 208–10, 281–2; Robert (1955), 86–8.

[58] SEG 51 (2001), 615: Ἀγαθῆ Τύ]χη· [τόπος Μά]ρ. Αὐρ. [Ἰούνκ[ου? Αἰμιλι?]ανοῦ Ὀνησίμ[ου δολιχ?]α[δρό]μου Πυθ[ιονείκ]ου· θ[εό]ς?· μεγάλη Τ[ύχη Δελφ]ῶν· μέγας ὁ Πύθ[ιος Ἀ]πόλλων· [ε]ὐτύχ[ει] Δαίδαλ[ε].

[59] SEG 51 (2001), 622: Ἀ[γ]αθ[ῆ Τύχη· εἷ]ς θεός· [μέγας Πύθιος] Ἀπ[ό]λ[λ]ων· [μεγάλη Τύ]χ[η Δελ]φῶν· [μεγάλη Ἀρ]τεμις· [μεγάλη] Ἑκάτη· τόπος Σεξ(τίου) Πρίμου).

the same acclamations as well as the formulae 'The Pythian god is great!' (Πύθιος θεὸς μέγας) and 'One god in heaven!' (εἷς θ[εὸς ἐν τῷ οὐρα]νῷ). An acclamation is devoted to Artemis Prothyraia, who was worshipped in Delphi, another one to 'Great Sacred Palaimon', who was worshipped at Isthmia; it is an allusion to the Isthmian games, possibly inscribed at the initiative of an athlete who had won both the Pythia and the Isthmia.[60]

These graffiti record acclamations that must have taken place during the celebration of the Pythian festival. They are addressed to athletes, to the Delphians and their city, and above all to the local god, not Apollo in general, but the *Pythian* Apollo, the god in Delphi. Not a single acclamation invokes Apollo without his epithet Pythios, and one invokes him simply as the Pythian god. The Delphic acclamations use a formulaic vocabulary known from the praise of a superior god. Characterised by a spirit of local patriotism, they stress the privileged relationship of Delphi with Apollo. The acclamations leave no doubt that Apollo Pythios was regarded as having a superior position; consequently his cult place had a privileged position among cult places. That a spirit of competition emerges in acclamations that take place during the celebration of an agonistic festival, while thousands of people experience competition, should not surprise us. In the same period, in Ephesos, Apollo's sister was called 'for ever the greatest among all the gods' (see n. 10).

In Delphi, the superior position of Apollo is evident in the acclamation in which he is named together with Artemis and Hekate (see n. 59): 'One god! Great is Apollo Pythios! Great is the Fortune of the Delphians! Great is Artemis! Great is Hekate!' All three divinities are designated as great, but only Apollo has a local epithet, only Apollo is honoured with the acclamation *heis theos*. This text is evidence not of monotheism but of competition. Similarly, when Aelius Aristides exclaimed εἷς in the sanctuary

[60] *SEG* 51 (2001), 617: Ἀ[γαθῇ Τύ]χῃ· εἷς θ[εὸς ἐν τῷ οὐρα]νῷ· μέγα[ς Πύθιος Ἀ]πόλλων· μ[εγάλη Τύχη Δ]ελφῶν· τ[όπος – – τοῦ] Θεοδούλο[υ.... παιδ]ὸς διαυ[λοδρόμου Π]υθιονί[κου ὑπὸ προστάτην – –] ('Good Fortune! One god in heaven! Great is Apollo Pythios! Great is the Fortune of the Delphians! Place of – – of Theodoulos, a boy long distance runner, winner at the Pythia, under the supervisor – –'); *SEG* 51 (2001), 618: [Ἀγαθῇ Τύχῃ· εἷς] θεός· μέ[γας Πύθιο]ς Ἀπόλλω[ν Δελφῶ]ν· [τόπος Σ]ωσικλῆ[ος παιδὸς διαυ]λοδρό[μου] Πυ[θιονίκου ὑπὸ π]ροστάτ[ην – –]μην Μ.Ν. [– –] Λακεδε[μ]όνιον· [μ]εγάλ[η Τ]ύχη τῆς π[ό]λε[ως]· εὐ[τ]υχῶ[ς] ('Good Fortune! One god! Great is Apollo Pythios of the Delphians! Place of Sosikles, a boy long distance runner, winner at the Pythia under the supervision of – – of Lakedaimon. Great is the Fortune of the city! Good luck!'); *SEG* 51 (2001), 623: [Μεγ]άλη Ἀρτεμ[ις Προ]θυραία. Μέγας ἅγιος Παλέμων ('Great is Artemis Prothyraia! Great is sacred Palaimon!'); *SEG* 51 (2001), 626: [Ἀγαθῇ Τ]ύχῃ· [εἷ]ς [θεὸς ἐν ο]ὐρανῷ· [μέγ]ας Π[ύθιο]ς Ἀπόλ[λων]· μεγά[λη] Τύχη [Δελ]φῶν· τόπος Θε[οδό]του Θεσπιαίως [παιδὸς?] διαυλοδρόμου.....τος κατὰ ΑΝ... ('Good Fortune! One god in heaven! Great is Apollo Pythios! Great is the Fortune of the Delphians! Place of Theodotos of Thespiai, a boy long distance runner – –').

of Asklepios in Pergamon, he was praising a god with whom he had established a personal relationship.[61] It has often been stressed that when the attribute *heis* is not used in a Christian context it underlines the uniqueness of one particular god.[62] Hardly any other evidence shows so clearly the competitive use of *heis* as these new Delphic graffiti or the honorary decree for the benefactor Epameinondas in Akraiphia in Boiotia. In a long narrative of his benefactions, Epameinondas is compared with other citizens and benefactors, whom he had surpassed in every respect. It is in this context of competition that we find the following allusion to acclamations in his honour:[63] 'He surpassed in magnanimity and virtue all men of the past, by devoting himself to the love of fame and virtue through continual expenditure, so that he is regarded as the one patriot and benefactor (εἷς φιλόπατρις καὶ εὐεργέτης)'.[64] The Akraiphians meant that Epameinondas was 'a unique patriot and benefactor', not the 'only patriot and benefactor'. The use of εἷς is not exclusive – as in Christian prayers and acclamations – but competitive.[65]

Let us return to the Delphic acclamations. Those which do not name a particular god (εἷς θεός, εἷς θεὸς ἐν τῶι οὐρανῶι, μέγιστον ὄνομα τοῦ θεοῦ) could be used by the worshippers of any god. In fact, they were used by the worshippers of exclusive monotheistic religions – the Jews and the Christians – and by pagans, who reserved a superior position in heaven for another Olympian or for another local god. In the case of Delphi, the agonistic context suggests that this convergence in formulaic acclamations was the result of competition; it presupposes knowledge of the ritual practices of other cult communities and assimilation not of concepts, but of linguistic expressions.

---

[61] *Hieroi logoi* 4.50: κἀγὼ περιχαρὴς τῇ τιμῇ γενόμενος καὶ ὅσον τῶν ἄλλων προὐκρίθην, ἐξεβόησα, 'εἷς', λέγων δὴ τὸν θεόν. Versnel (1990), 50 n. 32, observes that this acclamation is often connected with the soteriological qualities of a god. For its earliest attestation in *P. Gur.* 1 (third century BC), as a 'password' (εἷς Διόνυσος) in a Dionysiac initiation, see Versnel (1990), 205. On the Gurob papyrus see now Graf and Johnston (2007), 150–5.

[62] Peterson (1926), 268–70; Robert (1958), 128 n. 101; Herrmann and Polatkan (1969), 52–3; Lane (1976), 79–80; Versnel (1990), 35, 50, 235, (2000), 146–52; Markschies (2002); Belayche (2005c), 264–5, (2006a), 19–20, (2007b) and in this volume.

[63] For secular acclamations see Roueché (1984). Recent finds: *SEG* 38 (1988), 1172; 50 (2000), 1160; 51 (2001), 1813.

[64] *IG* VII, 2712 lines 52–5: [ὑπερβάλλετο] δὲ τῇ μεγαλοψυχίᾳ καὶ ἀρετῇ πάντας τοὺς [προτέρους τρέψας] ἑαυτὸν πρὸς τὸ φιλόδοξον [καὶ] φιλάγαθον ταῖς ἐπ[αλ]λή[λ]οις δαπάναις, εἷς φιλόπατρις καὶ εὐεργέτης νομιζόμενος. Discussion: Chaniotis (2008a).

[65] For this acclamation in Christian inscriptions see Peterson (1926), 1–140. Cf. e.g. *SEG* 49 (1999), 2054 (Caesarea Maritima, fourth century AD): εἷς θεὸς μόνος; Roueché (1989a), 126 no. 83 i (Aphrodisias, *c.* AD 480): εἷς τὸν κόσμον ὅλον εἷς ὁ θεός.

In the same period as that in which the worshippers at Delphi were stressing through acclamations the superior position of Apollo and Apollinic oracles were promoting the idea of a superior god,[66] a dedication in Iuliopolis was addressed to another god, using adjectives in the superlative.[67] The dedicant of an altar, Kattios Tergos, describes an anonymous god (a local Zeus?) as 'the best and greatest god, the one who listens to prayers, his saviour, and that of his children and all his oxen.' The dedication is followed by an epigram: 'To you, most revered among the Blessed, Tergos set up this well-constructed offering of honour, writing in poetry [literally 'with the letters of the Muses'] your deeds of grace, great, best, willing to listen, ruler of the world. May you care for him, for his children and for his livestock.' Both in the prose text and in the epigram, Tergos attempted to establish a personal relationship to the god, his personal saviour, a god who listened to his prayers. Similarly, the Athenian Diophantos sought Asklepios' assistance, emphasising both the god's unique power (μόνος εἶ σύ, μάκαρ θεῖε, σθένων) and his personal devotion (ὅππως σ' ἐσίδω, τὸν ἐμὸν θεόν).[68]

The most striking stylistic feature in Tergos' dedication is a preference for superlatives (ἄριστος, μέγιστος, κύδιστος). This feature is not an innovation of the imperial period; it can already be observed, for instance, in the hymn for Demetrios the Besieger in the early third century BC,[69] or in a decree at Mylasa in the first century BC, in which Zeus Osogo is designated as 'the greatest of the gods, rescuer and benefactor of the city' (τοῦ μεγίστου τῶν [θεῶν Διὸς Ὀσογ]ω, σωτῆρος καὶ εὐεργέτου τῆς πόλεως).[70] But it became very common in the imperial period, when divinities were often designated with attributes such as ἁγιώτατος, ἄριστος, δικαιότατος, ἐπιφανέστατος, κράτιστος, κύδιστος, μέγιστος, πανύψιστος, ὕψιστος, etc.[71] The designation of a deity with an epithet in the superlative is a form of exaggerated, affective and ostentatious praise, which probably originated

---

[66] Busine (2005), 202–8.

[67] *SEG* 50 (2000), 1222 (second/third century AD): Ἀγαθῇ Τύχῃ· Θεῷ ἀρίστῳ μεγίστῳ ἐπηκόῳ σωτῆρι ἑαυτοῦ καὶ τῶν τέκνων αὐτοῦ καὶ πάντων τῶν [βο]ῶν Κάττιος Τέργος εὐχήν. Σοὶ μακάρων κύδιστε γέρας τόδε Τέργος ἔθηκεν | εὔτυκτον Μ[ου]σῶν γράμμασι γραψάμενος | σὰς χάριτας, μεγ' ἄριστε, φιλήκοε, κοίρανε κόσμου | σοὶ δ' αὐ|τός τε μέλοι τέκνα τε κα[ὶ κτέ]|ανα.

[68] *IG* ιι², 4514 (Athens, mid second century AD); cf. Versnel (1990), 195 n. 335.

[69] Douris, *FGrH* 76 F 13; Demochares, *FGrH* 75 F 2: μέγιστος, φίλτατος, κράτιστος. Discussion: Ehrenberg (1965), 503–19; Mikalson (1998), 94–7; Chaniotis (2010). Cf. the epigram referred to below, n. 73.

[70] *I.Mylasa* 306. Cf. the hymn for Apollo in Susa (*SEG* 7, 14 = *I.Estremo Oriente* 221 = *SGO* ιιι, 12/03/1, first century AD): ὕπατος [θεῶν].

[71] For examples see notes 10, 37, 82, 85, 94, 115, 118–19. Cf. *IG* ιι², 4514: σθεναρώτατε.

in acclamations.[72] Such 'acclamatory hyperbole' characterises non-religious texts as well. As early as the mid second century BC, for instance, the Graeco-Baktrian king Euthydemos was designated in an epigram, which possibly reflects acclamations, as 'the greatest of all kings' (τὸμ πάντων μέγιστον Εὐθύδημον βασιλέων).[73] In the imperial period, we observe 'acclamatory hyperbole' in an Ephesian graffito which gives assurance that Rome's power will never be destroyed,[74] in the designation of Caracalla as a lord 'who will live in eternity',[75] in the claim that Perge was 'the only inviolable city',[76] and in attributes of emperors.

It is quite probable that such a 'superlativism', which can also be observed in contemporary honorary inscriptions and epitaphs,[77] was enforced by the influence of Latin style and phraseology. This is evident e.g. in the case of Ζεὺς Κράτιστος Μέγιστος Φροντιστής, the Greek translation of *Iuppiter Optimus Maximus Tutor*,[78] or σεβασμιωτάτη Ἀφροδείτη, the translation of *Venus augustissima*.[79] As acclamations were experienced not only by those who performed them, but also by the audiences which attended festivals and processions, a koine of 'acclamatory epithets' could easily be developed and an epiklesis transferred from one divinity to another.[80]

---

[72] Chaniotis (2008a), 81–4 and (2008b), 210–13. Versnel (1990), 248 has collected examples of parody of such rhetorical extravagances.

[73] Rougemont (2004); *SEG* 54 (2004), 1569.

[74] *I.Ephesos* 599 with the new reading of Taeuber (2003), 94 n. 9: Ῥώμη πανβασίλια, τὸ σὸν κράτος οὔποτ' ὀλῆται.

[75] *SEG* 48 (1998), 1961–2, 1964–5 (Alexandria, c. AD 201): γῆς καὶ θαλάσσης δεσπότην καὶ φιλοσάραπιν ἀεὶ ζῶντα.

[76] *I.Perge* 331 (AD 275/6): αὖξε Πέργη, ἡ μόνη ἄσυλος. The same hyperbole can be observed e.g. in the Susan hymn for Apollo referred to in n. 70 (*SEG* 7, 14 = *I.Estremo Oriente* 221 = *SGO* III, 12/03/1, first century AD): ἐπεὶ σέβας μ[οῦνο]ς ἔσκε[ς] ἁπάντων.

[77] See e.g. Chaniotis (2004b), 378 no. 1 (*SEG* 54 (2004), 1020, honorary inscription from Aphrodisias, c. 50 BC): τῶν πρώτων καὶ ἐνδοξοτάτων πολειτῶν, προγόνων ὑπάρχων τῶν μεγίστων καὶ συνεκτικότων τὸν δῆμον καὶ ἐν ἀρετῆι καὶ φιλοδοξίαις καὶ ἐπαγγελίαις πλείσταις καὶ τοῖς καλλίστοις ἔργοις πρὸς τὴν πατρίδα βε<βι>ωκότων . . . πρὸς θεοὺς εὐσεβέστατα διακείμενος καὶ πρὸς τὴν [π]ατρίδα, φιλοδοξότατα κοσμήσας αὐτὴν ἐπαγγελίαις καλλίσ[τ]αις καὶ ἀναθήμασιν, εἰς πολλὰς δὲ πρεσβήας καὶ ἀνανκαιοτάτας [πρ]οχειρισθεὶς καὶ εἰς ἀγῶνας κατὰ τὸ κάλλιστον ἐτέλεσεν [π]άντα, . . . παρά τε ταῖς ἐξουσίαις καὶ τοῖς ἡγουμένοις πλείστην γνῶσιν καὶ σύστασιν σχὼν εὐεργέτησεν καὶ διὰ τούτων μέγιστα τὴν πόλιν; cf. *MAMA* VIII, 471: τελέσαντα τὰς λειτουργίας πολυτελέστατ[α] καὶ λαμπρότατα καὶ τὰς μεγίστας ἀρχὰς πάσας ἄρξαντα κατὰ τὸ κάλιστον, τελέσαντα δὲ καὶ πρεσβείας ἄλλας τε πλείστας καὶ εἰς Ῥώμην; *MAMA* VIII, 477: ἐτείμησαν . . . ταῖς καλλίσταις καὶ μεγίσταις τειμαῖς . . . ἄνδρα γένους πρώτου καὶ ἐνδοξοτάτου . . . πάσας παραρχόμενον τῇ πατρίδι φιλοδόξους καὶ λαμπροτάτας λιτουργίας καὶ τὴν ἰδίαν πρὸς αὐτὴν εὐνουστάτην διάθεσιν ἀθανάτοις ἑαυτοῦ προεντυπωσάμενος τοῦ βίου ὑπομνήσεσιν.

[78] *I.Iznik* 1141–2 (Nikaia, second century AD).

[79] *SEG* 51 (2001), 2074. Similarly, the attribute γλυκύτατος in epitaphs is the Greek rendering of *dulcissimus*.

[80] I designate as 'acclamatory epithets' a group of epithets which were not exclusively used in the worship of a particular god but could praise any divinity and its power in rather general terms:

In the light of these observations, it is legitimate to doubt that the expression 'the One and Only God' (εἷς καὶ μόνος θεός), used by the priest of this god and of Hosion kai Dikaion,[81] is to be taken literally. This expression did not mean that the anonymous god (Theos Hypsistos?) was the only god in a genuinely monotheistic theology, with the Holy and the Just serving as his angels. It was simply intended to attribute this god a superior position. Exactly as in the acclamations from Perge the Pamphylian city was called 'the only inviolable city' (ἡ μόνη ἄσυλος), in the sense that it was the only city which truly deserved this honour in the context of a competition among cities, the author of this dedication intended to say that the god whom he served as priest was the only deity which truly deserved the designation *theos*. It is an 'acclamatory hyperbole'.

Another stylistic feature in Tergos' language of worship is his preference for variation. When he designated his anonymous god as 'the one who listens to prayers', he avoided using the very common epithet ἐπήκοος, using instead the rare variant φιλήκοος. Analogous variations in standard epithets are not unusual. For example, πανύψιστος is a reinforced variant of the standard ὕψιστος.[82] Epithets such as προηγέτης and προκαθηγέτης are variants of the more common ἀρχηγέτης, καθηγεμών and προκαθηγεμών.[83] Such deviations from standard formulae served two purposes: they emphasised the personal devotion of a worshipper, who distinguished himself from other dedicants through the personal, idiosyncratic language he used in communicating with a deity; and they were a means of differentiation between deities.

Finally, Tergos attributed to his saviour god a prominent position among the gods by describing him as the most revered among them, the ruler of

---

e.g. ἀγαθός, ἅγιος, ἁγιώτατος, ἀθάνατος, ἀνείκητος, ἀρωγός, βασιλεύς, βοηθός, δεσπότης/ δέσποινα, ἐνάρετος, ἐπήκοος, ἐπιδήμιος, ἐπιφανής, ἐπιφανέστατος, εὐάγγελος, εὐεργέτης, εὐμενής, καλοκἀγαθιος, κύριος, μέγας, μέγιστος, οὐράνιος, παντοκράτωρ, προστάτης, σωτήρ, σώτειρα, ὕπατος, ὕψιστος, φιλάνθρωπος etc. Such epithets were very popular from the Hellenistic period onwards. For examples see the indices in *SEG*.

[81] *TAM* v.1, 246 (Kula, AD 256/7): τοῦ ἑνὸς καὶ μόνου θεοῦ [ἱ]ερεὺς καὶ τοῦ Ὁσίου καὶ Δικαίου... ('the priest of the One and Only God and of the Holy and the Just'); cf. Versnel (1990), 235 n. 145; Belayche (2006a), 19–21 and her discussion in this volume, p. 153 with p. 154 Fig. 1. Mitchell (1999), 63 associates this text with the worship of Theos Hypsistos. I assume that we have an example for the affective use of μόνος. Cf. the passages cited in nn. 68 and 76, and the praise of Isis from Maroneia (Totti (1985), 61 no. 19 line 20): μόνους γὰρ ὁ βίος ὑμᾶς [Isis and Sarapis] θεοὺς οἶδεν; cf. the affective use of μόνος/μοῦνος in the Orphic hymns: 16.7 (Hera) and 68.1 (Hygieia): πάντων γὰρ κρατέεις μούνη πάντεσσί τ᾿ ἀνάσσεις; 29.11 (Persephone): μόνη θνητοῖσι ποθεινή. Cf. Versnel (2000), 151; Belayche, in this volume.

[82] See below, n. 119: Ζηνὶ πανυψίστῳ.

[83] Προηγέτης: *TAM* II, 188 (Artemis and Apollo); προκαθηγέτης: *IG* v.2, 93 (Pan); *TAM* II, 189. For ἀρχηγέτης: *LSAM* 33 (Artemis); καθηγεμών: *LSAM* 15 (Dionysos); προκαθηγεμών: *I.Ephesos* 26 (Artemis); *LSAM* 28 (Dionysos). On the significance of these epithets see below, n. 91.

the world. He praised his god with an impressive list of epithets: ἄριστος, μέγιστος, ἐπήκοος, σωτήρ, κύδιστος, μέγας, φιλήκοος and κοίρανος. Interestingly, a god invoked with so many epithets lacks a name. He was conceived as πολυώνυμος, exactly as Artemis in a hymn in Samos, Isis in several aretalogies, Dionysos in the Orphic hymns and God in the Klarian oracle.[84] To leave the addressee of the dedication unnamed, in a text otherwise written with great care and a deliberate use of hyperbole and variation, was a conscious choice. One has the impression that Tergos avoided using a name, as if the properties and powers of his divine saviour were 'not contained in a name' (οὔνομα μὴ χωρῶν) – to quote, again, the oracle of Klaros – as if the many different epithets were more adequate to describe his properties.

If Tergos was influenced by the oracle of Apollo, why did he not use for his god the attribute *hypsistos*, as the author of the aforementioned dedication from Amastris (p. 117 with n. 22)? Why did he avoid the only attribute that would have made an unequivocal identification possible? Was Tergos a worshipper of Theos Hypsistos or was he praising a local god using the language of those who exalted Theos Hypsistos? Is convergence of language evidence of homogeneous concepts, of influence, or of competition?

MEGAS THEOS: THE CONSTRUCTION OF THE ALMIGHTY GOD

The few selected texts which I have discussed here share a common language without necessarily sharing a common conception of the divine or a common faith. While many of them praise a particular, superior, god, none of them praises a single god whose existence excludes that of other gods. Their rhetorical and stylistic strategies aimed at stressing the properties of the almighty god whom they praised – Zeus, Mes, Apollo, Theos Hypsistos, the anonymous saviour of Tergos. They reveal a concept of the divine with several recurring elements: the power, righteousness and efficacy of these gods; their demand for continual public praise; their willingness to offer assistance; and their presence. The faith of the authors, like that of

---

[84] Artemis: *IG* XII.6, 604 (third century AD); Isis: *I.Kios* 21 (first century BC); Bernand (1969), 632–3 no. 175 I = Totti (1985), 77 no. 21 lines 23–6 (Medinet-Madi, first century BC): ὅτι μούνη εἶ σὺ ἅπασαι αἱ ὑπὸ τῶν ἐθνῶν ὀνομαζόμεναι θεαὶ ἄλλαι... σώτειρ᾽ ἀθάνατη, πολυώνυμε Ἴσι μεγίστη; Orphic hymns 2.1 (Prothyraia), 10.13 (Physis), 11.10 (Pan), 16.9 (Hera), 27.4. (Meter Theon), 36.1 (Artemis), 40.1 (Demeter), 41.1 (Meter Antaia), 42.2 (Mise), 45.2, 50.2, 52.1 (Dionysos), 56.1 (Adonis), 59.2 (Moirai); Klarian oracle: see n. 17. Cf. the hymn for Apollo in Susa (*SEG* 7, 14 = *I.Estremo Oriente* 221 = *SGO* III, 12/03/1, first century AD): τοὶ γὰρ ἔθν[εα] καὶ πόλεις πολυ[ώ]νυμο[ν ὄμ]μα ὡσίωσαν. On *polyonymia* in the religions of the Roman Empire, see MacMullen (1981), 90 with n. 57; in Greek religion, see Versnel (2000); Aubriot (2005), 482–6.

Aelius Aristides in the *Hieroi logoi*, was based on a personal experience of divine power, on divine assistance provided in time of need.[85]

'You have given me satisfaction. I praise you.' With these words Glykon completed his praise of Mes (p. 122 with n. 44) – a nice expression of the principle of *do ut des* in ancient religion.[86] The personal relationship between a mortal and an almighty god, as the one implied in the epigram of Tergos (p. 129 with n. 67), was established through complex strategies of persuasion. A grave stele of a fifteen-year-old boy may exemplify this.[87] It is inscribed with an appeal to divine justice and revenge: 'Lord the Almighty, you have made me, but an evil man has destroyed me. Revenge my death fast!' In order to attract the god's personal interest in this affair the author made the god a victim of the offender: the murderer is presented as someone who has destroyed the god's personal creation (σὺ μὲ ἔκτισες). Thus his punishment became the god's personal concern. A second element of his persuasion strategy consists in stressing the god's power (Κύριε Παντοκράτωρ; cf. n. 115). The god is invited in a subtle way to prove his endless power not only by punishing the murderer, but also by inflicting the punishment fast (ἐν τάχι). This is a strategy known from magical texts. In order to provoke the anger of the gods and demons, the magician often applied a method described as *diabole*, i.e. he accused his opponent of offences against the divinity.[88] Magical texts regularly urge the divine powers to fulfil the magician's wish fast (ἤδη ἤδη, ταχὺ ταχύ).[89]

This personal experience of the divine bridged the gap between mortals and gods. One of the most obvious objectives of religious texts in the imperial period was to insinuate the tangible, continuous and effective

[85] Cf. e.g. *I.Sultan Daği* 44 (Philomelion): [Λητ]οῖδη Σώζοντι καὶ Ἡελίῳ βασιλῆι [εὔξ]ατο βωμὸν ἀνὴρ υἱὸς Ἐπατόριγος [ἱερ]ὸν ἀθανάτοισι Μενέστρατος, ὃν δι[ασωθεὶς] θῆκε δικαιοτάτοις ἠδ' ὁσίοισι θ[εοῖς] ('To the immortals, the son of Leto, the Saviour, and the Sun, the king, Menestratos, son of Epatorix, promised a sacred altar; now that he has been saved he erected it, to the most just and holy gods'); *SEG* 51 (2001), 1801 (Nakoleia, imperial period): [Ἡε]λίῳ Τειτᾶνι κὲ Ὁ[– –]ΑΕΙΔΑΙ Ὁσ[ίῳ] Δικέῳ κὲ θείῳ πα[ντ]οδυνάστῃ ἔνθ[α] Πολυξενία, ὡς η[ὔξ]αντο κὲ ἐκέλευσ[α]ς, ἥκον κὲ Νείκην χ[ρυ]σοστέφανον [– –]σαν εὐξάμενοί σε, μάκαρ, περὶ ἑαυτῶν κὲ τεκέεσσιν, οἷς ἱκέτα<ι>ς ἐπάκουε κὲ εἴλ[ε]ος, οὐράνιον φῶς ('Helios Titan and – – the Holy, Just and Divine, ruler of all, here came Polyxenia, as they had vowed and as you ordered, and (erected a statue) of Nike with a golden crown, praying to you, Blessed, for themselves and for their children; listen to the prayers of these suppliants and show them mercy, heavenly light'). See also above, n. 50. On aspects of faith in the inscriptions of Asia Minor see Belayche (2007b), 78–90.
[86] On reciprocity in Greek religion see Parker (1998), 105–25.
[87] *SEG* 50 (2000), 1233 (Neoklaudiopolis, AD 237): Κύριε Παντοκράτωρ· σύ με ἔκτισες, κακὸς δέ με ἄνθρωπος ἀπώλεσεν· ἐγδίκησόν με ἐν τάχι.
[88] For this strategy see Graf (1996), 163–6. Good examples are *PGM* IV, 2471–9 and Jordan (2004), 693–710.
[89] E.g. *PGM* I, 262; II, 83 and 98; IV, 1924, 2037 and 2098; VII, 330; XIV, 11; *SEG* 46 (1996), 1726 I; 53 (2003), 1763 line 154; *IJO* I, Ach no. 70 (τὴν ταχίστην).

presence of the gods in the world of the mortals. This was achieved through a variety of media: through narratives of epiphanies and miracles; through references to the appearance of gods in dreams, which was perceived as a close physical presence;[90] through epithets deriving from place names and thus evoking a close relationship between a divinity and a community; through epithets which expressed the protection offered by a patron god and presented him as the leader of a community (ἀρχηγέτης, καθηγέτης, καθηγεμών), its supervisor (προεστώς),[91] and its continual protector (προστατοῦσα).[92] Such epithets (μεδέων, πολιεύς/πολιάς etc.) are already attested in the classical period, but most of them appeared for the first time in the Hellenistic period and were used in the imperial period in an impressive range of variations, as if every new variation was meant to reinforce the presence of a deity in a place. The epithet ἔνδημος ('present in the community') is a nice example; it linguistically deprived a deity of the possibility to leave.[93]

Μέγας, the most common and oldest among the 'acclamatory epithets', is closely connected with this need of the mortals to experience the presence of a god.[94] What made a god μέγας were power (δύναμις), efficacy (ἀρετή), presence (ἐπιφάνεια), infallible justice (νέμεσις, δίκαιον), visible holiness (ὅσιον), willingness to listen to the just prayers of humans (ἐπήκοος). One of the best examples is the narrative of a miracle at Panamara, when the sanctuary of Zeus and Hekate was attacked by the troops of Labienus

90 E.g. in a confession inscription (Ortaköy, second/third century AD) the sinner reports that he saw in his dreams the god standing by him: Petzl (1994), 122–5 no. 106: [κ]αὶ ὀνείροις μοι παρεστάθη καὶ [εἶ]πεν. See also below, p. 136 with n. 105.

91 Epithets stressing the presence of a divinity in a locality are e.g. ἀρχηγέτης/ἀρχηγέτις τῆς πόλεως, ἔνδημος, καθηγέτης, καθηγεμών, μεδέων, προηγέτης, προκαθηγεμών, προκαθηγέτης, πάτριος, πατρῷος, πατρῷος κτίστης, προπάτωρ, πολίαρχος, πολιεύς/πολιάς, προεστώς/ προεστῶσα τῆς πόλεως, προκαθήμενος/προκαθημένη τῆς πόλεως, προκαθεζομένη θεός; see Nollé (1993), 105–6; Chaniotis (2003), 185 n. 35; Hübner (2003), 187–8. I assume that the epithets, which characterise the gods as kings and rulers of a place, do not only show their superior position, as rightly observed by Belayche (2005c), but also fulfil a similar function, connecting a divinity with a place.

92 IOSPE I², 352 line 23–4 (Olbia, late second century BC): ἡ διὰ παντὸς Χερσανασιτᾶν προστα-τοῦσα [Πα]ρθένος.

93 Ἔνδημος: MAMA x, 158 (Hosion kai Dikaion, Appia, imperial period). Cf. ἐπιδήμιος: Marek (1993), 193 no. 19 (Zeus, Kaisareia) and Callimachus, Hymn to Artemis 224–5: χαῖρε, Χιτώνη | Μιλήτῳ ἐπίδημε.

94 For a still useful collection of testimonia see Müller (1913); Peterson (1926), 196–208; cf. Lane (1976), 79. For examples of μέγας and μέγιστος see nn. 39, 44, 50–1, 54, 57–60, 67, 69, 96–7, 105, 107, 115, 118 and 130 in this chapter. Cf. e.g. I.Ephesos 27 lines 224 and 324 (Artemis, μεγίστη θεός); I.Stratonikeia 513, 523 and 527 (Hekate, μεγίστη θεά), 1101 (Zeus and Hekate, μέγιστοι θεοί); Habicht (1969), 128 no. 113b (Pergamon: μεγ' ἄριστε θεῶν, [Ἀσ]κληπιέ); SEG 50 (2000), 1222 (. . . μεγ' ἄριστε, φιλήκοε; see above, n. 67).

(40 BC).⁹⁵ Zeus's fire burned the weapons of the enemy, and a sudden storm, with thunder and lightning, terrified the assailants to such an extent that 'many were those who were deserting, asking for forgiveness and crying out with loud voice "Great is Zeus Panamaros!"' (ἔτι δὲ ἀναβοών[των] μεγάλῃ τῇ φωνῇ Μέγαν εἶναι Δία Πανάμαρον). Similarly, Aelius Aristides shouted 'Asklepios is great!' and Glykon 'Great Mes!' because they had witnessed the god's power.⁹⁶

Acclamations and 'acclamatory epithets' became in the imperial period an important medium for the conceptualisation of divine presence and efficacy. The aforementioned acclamations for Mes, for instance, list essential properties of the god: he is powerful, holy and just; he gives victory and success; he punishes the unjust; he dwells in heaven; he is unique.⁹⁷ A common expectation expressed by praises was that the god watched everything as παντεπόπτης and punished the unjust.⁹⁸ The divine power knew no limits, as we read in a confession inscription: 'I thank Meter Leto, for she makes the impossible things possible.'⁹⁹

It was a traditional function of divine epithets to describe the properties of gods. New in the imperial period is, however, the increase in the number of epithets and in their rhetorical qualities. The traditional epithets, which stressed the protective powers of gods – such as ἀσφάλειος, ἀποτρόπαιος and σωτήρ – seemed no longer sufficient to describe the benevolent and continuous presence of an almighty deity; they had to be supplemented

---

⁹⁵ *I.Stratonikeia* 10. Discussions: Roussel (1931); Chaniotis (1998), 408–10; cf. Girone (2003). Already Peterson (1926), 193–5, 213–22 established the connection between miracles and spontaneous acclamations.

⁹⁶ Aelius Aristides, *Hieroi logoi* 2.7: μέγας ὁ Ἀσκληπιός. An inscription in the Asklepieion in Pergamon records this acclamation: Habicht (1969), 129 no. 114; cf. Schröder (1986), 43 n. 16. Glykon: see above, n. 44. Cf. an aretalogy of Sarapis (*P.Oxy.* XI, 1382 = Totti (1985), 32–3 no. 13): οἱ παρόντες εἴπατε 'εἷς Ζεὺς Σάραπις'. Cf. *Acta Pauli et Theclae* 38: αἱ δὲ γυναῖκες πᾶσαι ἔκραξαν φωνῇ μεγάλῃ.

⁹⁷ See above, n. 44. Cf. *I.Ephesos* 3100 (cf. *SEG* 41 (1991), 982): Μέγα τὸ ὄνομα τοῦ θεοῦ, μέγα τὸ ὅσιον, μέγα τὸ ἀγαθόν; *TAM* v.1, 75 (Saittai): Εἷς θεὸς ἐν οὐρανοῖς. Μέγας Μὴς Οὐράνιος. Μεγάλη δύναμις τοῦ ἀθανάτου θεοῦ ('One god in heaven! Great is Heavenly Mes! Great is the power of the immortal god!'); cf. Lane (1976), 79.

⁹⁸ Παντεπόπτης: Robert (1971), 615; Marek (2000), 136–7; *SEG* 37 (1987), 1036 (Helios, Bithynia, second/third century AD); cf. πανδερκής: Robert (1971), 615 (Aither); *I.Kios* 21 (Isis); *Theosophia Tubingensis* 22 (*Theosophorum Graecorum fragmenta* p. 15 Erbse): Ζηνὸς πανδερκέος ἄφθιτον ὄμμα; *Poetae epici Graeci* II.1 frg. 102 F line 2 Bernabé (Apollo); Orphic hymns 4.8 (Ouranos), 8.1 (Helios), 9.7 (Selene), 34.8 (Apollo), 61.2 (Nemesis), 62.1 (Dike); cf. πανόπτης: *Poetae epici Graeci* II.1 frg. 141 F Bernabé: Ζεὺς ὁ πανόπτης; παντόπτης (Apollo): *SEG* 7, 14 = *I.Estremo Oriente* 221 = *SGO* III, 12/03/1 (first century AD).

⁹⁹ Petzl (1994), 140–1 no. 122 (Ortaköy, second/third century AD): εὐχαριστῶ Μητρὶ Λητώ, ὅτι ἐξ ἀδυνάτων δυνατὰ ποιεῖ.

by new attributes such as ἀγαθοποιός, καλοκἀγάθιος and ἁγιώτατος.[100] Such a deity demanded from the worshippers more than the traditional expression of devotion through sacrifices; it demanded spiritual worship through hymns, acclamations and eulogies, which had a lasting effect because they were regularly performed, written down in inscriptions, and read (or read out aloud).[101] The existence of a god would be irrelevant if those who had witnessed his power kept this experience to themselves. A new confession inscription reports how a man was not allowed by his sons to confess a sin and testify to the power of god (ἐκράτησαν ἐξομολογούμενον τὰς δυνάμις τῶν θεῶν); consequently, he did not acquire forgiveness and died, probably killed by an animal.[102] Such confession inscriptions would not have existed if the gods had not demanded a written record of their punishing power;[103] and dedications would not exist if the worshippers neglected to set up thanksgiving texts.[104] Worshippers often believed that the god had appeared in a dream, demanding public praise of his power.[105] This took place in sanctuaries and consisted in ritual gestures, such as raising the right hand and falling on the knees in front of a statue, and in the performance of hymns, eulogies and acclamations.[106] All this gave the worship a more spiritual character and contributed to the conceptualisation of the almighty god.

An interesting feature of the epithets used to describe the properties of a superior god is the fact that they implicitly responded to criticism,

---

[100] *SEG* 6, 550: Ζεὺς Καλοκἀγάθιος (Saghir, Pisidia, imperial period). For ἀγαθοποιός see Johnston (1992), 307 (the Thracian Rider God). For ἁγιώτατος see n. 111. Further material is quoted in nn. 108–17.

[101] For the emphasis on spiritual worship see Bradbury (1995); Chaniotis (2002c), 76–7; see already Nock (1933), 117. For the gradual decline of sacrifice see Stroumsa (2005). For acclamations and eulogies see above, nn. 46–7. See e.g. the oracle of Apollo Didymaios, in which the god expresses his preference for hymns over sacrifices (*I.Didyma* 217; Busine (2005), 448–9 no. 24); a dedication in Lydia (AD 235/6) reports that Mes allowed a woman to substitute the sacrifice of a bull with the dedication of a stele: *TAM* v.1, 453 = Petzl (1994), 78–9 no. 61.

[102] Herrmann and Malay (2007), 113–16 no. 85 (Kollyda, AD 205): . . . Ἐπὶ ἐκολάσθη[σ]αν οὗτοι, ὅτι τὸν πατέρα ἐκράτησαν ἐξομολογούμενον τὰς δυνάμις τῶν θεῶν. Καὶ ἐλημοσύνην μὴ λαβόντος τοῦ πατρὸς αὐτῶν, ἀλλὰ ἀποτελεσθέντος αὐτοῦ 'μή τίς ποτε παρευτελίσι τοὺς θεούς' διὰ τὰς π[ρ]ώτας προγραφὰς αὐτοῦ ἔγρα[ψ]αν καὶ ἀνέθηκαν εὐλογοῦντε[ς] τοῖς θεοῖς ('. . . For they have been punished because they seized their father, while he was acknowledging the powers of the gods. And their father did not obtain pity. But after his death, they wrote (?) on account of his first written declaration "nobody at any time should disparage the gods", and dedicated [the stele] praising the gods').

[103] E.g. Petzl (1994), 68–9 no. 57: ἐκέλευσεν στηλλογραφηθῆναι νέμεσιν. See Chaniotis (2009), 141.

[104] *SEG* 50 (2000), 1222 (second/third century AD): γραψάμενος σὰς χάριτας.

[105] E.g. *I.Ephesos* 3100: Μέγα τὸ ὄνομα τοῦ θεοῦ, μέγα τὸ ὅσιον, μέγα τὸ ἀγαθόν. Κατ᾽ ὄναρ: cf. Peterson (1926), 205–6; Robert (1955), 88 and 299; Mitchell (1999), 63.

[106] For a detailed analysis see Chaniotis (2009), 118–22, 139–40, 144; see now also Belayche (2006b).

uncertainties, or lack of faith. We cannot tell whether a confession inscription defended Mes's divine justice from critics when it described him as an infallible judge in heaven.[107] But to praise Apollo Grannus as the god 'who listens to prayers always and everywhere'[108] hints at the shortcomings of other gods in this respect. An anonymous god in Aspendos was called 'the one who does not lie' (ἀψευδής),[109] exactly as Perge was designated as the city which never lies in an acclamation directly connected with competition among the Pamphylian cities for privileges.[110] The claim that the same anonymous god at Aspendos was 'not made by mortal hands' (ἀχειροποίητος) implicitly made a distinction between true and false faith. Acclamatory epithets designating a deity as 'most sacred' (ἁγιώτατος),[111] 'immortal' (ἀθάνατος) and indestructible (ἄφθιτος),[112] 'truly just' (δικαιότατος),[113] 'unforgiving in his anger' (ἄλυτος),[114] 'almighty' (παντοδυνάστης, παντοκράτωρ),[115] 'with visible power' (ἐπιφανέστατος),[116]

[107] Herrmann and Malay (2007), 75–6 no. 51 (Hamidiye, AD 102): Μέγας Μεὶς Οὐράνιος Ἀρτεμιδώρου Ἄξιοττα κατέχων καὶ ἡ δύναμις αὐτοῦ, κρ[ι]τὴς ἀλάθητος ἐν οὐρανῷ ('Great is Heavenly Mes, founded by Artemidoros, the ruler over Axiotta, and his power, an infallible judge in heaven').

[108] SEG 35 (1985), 589 (Ulpia Traiana): αἰεὶ καὶ πανταχοῦ ἐπηκόῳ. Cf. MAMA I, 8 (Laodikeia Combusta, second/third century AD): πανεπηκόῳ θεῷ.

[109] SEG 38 (1988), 1335 (first/second century AD): Θεῷ ἀψευδ[εῖ καὶ] ἀχειροποιήτῳ εὐχήν. See Ameling (2004), 458–61 no. 258, with further bibliography. To the examples collected by Ameling, add the attribute ἄψευστος used for Bes as an oracular god in Abydos (SEG 47 (1997), 2098). See also Mitchell, p. 176 below.

[110] I.Perge 331: αὔξε Πέργη, ἡ μηδὲ[ὲ]ν ψευδομένη. Cf. above, n. 76.

[111] E.g. Milet VI.2, 699 (Apollon Didymeus, second/third century AD); I.Side TEp 3a (Athena, second century AD). For Artemis Ephesia see Engelman (2001). Cf. Robert (1971), 594.

[112] Ἀθάνατος: Fraser (1962), 25–7: πατρὶ θεῶι Σαμοθρᾶκι ἀθανάτωι ὑψίσ[τωι] (Kyrene, imperial period); Marek (1993), 194 no. 24: [Θεῷ] Ὑψίστῳ . . . Θεῷ ἀθανάτῳ (Kaisareia); I.Sultan Dağı 44 (Apollo and Helios, Philomelion); Eusebius, Praep. evang. 3.15.3 (oracle of Apollo). Cf. Mitchell (1999), 63. For the use of this attribute by Jews and Christians see Ameling (2004), 397–8. Ἄφθιτος: I.Kios 21 (Anoubis); SEG 45 (1995), 1612 (Zeus); Orphic hymns 10.5 (Physis), 15.1 (Zeus), 83.1 (Okeanos); Orphicorum fragmenta 248.5 Kern (Zeus).

[113] SEG 1, 463 (Apollo and Helios).   [114] Petzl (1994), 5–6 no. 4 (Theos Tarsios).

[115] Παντοδυνάστης: SEG 51 (2001), 1801 (Helios?, Nakoleia, imperial period); cf. Orphic hymns 12.4 (Herakles), 45.2 (Dionysos). Παντοκράτωρ: see above, n. 87; cf. I.Cret. II.28.2 + SEG 33 (1983), 736 (Hermes Eriounios, Tallaion Antron, Crete, second century AD); I.Iznik 1121 and 1512 (Zeus, Nikaia, second/third century AD); IG IX.2, 1201 (Methone in Thessaly, imperial period): Βασιλέα θεὸν μέγιστον παντοκράτορα κτίστην ὅλων καὶ θεοὺς πάντας καὶ θεοὺς ἥρωας καὶ αὐτὴν τὴν Δέσποιναν βασιλίδα; Kayser (1994), 198–9 no. 59 (Alexandria, second century AD): Isis Παντοκράτειρα; Orphic hymns 10.4 (Physis), 29.10 (Plouton), 2.10 (Persephone); Theosophia Tubingensis 27 (Theosophorum Graecorum fragmenta p. 19 Erbse). Cf. the epithet πανκράτωρ in SEG 7, 12–13 (Susa, first century BC). For the same conception in magic see e.g. SEG 45 (1995), 1897: Ἰάω, πάντων δεσπότης. For Jewish examples see Ameling (2004), 487–8.

[116] E.g. SEG 50 (2000), 1244 (Helios Apollon, Bahadinlar, Phrygia, AD 255), 1256 and 1270 (Apollo Lairbenos, Motela, second/third century AD); I.Ephesos 27 line 344 (Artemis, AD 104); I.Side 377 (Ares, second/third century AD); I.Stratonikeia 197, 224, 291, 527, 1101 (Zeus Panamaros and Hekate, second century AD).

and 'supreme rescuer' (πανυπείροχος σωτήρ),[117] fulfilled the same function: they expressed the superior status of a deity. The emphatic use of such an epithet for a particular god implied that he had properties which divinities lacked. As we have already seen, a common strategy in the effort to underline the priority and uniqueness of a god was to use long lists of epithets and superlatives;[118] through their rhythmical repetition during acclamations, such epithets became an effective medium for the propagation of the cult of a deity. The creation of new words such as πανυπέροχος and πανύψιστος is to be seen in the context of competition.[119]

THE PERSONAL WORSHIP OF AN ALMIGHTY GOD AND MONOTHEISTIC TRENDS

How is this emphatic form of devotion towards gods who were regarded by their worshippers as particularly powerful or even more powerful than others related to monotheistic tendencies? I would be inconsistent with my own programme of stressing the heterogeneity of religious mentality in the imperial period if I were to give one single answer to these questions. Our sources rather suggest a dynamic relationship between various factors: philosophy, exclusive monotheistic religions, the initiatives of cult founders and holy men, the teachings and performances of mystery cults, the survivals and revivals of local cultic traditions, and probably magical practices.

Some of the texts discussed above reflect the religious trends epitomised in the theosophical oracle of Klaros. The first line of this oracle lists attributes of god, all of them beginning with the letter *alpha*, as if its author

---

[117] *SEG* 37 (1987), 840 (Deva, Chester, third century AD): πανυπειρόχας ἀνθρώπων σωτῆρας ἐν ἀθανάτοισιν (Asklepios and Hygieia). For πανυπείροχοι θεοί cf. *IG* ii², 4514 (Athens, second century AD).

[118] See e.g. the texts quoted above, nn. 67 and 97. Cf. e.g. *I.Kios* 21: μάκαιρα θεὰ μήτηρ πολυώνυμος Ἶσις; *IGUR* 105 (second century AD): Ἀσκληπιῷ θε[ῷ] μεγίστῳ, [σ]ωτῆ[ρι], εὐερ[γ]έτῃ; *IGUR* 194 (early third century AD): Διὶ Ἡλίῳ Μεγάλῳ Σαράπιδι, σωτῆρι, πλουτοδότῃ, ἐπηκόῳ, εὐεργέτῃ, ἀνεικήτῳ Μίθρᾳ; *MAMA* x, 158 (Appia, imperial period): Μητρὶ μακαρίᾳ ὁσίᾳ δικαίᾳ; *CIG* 4502 (Palmyra, second century AD): Διὶ ὑψίστῳ μεγίστῳ καὶ ἐπηκόῳ. The long lists of divine epithets and attributes in the Orphic hymns, in the aretalogies of Isis (below, n. 121) and in magical texts are a related phenomenon.

[119] Drew-Bear, Thomas and Yildizturan (1999), 236 no. 364: Ζηνὶ πανυψίστῳ (Kurudere, Phrygia, c. AD 170). Cf. the attributes πανυπέρτατος in the Orphic hymns 4.8 (Ouranos), 8.17 (Helios), 10.4 (Physis), 12.6 (Herakles), 19.2 (Zeus), 61.6 (Nemesis), 66.5 (Hephaistos), and βασιλέστατος in *Theosophia Tubingensis* 27 (*Theosophorum Graecorum fragmenta* p. 19 Erbse). However, the double superlative μεγίστατος in Peterson (1926), 281–2 (acclamation in Cyprus: εἷς θεὸς, τὸ μεγίστατον, τὸ ἐνδοξότατον ὄνομα· βοήθη πᾶσι, δεόμεθε. Ἥλιος) does not exist; the reading has been corrected by Robert (1955), 87–8.

was using a lexicon of epithets and did not manage to reach the second letter of the alphabet: αὐτοφυής, ἀδίδακτος, ἀμήτωρ, ἀστυφέλικτος.[120] Such a listing of epithets is a stylistic feature of many contemporary groups of religious texts: the Orphic hymns, the 'aretalogies' of the Egyptian gods, magical texts, and dedications.[121] It originates in the belief that a single word or name is not adequate to comprise the entire concept of the divine. According to the Klarian oracle, god lives in fire; similarly, in contemporary texts the almighty god is often associated with heavenly bodies or is given a dwelling in heaven;[122] from his heavenly throne the god sees all. The Klarian god required a daily personal worship with ritual gestures (turning to the east in the theosophical oracle) and oral performances (εὔχεσθαι). Again, this corresponds to a general trend in this period; both cult regulations and oracles propagated a spiritual worship consisting in the singing of hymns (see n. 101); the confession inscriptions of Lydia and Phrygia stereotypically end with the phrase καὶ ἀπὸ νῦν εὐλογῶ ('and from now on, I praise'), possibly a speech act with which the conflict between sinner and god came to an end.[123]

Finally, the heavenly dwelling of the god made messengers necessary for his communication with the mortals (μεικρὰ δὲ θεοῦ μερὶς ἄνγελοι ἡμεῖς). In this respect, there is again a convergence between the Klarian oracle and religious texts which either imply or explicitly refer to divine mediators between the mortals and a superior god. The inscriptions of Asia Minor often refer to gods who served as messengers (ἄγγελοι) of a superior god.[124] A confession inscription presents Zeus in the role of such an intermediary between a man and Mes, serving as the 'advocate' (παράκλητος) of a sinner (see n. 55). But this concept was by no means limited to Asia Minor. The Orphic theology also knew of angels of a superior god, his πολύμοχθοι ἄγγελοι (see n. 20). In his hymn on Eros at Thespiai, Hadrian asked Eros/Antinoos to serve as an intermediary between earth and heaven

---

[120] For a Greek–Latin lexicon of epithets see Krämer (2004), 43–62. Cf. the list of epithets of Zeus in Miletos (*SEG* 45 (1995), 1612, second century AD). Only epithets beginning with the letter alpha are preserved. The same interest in epithets beginning with the letter alpha can be observed in oracles quoted in the *Theosophia Tubingensis* 42 (*Theosophorum Graecorum fragmenta* p. 27 Erbse): ἄναξ πάντων, αὐτόσπορος, αὐτογένεθλος; 21 (p. 15 Erbse): αὐτοφανής, ἀλόχευτος, ἀσώματος, ἄϋλος; 48 (p. 31 Erbse): αὐτογένεθλον ἀείναον... ἀγνὸν... ἀγλαόν. See also Gregory of Nazianzus, *Carmina*, *PG* 37, 1571: αὐτοπάτωρ, ἀλόχευτος, ἀμήτωρ.

[121] For the 'aretalogies' of the Egyptian gods see e.g. Totti (1985), 5–10 no. 2 (= *IG* XII.5, 739), 15–6 no. 6 lines 9–11, 62–75 no. 20 (= *P.Oxy.* XI, 1380), 76–82 nos. 21–4.

[122] Ἐν οὐρανοῖς: see notes 53 and 97.

[123] Petzl (1994), nos. 20, 33, 34, 37, 44, 62, 64, 69; Herrmann and Malay (2007), 81–2 no. 55. Cf. Chaniotis (2009), 139.

[124] Robert (1964), 28–30; Pleket (1981), 183–9; Mitchell (1993), 36. Angels in 'confession inscriptions': Petzl (1994), 3–5 no. 3, 47–8 no. 38; Petzl (1998), 13; de Hoz (1999), 122; Belayche (2005a), 43.

(line 6: ἄγγελον τόνδε).¹²⁵ The same concept underlies a dedication to Janus in Latium, in which Janus is asked to mediate between a man and Jupiter.¹²⁶

This convergence should not be misunderstood as evidence for a homogeneity of religious concepts. The worship of Mes, originally an Iranian moon god, is perhaps the best example of how the convergence of concepts could go along with the construction of the distinct profile of a *megas theos*.¹²⁷ Despite his similarities with Theos Hypsistos or, for instance, with the supreme Orphic god, Mes cannot be confused with either of them. He is not 'motherless' (*ametor*); on the contrary, several texts emphatically praise his mother (n. 51). Not unlike Theos Hypsistos he resides in heaven (as Ouranios), not representing the rising sun of the Klarian oracle but another heavenly body, the moon. He is served by angels; he is addressed with epithets that designate him as a ruler; and he has a superior position presiding over a council of gods (see nn. 54–5). This superior god is not a monotheistic god; he is a *megas theos*. The construction of such an image, with these striking similarities and differentiations from that of Theos Hypsistos or other deities, probably goes back to the initiative of a religious figure, a cult founder,¹²⁸ a holy man, a prophet – such as Alexander of Abonou Teichos in the case of Glykon New Asklepios.

The acclamatory phrase 'One god in heaven!' (εἷς θεὸς ἐν οὐρανῷ) epitomises both convergence in religious vocabulary and conscious differentiations in conceptions of the almighty god. In Delphi, this acclamation was used for Apollo Pythios, in Lydia for Mes Ouranios,¹²⁹ in Aizanoi in Phrygia for an anonymous god, who may be Theos Hypsistos,¹³⁰ in countless texts all over the Empire for the Christian God.¹³¹ This affective phrase, far from being evidence for monotheism or for an assimilation of cults, is evidence for the use of the same religious attributes for different gods and for the competition between their devotees.

¹²⁵ *IG* vii, 1828 (AD 134?). Discussion: Goukowsky (2002), 227–9.
¹²⁶ *AE* 1996, no. 370 (Signia, second/third century AD): [*et fa*]*ciles aditus da Iovis ad s*[*peciem*] ('and grant an easy approach to the presence of Jupiter').
¹²⁷ For the cult of Mes see Lane (1976); de Hoz (2002); Le Dinahet (2002); Labarre and Taşlıalan (2002), 257–312; Hübner (2003).
¹²⁸ For founders of sanctuaries of Mes see Hübner (2003), 188–90.
¹²⁹ *TAM* v.1, 75 = Lane (1976), 79: Εἷς θεὸς ἐν οὐρανοῖς. Μέγας Μὴς Οὐράνιος. Cf. Ramsay (1883), 322 no. 52 (Cappadocia): Μέγας Ζεὺς ἐν οὐραν[ῷ].
¹³⁰ *SEG* 42 (1992), 1192 (Aizanoi): Ἷς θεὸς ἐν οὐρανῷ. Μέγα τὸ Ὅσιον, μέγα τὸ Δίκεον. For another example (in Egypt) see Belayche (2006a), 21 and (2007b), 96–7.
¹³¹ Peterson (1926), 78 and 85.

CHAPTER 8

Deus deum ... summorum maximus (Apuleius): ritual expressions of distinction in the divine world in the imperial period

Nicole Belayche

Some, throwing out all the others, grant rulership over the universe to one god alone (ἑνὶ μόνῳ τὴν τῶν ὅλων ἀρχὴν)... But others, less greedily, assure us that there are several. They divide them into classes, call one the first god (τὸν μέν τινα πρῶτον θεόν) and assign the second and the third rank of divinity (τῆς θεότητος) to the others.

(Lucian, *Icaromenippos* 9)

The hermeneutic investigation of how religion evolved in late antiquity has expanded since historians widened their cognitive concepts by deploying approaches to the problems drawn from the social sciences. Students of late antique religion have now begun to ask questions about the fabric of polytheisms (how and why a god, 'all the gods' or *the* god are constructed), about their structures, and how they functioned. Since these divine worlds were open to change and naturally adaptable, the configurations of the evidence throw light on empirical processes – a sort of *bricolage* – that are determined by context rather than matters of dogma. Such research, in a word, is concerned with religion's dynamic development. The 'organigramme' of the pantheon that is invoked is always specific to the occasion or the place where it occurs, even if its starting point consists in a hierarchical representation fixed by institutions or conventions. Accordingly, the construction or reconstruction of the pantheon was a continuous process, which might modify the hierarchical order case by case, add new divine figures, or modify the outline of old ones. This research involves using and testing the validity of heuristic tools borrowed from various disciplines: sociology provides approaches for analysing religious pluralism and its market place, and for resolving questions of identity, hybridisation and the cross-fertilisation of the higher powers; philosophy and the cognitive sciences suggest typologies of how the divine worlds were represented; and historiography makes it possible to depict the nuances of periodisation.

In 1999 Athanassiadi, Frede and their colleagues re-examined the 'trend towards monotheism', already emphasised in studies from the first half of the twentieth century, which wittingly or unwittingly followed the direction of Christian apologetic argument in late antiquity. Since then a scholarly debate has developed about the capacity of pagan monotheism to be used as one of the interpretative tools for providing connections between the dispersed documentary data, making it possible to define a comprehensive vision, and even the rationale behind the development of these phenomena.[1]

THE *KAIROS* OF THE EVIDENCE AND THE -*ETIC* CATEGORIES

We need to start by acknowledging that the notion of pagan monotheism rests on at least two interlocking assumptions, one hermeneutic and the other ideological. The hermeneutic assumption is that the documentary material, which is the evidence for the pre-eminent or indeed unique position ascribed to divine figures addressed as *heis theos* that were endowed with exceptional and universal qualities and placed at or near the summit of the hierarchy, attests a unitary religious conception,[2] to be understood as the *doxa* or *communis opinio* of late antiquity, its theological koine.[3] However, just as the documents which illustrate this tendency in fact derive from varied milieux, and extend geographically to the limits of the Roman Empire itself (from the Spanish peninsula to the eastern *limes*), so their nature, function and contexts are very different from one another. They range from acclamations which hailed an epiphany, declarations of identity in competitive religious environments,[4] to commonplace religious dedications, expositions of speculative theology and revelatory utterances from the mouthpiece of the god. The assumption of unity consequently runs the risk of obscuring the contexts of these religious statements, which naturally make up their historical substance.

At an ideological level, the choice of the word monotheism for the *heis theos* formula involves giving a privileged perspective to the model of a unique god. Among the many possible processes, the One that is selected

---

[1] Athanassiadi and Frede (1999); see the excellent contribution of Peter Van Nuffelen to this volume. I am grateful to Stephen Mitchell for the English translation and to the editors for giving me the chance to present this study, several detailed aspects of which have appeared in previous publications; cf. Belayche (2005a), (2005b), (2005c), (2006a) and (2007b).

[2] The assumption, for example, of Mitchell (1999) concerning Theos Hypsistos. Against this see Bowersock (2002), 363: 'Ancient religion always allowed for local diversity, and never more than in the kaleidoscope of cults of the Highest God'; and Belayche (2005b), 427–8.

[3] See Foschia (2005), 461–6; Athanassiadi (forthcoming), whom I thank for a view of her manuscript.

[4] See the silversmiths of Ephesus, Acts 19:34, and the house doorways inscribed with the words *heis theos* to affirm that they belonged to the Jewish, Christian or Samaritan community of Palestine in late antiquity. See Di Segni (1994), 111–13 (summary table) and Markschies, in this volume.

is deemed to be generated by the aggregation and simplification of multiple entities,[5] a process which is variously described as syncretic, spiritualist etc. One should note at once, however, that in speculation about the unity of the divine, which can be traced in a continuous line since the Ionian philosophers of the sixth century BC,[6] and provides the guidelines for the conceptualisation of pagan monotheism,[7] the process is reversed. According to the general principles of Platonic theology that permeate the thinking of the middle and late imperial periods, for example, the multiplicity of beings derived from the One, the Supreme Good, by successive emanations which are explained as successive hypostases. In contrast, pagan monotheism is seen as the product of a simplification or purification of the divine world, culminating in the recognition of the existence of a single superior universal power, perfect and impersonal. The traditional gods in such a scheme merely represent assistants, whose special functions related to the lower form of existence experienced by mankind, *pro ratione officiorum nostrorum*, according to the rationale of the tasks that they fulfil for us.[8]

Factual objections should be added to these methodological precautions. Systematic philosophical pronouncements about a single god in Greek and later Roman societies, as well as poetic expressions in the same sense,[9] always existed alongside evidence of religious devotion in the pluralist tradition.[10] Given this fact, it could paradoxically be argued that in some circumstances monotheism might be regarded as a modality of polytheism, and yet this model is also much too dichotomous to grasp helpfully the variety of ways in which the divine realm should be approached. The fact holds true even when one or several divinities were called by epithets which could also be applied to the unique god in other religious systems with different structures. This is the case with Hypsistos, which is one of the translations of

---

[5] See for example Turcan (1999), 394: 'un hénothéisme qui le [le paganisme] condamne à terme en le menant au monothéisme'. Assmann (2003), 24–8 distinguished an 'evolutionary monotheism', which 'may be seen as the final stage of polytheism', from a 'revolutionary monotheism'.

[6] For example Kenney (1986) and West (1999), 32–40, who illustrates the gap that exists and was never bridged by monotheism in ancient cultures.

[7] See e.g. Moreschini (1983).

[8] Servius, ad *G.* 1.5: *Stoici dicunt non esse nisi unum deum et unam eandemque potestatem quae pro ratione officiorum nostrorum variis nominibus appellatur* (*Stoicorum Veterum fragmenta* II, p. 313 no. 1070).

[9] The most famous is Aeschylus, *Supp.* 524: 'King of kings, fortunate among the fortunate, sovereign power among all powers . . .', echoed by Apul., *Met.* 11.30; cf. Rose and others (1954) and Decharme (1966).

[10] See the sacrificial relief and table of offerings (?) discovered in the house said to belong to Proclus on a slope of the Athenian acropolis (in the street of Dionysius the Areopagite), and the hymns composed by Proclus, reported by Marinus, *Proclus (On Happiness)* 19, 20–6.

the name of the Jewish God in the Septuagint.[11] A historian of religions cannot overlook this paradoxical panorama in one of his objects of study, the
representation of the divine. This topic has been investigated with different
objectives, either in studies concerned with the definition and singularity
of polytheism,[12] or in order to elucidate documents which assert oneness
in societies that claim several gods.[13] This documentation has encouraged
some to 'think polytheism'[14] by employing heuristic tools which are judged
better to represent the various aspects of the divine, including the 'inclusive
or exclusive polytheism' of J. Boulogne, and the 'inclusive monotheism' of
P. Athanassiadi following others.[15] The current debate has been made all the
more complex by the meanings attributed to 'divine' and 'divinity'. At all
events, it has not been possible to resolve the argument by retaining these
hermeneutic and ideological categories.[16] Efforts made to adapt these categories to recalcitrant religious or intellectual realities, which themselves are
already problematic,[17] have not produced a more functional interpretative

---

[11] For Hypsistos see Ustinova (1999), 221–8; Bowersock (2002), 355–7; Belayche (2005a and b). Against,
     see Mitchell (1999), who suggests that the Oinoanda oracle provides the theological representation ('a
     common pattern of religious belief') of all the dedications to Theos Hypsistos. See already Mitchell
     (1998), 64: 'without the god-fearers, it would be almost impossible to imagine the transformation
     of the pagan world to Christian monotheism'; compare Fürst (2006a).

[12] Note François (1957) for lexical analysis; Rudhardt (1966), 362–3: 'le Grec [est] sensible à la
     prééminence éthique de l'unité; mais, il se refuse à exclure de la réalité divine une multiplicité
     dont témoigne la variété des expériences qu'il en fait et dont le rejet constituerait à ses yeux un
     affaiblissement du divin' ('the Greek is aware of the ethical preference for unity; but he refuses to
     exclude that divine reality contains a multiplicity of beings, to which the variety of his experiences
     bears witness, and to reject which would amount in his eyes to the enfeebling of divinity'); Vernant
     (1985), 363: 'Les diverses puissances surnaturelles dont la collection forme la société divine dans son
     ensemble peuvent elles-mêmes être appréhendées sous la forme du singulier, ὁ θεός, la puissance
     divine, le dieu, sans qu'il s'agisse pour autant de monothéisme' ('the various supernatural powers
     which together make up the divine society can themselves be grasped in singular form as ὁ θεός, the divine
     power, the god, without this being a case of monotheism'); Assmann (2003), 16: 'Unity in this case
     does not mean the exclusive worship of one God, but the structure and coherence of the divine
     world, which is not just an accumulation of deities, but a whole structure, a pantheon'; etc.

[13] Bonner (1950), 174: 'when used of a pagan god, εἷς expresses the great power or the preeminence of
     the deity, rather than definitely monotheistic belief'. Robert (1983), 583 n. 1: 'εἷς est l'acclamation
     au superlatif... elle n'implique pas une tendance au monothéisme' ('εἷς is a superlative acclama-
     tion... it does not imply any tendency towards monotheism'). Max Müller, in a lecture published
     as early as 1859, wrote: 'Il est perçu à ce moment comme une divinité... suprême et absolue, en
     dépit des limitations nécessaires qu'une pluralité ne manque d'imposer à chaque dieu en particulier,
     dans notre esprit' ('he is perceived at this moment as a... supreme and absolute divinity, despite
     the necessary limitations which are inevitably imposed on each individual god by the existence of
     a plurality'); cited by Hornung (1986), 215, in a study concerned with the relationship between the
     One and the many in Egypt.

[14] Schmidt (1988).   [15] Boulogne (1997); Athanassiadi (forthcoming).

[16] Compare Sfameni Gasparro (2003), 101: 'l'ossimoro di un "monoteismo politeistico"' ('the oxy-
     moron of polytheistic monotheism'); compare also Wallraff (2003).

[17] That is without returning to the often repeated reservations about the terms 'polytheism' and
     'paganism'. See the methodological and historiographical analysis of Ahn (1993), the attempt at
     typology by Dillon (1999), 69, and Markschies (2002) on Christianity.

model. The reason might lie in the fact that the fundamental antinomy between mono- and poly-theism that they try to surmount is the result of post-antique classification.[18] Accordingly, such attempts are forced to mix together emic and etic approaches. I would cite as a demonstration the way in which the emperor Julian, who as a philosopher was fully aware of the ontology of the transcendent god, viewed the Jewish God as 'the very powerful and excellent god, who controls the sensible world, and whom we ourselves revere, as I know, under other names'. Julian's observation was shaped by the fact that he classified the Jewish God as an ethnic god, as indeed he also was.[19]

If these sophisticated classifications of how the divine world is represented do not successfully account for the ways in which the religious landscape was structured and risk posing an epistemological obstacle, should we not modify the perspective and give preference to a reconstruction based on what can be known about the ritual context of these documents? In traditional ancient religions it was not speculative exposition but rites and ritual actions which designated the representation of the superior world and guided religious life.[20] I propose, therefore, to re-examine the ritual expressions used to denote pre-eminence or 'distinction' which were attached to certain divine personalised figures or to divinity itself, and pay special consideration to their functions. Although these are infinitely rarer than Jewish (or Samaritan) and Christian attestations of the term, the most intriguing forms are those which acclaimed a divinity as *heis theos* among other gods.[21] The work of reference remains the study of Eric Peterson.[22] The Bonn scholar rightly underlined the communicative character of the formula and concluded that even for Christians 'die εῖς θεός-Formel ist Akklamation, aber nicht Glaubensbekenntnis' ('the formula εῖς θεός is an acclamation, but not a statement of belief'), even while he recognised that it could slide 'von der Akklamation zur begrifflichen Einheitsformel' ('from an acclamation to a formulation of conceptual uniqueness').[23] His collection of evidence assembles the pagan examples of the formula as a backdrop to a larger dossier, whose perspective was explicitly Christian

---

[18] Alongside the debate about the multiplicity of gods, early Christian apologetic from the time of Tertullian and Origen brought many proofs to bear on the false, demoniac, nature of the traditional gods; see e.g. Fédou (1988), 264–81.

[19] Julian, *Ep. et leg.* no. 89, 454a Bidez/Cumont.   [20] Scheid (2007).

[21] For Palestine see e.g. Di Segni (1994). On the use of the formula *heis theos* and its connection to the stages of Christianisation see Trombley (1993–4) I, 120–2 and II, 313–15.

[22] Peterson (1926). A new edition with an updated catalogue is awaited: Markschies (forthcoming).

[23] Peterson (1926), 302 and 305 (cf. 216: a 'propagandistic formula' of Jewish origin in the Hellenistic period).

and concerned principally with Christological disputes.[24] This more or
less deliberately placed his investigation in a framework of enquiry about
monotheism. Since then H. S. Versnel has written, to my mind definitively,
about the 'acclamatory-elative' nature of *heis*, although he has prudently
supposed that 'the henotheistic element gradually increased at the cost of
the acclamatory-elative component'.[25] Regardless of the elaboration of the
two categories, already presupposing monotheist against polytheist,[26]
the opposition of these antinomic representations of the divine world
in the ancient sources was a main component of intellectual and religious
polemic, rather than a feature of religious life itself. It has hence caused
difficulties for modern scholars wishing to give labels to the religious associations of this or that item of evidence. It is essential to be aware of
the contexts of these expressions in order to locate their primariness and
pre-eminence within the divine landscape.

Like all ritual practice, these acclamations, which reveal religious actions,
are a medium for understanding the representation of the pantheon. Compared to other evidence for religious devotion, they offer an emphatic form
of homage to the *time* of the gods, which is to be found in the Greek epic
and poetic traditions, in epigraphic practice,[27] and in Latin theatrical works
of the late republican period, even if there it is a humorous topic.[28] The
new religious attitude contained in these attestations is to be identified, in
my opinion, as the expression of a relationship with a privileged divinity.
Instead of being structured solely according to a contractual votive ritualism, this expression enhanced the theological quality and ontology of
the power invoked, frequently as a result of a direct personal experience.
Rather than being a simplified representation of the structures of the divine
world, these attestations may be evidence for a different sort of religious
communication and a new way of articulating the presence of divine beings

---

[24] Peterson (1926), preface: 'the original object of my work was to collect and interpret the ΕΙΣ ΘΕΟΣ
inscriptions in Christian epigraphy. I went beyond the envisaged boundaries in the course of the
investigation. The concept of the acclamation needed to be treated in depth, and the altered stance
of the philological and religious-historical research led to new questions being asked.' See the
historiographical analysis of Markschies (2001).

[25] Versnel (1990), 25 (nuanced in Versnel (2000), 155: 'an affective exclusion of other gods'); cf. 190–
205 (repeated in Versnel (2000), 138–46) for his model of the nine characteristics of 'henotheistic
religiosity', which principally emphasise the state of mind of devotees.

[26] Cf. Sfameni Gasparro (2003), 101–7.

[27] See Tod (1949), 110–12 for the social context of the hyperbole conveyed by εἷς, πρῶτος and μόνος.

[28] See e.g. Plautus, *Trin.* 823–4: 'as for me I am grateful to you, Neptune, and give thanks to you
above the other gods to the highest degree (*tibi ante alios deos gratias ago atque habeo summas*)'. Cf.
Belayche (2006a). *Summus* had been used by philosophers and Christian authors to describe the
supreme god at the same time as *altissimus*: Battifol (1929), 188–201.

in the world, their *être-au-monde*.[29] Among the 'theological oracles' of the sanctuaries of Claros and Didyma, which articulated contemporary theological speculation about the supreme divinity, only one appears to be the answer to an explicit question about the literal uniqueness of an ineffable god, while three others concern such a god's place in the pantheon.[30] The majority of these revelatory texts provided an analysis of the qualities of the divine being, from which its uniqueness could be inferred. These acclamations can be much better interpreted as part of the trend to individualise relationships between men and the gods, well illustrated by Versnel and his followers,[31] for which they provided a convenient rhetoric of communication.

THE ENUNCIATORY CONTEXTS AND FUNCTIONALITY OF *HEIS THEOS* ACCLAMATIONS

The attestations of *heis theos* can be divided into two groups: ritual documents, notably inscriptions, amulets and gems; and speculative or philosophical expositions, which were literary compositions designed for demonstrative purposes. By nature these belong to different registers, which can nevertheless overlap with one another. Independently of philosophical exegesis, which controlled and turned public religious life into a *religio necessaria*,[32] Cicero in his treatise *On the Nature of the Gods* already distinguished the *ratio religionis*, which he expected from the philosophers, from expressions of belief or piety anchored in the ancestral tradition.[33]

Christian fathers already began to make assertions about a possible 'pagan monotheism' in works that were mostly reflective or speculative.[34] These texts took their probative force from three kinds of argument: etymological games about naming; the heritage of philosophical and poetic tradition, which could be followed from oldest antiquity; and the authority of mystic and oracular revelation in the Orphic and Apollonian traditions.[35] In these writings ancient authors regularly distinguished speculation from cult practice. Macrobius, after reporting an oracle given to Nicocreon,

---

[29] Contra Mitchell (1999), 104: 'a group of acclamations . . . which clearly relate to a form of monotheistic worship'.
[30] Respectively Erbse (1995), 38 lines 1 and 7 (εἷς . . . θεός, ἐξ ἑνός εἰς ἓν ἰόντα), 42 (Hypsistos), 39 (another god whose power was *meizona*); Macrobius, *Sat.* 1.18.20 (*hypatos*). In Erbse (1995), 35 the immortal god who alone (μόνος) should be respected is μακάρων βασιλεὺς μέγιστος. Compare Busine (2005), 203–8, and see also Suarez de la Torre (2003).
[31] Versnel (1981b); see also Veyne (1986).   [32] Cicero, *Nat. D.* 3.1.6.
[33] Belayche (2007b).   [34] Hirsch-Luipold (2005).
[35] See the three types of material in the presentation of Praetextatus: Macrobius, *Sat.* 1.17.2–7; see now Kahlos (2002).

the king of Cyprus, which declared the Sun or Sarapis to be the *deus maximus*, and called him εἶς τὸ πᾶν, 'the unified totality', in a preceding chapter, continued: *Isis iuncta religione celebratur* ('Isis is joined with him in the cult').[36] These roles could be reversed, as on a gem which shows a seated Sarapis-Hades with Isis standing in front of him, while the inscription acclaims the female figure of the pair: Η ΚΥΡΙΑ CICIC (*sic*) ΑΓΝΗ. In another example the two figures, both equally exalted as mighty, are portrayed on the two sides of a gem.[37] The reaction of the listeners to Praetextatus' speech at the Saturnalian banquet shows explicitly that the investigation (*hermeneia*) of divine matters by exegesis[38] was connected to educated culture and rhetoric, that is to say it was a form of dialectic which assimilated religious experience by means of an interpretative priestly tradition.

Then one began to commend his memory, another his learning (*doctrina*), everyone his religious knowedge (*religio*).[39] Each proclaimed that he was the only person who was privy (*conscium*) to the secrets of the nature of the gods, who was capable both of pursuing divine matters through the application of intelligence (*adsequi animo*) and of expounding them by his talent (*eloqui ingenio*).[40]

Late Roman intellectuals were certainly proud of signifying their social distinction in this way: 'the divinities have always preferred to be known and worshipped (*et sciri et coli*) in the way that tales of antiquity have been told to the common people (*qualiter in vulgus antiquitas fabulata est*), by assigning images and statues to them, although they have nothing to do with such forms (*talium prorsus alienis*).'[41] Whatever was said, the philosophical life itself encouraged one to honour all the gods, and not only those of one's ancestral tradition, and this was something that Proclus put into practice in his hymns, because the philosopher 'ought in every case to be the hierophant of the entire world'.[42]

---

[36] Macrobius, *Sat.* 1.20.18. Dio Chrysostom, *Or.* 31.11 (to the Rhodians) proposed drawing a different conclusion from this 'henotheism': 'plenty of others simply bring all the gods together in a single force and power, so much so that it matters little whether one or another is honoured (ὥστε μηδὲν διαφέρειν τὸ τοῦτον ἢ ἐκεῖνον τιμᾶν)'. The evidence of acclamations shows that this was not common practice.

[37] See, respectively, Richter (1956), no. 346 (to be compared with a graffito from Ptolemais in Egypt, Peterson (1926), 238: Ἲς Ζεὺς Σέραπις καὶ Ἥλιος Ἑρμανοῦβις) and Bonner and Nock (1948) (Κύριος Σάραπις and Ἀνίκητος Νεωτέρα).

[38] Macrobius, *Sat.* 1.19.9.

[39] This sense may be deduced from the priestly functions of Praetextatus.

[40] Macrobius, *Sat.* 1.24.2; cf. Liebeschuetz (1999).

[41] Macrobius, *In somn.* 1.2.20. According to Frede (1999), 56–7, the *communis opinio* of antiquity would consider that 'if you were a philosopher you would usually assume that there is a god, the God'.

[42] Marinus, *Proclus* (*On Happiness*) 19.29–30. Already according to Porphyry, *Abst.* 2.49, the philosopher who had understood the ordering of the world is ὁ τοῦ ἐπὶ πᾶσι θεοῦ ἱερεύς.

The relationship between speculation and *praxis* requires us, therefore, to pay attention to the nature of the documents that are cited. Every pantheon, because it is a plurality, necessarily displays protocols of order, an etiquette which was fixed by local and trans-local or functional configurations, according to which men organised the co-existence of beings, who were all equally godly. The act of emphasising or reinforcing the hierarchy in one or another organigramme of divine powers did not imply *ipso facto* that men were changing the general principles of its architecture, as is evident when a man consulting Apollo demanded 'if another god (ἕτερος θεός) exists who possesses greater (μείζονα) power than yours'.[43] Varro, as reported by Augustine, insisted at a much earlier date on the distinction between the gods' ontology, reflected in philosophical thinking, and their spheres of competence in their relation to the world: 'It is fruitless to know that Aesculapius is a god if one does not know that he cures illnesses, if one is ignorant of why it is necessary to pray to him.'[44]

The Latin antiquarian's remark helpfully draws attention to the fact that documents addressing *heis theos* should be considered with regard to their ritual function. The acclamations attested epigraphically or in literature in hymnic narratives, which are by nature exalted texts,[45] served as means of communication, and the amulets inscribed *heis theos* had a protective or apotropaic object. Εἷς Ζεὺς | Σαράπις· ἱλέως τῶι φοροῦντι was the text explicitly carved on a gem in the British Museum.[46] In both cases the function was one of emphasis and exaltation. The formula does not occur *expressis verbis* in the ritual protocols of the so-called magical papyri edited by K. Preisendanz, in spite of their numerous borrowings from the Jewish tradition and their closeness to the amulets.[47] We nevertheless encounter invocations to *megas theos*, or even to 'the one and blessed of the Aeons, and father of the world' (τὸν ἕνα καὶ μάκαρα τῶν Αἰώνων) in a prayer formula addressed to a unique and holy power.[48]

The dedication of the Mithraeum at the Baths of Caracalla shows how the different forms of exaltation of divine figures demanded different forms of address. Side B of the altar carries a normal votive formula to the composite divinity 'Zeus Sarapis megas Sarapis', a form of the god which had developed in Roman milieux maintained by the priests of the Sarapeum at Alexandria, supplemented with theological epithets,

[43] Erbse (1995), no. 39.   [44] Varro, *Antiquitates*. 1.3, quoted by Augustine, *De civ. D.* 4.22.
[45] See e.g. the *dipinto* text in the *mithraeum* of St Prisca at Rome, Vermaseren and Van Essen (1965), 187 for a ritual hymn (line 12: *per ritum*), and 155 for the acclamation of the grades. For Isiac hymns see below, pp. 151–2.
[46] Michel (2001), no. 543.
[47] For the use of rings and inscribed bracelets in these rituals see below, n. 101.
[48] *PGM* iv, 1169–70.

σωτῆρι, πλουτοδότῃ, ἐπηκόῳ, ἀνεικήτῳ, which could form part of the prayer.[49] On side A the formulaic acclamation εἷς Ζεὺς Σάραπις also included identification with the sun god (Ἥλιος) and accounted for the two qualities which made him a supreme god. He was κοσμοκράτωρ and ἀνείκητος. Similar expressions, varying according to the contexts in which they were pronounced, are to be found on an Oxyrhynchus papyrus which narrates the miraculous intervention of the *arete* of Zeus Helios Megas Sarapis, but also shows that a public acclamation (οἱ πάροντες εἴπατε) followed the formulaic slogan Εἷς Ζεὺς Σάραπις.[50]

HEIS AND MONOS AND THE MONOTHEIST FORMULAE

Turning to the variety of formulations of the εἷς θεός acclamations, we should first note those that are connected in at least one respect to traditional representations of the divine world. They are not numerous, except on gems,[51] and in any case are much rarer than the formulae which acclaimed the greatness of one or another divine figure.[52] The protective formula εἷς θεὸς βοήθει ('one god, protect'), which is unusual in non-Semitic pagan contexts,[53] was especially addressed to gods with healing powers, such as Sarapis, or those that delivered justice, such as Nemesis. It may also indicate the permeability of confessional religious milieux under the influence of Christian formulae in the later period. The appeal for protection explains why it was carved on amulets, like an example from fifth-century Palestine, which placed the wearer under the protection of a god from the traditional pantheon, Poseidon: Θεὸς βοηθός, Ποσείδων βοήθει.[54]

The first part of the formula, θεός βοηθός, recalls acclamations of devout Jews and Christians which are echoed in the apocryphal *Acts of John* as these report the episode at Ephesus: Ἡ μεγάλη Ἄρτεμις Ἐφεσίων βοήθει. This is less faithful to pagan formulae of acclamation of the deity's greatness than the formula to be found in the canonical version of Luke-Acts: Μεγάλη Ἄρτεμις Ἐφεσίων.[55] Few of the monotheistic *heis theos* formulae catalogued by E. Peterson were used by pagans. The appeal to a *heis theos* as saviour,

---

49 *CIMRM* I, 463 side B. Mithras was added later on the grounds of the heliac identity of the gods.
50 *P.Oxy.* XI, 235 no. 1382, II 15–21 = Totti (1985), 32 no. 13.
51 The additions to the *heis theos* corpus, which are expected to be considerable, will appear in the eagerly awaited new edition of Markschies (forthcoming). Most of them are Jewish, Samaritan and Christian documents.
52 Müller (1913); cf. Chaniotis, in this volume.
53 Note an amulet of the second century AD depicting an enthroned Sarapis, inscribed Βοήθει μοι ὁ θεός, Michel (2001) no. 31. For a collection of examples of the formula see Peterson (1926), 3–5.
54 Manns (1977), 236–7 no. 3. 55 *Acts of John* 26.5; Acts 19:34.

which is well attested in a monotheistic milieu or on apotropaic objects that are difficult to attribute to any specific religion,[56] occurs very unusually in a Sarapiac context, although the god is regularly honoured and acclaimed as σωτήρ.[57] *Heis theos monos* is another formula which is almost exclusively Jewish or Christian, and its exclusivity emphasises the uniqueness of the deity.[58] However, it is not entirely unknown in documents which depict a pluralist divine world. So, a gem in the Cairo Museum places images of Zeus, Asclepius and Hygia beside the formula μόνος θηὸς (*sic*) ἐν οὐρανῷ. The same formula was also used at Thasos and in Anatolia to glorify the god Men.[59] The original formula of acclamation is constructed like the commoner formula *heis Zeus Sarapis*, which proclaims the identity of the two gods,[60] but the figured image of the Cairo gem reflects the individuality of the three gods, indicating the pre-eminent positions of Zeus and Asclepius, and the familial relationship and shared competences of Asclepius and Hygia.

The tendency to the varied deployment of one, a pair, a triad and multiple figures was common in Isiac contexts. The elogium preserved on a stele of Isis found at Maronea begins with Isis as she was first generated; then it celebrates the pair that she formed with Sarapis, both being honoured as *monoi theoi*. Subsequently they acquire a multiplicity of names from being invoked in a liturgical hymn praising their virtues and powers. Its form is stereotyped and portrayed a presence that was civilising, universal, omnipotent and providential.[61] However, the successive steps of the narrative are not placed in the same register. The primordial couple, which established the divine law, is articulated with the natural elements, the sun and the moon, and placed in the cosmic register, the location both of the theogony and of the ordering of the world. The ritual level, that of religious life, is the one where polyonymy is featured, thus showing how the special functions of the gods were distributed among various divine figures.[62] The distinction of the couple in the experience of their devotees as *monoi theoi*, unique gods but not alone, illustrates the belief that Isis and Sarapis united in themselves the multiple individual representations of divine beings, something that was

---

[56] See e.g. Di Segni (1994), no. 27.

[57] See Peterson (1926), 91 and 237: a ring inscribed Εῗς Ζεὺς Σέραπις ἐπιφανὴς Ἀσκλήπιος σωτήρ.

[58] Compare Mauser (1986); and an oracle preserved in the *Theosophia Tubingensis* (Erbse (1995), no. 42): εἰ μόνος ὁ Ὕψιστος ἐστιν ἄναρχος καὶ ἀτέλευτος.

[59] Cited by Peterson (1926), 196; for Men see below, p. 156. [60] See below, p. 157.

[61] *RICIS* I, 114/0202 lines 16, 19–20, 22; cf. Grandjean (1975). The hymn form was an excellent medium for communicating the exaltation of the gods; see Herrero de Jáuregui (2009).

[62] See the teasing rhetorical *captatio benevolentiae* insisting on the difficulty of evoking numerous gods: Grandjean (1975), lines 20–2.

a *locus classicus* of Stoic and Middle Platonic philosophy.[63] As in the reading which historians now propose for Deuteronomy 6:4, 'Hear Israel *Yhwh* your *Elohim*, *Yhwh* alone',[64] the term *monos* appears to me to be an expression of privilege and exaltation through hymnic rhetoric, and not a declaration of uniqueness. The Cyrene stele plays on the same registers. Although it is dedicated to Isis and Sarapis, like the god of Stratonikos in Lydia,[65] Isis as a ruler of the cosmic realm is described as *mia* and *mone*, pre-eminent and unique among her divine peers, ὑψίστην θεόν, πάντων μεγίστην τῶν ἐν οὐρανῶι θεῶν.[66] At Cyrene she is pre-eminent and unique (*mia*) among her divine peers, ὑψίστων μεδέουσα θεῶν. Similarly, at Medinet-Madi she is ὑψίστη and παντοκράτειρα, ὑψίστων μεδέουσα θεῶν.[67] Yet she never formally receives the acclamation *heis theos*, which was so current for Sarapis, and which was given to other female divinities. A gem of the second or first century BC from a Greek-speaking Egyptian environment carries an acclamation of Hathor and her power within a trinity, *trimorphos theos*, which she forms with Horus and a local god: *Heis Bait Horus, heis Athor, mia ton bia, heis de Akori...* [68] The Phrygian god Men was also exalted as *heis theos*, his powers and greatness being acclaimed in the company of other gods. In classical Greek, when the numeral *heis* was used for rhetorical emphasis, it was supplemented by the use of οἶος/οἴα or by μόνος to convey the notion of uniqueness.[69] It is used in a similar way in passages of religious speculation which exploit its semantic diversity. Plutarch made a play on the etymologies of the various names used to designate Apollo's uniqueness: 'the name of Apollo is opposed to plurality and excludes multiplicity; that of Eios signifies that he is one and only, εἶς καὶ μόνος'.[70]

This tradition of interpretation goes back to Plato, and Latin writers adopted the same linguistic device. Cicero, for example, makes a connection between *Sol* and *solus*.[71] At the beginning of the fifth century AD Macrobius continues to allude to these hermeneutic games: 'Chrysippus has written that he is called Apollo . . . in virtue of the fact that he is unique and not multiple (μόνος ἐστι καὶ οὐχὶ πολλοί), and in fact Latin speakers also called

[63] See already Cleanthes, *Hymn to Zeus*; Thom (2005).   [64] Cf. Sérandour (2004), 48–51.
[65] See below, n. 74.   [66] *RICIS* II, 701/0103 lines 7–8.
[67] *SBAU* V, 8138, I, lines 2 and 3, III line 1.
[68] Michel (2001), no. 24. Cf also Kore and Hekate, below, n. 83.
[69] Homer, *Il.* 4.397 and *Od.* 7.65; Herodotus 1.119; Dionysius of Halicarnassus 1.74. Cf. Versnel (1990), 235 n. 145 for *unicus*.
[70] Plutarch, *On the E at Delphi* 20 (393C). On 'the place of the name (ΤΟΠΟΣ ΑΠΟ ΤΟΥ ΟΝΟΜΑΤΟΣ)': Pernot (2005).
[71] Cicero, *Nat. d.* 2.27. For the *solus* formula see Versnel (1990), 213–16.

him the sun, because he is the one god to have such a great impact.'[72] These observations, arising from ritual and conceptual contexts alike, can throw light on a Lydian dedication made by a certain Stratonikos, 'priest of the One and Only God and of Hosios kai Dikaios' (τοῦ Ἑνὸς καὶ Μόνου Θεοῦ ἱερεὺς καὶ τοῦ Ὁσίου καὶ Δικαίου).[73] There is nothing unusual in the same person taking several priesthoods; the fact is a feature of religious pluralism. He and his wife Asclepiaia had a traditional contractual votive relationship with the superior beings (εὐξάμενοι . . . εὐχαριστοῦντες, lines 4 and 5). The couple had themselves depicted standing on either side of an altar, on which Asclepiaia makes an offering of incense, following the iconographic code for depicting sacrificial honours (Figure 1). The identity of the recipient(s) might appear obscure, because the construction of the first two lines is not the usual one in votive epigraphy,[74] and the deities are addressed impersonally. In the relief on the pediment of the stele, which usually houses the representation of the god being honoured, we should recognise Hosios kai Dikaios, the Holy and the Just, represented as a unique entity in the form of a god on horseback. This is rarer than the common form in which they were represented as a pair of divine beings identified by their attributes, the sceptre and the weighing scale.[75] The impersonal form of address should not lead us to suppose that they were depersonalised. In Lydia they are equally honoured in a gendered form, 'to the god Hosios kai Dikaios and to Hosia kai Dikaia', or as an indefinite plurality of powers or qualities, Hosiois kai Dikaiois.[76]

It is more hazardous to try to establish the precise relationship between 'the One and Only God' and 'the Holy and the Just'. S. Mitchell has envisaged that the latter were agents of a transcendent god, basing his argument on the Oinoanda oracle and the architecture of Platonic theology.[77] This interpretation, however, seems to be rather distant from the features that reveal the context of this document: the relief, the two priesthoods, the

---

[72] Macrobius, *Sat.* 1.17.7.

[73] *TAM* v.1, 246 (Kula, Lydia) = Ricl (1991–2), 18, no. 2. Cf. Versnel (1990), 235 n. 145 and de Hoz (1999), 61: 'Μόνος bedeutet jedoch nicht "einzig", sondern "einzigartig"'. Contra Mitchell (1999), 103–4: 'no doubt that he [Stratonikos] should be identified as a believer in the monotheistic theology of the Oenoanda oracle'.

[74] The normal formula is *ho hiereus* followed by the name of the god who is served; cf., for Lydia, de Hoz (1999), 352 (index).

[75] Ricl (1991–2), 93–7.

[76] *TAM* v.1, 247 (compare Petzl (1998), 14–21); Ricl (1991–2) 18, nos. 95 and 96.

[77] See Mitchell (1999), 104–5 (cf. Mitchell (1993), 45), although he acknowledges the conclusion of Eric Peterson on the non-monotheist character of the acclamation *Heis theos*. Hypsistos and Hosios were sufficiently closely linked that a lapicide was able to confuse them, cf. Malay (1994), 181 and Petzl (1998), 22–3 (*SEG* 48 (1998), 1427).

Figure 1 Lydian dedication of Stratonikos, priest of
the One and Only God and of Hosios kai Dikaios

ritual and votive environment, the pluralist logic according to which the exalted divinity is honoured at the same time as his anthropomorphised qualities, and, finally, a formula that is identical to that found in the Isis *elogia* discussed above.[78] In addition, the formulation of the text evokes another acclamation found near Ephesus, Μέγα τὸ ὄνομα τοῦ θεοῦ, | μέγα τὸ ὅσιον, | μέγα τὸ ἀγαθὸν | κατ᾽ ὄναρ,[79] in which the great god communicates directly with his devotee despite its exalted grandeur.

HEIS AND MEGAS AS ACCLAIMING THE DIVINITY'S SUPERIORITY

In contrast to these examples, which use possibly monotheist language but always in an ambiance of a plural divine world, the combination of *heis* and *monos* does not seem to occur regularly in a monotheist milieu, even if the expression ὁ μέγας ἐν οὐρανῷ was familiar from the language of the Psalms.[80] When the Christian God was acclaimed as 'great', the expression is put in the mouth of pagans who have been converted by miraculous events, as at Gaza in Palestine: 'and all those who witnessed, stupefied, cried out (ἔκραξαν), "Great is the God of the Christians (Μέγας ὁ θεὸς τῶν Χριστιανῶν)!" "Great is the priest Porphyry" (Μέγας ὁ ἱερεὺς Πορφύριος)!"'[81] The acclamation of the epiphanic power of God is thus extended to his servant and protégé, as happens at Delphi, where a painted text on the wall of the *xystis* acclaimed the winner of a race after his protective goddess: Μεγάλη Ἄρτεμις Προθυραία. Μέγας ἅγιος Παλέμων.[82]

The juxtaposition of the two acclamations, 'One is . . .' and 'Great is . . .', is a precious indication of how we should interpret *heis theos*. At Sebaste in Samaria, the goddess Kore is acclaimed in a text which first glorifies her with a formula in the masculine: Εἷς θεός, ὁ παντῶν δεσπότης, 'One god, master of everything', and then with the personalised invocation: Μεγάλη Κόρη, ἡ ἀνείκητος, 'Great Kore, invincible'.[83] The emphasis placed on

[78] See Belayche (2005a), 40–4. In Carian Stratonicea, the Divine is addressed as θείῳ πολυμόρφῳ: Şahin (2002), 17 no. 38. When it is addressed coupled with another divine figure (Zeus, less often Theos, Hypsistos), it holds the second rank, but with glorifying epithets: *basilikos* (*I. Stratonikeia* nos. 509, 1115, 1116), *megas* (no. 1111).
[79] Ricl (1991–2), 47 no. 105 = *I.Ephesos* VII.1, 3100. An identical text at Thasos (*IG* XII.8, 613) contains no indication of the manner of communication. To be compared with a Jewish or Christian gem of the fifth century, Peterson (1926), 209 (Μέγα τὸ ὄνομα τοῦ μόνου θεοῦ).
[80] Cf. Michel (2001), no. 563.　　[81] Mark the Deacon, *Life of Porphyry* 31.2.
[82] Queyrel (2001), 357–8 no. 11.
[83] Flusser (1975); Di Segni (1994), 100. Di Segni imagines that the transition from masculine to feminine is evidence for two divinities: a masculine Sarapis-Helios, and a feminine Isis-Kore, but the adjective *aniketos* is attached to Kore and not to the supposed masculine god who might be

the universal domination of *Kyria Kore* is a reference to her pre-eminent but not exclusive position in the city where she had two cult places.[84] In Lydia the heavenly god Men is given pre-eminence in an acclamation which requires a sharper analysis before it can be assigned to the dossier of 'pagan monotheism':[85] Εἷς θεός ἐν οὐρανοῖς, μέγας Μὴν Οὐράνιος, μεγάλη δύναμις τοῦ ἀθανάτου θεοῦ.[86] The first expression, 'One god in heaven', was not exclusively reserved for this great god of non-Greek origin, also called *Tyrannos*, master of territory and dispenser of justice, whose devotees recalled the extreme forms of the power that they experienced from him.[87] Apollo at Delphi was also exalted as εἷς θεός ἐν οὐρανῶι.[88] The Lydian acclamation defines Men explicitly as a god of the cosmic world, as he might be experienced by men, comparable to those whom the proconsul who judged Pionius at Smyrna called 'the gods and the heaven, and the gods who are in heaven'.[89] Thus a pair of dedicants could offer a prayer (*eulogia*) to Men and celebrate in a prayer rhetorically constructed as a litany his great holiness, μέγα σοι τὸ ὅσιον, his great justice, μέγα σοι τὸ δίκαιον, and his great powers of vengeance, μεγάλαι (αἱ) σαὶ νεμέσεις, while also paying homage to the twelve gods who probably shared his local sanctuary, μέγα σοι τὸ δωδεκάθεον τὸ παρὰ σοὶ κατεκτισμένον.[90] In this *eulogia* Men was experienced as an exceptional power, mighty and celestial, within the superior world. In other circumstances and by other devotees, such universal mastery was attributed to other divinities, as befitted the nature of polytheism, whose structure, as G. Dumézil has demonstrated, could be given various polarisations according to place and occasion. Nemesis, for example, took the role of *kosmokrator* in an acclamation from Rome: Μεγάλη Νέμεσις ἡ βασιλεύουσα τοῦ κόσ(μου).[91] In the Lydian document cited above, cosmic Men is acclaimed as *heis theos*. This contrasts with the speculative tradition, which, like the monotheistic hermeneutic, reserves this qualification for the ineffable and transcendent god, referred to as 'the immortal god' in the acclamation. Heavenly Men is hailed as one of his

concealed in the first part of the acclamation (for another feminine figure, Neotera, described as *aniketos* on a gem from Beirut see Bonner and Nock (1948)). The mix of genres occurs also on an entaglio in the Louvre showing Hecate and inscribed εἷς θεὸς ὕψιστος: Delaporte (1923), 219 no. A 1270.

84 Crowfoot, Crowfoot and Kenyon (1954), 37 no. 14 and 36 no. 9; Belayche (2001), 212–15.
85 See Mitchell (1999), 101.   86 *CMRDM* I, 83; *TAM* v.1, 75.
87 See Herrmann (1978) and Belayche (2005c); and the so-called confession steles: Petzl (1994).
88 Cf. Queyrel (2001), 350 no. 5 and 364 no. 14; also Queyrel (1992) for a study of the acclamations (with earlier bibliography).
89 *Martyrium Pionii* 19.10.   90 Malay (2003) (*SEG* 53 (2003), 1344).   91 *CIL* vi, 532.

powers, albeit a unique one.[92] So far as one can decide for each individual testimony, according to the starkly hierarchical representation of the divine world which is one of its main features in the imperial period, the *heis theos* of ritual documents is not similar to the transcendent first principle, a philosophical concept that might be labelled monotheistic in theoretical theology.[93]

HEIS THEOS AND HEIS ZEUS SARAPIS

The commonest and earliest acclamatory formula is *Heis Zeus Sarapis* (or *Serapis*).[94] This short acclamation proclaims the identity of two great gods who belong to different cultural traditions: 'Zeus and Sarapis are only one.'[95] When the acclamatory mode demonstrates both their places in the divine architecture, it defines the relationship between the gods. The formula derives, as has been seen, from the tradition of glorifying the gods in Ptolemaic Egypt and, more broadly, from social and political practices in the Hellenistic kingdoms.[96] We read the formula engraved on a little aniconic bronze medallion of the first century AD, which was discovered near Jerusalem, where it reinforces the old and more typical elogium of the god's greatness and readiness to listen: Εἷς Ζεὺς | Σαράπις | μέγας ὁ | ἐπήκοος | Σαράπις ('One is Zeus-Sarapis, great is Sarapis who listens to prayers').[97]

If one compares the formulae used during the triumphal entry of Vespasian into Alexandria, to which I shall return shortly, it appears quite possible that this medallion, found out of context, belonged to a soldier travelling from the city.[98] According to Pliny these amulets or protective objects, sometimes set with jewels, became fashionable at precisely this period,[99] and were ideal mountings for this sort of slogan. Accordingly

---

[92] Cf. a gem of the fourth century AD, engraved with depictions of the animals that usually accompany Harpocrates, inscribed δύναμις μέγας [sic] (θεοῦ ?): Michel (2001), no. 484.

[93] See e.g. Suarez de la Torre (2003).

[94] Peterson (1926), 227–40. Cf. Richter (1956), no. 253, dated to the first or second century AD on palaeographical grounds, and Philipp (1986), no. 55, possibly first century AD.

[95] For *heis* as an expression of identity see Numenius, *Fragments* 11.13–14 Des Places: 'and so the god who is second or third is in truth simply one', and an oracle cited by Julian, *Or.* 11, *Basileus Helios* 10, 136A, and Macrobius, *Sat.* 1.18.18: Εἷς Ζεύς, εἷς Ἀίδης, εἷς Ἥλιός ἐστι Σάραπις.

[96] The first attestation in Greek of the form '*heis* + a theonym' occurs on a Gurob papyrus of the third century BC and exalts Dionysus (*Heis Dionysos*): Brisson (1990), 2928–9 and Versnel (2000), 152–3.

[97] Di Segni (1994), no. 28; cf. Bricault (2005b). [98] See p. 160.

[99] Pliny, *HN* 33.12.41. Numerous examples date between the second and fourth centuries AD.

we find that the engraved text *Heis Zeus Sarapis* accompanies a representation of a solar Harpocrates, a divinity who belonged in the circle of the
acclaimed god.[100] In the religious practice documented by these examples
the superior powers who were acclaimed as 'great' or 'one' continued to be
accompanied by their peers.

Another type of document confirms that the formula *Heis Zeus Sarapis*
was not theologically exclusive. A ritual described in the great magical
papyrus of Paris shows how these ornaments may have been used and
illuminates the subtlety of the links between the divine figures:

> Ὀρκίζω γῆν καὶ οὐρανὸν καὶ
> φῶς καὶ σκότος καὶ τὸν πάντα
> κτίσαντα θεὸν μέγαν Σαρου-
> σιν σὲ τὸ παραστὼς ἀγαθὸν
> δαιμόνιον πάντα μοι τέ-
> λεσαι διὰ τῆς χρείας ταύτης
> τοῦς δακτυλίου τούτου ἢ οὗ ἐὰν
> τέλῃς. λέγε. Εἷς Ζεὺς Σάραπις.[101]

Two figures appear beside the structural elements of the cosmos, earth and
heaven, light and darkness: a great (*megas*) creator god, Sarousin, and the
god Zeus Sarapis, glorified in his unity at the closure of the ritual. An
acclamation for him would certainly have been inscribed on the ring that
was used. This figure, unique in his double appearance, is distinguished
from the supreme creator god. Acting within the cosmos, he is a benevolent
assisting figure, an *agathon Daimonion*, who is personally appealed to
(σέ, l. 1711), and whose glory is acclaimed by a ritualised formula, which
brings the ritual process to a successful completion. As on the so-called
gnostic gems, the supreme power is regularly accompanied by angelic or
archangelic associates, who can be divinities from the traditional pantheon.
They are not to be reduced to intermediaries with the task of covering the
distance between a unique god and his devotees, as in the Oinoanda oracle
or the heliac theology of the emperor Julian.[102] They possess their own
power in their level of cosmic reality.

---

[100] Sanzi (2002), 219 fig. 6; cf. also Spier (1992), no. 359, a gem showing Aphrodite Anadyomene, but
inscribed Ζεὺς Οὐρανοῦ.

[101] *PGM* IV, 1708–15; 'I conjure earth and heaven and light and darkness and the great god who created
all, SAROUSIN, you Agathon Daimonion the helper, to accomplish for me everything [done]
by the use of this ring. When you complete [the consecration], say, "the one Zeus is Sarapis"'
(translation M. Smith, *PGMTr*, 69).

[102] See, respectively, Mitchell (1999), 91, and Julian, *Oration to the Sun King* 16.157A, who positions
Helios as mediator, both co-ordinating agent and link between the *heis demiourgos* and the *polloi
demiourgikoi theoi*.

THE ACCLAMATION AS A TOOL OF GOVERNMENT:
DECISION AND DISTINCTION

Although it did not become a weapon of exclusivity and intolerance before the radicalisation of the religious conflicts of the fourth century AD, the acclamation of the grandeur of Artemis of Ephesus, recalled in Acts 19:34, properly embeds this tool in the practical equipment of government in competitive societies. The tradition of *ekboeseis, phonai* or *euphemiai*, and then of *acclamationes* or *succlamationes* in the Roman world, had become part of the scheme of socio-political communication since the Hellenistic period.[103] The use of acclamations by Christians in ecclesiastical assemblies, including the elections of bishops, and the proceedings of Church councils, and in hagiographic accounts follows this habit. The uttering of shouts was a form of decision-making in competitive civic or imperial society.[104] The shouts that hailed an individual acknowledged his virtues and thus legitimated his *time*;[105] the shouts that glorified a divinity put on show its manifest power and *dynamis*. The devotees spontaneously, or in response to a command, praised the god's *arete* or *aretai*, and disseminated them in enduring *eulogiai* by means of inscribed texts or reliefs.[106] In his contribution to this volume A. Chaniotis has documented the double acclamations of the victors at the Pythian games and their patron gods, Apollo and the Tyche of the Delphians, who were hailed as *megas/megale, megistos* and *heis theos* alongside other divinities during the imperial period.[107] Like today's applause meters, an acclamation objectivised the hierarchical ranking of contemporary society; it belonged pre-eminently to a world of relative positioning. It highlighted an individual in relation to others. It classified without rejecting anyone.[108] When supra-human personalities, and divinities all the more, were hailed, acclamations paid homage to, or prayed for, their power, as Ovid shows by drawing attention to the link between the

---

[103] Cf. Robert OMS VI, 454; *RE* I.I (1893), 147–50 s.v. *acclamatio* (J. Schmidt). See, in a law of Constantine, *Cod. Theod.* 1.16.6.

[104] Cf. Colin (1965) and Wiemer (2004).

[105] For agonistic acclamations see e.g. Nero returning from victory at the Pythian games (Cassius Dio 63.20.5) and Tertullian, *De spect.* 25.5; cf. Tod (1949), 110: Robert (1938), 108–11 and (1969), 275–6. Note the title *primus omnium* in Italian towns (Mrozek (1971)), and the titles (such as 'first') claimed by cities (Heller (2006)).

[106] Petzl (1994), 58–9 no. 50 (the god gives instructions for his *arete* to be inscribed) and Belayche (2006b) and (2008).

[107] Cf. Queyrel (2001), 356–7 no. 10 (Pythian Apollo, Tyche of the Delphians, Artemis, Hecate). Robert (1958), 128 made a pertinent note of 'the virtual equivalence of *heis* and *megas* (supreme, certainly not "unique god")'. Pleket (1981), 179 reflects that the social structure offered favourable terrain for this 'ideology of power'.

[108] See Tod (1949), 112: 'the Greeks of all periods were keenly interested in records'.

surname *Augustus* given to Octavian and the verb *augere* 'to increase'.[109] The appeal to provide increase was not confined to individuals, but could be addressed to institutions or communities through the acclamation of their divine protector, Tyche.[110] The regular procedure within Greek or Roman religious ritual was thus taken to an extreme. It began precisely by recognising the superior *time* of the divine being that was addressed, and this established the relationship between men and gods. In Roman public ritual, this was the function of the *praefatio*, which is so often represented on reliefs. The same interpretation can be deduced from reliefs that showed divinities holding a *phiale*.[111]

In the communication between gods and men as conceived in Greek and Roman polytheisms, the public acclamation of the gods, given permanent expression by inscriptions, is to be seen as an intensification of a form of homage, designed to salute an interlocutor on a different plane of existence. If we recall the prayers of gratitude which occur in Latin comedy in the second century BC and already exalted the glory of the gods in the manner of contemporary or imperial aretalogies, this was not new. But for late republican authors and advocates of Roman traditional religion, these excessive displays of piety were often classified as *superstitio* and shown on the theatrical stage as a matter for ridicule.[112]

An Egyptian papyrus of the first century AD, which has not, to my knowledge, previously been taken into consideration, provides an eloquent model for investigating the *heis theos* acclamation in more depth.[113] The surviving fragments of this tantalising document allow us to reconstruct the *adventus* of Vespasian into Alexandria at the beginning of AD 70. The *imperator* was returning victorious from the war in Judaea, illuminated by the halo of two predictions of his imperial destiny. In the hippodrome he was hailed with classic vows for his well-being and acclaimed as 'Master Caesar Vespasian, the one saviour and benefactor (εῖς σωτὴρ καὶ εὐεργέτης)', 'Master Augustus', the protégé or beloved most probably of Sarapis, 'son of Ammon' according to the Pharaonic conception, 'god (θεός) Caesar Vespasian'.[114] The acclamations *heis* and *soter*[115] were inspired by the

---

[109] Ovid, *Fasti* 1.611–13.   [110] See *SEG* 37 (1987), 1145 for a Syrian town, Aïnkania.

[111] Scheid (2005), 44–50 and Veyne (1990). In Lydia, a devotee was punished for not respecting the hierarchy of honours between gods and men: Petzl (1994), 73–6 no. 59 lines 22–3.

[112] Belayche (2006a), 22–3.

[113] Note, however, that Peterson (1926), 217 n. 4 had a sense that the formula *Heis Zeus Sarapis* could be dated to the period of Vespasian's visit to Egypt. Robert (1955), 61 cited the document only to support the idea that the origin of the acclamation was not religious.

[114] *Acta Alexandrinorum*, pp. 20–1 lines 11–20 Musurillo.

[115] See also the honorific decree cited by Chaniotis in his contribution to this volume, *IG* VII, 2712 line 55: εῖς φιλόπατρις καὶ εὐεργέτης. Flavius Josephus, *Autobiography* 244, was simply acclaimed as *euergetes* and *soter*.

qualities and forms of address of Sarapis, who had passed on his powers, including the working of miraculous cures.[116] This imperial acclamation is the first in a richly documented series for the emperors of the second and third centuries, principally designed to glorify their role as victors, and the privileged assistance that they received from the gods. The acclamations that saluted the emperor Julian in the middle of the fourth century[117] resumed the many themes that had been registered since Vespasian: Εἷς θεός. Νίκα Ἰουλιανέ, 'A single god! Be victorious, Julian!'[118]

This acclamation from Ascalon is unique in Palestine and generally related to the so-called 'pagan reaction', which led to martyrdoms at Ascalon and Gaza according to the Church historians.[119] The choice of the formula *heis theos* could then be read in the context of the religious struggle between the cult of the gods restored by Julian and the Christian God.[120] However, the acclamation is not isolated in the wider Near Eastern context during the period when Julian was wintering at Antioch before his Persian expedition. It can be set alongside a series of inscribed milestones with which the governor of Arabia, the orator Belaeus, marked out the route from Gerasa to Philadelphia.[121] The very fact that these acclamations, repeated in the form of slogans, had been inscribed beside a road which the emperor might have followed places us in the context of a triumphal entrance, of the acclamation of an imperial *adventus* which greeted the man whose supreme victory and virtues were thus acknowledged.[122] That is also the explanation for the slogan when it appeared on inscriptions and amulets for the gods.

It is unnecessary to illustrate further the universality of acclamations, which always occur in a context of victory and sovereign power in Graeco-Hellenistic civic society. The fact that this type of expression was adopted in Christian communities confirms this. The acclamation was sometimes an institutionalised way of taking decisions in the setting of assemblies and councils. On other occasions it was a form of public homage for

[116] See Michel (2001), no. 37, an amulet with the inscription: Νίκα ὁ Σέραπις τὸν φθόνον. Cf. Sfameni Gasparro (2006), 21–31.
[117] Peterson (1926), 143–4. [118] Avi Yonah (1944), 160–1 no. 1 = Di Segni (1994), 104 no. 31.
[119] Cf. Belayche (2001), 299–303.
[120] One might also imagine that this was the proposition of a Jew who recognised the providence of his own God in the emperor's person; for it dates to the time of Julian's stay in Antioch, in 362–3, from where the emperor informed the Jews by letter that he wished to see the Temple at Jerusalem rebuilt: 'I invest all my enthusiasm (μετὰ πάσης προθυμίας) in restoring the temple of the Highest God (τὸν ναὸν τοῦ Ὑψίστου Θεοῦ)': Julian, *Ep. et leg.* no. 134 Bidez/Cumont. Compare Stemberger (1987), 160–74.
[121] Peterson (1926), 270–3; Welles (1938), nos. 345–8.
[122] Cf. Peterson (1926), 152–63 ('Die Νίκα-Akklamation').

exceptional figures, notably the emperor and of course the gods, a way
of marking out someone from the normality of a group and setting him
above competition, and thus signifying that he was beyond comparison,
'unique', *heis*. In a broader sense it was a tool employed in situations of
rivalry or conflict, and thus, to use the language of sociology, became
a way of demonstrating public opinion. Consequently it is by nature a
method of public expression in cases of real or potential comparison.
In this perspective, the exemplary episode of the acclamation of Artemis
by the silversmiths of Ephesus, when Paul decried the sanctity of their
offerings, simply expressed the support of the Ephesians for their great
civic goddess. It is readily evident from the local religious epigraphy that
such acclamations did not imply a simplified or unified representation of
their divine world. On the other hand, the fact that *ekboesis* was a tool
of competition meant that it could also be used as a tool of exclusion
in the fourth century AD, when the positions of the opposed camps had
been radicalised. Although acclamations of a divine power as *heis* were
probably derived from experience of a divinity, or preserved the memory
of an epiphany, they do not demonstrate an *enthousiasmos* created by the
presence of the god, as E. Peterson envisaged,[123] at least in the etymological
sense of the word. This interpretation seems to be excessively tinged by the
Christian notion that God acts within the world through the Spirit that
houses figures who are regarded as sanctified.[124]

HEIS THEOS AND 'PAGAN MONOTHEISM'

With respect to the particular relationship which the devotee established
with the god, it seems to me that it makes no major difference whether a
divinity is acclaimed as great (*megas, megale*), or as unique (*heis*).[125] *Heis*
is a term of intensification, as we saw at Alexandria where Vespasian was
heis, soter, euergetes, theos, without detracting in any way from the saving
quality of Sarapis, whose power he, like the Pharaohs, shares. Similarly, for
Aelius Aristides, calling Asclepius *heis* was a way of stating his pre-eminent
position in the pantheon: 'I would cry out: "One only!"', wishing to denote

---

[123] Peterson (1926), 145. No more did miracles indicate *enthousiasmos* in the aretalogies, even when
there is a claim to have experienced an epiphany; cf. the reactions of astonishment and terror, but
not of religious possession, according to the traditional scheme of the effects of epiphanies, that
are recorded in the aretalogy of Sarapeion A at Delos, *RICIS* I, 202/0101.

[124] For the accent placed on the prophetic spirit see Waldner (2007).

[125] Cf. Henig and McGregor (2004) no. 13.29: a gem inscribed *Megas Sarapis* instead of the usual *Heis
Zeus Sarapis*.

the god'.[126] His explanation also recalls the fact that the use of the noun *theos* instead of the individual name of the god is not in itself a sign of the depersonalisation of the superior powers, leading to the unity of the idea of god. It was not rare for a god simply to be designated by reference to his superior status when the context sufficed to identify him.[127] But it is true that writers in the Christian tradition took advantage of these attestations to apply the template of a monotheistic reading to them. Minucius Felix observed: 'I hear the common voice of men speaking; when they extend their hands towards heaven, they say only "God!" or "God is great", "God speaks the truth", and "if God allows it".'[128]

It also appears to make no further natural difference whether one exalts *heis theos* or *heis* combined with the god's name, Sarapis, Men, Apollo, Kore etc. Divinities who were called upon by impersonal forms of address that were inspired by their qualities were perfectly personalised in the conception of their devotees. The most exemplary case in my opinion, albeit one that remains a subject for debate,[129] is that of Theos Hypsistos, which is neither always as enigmatic as it may appear, nor always indicative of a break in the representation of the divine world, as the term itself might suggest. Theos Hypsistos was used to qualify personalised beings such as the god Men at Andeda,[130] or Zeus Megistos at Iconium, who is known as an agrarian deity according to his epiclesis *epikarpios* and his figuration,[131] or the Zeus at Tavium attested by Strabo, who received a dedication as Theos Hypsistos from a local trader from Ancyra.[132] This observation holds true in official contexts as well. An honorific inscription set up at Miletus for a high-ranking Roman citizen, Ulpius Carpus, prophet of Apollo at Didyma, calls the god 'very holy god *hypsistos* saviour'.[133] The origin of the

---

[126] Aelius Aristides, *Sacred Tales* 4.50. Compare a stele of Megalopolis in Arcadia which publishes the rules of entry to the sanctuary of Isis, Sarapis and Anubis, and whose text begins with an acclamatory address: Στάλα Ἴσιος Σαράπιος. Θεός. Τύχα ἀγαθά: *SEG* 28 (1978), 421.

[127] See, for example, from Nemea in the Peloponnese, an offering table inscribed ΤΩΙ ΘΕΩΙ which designated the local Zeus (*c.* 300 BC), Museum inv. ST 783; compare also *IG* xiv, 966 at Epidaurus: ηὐχαρίστησεν δημοσίᾳ τῷ θεῷ.

[128] Minucius Felix, *Octavius* 18.11. According to Acts 17:23 this was already the interpretation of Paul, expressed in his speech on the Areopagus, evoking an altar dedicated 'to the unknown god', the equivalent of the expression *sive deus, sive dea* found in Roman practice.

[129] See above, n. 11 and Mitchell, in this volume.   [130] *CMRDM* I, 129.

[131] *MAMA* VIII, 298. Compare Mitchell (1993), 23. Four Phrygian dedications to Theos Hypsistos carry ears of corn: *MAMA* v, 186 and 211, and x, 261; and *SEG* 40 (1990), 1227.

[132] *RECAM* II, 317–18 no. 418; cf. Strabo 12.5.2. Nothing (chronology, onomastics, epigraphic formula) points towards an identification with the Jewish God honoured near Ancyra, *RECAM* II, 177–8 no. 209b.

[133] *OGI* II, 755 and 756. The same person also worships Sarapis, cf. Robert (1968), 594 and Belayche (2005b), 441.

text is all the more noteworthy because Didyma (admittedly less explicitly than Claros) was one of the sanctuaries that produced 'theological
oracles'. There is also abundant evidence that these divinities, exalted in
an impersonal fashion, belonged to a plural pantheon.[134] It will suffice to
cite the Lycian text that pays homage to a traditional pair of magisterial
deities, Theos Hypsistos and a Meter Oreia, and 'to all the gods and all the
goddesses'.[135]

In the personalised polyonymous formulae, which are well attested
throughout the imperial period,[136] the acclamation of various divine figures (generally Zeus Sarapis, but also Helios, Asclepius, Kore and others)
as *heis* proclaims an assimilation of dominant or supervisory figures, whose
theonyms vary. A model for this process can be found in the aretalogies
for Isis, who is celebrated with the names of the great female divinities
of different peoples. Isidore's hymn to Isis at Medinet-Madi supplied the
Egyptian equivalent of the Greek *heis*. After rolling out the litany of names
of the goddess in all the nations, the devotee continues: 'but the Egyp-
tians call you *Thiouis* (the unique), because you, and you alone are all the
goddesses that the peoples name by other names'.[137]

Since acclamations were one of the means of bringing the gods into
communication with societies, they were always concerned with gods as
objects of religious experience, a presence within the world, and not with
a god set apart beyond the cosmos, inhabiting the sphere of the heavenly
bodies, like the unique and transcendent principle of late antique philosophical speculation.[138] As social expressions, the documents that have
been examined so far do not throw light on the meaning of the 'unique
entirety' (ἓν τὸ πᾶν), evoked in the theological exposition of Praetextatus,
as recorded by Macrobius. The 'unique' divine power might embrace fields
of competence that were previously specialised,[139] while it still continued
to be connected with the multiplicity of the great gods. A hymn preserved
in a magical papyrus of the fourth–fifth century, which set out a ritual of

---

[134] See Belayche (2005a).
[135] *TAM* II.2, 737. The editor has restored a third god (καὶ Κελε[ναίῳ], but S. Mitchell suggests, more
appropriately, κα(τὰ) κέλε[υσιν]. See Mitchell, in this volume p. 182.
[136] Avienus, when asking of Praetextatus 'the reason for such a great diversity among the names given
to a single divine figure' (Macrobius, *Sat.* 1.17.1) echoes, at a distance of four centuries, Valerius
Soranus, who celebrated *Iuppiter* as *omnipotens... deus unus et omnes* (cited at Augustine, *De civ.
D.* 7.9).
[137] Vanderlip (1972) I, 23–4.
[138] Compare the god of the Oinoanda oracle, ἐν πύρι ναίων: Mitchell (1999), 86 line 2.
[139] Even in these cases, the first competence continued to be the dominant one, as is shown by the
gems which call on the healing power of Sarapis: see above, nn. 46 and 57, and the expression
'One is Zeus Sarapis, may he be propitious for my sleeping', found on entaglios of Pannonia and
Moesia (I thank R. Veymiers for showing me these documents to me).

lychnomancy during which the Delphic Apollo is invoked,[140] shows how the ontological qualities of the transcendent god participate in a ritual process peculiar for the way in which it worked to activate the manifestation of a divine power. In this ritual context, the search for power that is beyond other powers, i.e. perfect effectiveness, operates by juxtaposing various representations of the divine world. Geography, mythography and a pantheon in the Olympian tradition appear alongside figures of power belonging to the hermetic-magical tradition, such as Abrasax and Iaô, and an abstract theology represented by an uncreated Nature. Because we are at the level of ritual the world of these powers was densely populated. The accumulation of the divine figures guaranteed that the infinite world had been circumscribed, as though the idea of the fullness of the Universe could only be experienced through the sum of its constituent parts. If this reading of the evidence is right, it can be matched to the conception of a pluralistic divine world, which was analytical in structure and based on the sum of the fields of competence that were assumed by individual divine figures, even when one of them had been placed at their forefront.

Even the 'theological oracles', first given this name by A. D. Nock,[141] display this sort of tension between the one inexpressible and transcendent god, conceived by spiritualistic speculation, and the multitude of gods that function within the cosmos and are the recipients of the acclamations. Whatever transcendent definition may have been given to an uncreated God who resides beyond the cosmos, this did not abolish belief in the gods who operated on, and in, the world. They are represented according to ancestral tradition, as much in the names that they bear (Horus, Osiris,[142] Apollo, Zeus[143]) as in their genealogical identity (e.g. Apollo is the son of Zeus). The homage which they received, for example the acclamation of their exceptional personalities, drew on the repertoire of social communication. At least these forms of rhetorical homage throw some light on their ontology and theology, given the interaction between religion and philosophy which was characteristic of the Second Sophistic.

CONCLUSION

This examination of the acclamations *heis theos* confirms the relevance and value of an approach which fuses anthropological and social enquiry in

---

[140] *PGM* I, 296–327.   [141] Nock (1928).

[142] His name is inscribed *heis* on a gem within a serpent *ouroboros*, and qualified by a traditional Egyptian epithet (Onophris): Michel (2001), no. 334; cf. also no. 338, Chnoubis.

[143] Compare Heraclitus frg. B 32: ἓν τὸ σοφοῦ μοῦνον λέγεσθαι οὐκ ἐθέλει καὶ ἐθέλει Ζηνὸς ὄνομα ('the unique principle, the principle of wisdom, does not wish and wishes to be called by the name of Zeus').

166   NICOLE BELAYCHE

the study of religious questions. The evidence can be correlated with the competitive spirit which governed social relations in the Roman Empire, whether it concerned the central power, members of the elites, associations, the cities, or other entities. On these different levels, the *agon* was not a symbol of exclusion, or a way of negating the competitors, except for those who challenged the emperors. The monarchic model of divine *basileia* did not annul plurality in the religious sphere. The comparison was developed at length by Apuleius: '[the supreme god] occupies an outstanding and superior position (*praestantem ac sublimem sedem tenere*); in the *elogia* of the poets he receives as additional names the titles which designate consuls and kings, and he has a consecrated throne on the highest citadels of heaven (*in arduis arcibus habere solium consecratum*)'.[144] The term *heis theos*, 'alone/unique', signifies that the divinity was alone of its type, unmatched (*praestans* in Apuleius' words), capable of achieving the impossible,[145] but not one god as such. It is the equivalent of a relative superlative form, like *hypsistos*, designed to affirm the unequalled characteristics of the god celebrated. These acclamations, which are the intensified form of an act of thanksgiving, accompany other ritual forms of exaltation, for example the use of epithets or theonyms of glorification and praise. This redesigning of the architecture of the divine world does not require the *heis theos* to be exclusive; on the contrary, the exaltation of a divinity takes on greater significance in a pluralistic context. We here encounter an intrinsic quality of polytheism, which was pluralist and capable of organising the pantheon according to hierarchies that varied according to the contexts.

[144] Apuleius, *De mundo* 25 [343]. See also 346ff., where Apuleius takes as his example the centralised administrative structure of the Persian kingdom. For this monarchic scheme see also Firmicus Maternus, *Mathesis* 5, *praef.* These passages all come from speculative philosophical works.
[145] Petzl (1994), 140 no. 122 lines 4–5: ἐξ ἀδυνάτων δύνατα πυεῖ (*sic*).

CHAPTER 9

Further thoughts on the cult of Theos Hypsistos

Stephen Mitchell

PRELIMINARY OBSERVATIONS

My own earlier study of the cult of Theos Hypsistos, published in Athanas-siadi and Frede (1999), was an attempt to ascertain whether any form of monotheistic worship could be identified apart from Judaism and Chris-tianity in the Roman and late Roman worlds. The material central to the analysis was the corpus of almost 300 inscriptions, mostly votive dedica-tions, addressed to Theos Hypsistos (180 texts), Zeus Hypsistos (88 texts), or simply Hypsistos (24 texts), dated between the second century BC and the early fourth century AD, which had been identified at find-spots across the east Mediterranean basin, around the Black Sea, in Egypt and in the Near East. Since that study was written, evidence has continued to accrue. By my reckoning, which is certainly not exhaustive, new discoveries have increased the figures for the three groups to 220, 121 and 34 texts respectively, a total of 375. I present a catalogue of these additional texts, geographically organised, as an appendix to this paper, and will cite them as appropriate by the numbers **A1** etc., retaining the simple numerals **1** etc. for the items listed in my earlier study.[1] The majority of the new discoveries fit within the pattern of those that were previously known, although some of this evidence prompts further substantial analysis. More important than these finds have been the responses of other scholars, which have called not only the main hypothesis but also my basic approach into question.

The main object of this paper is to address the arguments of these critics and to assess the consequences for the conclusions that I reached in 1999. Inevitably it will be necessary to deal with the various points that have been made *ad hominem* and in some detail, but it is helpful to spell out the central question of method. My own approach, deliberately adopted, was

---

[1] Cf. Belayche (2005a), 35 n. 7: 'près de 360 attestations'; Belayche (2005b), 427 n. 2: 'près de 375 attestations, soit c. 75 de plus que la liste etablie par S. Mitchell'. My own updated count omits a number of clearly Christian attestations in inscriptions of the fifth and sixth centuries AD.

to assemble the epigraphic evidence in its entirety and treat it as a whole. The aim was to establish whether the documentation for the worship of Theos and Zeus Hypsistos could be interpreted as part of an overall pattern that was cogent and historically convincing. Part of the justification for this approach was the fact that four Greek Christian authors of the fourth and fifth centuries (Epiphanius, Gregory of Nazianzus, Gregory of Nyssa and Cyril of Alexandria) more or less explicitly identified the worshippers of a Highest God as a coherent group of quasi-monotheist worshippers, whose religious ideas were acknowledged to contain a mixture of pagan Greek and Jewish or judaising elements.[2]

Criticism of my earlier approach has focused on the argument that this attempt to lump together the evidence simply does not take into account a fundamental fact of Graeco-Roman pagan religion, that it was multifarious, polytheistic and localised. 'Es hat nicht einen einheitlichen Kult für einen bestimmten Gott gegeben, sondern unter dem Namen Theos Hypsistos bzw. Hypsistos wurden verschiedene Gottheiten verehrt.'[3] 'Ancient religion always allowed for local diversity, and never more than in the kaleidoscope of cults of the Highest God.'[4] 'Dans la perspective méthodologique qui guide nos travaux et par suite de l'impossibilité de développer l'ensemble d'un dossier complexe, j'ai retenu quelques aspects qui démontrent que les sens multiples de cette epiclèse [*hypsistos*] fragilisent au fond toute interprétation qui chercherait à être générale et gommerait par là même la diversité des attitudes religieuses que recouvrait précisément le vocable et qui caractérisait le monde romain.'[5]

As a first response, there is an obvious point to be made. The great gods of the Greek Olympian pantheon, Zeus, Apollo, Artemis, Dionysus and the rest, were worshipped under these names throughout and beyond the Mediterranean world during the whole of classical antiquity. There were innumerable diverse local cults for all of these gods, but they had identifiable unified divine personalities, acknowledged or rather moulded by the beliefs of worshippers in antiquity, as they are recognised today by modern scholars. If this were not the case, any attempt to treat them as the object of synthetic discussion would be condemned from the start to incoherence. My approach was to treat Hypsistos in exactly this sense. The assumption and hypothesis built into this approach are that Hypsistos worshippers retained a common underlying concept of a specific divine personality behind this appellation, even if their god, by contrast with

---

[2] Mitchell (1999), 92–7. Here, as in many other aspects, I was anticipated and influenced by the classic paper of Schürer (1897).
[3] Stein (2001), 124.   [4] Bowersock (2002), 362.   [5] Belayche (2005b), 428.

the Olympians, was remote, abstracted and usually nameless. Since the enquiry is about religious beliefs, it cannot be settled by crude empirical data. The god or gods in question do not verifiably exist in a way that can be demonstrated by adducing decisive material evidence or deduced by logical argument for the divinity's existence, singular or multifarious. For the historian, divinity exists only as a construct of its worshippers, and therefore can only be inferred from reconstructing the historical behaviour of those worshippers, and the propositions they make about their god or gods. Is it then convincing historically to interpret the evidence for the worship of Hypsistos as a conceptual unity, in the same way as the worship of Apollo or Dionysus is so understood, or is *hypsistos* merely a generic adjective applicable to many forms of divinity, which had nothing in common beyond sharing this common descriptor?

There is a further preliminary point. Classical polytheism by its nature generated an uncountable variety of gods and cults, each specific to a given community, or even, in extreme cases, to the imagination of individual worshippers. This diversity is especially marked in the endless variation of deities and cults to be found in the *polis* communities of the Greek world, each tailored to the locality where it occurred. However, the Greek and Roman worlds were also united by common religious ideas, which were part of their shared cultures. More specifically than this, the Roman Empire created a framework which promoted the wide and effective diffusion of religious ideas. We see this, most obviously, in the spread of Christianity in the early centuries, in Diaspora Judaism, or in the dissemination of eastern cults such as that of Jupiter Dolichenus or Mithras to the western parts of the Roman world.[6] Moreover, we can readily identify certain conditions that led to the spread of these religious ideas, even if we are not always able to assess their precise impact in individual cases: common language use (Latin and Greek), abetted by increasing literacy; communication by letters; peaceful and relatively secure conditions of travel by land and sea; individual movement through the Empire for private or official reasons; and the dissemination of documents of religious authority, especially oracles.[7] Thus new extraneous forms of religious activity became increasingly visible alongside the cults of any given locality or region. We would reasonably expect the local and ecumenical aspects of religious belief and behaviour to have influenced one another. Local cults may have taken new forms in response to influences from outside, and the

---

[6] See Anna Collar, 'Networks and religious innovation in the Roman Empire' (Exeter PhD 2008), a thesis written as part of the Exeter Pagan Monotheism project, funded by the AHRC.
[7] See, provisionally, Mitchell (2008).

'international' cults will have taken on local character as they spread to new locations. This was especially true between the first and fourth centuries AD, when the conditions of Roman rule enormously facilitated communication, but before the Christian-Roman state emerged to restrict and control forms of religious activity. W. Wischmeyer, in a recent discussion of Theos Hypsistos, has made similar observations in reference to the language of cult, which developed common forms of expression in late antiquity, and demonstrated, among other things, a tendency to present deities in an anonymous form or with an abstract character.[8] It is neither intrinsically impossible nor implausible that a common cult of Theos Hypsistos should have emerged across a large swathe of the eastern Roman Empire between the second and fourth centuries AD, especially as this is precisely the period which saw a parallel development in both Christianity and Judaism.

ZEUS HYPSISTOS

The largest body of additions to the Hypsistos corpus in recent years has come from archaeological and epigraphic discoveries relating to the worship of Zeus Hypsistos in northern Greece, especially Macedonia (**A8–10** Thessaly, **A11–29** Macedonia). Two sanctuaries of the god have been convincingly located, outside the city walls of Beroia,[9] and at Dion.[10] None of these finds suggests that the worship of Zeus Hypsistos differed significantly from that of other Greek Olympian cults. Visually explicit votive monuments included statues or figured reliefs of the god (**A13, A14, A24**). Fourteen reliefs of eagles were excavated at Dion, and the eagle is represented widely elsewhere in connection with the cult (**A15, A18, A19, A22, A26**). The cities of Western Macedonia were adjacent to Mount Olympus, mythical home of the Olympian pantheon, and this surely explains the presence of several sanctuaries of Zeus Hypsistos in them. The choice of the adjective *hypsistos* may in this context have been influenced by worshippers' notions about the physical location of the home of the gods, on the highest summit of their region, but here, as elsewhere, the connotations of loftiness should generally be understood in an abstract, rather than a literal, sense.[11] This large and growing Macedonian group of

[8] Wischmeyer (2005), 156, who discusses the 'Potentialisierung regionaler Kulte und ihrer Gottheiten durch "Anonymisierung" und "Abstraktion in einer ökumenischen Koine der religiosen Sprache"'.
[9] Chrysostomou (1996) collects all the testimonia for Zeus Hypsistos in Macedonia and discusses the iconography of Zeus Hypsistos on p. 61; see also Chrysostomou (1991). There are updated references to the epigraphic literature in the commentaries of Gounaropoulou and Hatzopoulos (1998), nos. 25–8.
[10] Pandermalis (2005).   [11] Belayche (2005a), 44–7.

examples has a special place in the Hypsistos corpus. In my previous study I attempted to bring them within the same interpretative framework as the rest of the documentation, but it is prudent for the moment to set them aside.[12] Whether or not they can be interpreted as evidence for a cult that favoured the exaltation of one god at the expense of others (if not to the point of 'monotheism'), they must be distinguished in very important ways from the Theos Hypsistos material. In particular, this god was certainly neither aniconic nor anonymous. He was also never, in Macedonia or Thessaly, addressed as Theos Hypsistos.[13]

Other instances of the worship of Zeus Hypsistos are not so clearly separable from the rest of the evidence. In many sanctuaries where Theos Hypsistos was worshipped, the god might also sometimes be called Zeus: at Athens, Nicomedia, Stratonicea, Seleucia on the Calycadnus, and perhaps at Thessalonica (**A28**) and Philippopolis (**A33**).[14] Moreover, the eagle was a common symbol associated with Theos Hypsistos throughout the whole area where the cult had spread. Here it is still necessary to keep both forms of worship in view.

WHICH GODS WERE WORSHIPPED AS *HYPSISTOS*?

My arguments for treating the Hypsistos cults as a unity depend in part on the observation that the adjective was very rarely applied to gods other than Theos and Zeus. Apart from Pausanias, who reported the presence of cults of Zeus Hypsistos at Corinth, Olympia and Thebes,[15] it is very striking that Greek writers of the imperial period, who wrote extensively on religious subjects, never used the term in relation to Greek cult.[16] This suggests strongly that *hypsistos* was not a common or conventional adjective of exaltation, like *megas, megistos*, as is suggested by A. Chaniotis in his contribution to this volume. I propose that it is a term with a stricter theological connotation. N. Belayche has contested this, but I am not swayed by the examples or arguments that have been adduced.[17] *Hypsistos*

---

[12] Apart from the name, the one important common feature linking Macedonian Zeus Hypsistos and Theos Hypsistos was the office of *archisynagogos* at Pydna, which is mildly suggestive of a link to Diaspora Judaism, but not probative; Mitchell (1999), 100–1 with nn. 40–1.

[13] Mitchell (1999), 101.   [14] Mitchell (1999), 99.

[15] Pausanias 2.28, 5.15.5, and 9.8.5. These conform with the epigraphic evidence for Zeus Hypsistos in mainland Greece.

[16] Observed by Bowersock (2002), 355–6: absent from Strabo, Dio Chrysostom, Plutarch, Chariton, Aelius Aristides, Achilles Tatius, Artemidorus, Lucian, Maximus of Tyre, Athenaeus, Galen, Plotinus, Himerius, Libanius and Proclus.

[17] Belayche (2005a), 40: 'Les dédicaces honorant une divinité comme *hypsistos* en même temps que d'autres compagnons divins ne sont pas rares. Les trente attestations des divinités personnalisées

occurs, extremely rarely, as a term of exaltation, in the hellenised Egyptian cults of Sarapis and Isis, which are attested throughout the Empire by a huge documentation.[18] Sarapis was called *hypsistos* at an unusual rock sanctuary of Panoias in north Portugal (Hispania Citerior) on one of a group of rock cut inscriptions set up by a Roman official, possibly of Pamphylian origin, in the third century AD.[19] The term also occurs in the aretalogical hymns for his consort Isis. Verses from the Serapeum at Cyrene proclaim ἐγὼ τύραννος Εἶσις αἰῶνος μόνη | πόντου τε καὶ γῆς τέρμονάς τ᾽ἐπιβλέπω | καὶ σκηπτρ᾽ἔχουσα καὶ μί᾽οὖσ᾽ἐπιβλέπω. | καλοῦσι δή με πάντες ὑψίστην θεόν,[20] and the adjective occurs in a passage of the third-century BC verse hymn from the island of Andros.[21] In Egypt itself she is equated with Δηοῖ ὑψίστη, apparently an equation of Isis with Cybele, in the inscribed aretalogy from Medinet-Madi.[22] This appears to be the sum of the evidence. Amid the prolific documentary and literary attestations of the cults of the Egyptian gods, these instances are rare and isolated. Belayche herself rightly concedes the exceptional character of 'les hymnes isiaques, dont on sait combien ils sont exemplaires d'une recomposition hénothéiste du panthéon à l'époque impériale'.[23] It seems to me more significant that Sarapis, who was equated explicitly with virtually all the great gods of the increasingly cosmopolitan pantheon under the Roman

---

(Zeus, Cybele, Sérapis, Mithra) n'ont rien d'originale dans un système polythéiste.' This claim is highly misleading. The only reference to Cybele as *hypsiste* is as the Δηοῖ ὑψίστη of the Egyptian Isis aretalogies. There is one outlying example for Sarapis (see below, n. 19), and the relevant text relating to Mithras shows him in a complex form of syncretism with Zeus and other deities (**A71**). All the other examples relate to Zeus Hypsistos, in the company of another divinity.

[18] See especially Bricault (2005a) (*RICIS*) and Merkelbach (2001).
[19] *RICIS* II, 602/0501; see Alföldy (1997), who reads the text as ὑψίστῳ Σεράπιδι σὺν γάστρᾳ καὶ μυστορίοις G. C. Calp. *Rufinus v(ir) c(larissimus)*. The dedicator, according to Alföldy, may have been a Roman official called C. C(ornelius) or C(aecilius) Calp(urnius) Rufinus originating from Perge or Attaleia in Pamphylia. It would be better to expand Calp. to the cognominal form Calpurnianus. Alföldy (1997), 231 n. 132 notes the rarity of the term *hypsistos* and cites this as the only example for Sarapis apart from an unpublished inscription from Lepcis Magna. In fact this unpublished text is presumably the inscription for Zeus Hypsistos found in front of the Serapeum at Lepcis (**A38**). Bricault observes that the inscription from Portugal is the only text for Sarapis outside Egypt calling him *hypsistos*, but also quotes no Egyptian examples.
[20] 'I am the tyrant Isis, alone of eternity, and I look out over the boundaries of the sea and the land, and holding sceptres, being unique I look out. Everyone indeed calls me the Highest Goddess': *RICIS* II, 701/0103.
[21] Peek (1930) = *IG* XII.5, 739.7–8.
[22] *SEG* 8 548.3, 550.1, 551.4; Bernand (1969), 631–5 no. 175.1.1; III.1, v.4. Belayche (2005a), 38 n. 24 also cites *SEG* 38 (1988), 748, a verse dedication recorded at Chersonesus on the north shore of the Black Sea, restored by L. Moretti as follows: τὰν σεμν[άν, ὑψίσταν] | τοῖς μὲν [ἐπὶ χθο]|νὶ θνατο[ῖς] | στᾶσεν Ἀλέξ[ανδρος] | τὰν ἱερὰν [δ᾽ Εἶσιν. Both the name of the goddess and her epithet are supplied by the editor, the latter *contra metrum*.
[23] Belayche (2005a), 39.

Empire, including Zeus, Helios, Mithras, Asclepius, Aion and even Yahwe, was never thus matched with Theos Hypsistos.[24]

A Hellenistic poet, Arion of Methymna, apostrophised Poseidon as ὕψιστε θεῶν.[25] About half a millennium later, the Phrygian divinity Attis was also called *hypsistos* in the Greek verses which preface the dedication of a taurobolium to Mithras by a Roman senator during the final flourish of paganism in the governing class at Rome around AD 370. The verses, hyperexalted in tone and developing the religious–philosophical ideas of the later fourth century, also refer to Attis as συνεχὼν τὸ πᾶν, embracing the universal.[26] A Roman relief of the second century AD depicts an oriental goddess on a lion, and carries the unambiguous inscription θεᾷ ὑψίστη Ἀστάρτῃ. This is the only clear example in a straightforward dedication of the phenomenon that Belayche supposes to be widespread.[27] We may discount the reference to Apollo as Theos Hypsistos on a text from the Phrygian sanctuary of Apollo Lairbenos, as it is based on a flimsy restoration.[28] There remains a curious Greek text from Cyrene reading πατρὶ | θεῶι | Σαμοθρᾳκι | ἀθανάτωι | ὑψίσ[τωι], which may best be interpreted as an eccentric and personalised dedication to the anonymous Theos Hypsistos (**A72**).[29]

These appear to be all the attestations of *hypsistos* applied to named gods other than Zeus. Belayche claims that 'à peu près partout, un grand dieu a été exalté localement comme ὕψιστος, donc placé en première place par ses fidèles'. But her other examples all depend on the assumption that in a given context the presence of Theos Hypsistos (or the two instances from the Lydian sanctuary at Collyda for Thea Hypsiste) in fact conceals, or represents, a specific local god, known by another name. Thus for Belayche Theos Hypsistos at Tavium (**204**), Aezani (**208–12**) and Iconium (**236**) was simply a term to designate respectively the famous Zeus of Tavium, whose cult was described by Strabo,[30] the even more prominent Zeus worshipped at Aezani, in the great temple which still dominates the

---

[24] Merkelbach (2001), 77–9; and see the exhaustive documentation of the divine composita which are such a feature of the Isis and Sarapis cults under the Empire in the indexes of *RICIS*.

[25] *PMG* 939 Page.

[26] *IGUR* I, 129; *CIL* VI, 50: μήτερι τῇ πάντων Ῥείῃ [. . . .] τε γενέθλῳ | Ἄττι τ' ὑψίστῳ καὶ συ[νέχο]ντι τὸ πᾶν. There is helpful commentary on the last phrase by Cumont (1924), 59 and 227 n. 57.

[27] *IGUR* I, 136. The relief is a fine one and must have fitted into a larger architectural ensemble, which might have told us more about the identity and circumstances of the dedicator(s).

[28] Ramsay (1889), 223 no. 11: [− − Ἀπόλ]|λωνι Λ[αιρβ]|ηνῷ [− −] | θεῷ Υ − −.

[29] Fraser (1962), 25–7 speculated along these lines; the Roberts, *Bull. Ép.* 1964, 561, were sceptical, but puzzled.

[30] Strabo 12.5.2, 567.

site,[31] or the farmers' god Zeus Megistos, who is well attested in the rural communities of Lycaonia and Phrygia. She suggests that Theos Hypsistos, addressed as *soter* at Thessalonica (55) and at Miletus (135), should be equated respectively with Sarapis and Men.[32] However, there is no evidence to support these or other identifications, which rest on the presupposition that the term Theos Hypsistos was simply a formula that exalted an otherwise named divinity. In the entire epigraphic corpus, the identification of Theos Hypsistos with another named deity occurs only once, at Pergamum, and this itself depends on a restoration: the modest dedication of a certain Tation [Ἡλ]ίωι | θ[ε]ῶι | ὑψ[ί]στωι (186).[33] Theos Hypsistos may here be equated with the sun god, Helios. The strong associations between the worship of Hypsistos and light and fire, including specifically that of the sun, makes this equation intelligible and readily explicable.

THE DISTINCTIVENESS OF HYPSISTOS WORSHIP

In my earlier study I made the point that for the most part the format of Theos Hypsistos worship did not differ from the common patterns of pagan cult. Men and women provided material evidence for their prayers in the form of inscribed monuments and used conventional formulae to describe their actions (εὐχήν, εὐξάμενος, εὐχαριστῶν, ἀνέθηκε). They did so in response to dreams, oracles and other signs that could be interpreted as evidence for the god's will. Moreover, such prayers were offered in the usual contexts of intensified religious activity, at moments when something significant was at stake for the worshippers, including their concerns about health, harvests, the risks of travel, and personal security.[34] These aspects imply that the worship of Theos Hypsistos was not functionally distinct from other forms of cult. However, there are significant differences. None of the evidence, old or new, suggests that animal sacrifice had a part to play in any ritual.[35] The worship of Theos Hypsistos was also, it seems,

---

[31] The temple is now shown to have been completed and dedicated to Zeus under Domitian, not Hadrian: see Posamentir and Wörrle (2006).

[32] Belayche (2005b), 437 n. 70. The equation with Sarapis at Thessalonica depends on the report that the main group of texts for Theos Hypsistos there (55–6, see also A28) was found near the site of the Serapeum (which has produced over seventy inscriptions for the Egyptian cults). Four of them are marble columns, some 3 metres high, and probably came from a portico associated with a dining or sympotic association linked to the cult (see especially *IG* x.2, 69 and 70 (AD 66–7), and below, n. 63).

[33] Another possible instance is at Amastris (196), where the dedication could be read as θεῶι ὑψίστωι | ἐπηκό[ω]ι Ἡλ[ίωι] rather than treating the last word as the name of the dedicator, Helios.

[34] Belayche (2005a), 47–51; Mitchell (1999), 106–7.

[35] Bucrania appear on A1 (which may not be a dedication to Theos but to Zeus Hypsistos, or even to a god called μέγιστος); A9 (Z. H.), and A20 (on a lamp for Hypsistos). These indications are

rigorously aniconic. The seated Thea Larmene, carrying a staff, appears on **172**, but there is no representation of Theos Hypsistos or *to theion*, also named in this text. A mounted horseman appears on one of the Tanais stelae, but the identification of this figure as the Highest God in person is highly contestable.[36] The cult is represented in visual form by the eagles which appear on several of the Tanais monuments (**89, 90, 92, 96**), and widely elsewhere, a point to which we shall return.

Anonymity was an important aspect of the cult for the majority, but not all, of the god's worshippers. The occurrence of votives to Zeus Hypsistos alongside those to Theos Hypsistos within the same sanctuary shows that a significant minority of devotees was ready to identify Theos Hypsistos with the supreme Hellenic divinity Zeus. Pagan theological literature from Cleanthes' famous Stoic *Hymn to Zeus* to Orphic and other writers of the later Roman period provides plenty of material to illuminate contemporary understanding of an all-powerful, transcendent Zeus.[37]

Nevertheless, a majority of worshippers chose to call their god Theos Hypsistos without naming him in a way that linked him to the intricate complexities of the Olympian pantheon. In such cases anonymity was not designed to conceal the divinity's true identity. The nature of the worshippers' beliefs was eloquently articulated in the first couplet of the Oinoanda oracle: αὐτοφύης, ἀδίδακτος, ἀμήτωρ, ἀστυφελίκτος, οὔνομα μὴ χωρῶν, πολυώνυμος, ἐν πύρι ναίων.[38] The claim that the god had no names but also many names cannot be taken as support for the view that he could be identified at will with other Greek or Egyptian gods, for that would contradict the famous negative theology of the previous verse, which emphatically disassociated the supreme divinity from all others. Moreover, as we have seen, such equations are almost entirely absent from the evidence.[39]

From time to time inscriptions provide us with views of the Highest God in a variant guise. A text from Pergamum, included in my first catalogue as **188**, marks the dedication of an altar, a torch-carrier and a torch-bracket to

insufficient to countermand the general hypothesis. Bucrania had entered the generic decorative repertoire and by no means always evoked the sacrificial ritual.

[36] Ustinova (1991) and (1999). See Mitchell (1999), 117 n. 106. Belayche (2005a), 50 supposes that a larger niche than the others in the Pnyx sanctuary at Athens could have contained a statue of the god, but there is no evidence for this.

[37] Mitchell (1999), 101–2. For Cleanthes see now Thom (2005), and for the Orphic literature, Herrero de Jáuregui (2009).

[38] *SEG* 27 (1977), 933; Mitchell (1999), 86.

[39] See above, pp. 171–3. For the negative theology, which was especially emphasised in other contemporary oracular texts, see Robert (1971), Chaniotis, in this volume, p. 139 n. 120, and especially Lane Fox (1986), 170.

θεὸς κύριος ὁ ὢν εἰς ἀεί. The association with fire and torch-light helps to harden the supposition that this inscription alludes to Theos Hypsistos.[40] A large block, apparently from a building, has been recovered from Uylupınar, a village site in the Cibyratis, inscribed with the text κυρίῳ ἄνω θεῷ Ἔπριος | Ἀγαθεῖνος. An almost identical block, certainly from the same building, has the parallel dedication θεοῖς μεγάλοις συννάοις | Ἔ[π]ριο[ς] Ἀγαθεῖνος.[41] If the first of these inscriptions is also rightly interpreted as evidence for the worship of Theos Hypsistos, it is one of the relatively small number of texts which associated him explicitly with other, although also unnamed, gods (see p. 180). A small cylindrical altar, on the scale typical for most *hypsistos* dedications, has been found at Aspendos in Pamphylia, reading θεῷ ἀψευ[δεῖ καὶ] | ἀχειροποιήτῳ | εὐχήν.[42] Walter Ameling includes it in his corpus of Jewish inscriptions from Asia Minor, suggesting that it at least shows Jewish influence, but his excellent commentary draws attention to the fact that neither adjective finds a good parallel in Jewish writings, while both occur in late oracular literature.[43] This small votive could readily have been produced by a worshipper of the Highest God. Both this and the Pergemene inscription have reasonably been interpreted as the work of god-fearers.[44]

Lamps played an important part in the worship of Theos Hypsistos, although this feature was not exclusive to his cult. The new evidence includes a lamp, depicting an eagle and a bucranion inscribed ὑψίστου, from Pella in Macedonia (**A20**). Moreover, the small dedicatory altar from Gortyn in Crete is reported to have been found close to a larger, uninscribed altar, which probably served the same cult, and to have been associated with many terracotta lamps (**A36**). However, this feature is particularly well illustrated by N. Franken's study of several bronze appliances belonging to hanging lamps, which included inscribed *tabulae ansatae* to identify the nature of the dedication. In three cases these were for Theos Hypsistos (**290, A78–79**). It is probable that some of the other inscribed bronze *tabulae* in the Theos Hypsistos corpus belong to this genre (**291, 292, A27**). These elaborate lamps had a ritual rather than a narrowly functional

---

[40] Further bibliography at *SEG* 54 (2004), 1243 bis; cf. the reference at n. 45 below.
[41] T. Corsten, *I.Kibyra* I, 93–4; *SEG* 47 (1997), 1810–11; G. Horsley, *RECAM* v (2007), nos. 103 and 184 shows that both these inscribed stones and other blocks evidently from the same building were subsequently reused to make a Christian *baptisterion*.
[42] Brixhe and Hodot (1988), 124 no. 88; *SEG* 38 (1988), 1335.
[43] Ameling, *IJO* II, no. 218; see also Chaniotis, in this volume p. 137 n. 109.
[44] Van der Horst (1992); Delling (1964/5). As at Mitchell (1999), 122, I would recall again Paul's appeal to the altar of the ἄγνωστος θεός as he began his speech to the Areopagus at Athens, which fits well into this milieu.

significance. They show part of the theological apparatus of the cult, which was symbolised also by prayers offered to the rising sun, and implied reverence for the divine fire of the supreme deity revealed in the Oinoanda oracle.[45]

The new discoveries draw attention to a further characteristic of Theos Hypsistos worship: most of the votive monuments set up by individual worshippers were small and unpretentious. This requires discussion and explanation. In my earlier study I drew attention to the cult's wide appeal, in that evidence is found in cities and in the countryside, and worshippers can be found from many strata of ancient society. Several inscriptions mention Roman citizens (**1**, **12**, **55–7**, **68–9**, **78–9**, **115–17**, **125**, **136**, **149**, **151**, **153**, **161**, **192**, **198**, **201**, **228**, **236**, **A36–7**).[46] A handful of the dedications were indeed prayers for the benefit of the ruling élite, including one by the Jews of Athribis for Ptolemy V and Cleopatra in the mid second century BC (**285**), two set up on behalf of the Thracian royal family in the second quarter of the first century AD (**60**, **68**), the dedication from Amastris of AD 45, which is physically adjacent to a prestigious monumental dedication on behalf of the emperor Claudius (**195**), and, much later, the dedication of AD 306 from Panticapaeum, set up by a high-ranking local friend of the tetrarchs (**88**).

It is also clear that cult associations were created for the worship of Theos Hypsistos. This is most evident in the much discussed inscriptions from Tanais, which date between the first half of the second and the middle of the third century AD, and belonged without question to the dominant religious institutions of this community at the far north-east extremity of the Graeco-Roman world (**89–103**). They are not an isolated phenomenon. The cult was formally organised by an association at Thessalonica in the AD 60s and 70s, where forty names appear on the column dedicated on behalf of the triklinarch T. Flavius Euktimenos (**56**), as also at Pydna (**51**) and at Pirot in Serbia (**75**) in the middle of the third century AD, and in late Hellenistic Egypt (**287**). In this respect Theos Hypsistos worshippers behaved in a similar fashion to their counterparts in other cults.[47] The same was true, of course, of the earliest Christian groups that Pliny encountered in Pontus at the beginning of the second century.[48]

---

[45] Mitchell (1999), 91–2.   [46] Mitchell (1999), 105–6.
[47] See Harland (2003). Robert (1937), 288 n. 3 and (independently) Harland (2003), 32 suggest that the term ἀδελφοί in **198** from Sinope may also refer to an association, but it can also be understood there in its normal sense, referring to four named male siblings.
[48] Pliny, *Ep.* 10.96.

Most forms of pagan worship in the imperial period, especially during the second and third centuries AD, including the cult of Zeus Hypsistos in Macedonia, created opportunities for devotees to show off their wealth in homage to the gods, by funding buildings and statues, games and festivals. This feature is largely absent from the cult of Theos Hypsistos. Very little of the evidence for Theos Hypsistos comes into this category. In Phrygia at the beginning of the fourth century, a family dedicated columns and a propylon to a sanctuary (215). A new text carved on an architrave found in the territory of Amaseia in Pontus suggests that a man who had been saved by the god's intervention from great peril may have put up part or all of a building for Theos Hypsistos (A49). Some building inscriptions indicate that worshippers contributed as part of a collective group, as in the case of the forty *synklitai* at Thessalonica (56).[49] The most lavish donor in the entire corpus of documents was Herennia Procula at Thessalonica, who paid for four columns with bases and capitals promised in her father's estate.[50] Lavish architecture, however, seems to have been the exception rather than the rule. My own reconstruction of the architectural context associated with the one surviving Greek version of the Clarian oracular text, which prescribed worship 'to the gods and goddesses', was that this had been erected in a modest apsidal cult room located in the upper storey of a house in the Pisidian city at Melli, at some distance from the city centre. I also argued that this should be interpreted as a chapel intended for Hypsistos worship. Here, as very likely at Nysa in Lycia (232, see below), the inclusion of other gods in local cult practice followed reference to an oracle.[51]

To an overwhelming degree, the dedications of individuals were the humble offerings of humble people. Most were votive *tabulae*, simple altars, or plain circular *cippi*, rarely more than 40 cm high, carrying unpretentious texts (see A25, A26, A28, A30, A34, A36, A37, A41, A45, A47, A49, A50, A51, A52, A54, A55, A56, A61, A62, A63, A64, A65, A68, A83). The simple inference would be that the cult was favoured by the poor or the relatively disadvantaged in society, and that may be supported by

[49] Note Ameling's observations on the Jews and godfearers who contributed to the decoration of the Sardis synagogue in the later fourth century AD, *IJO* II, 230: 'Hervorzuheben ist jedenfalls, daß nicht wenige große Stiftern die Synagoge ausgeschmückt hatten, sondern viele Einzelpersonen ganz unterschiedlicher sozialer Stellung. Trotz einiger Ratsherren in der Gemeinde gab es offenbar kein überragendes Individuum mehr, der als Stifter der ganzen Synagoge oder ihrer Dekoration auftreten konnte – ein Befund, der auch für den Kirchenbau der Zeit gilt.'

[50] *IG* x.2, 70.

[51] Mitchell (2003), 151–5 no. 13 (*SEG* 53 (2003), 1587); see below, n. 68 for the debate about interpreting this inscription. Jones (2005) and (2006) does not attempt to explain the archaeological context.

the fact that a significant proportion of dedicators were female (73 women, compared with 152 men, are attested in the surviving evidence for individual dedications, excluding those of non-familial collective groups). However, even the monuments set up by worshippers of higher status, such as the Roman citizens, have an unassuming quality. Their behaviour is clearly not aligned to the extravagant cultic competition that is to be found in the civic religious life of the eastern Roman Empire in the second and third centuries, and the character of the dedications and the monuments that they set up suggests that there was a theological as well as an economic explanation. Confronted with the Highest God, it was fitting for every worshipper to emphasise his or her humility. Gregory of Nazianzus' account of the Hypsistarioi stresses exactly this point about the social origins and humility of the worshippers in the face of the universal power of their god: Ὑψιστάριοι τοῖς ταπεινοῖς ὄνομα, καὶ ὁ παντοκράτωρ δὴ μόνος αὐτοῖς σεβάσμιος ('to the humble by name they are Hypsistarians, and the all-mighty is indeed their only object of reverence').[52]

WHAT SORT OF MONOTHEISM?

There was no Greek or Latin word corresponding to the modern term monotheism. In so far as polytheists and followers of monotheistic religions such as Christianity did refer to their own or other forms of belief, or lack of it, they tended to do so by using the generalised vocabulary describing piety (*eusebeia*) or its absence (*asebeia*).[53] Monotheism, henotheism and other terms are all modern coinages, as Peter Van Nuffelen shows in his paper for this volume. Following the lead of Athanassiadi and Frede, I contented myself in 1999 with the commonest of these generic terms, monotheism, to identify the phenomenon that was being investigated. It was obvious to all the contributors to the 1999 volume that we were not, for the most part, dealing with monotheism in an exclusive sense, the worship of one god alone, to the strict exclusion of all other divine beings or powers, but with what John Dillon called 'soft monotheism', belief in an overwhelmingly superior divine power, but one that tolerated the existence and functionality of various lesser divine beings.[54] This usage has appeared too casual to those who prefer a strictly Mosaic interpretation of

---

[52] Gregory of Nazianzus, *Oratio* 18.5.
[53] Mitchell (2003b). The issues connected to the absence of any fixed terminology of monotheism, and their implications for the concept of monotheism as a whole, are discussed, with overlapping perspectives, by Van Nuffelen, North, Fürst, Markschies and Belayche in this volume.
[54] Dillon (1999), 69.

the term monotheism, 'I shall have no other gods before me'.[55] There is a tendency in modern scholarship to favour the commonest alternative modern coinage, henotheism, to denote religious concepts which express the preferential belief in and worship of a supreme god, but not to the exclusion of lesser divinities.[56] This identifies exclusiveness as the key criterion for 'true' monotheism. The terminological distinction between monotheism and henotheism may be useful, but it is important to remember that monotheism used in this sense is not only a modern coinage, but one that is heavily value-laden, in that the standard for monotheism is explicitly established by the views of Christians or Muslims in relation to earlier religious thinking and practice.[57]

Whether or not the cult of Theos Hypsistos is regarded as tending towards monotheism, it was not rigorously exclusive. A small part of the epigraphic documentation explicitly associates the god with another divinity, sometimes more than one. A sacred slave of the Meter Theon at Beroia made a dedication to the god (τῷ θεῷ) κατ᾽ ἐπιταγὴν θεοῦ ὑψίστου (37). At a sanctuary near the small Lydian city of Saittai a worshipper dedicated a statue of Thea Larmene, a local goddess, to Theos Hypsistos and an abstract divinity called *mega theion* (172), thereby bringing three divine entities into play. A priest of Men Ouranios in Pisidia erected a dedication to Theos Hypsistos at the prompting of an oracle (230). Nothing indicates in this case that these gods were identical with one another, but Men, here at least, was regarded as one of the Highest God's heavenly associates.[58] In the Cibyratis the dedication to the 'lord god above', who may perhaps be identified with Theos Hypsistos, was paired with one to 'the great gods who share his temple'.[59] New discoveries at Oinoanda show that Artemis and Leto, both of whom were important figures in the city's regular pantheon, received dedications alongside Theos Hypsistos in his sanctuary by the old

---

[55] So Chaniotis, in this volume. He is, of course, concerned with the substantive, not merely the verbal point that the concept of worshipping only one god is unhelpful as an approach to understanding ancient paganism.

[56] Detailed analysis of the term has been much more complex than this, but, as Van Nuffelen shows, modern usage varies from writer to writer, and the variation does not materially affect the point that I am making.

[57] See further Mitchell (forthcoming). Edwards (2004) in his critique of Frede (1999) lays much stress on the fact that supposed non-Christian forms of monotheism fail to meet the requirement for exclusivity.

[58] Discussing this text, Belayche (2005b), 439 distinguishes the two divinities ('le dévot d'un dieu *hypsistos* oraculaire se présente comme prêtre du dieu anatolien Mên'), but at (2005a), 38 she identifies the gods with one another ('c'est Mên *ouranios* que son prêtre appelle Theos Hypsistos'); so also in this volume, p. 163 n. 130.

[59] See discussion above, n. 41.

Hellenistic city wall.[60] In an invocation inscribed at Alexandria, a young woman, dead before her time, is represented as invoking Theos Hypsistos, who sees all, Helios and Nemesis to take vengeance on those who had caused her death (**284**). Two of the manumission documents involving a dedication to Theos Hypsistos from Gorgippia, which have universally been recognised as Jewish,[61] end with the formula that manumission was guaranteed by an oath sworn to Zeus, Ge and Helios (**85, 86**). Here the simple explanation of most commentators has been that the formulaic oath had little strictly religious significance and was therefore admissible even in a Jewish context.[62] A newly discovered inscription from Thessalonica may also be added to this list, reportedly a dedication to Theos Hypsistos and the *symposiastai theoi*, gods who were present at the same symposium (**A22**).[63] It happens that another text from Thessalonica records the dedication of θεὰν δικαίαν Νέμεσιν (presumably a statue) to Zeus Hypsistos (**54**), although this does not seem to have been connected to the same sanctuary as the Theos Hypsistos text. We should also note that Ulpius Carpus, the prophet and priest of Theos Hypsistos at Miletus, is said to have consulted the oracle of Apollo at Didyma concerning the cult of Sarapis.[64] Finally, in this context, a broken inscription from Nysa in Lycia of the second century AD has been published as a dedication θεῷ ὑψίσ|[τῳ καὶ Μητρ]ὶ Ὀρείᾳ καὶ Κε|[– –] καὶ θεοῖς πᾶσι | [καὶ θεαῖς] πάσαις χαρισ|[τ]ήριον (**232**).[65]

The first observation to be made is, quite simply, that only ten out of a total of more than 250 texts explicitly name or indirectly refer to other gods in the same context as Theos Hypsistos or Hypsistos. This tiny proportion does not support the inference that Theos Hypsistos, however the term be interpreted, should normally be seen as part of a pantheon. A second point is that three of the associates, Nemesis, *to theion* and Helios, are associated with the workings of divine justice. This connection is particularly evident in the rich Anatolian evidence from the second and third centuries AD.

[60] **A59**; for Leto at Oinoanda see Hall (1977).
[61] See the editions by Noy, Panayotov and Bloedhorn, *IJO* II, BS no. 20 and BS no. 22.
[62] So Stein (2001), 124 n. 40 with references.
[63] Theos Hypsistos at Thessalonica was worshipped in the second half of the first century AD by associations of cult followers, including many Roman citizens, sometimes called *synklitai* (*IG* x.2, 70) and including a president of the banquets, *trikleinarches* (**56** and *IG* x.2, 69). The members of the association clubbed together to pay for the building where these gatherings would take place (see above, n. 32). The nature of this social context makes it clear why other gods of the symposium were admitted to the company of Theos Hypsistos. See Harland 2003, 56–7 for an illustration and discussion of the symposiac group that worshipped Zeus Hypsistos at Cyzicus (**282**), probably at the same period.
[64] **135** and **136** with Robert (1968).
[65] *TAM* II.3, 737; see above, n. 51 and pp. 182–3 for the restoration of this text.

The association between Theos Hypsistos and the Anatolian god Ὅσιος καὶ Δίκαιος, sometimes represented as a single god, sometimes as a pair of divinities, is accidentally but vividly illustrated by the stone cutter's (or dedicator's) error revealed in **A48**, where the engraver's first intention was to cut a stone for θεῷ ὑψίστῳ, before this was emended to θεῷ Ὁσίῳ. The status of *to theion* at Saittae was analogous to that of the subordinate divinity, variously called *to theion, theion basilikon,* or *theios angelos,* who was associated with Zeus Hypsistos at Carian Stratonicea (**141–57**). I see no reason to retract the arguments put forward in my first study that in Anatolia at least worship of Theos Hypsistos was often linked to the cults of lesser divinities or angelic beings, who brought divine justice to the level of the communities where these beliefs flourished.[66]

Three of the texts associate Theos Hypsistos with an unnamed goddess: the Mother of the gods at Leukopetra, the goddess of Larma, and the mountain mother in Lycia. Goddesses played a major part in Anatolian religion from early prehistoric times, and this dominance is still marked in the Hellenistic and Roman evidence. Given the strong local tradition of worshipping powerful female divinities, it is readily intelligible that some acknowledgement of female divine figures should have been accommodated within the cult of Theos Hypsistos, and this, I would argue, is the reason why worshippers at Oinoanda also included Artemis and Leto in their prayers. Apollo's oracle, inscribed in the same sanctuary, stated explicitly that Apollo himself and his fellows were a small part of god (**233**). We also note that two dedications from the same sanctuary at Gölde in Lydia were offered to Thea Hypsiste (**167, A40**), and I would interpret the evidence from Gölde as showing that in this particular sanctuary worshippers more readily believed in a supreme female divinity in place of a divine overlord.

The inscription from Nysa 'for Theos Hypsistos and the mountain mother and all the gods and goddesses' (**232**) warrants further discussion. Kalinka suggested the reading καὶ Κελ[εναίῳ], a reference to an otherwise unknown local god. It is probably better to read κα(τὰ) κέλ[ευσιν], according to divine instructions, which would restore a typical formula in such texts. This local worshipper of Theos Hypsistos associated the god with a local mountain mother goddess. The additional 'catch-all' inclusion of all the gods and all the goddesses in the same dedication is an unusual

[66] The literature is now very substantial, and there is a good deal of consensus about this hierarchic model in the structure of rural Anatolian religion, but one prop has been removed from earlier arguments. The Phrygian votive stele supposedly set up for the Holy and the Just by an association of angel lovers (these divinities were sometimes identified as *angeloi*) has been shown to be the product of a vine-growers' association, φιλανπέλων (not φιλανγέλων) συνβίωσις: Malay (2005).

feature for a votive inscription of this period and requires an explanation. Independently of the evidence about Theos Hypsistos, it is well known that there was serious debate in the middle and later Roman Empire about the nature and number of the gods. This particularly took the form of questions posed to oracles in the form 'Who is god?', 'Are you or another god?'[67] The famous inscribed oracle from Oinoanda provides the best known response to precisely this question: god was to be identified with Aether, while other beings, including Apollo who delivered this response, were divine messengers, angels. We cannot know in every case what will have prompted individuals to ask these or similar questions, but the issue was a source of serious anxiety. Specifically, did the elevation of one god to a preferential position entail the consequence that the worship of others could or should be neglected? We do not know the circumstances of the Nysa dedication, but plausibly the inscription was set up following an instruction (through a dream or an oracle) to extend the dedication beyond the one Theos Hypsistos not only to the mountain mother goddess, but also to all the gods and goddesses of the pantheon. This was the conjectural explanation that I suggested for the interpretation of the Clarian oracle, known from eleven copies, which prescribed worship of 'the gods and goddesses'. Perhaps during the universal emergency of the great plague between AD 165 and 180 the advice of the interpreters of oracles such as the famous text from Oinoanda was that, rather than restricting cult to one god alone, all the divinities in the pantheon should be worshipped.[68]

These reflections on the possible circumstances which caused particular dedications to Theos Hypsistos to be linked to the cult of other deities make no claim to be more than conjectures. But the examples in question are rare, and they rarely include the names of the familiar Olympian gods and goddesses. Although accommodation with other beliefs and practices was not excluded, the evidence as a whole does not suggest that Theos Hypsistos, whether we understand the cult as unified or as disaggregated, was normally conceived as being integrated into the wider pantheon of deities.

---

[67] Lane Fox (1986), 256–61; Athanassiadi and Frede (1999), 14–17; see now Busine (2005). Chaniotis, in this volume, asserts that the central issue for believers was not the quantity but the quality of their gods. However, these oracular enquiries point to concern on both counts.

[68] Mitchell (2003a), 151–5 links the response directly to the Oinoanda oracle text. Jones (2005) and (2006) offers an alternative explanation, that Claros gave general advice for universal worship as a response to the ravages of the Antonine plague. Chaniotis, in this volume pp. 117–18, suggests that the two explanations might be reconciled with one another. He also rightly draws attention to the relevance of the inscription from Amastris, **A48**, a verse dedication to Theos Hypsistos set up on the advice of an oracle of Apollo, almost certainly in the context of the plague.

Although a common pattern can be identified across the spectrum of
Theos Hypsistos dedications, which thereby identify the core beliefs of
the worshippers, there was as much room for local variation in the cult
as there was in the cults of other gods worshipped in the Roman world.
Monotheism as such was not the most critical issue in the beliefs of the
worshippers of Theos Hypsistos. If the majority of the dedications is any
guide, most men and women chose to restrict their worship to the Highest
God alone. Their dedications mention no other god, and their particular
form of monolatry may therefore have made them particularly susceptible
to the attractions of Judaism (see below, pp. 185–9). However, many others
were ready to acknowledge lesser divine beings within a theological scheme
which still emphasised the transcending power of Hypsistos. The cult was
flexible enough to allow variety, and this reflects both individual choices
and, to a much greater extent, distinctive local variations in the forms
that their worship took. In Lydia and Phrygia the cult of Theos Hypsistos emerged in regions where gods of divine justice, Hosios, Dikaios,
Helios and Nemesis, were widely worshipped. Along the Hermos and the
upper Maeander river basins rural sanctuaries of Men, Anaeitis and Apollo
have produced an ever-growing corpus of confession inscriptions, which
show religious courts dispensing divine justice at a local level. It is not
surprising therefore that this religious environment has lent colour to local
forms of Hypsistos worship. We see a different variation at Stratonicea in
Caria. In this more hellenised environment the supreme god was almost
always identified by name as Zeus Hypsistos, although his adjutants, 'the
divine', 'the divine angel', or 'the ruling divine spirit' (*theion basilikon*),
are clearly reminiscent of the messengers and abstract or depersonalised
agents of heavenly justice that are found in Lycia and Phrygia (**140–56**).
The inscriptions from Thessalonica show that there was a strong local
organisation, which met for symposia and provided funds for a substantial colonnaded building connected to the sanctuary of Theos Hypsistos
(**55–8, A28** with *IG* x.2, 69–70). Here too other gods were incorporated
within the cult activities and the behaviour of the cult association may have
been inspired to emulate the organisation of other religious associations in
the city, notably the followers of Sarapis and the Egyptian deities, whose
sanctuary seems to have been adjacent to theirs.[69] In contrast, the Cypriot
Theos Hypsistos votives, originating from at least nine different sanctuaries,
are homogeneous in appearance and rigorously monotheistic in character
(**243–65, A62–9**).

---

[69] See above, nn. 32 and 63.

Discussing the various forms of Hypsistos worship found around the north shore of the Black Sea, Glen Bowersock suggests that 'the disparate cults of the Black Sea cities can be seen as a microcosm of the even more disparate cults of the entire Greek East. *Theos Hypsistos* in his anonymous guise and in his various named incarnations, such as Zeus, Helios and Sarapis, was not one god.'[70] However, this is not the conclusion of Yulia Ustinova, whose views he cites with approval, in that she has argued that the Theos Hypsistos attested in Gorgippia, Panticapaeum and Tanais should all be identified with a sky god of Irano-Scythian origin, which developed to become the supreme male divinity in the Graeco-Scythian communities of the Crimean Bosporos.[71] Thus, within the south Russian region, a range of local cults, not all identical in form to one another, nevertheless represented a common religious phenomenon and were directed to the same god. The argument can be applied to the entire body of material. Like the cult of every other divinity worshipped in the Graeco-Roman world, including the Christian God, that of Theos Hypsistos underwent transformations as it adapted to particular social and religious environments. To assert that Apollo of Delphi has nothing to do with the Apollo worshipped in a rural sanctuary of Gaul or Phrygia, or that the Christian worship that we encounter at Santiago de Compostela has nothing to do with the Christianity to be found in Stockholm or Sarajevo, is absurd. The same is true, *mutatis mutandis*, of the cults of Theos Hypsistos, which cohere around a central body of beliefs and practices, although these are represented locally by significant and observable variations.

WHAT HAS THEOS HYPSISTOS TO DO WITH THE JEWS?

My earlier study was entitled 'The cult of Theos Hypsistos between pagans, Jews, and Christians'. Objections were raised to an interpretation that appears to make a single divinity the object of worship both by pagans and by Jews and Christians. 'Jews and Christians knew that their god was Hypsistos, but they can have been in no doubt that any of the other cults dedicated to a deity of that name had nothing to do with them.'[72] 'Dann aber unterscheidet sich die nach Mitchell aus paganen Wurzeln hervorgeganene Verehrung des Theos Hypsistos von derjenigen seitens der Diaspora-Juden in einem zentralen Punkt, in der Gottesvorstellung.

---

[70] Bowersock (2002), 361.   [71] Ustinova (1999).   [72] Bowersock (2002), 361–2.

Kann man in einem solchen Fall wirklich noch von einem einzelnen, umfassenden Kult sprechen?'[73]

No one will deny that pagans and Jews in the ancient world belonged to different religious traditions, and as such had different ideas about the nature of god. It is harder to define the pagan than the Jewish concepts. The term pagan is non-specific and normally defined negatively, as denoting the religious beliefs and behaviour of inhabitants of the classical ancient world who were neither Christian nor Jewish. Amid the prodigious variety of these beliefs, one factor common to most pagans was polytheism. Jewish religion, by contrast, was overwhelmingly monotheistic in nature and focused on belief in a single supreme god, Jehovah, Yahwe in the Hebrew tradition. In the Greek version of the Jewish bible, the Septuagint, produced in Alexandria in the third century BC, the Jewish God is very frequently identified as Theos Hypsistos, and this became a standard and widespread term in Greek-Jewish literature and among the communities of the Jewish diaspora in the late Hellenistic and imperial periods. Seventeen inscriptions in the Theos Hypsistos corpus should be understood precisely in this sense, as referring to the Jewish God, and they have been registered as such in the excellent recent collections of Jewish inscriptions.[74] A further group of references has been confidently and probably rightly claimed as Jewish, usually on the grounds that these texts are closely associated with other material or epigraphic evidence for a Jewish community in the same location.[75] Twenty-three texts for Theos Hypsistos have pagan associations, either because the Highest God is linked in the text to other gods of whatever provenance,[76] or because of the appearance of pagan iconography, most often the eagle, the common symbol of Zeus.[77] The

[73] Stein (2001), 121. The remark in Colpe and Löw (1993), 1054 that 'weder auf jüdischer noch auf heidnischer Seite liegen Verhältnisse vor, die zu einem Synkretismus hätten führen können' is contradicted by their following supposition that absorption and competition played a part as the two sides confronted one another. This concedes the obvious point, that contacts between Jews and pagans in this context were unavoidable.
[74] Especially 84–7 (IJO I, BS nos. 20, 21, 22, 27, Gorgippia), 88 (IJO I, BS no. 4, Panticapaeum), 207 (IJO II, no. 176, Acmonia), 230 (IJO II, no. 215, Sibidunda), 281 (Negev), 282 (Alexandria), 285 (Athribis).
[75] 106–9 (IJO I, Ach nos. 60–3, Delos); 110 (IJO I, Ach nos. 70–1, Rheneia), 206 (Acmonia, not accepted in IJO II, 375 n. 93), 288 (Leontopolis), A76 (Egypt).
[76] 37, 85–6, 172, 232, 284, 330; discussed above, pp. 180–2. As noted on p. 181, 85–6 name pagan gods but are almost certainly Jewish.
[77] Eagles unless otherwise specified: 1 (Athens), 69 (eagles in the sanctuary at Serdica), 89, 92, 96 (Tanais), 115 (Mytilene), 121 (Chersonesus, Crete), 158 (Tralles), 176 (Thyateira), 190 (Nicomedia, for Zeus Hypsistos with an eagle), 191 (Nicomedia, for Theos Hypsistos with an eagle), 195 (Amastris), 231 (Termessus, a bronze foot), A8 (Thessaly, Azoros Elassonas), A22 (Edessa), A26 (Pella).

remaining 178 inscriptions cannot be classified as either pagan or Jewish simply on internal grounds.[78]

What sense can we make of this pattern of evidence? I do not claim that all worshippers of the Highest God envisaged for themselves a divinity that explicitly combined identifiable elements found in Jewish and in pagan cult, i.e. that each and every instance of Theos Hypsistos worship contains a sort of religious mixture. Rather, worship of a Highest God was something that was generated by the beliefs of all Jews and of a significant number of pagans in the time of the Roman Empire.

The essence of the commonality that I am arguing for is shared belief in the existence and powers of a Highest God. The inscriptions for Theos Hypsistos are evidence for this widespread belief. By its nature the documentary and material information does not reveal the details of each worshipper's 'notion of god' even within the Jewish communities, still less in the pluralist world of paganism. Such insights come only when an individual, in whatever tradition, chooses to present them in explicit and self-conscious literary form. However, we are well enough informed about Judaism to make generalisations about collective Jewish beliefs, and I maintain that this is true in the case of Theos Hypsistos, although the documentation is naturally much less comprehensive. The epigraphic evidence presents Theos Hypsistos as a single supreme divinity who was not represented in human form. His essence was associated with light, fire, and the sun. Cult involved prayers, but no animal sacrifices. Worship was characterised by the humility of mortals in the face of divine supremacy. These can be claimed as the core beliefs and practices of his worshippers. His elevated, indeed transcendental, status caused believers to ask the question whether Theos Hypsistos was the only god. Pagan oracles, most notably the text preserved at Oinoanda, which was widely known and disseminated in the later Roman Empire, responded by allowing that other divinities might be acknowledged, but had a lesser status within the divine hierarchy, or to be precise, as the oracle stated, they were parts of god.[79] The cult, accordingly, was not exclusively monotheistic and, as usual in the environment of ancient paganism, was not governed by strict doctrinal rules.

In practice it was unusual for Theos Hypsistos to be worshipped with other gods, but local groups of worshippers did not necessarily disassociate the cult from the wider religious environment. As we have seen, in places

---

[78] The dilemma is nicely posed by **202** from the territory of Ancyra. Ameling excluded it from *IJO* II, 335 n. 4 (citing diverse opinions); for Belayche (2005b), 439 n. 97 and (2005a), 38 n. 30 it is plainly Jewish. I am more than happy to reaffirm my own agnostic position.

[79] For this distinction see the discussion of Cerutti (2009).

where the cult was popular, they formed cult associations, which gathered
for shared meals and symposia in the god's honour as well, no doubt, as for
ritual purposes. Theos Hypsistos was sometimes addressed as Zeus Hypsistos in sanctuaries such as those at Athens, Nicomedia and Seleucia on the
Calycadnus, where the anonymous dedications also occur. These phenomena confirm the pagan background of many Theos Hypsistos worshippers,
but do not conflict with their core beliefs about the Highest God.

Beliefs of this kind or at this level by no means depend on each individual believer having an identical notion of the nature of god. Stein asks how
worshippers, respectively from pagan and Jewish backgrounds, could con-
ceivably have influenced one another's religious culture when their ideas of
God's nature were fundamentally different. Did pagan Greek worshippers
of Theos Hypsistos now think that they were worshipping Jehovah? Did
Jews who allowed themselves to be influenced by the pagan environment
come to think that the Theos Hypsistos they worshipped was Jehovah no
longer?[80] For him such notions are absurd, and so, accordingly, is the idea
of a common religious culture. But, at a level of normal social interaction,
the response to this is simple. Worshippers from both traditions could
readily agree that they revered a Highest God, without denying the particular features, customs and traditions that anchored their god (or their
notion of god) in a Jewish or a non-Jewish tradition respectively. Such is
precisely the outcome of many conversations that I have held over the years
in the shadow of a mosque with the local *imam* and the old men sitting
with him. What is my religion? – Christian. What is theirs? – Muslim.
But do we not both believe in a single omnipotent god? On such we are
happy to agree, usually tolerantly enough, without probing further into our
doctrinal differences, or into the different traditions from which our own
religious beliefs have emerged. Such sharing of religious practices, based
on shared beliefs, was all the more acceptable in a non-dogmatic religious
environment.

Thus it was perfectly possible for a Jew, or a gentile enthusiast for Jewish
ways, or a priest of a pagan Anatolian cult, to affirm a common belief
in Theos Hypsistos, without having identical notions of who this god
was. None of these needed to be a proponent of a unified cult of a hybrid
pagan–Jewish character. Nor were all worshippers of Theos Hypsistos either

---

[80] Stein (2001), 121; Gordon (2003), 271; cf. Bowersock (2002), 356: 'what would be truly hard to
believe is that Jews or judaisers would share in the same cult as a priest of Mên Ouranios'; 356–7:
'[the bronze foot dedicated to Theos Hypsistos at Termessos] is so much at variance with Jewish or
Christian theology that it alone would suffice to invalidate any assumption that all dedications to
a highest god represent a single cult'.

pagans, who adopted some but not all of the religious traditions and behaviour of the Jews, or Jews, who were unable to prevent their own beliefs and sense of cultural/religious identity being modified and transformed under the influence of their gentile neighbours. Both parties could and did worship Theos Hypsistos within their own traditions.

This created the opportunity for bringing pagan and Jewish worshippers of Theos Hypsistos into much closer contact. Because individuals from different traditions came to share a common view of the Highest God, and expressed it by the same terminology in their religious dedications, they created common ground, as I call it, between themselves and their different religious communities. Pagans in particular had no tradition of exclusivity and were perfectly ready to adapt the forms of their cult in response to local conditions. This is demonstrated by the local variations in Hypsistos worship that I have already identified. From a pagan viewpoint adaptation and integration with Jewish ways needs to be understood as the product of a similar permissive religious mentality.

THE GOD-FEARERS AND THEOS HYPSISTOS

Few Jews, we may imagine, compromised their own notion of their faith by identifying themselves as Hypsistarians. Although they certainly subscribed to the core beliefs and practices of Hypsistos worship, as defined above, this was insufficient to define the essence of their own beliefs, which depended above all on acceptance of God's law as expounded to them in the Torah. Their religion demanded that they recognise no God but Yahwe.[81] However, this did not cause them to reject any association with pagan followers of Theos Hypsistos. On the contrary, it provided grounds for a rapprochement. Pagan worshippers of Theos Hypsistos, meanwhile, had more room for manoeuvre. They were not bound by doctrinal obligations and other forms of social and religious discipline, such as circumcision or dietary regulations, to an exclusive form of worship. Some presented themselves as severely monotheistic, others admitted the existence of lesser divinities. They cannot have failed to recognise that Jews in the Diaspora communities held a belief in a Highest God that resembled their own, and also subscribed to the core practices of their own cult.

---

[81] Although we have seen (p. 181) that some Jews admitted some aspects of pagan cult behaviour into their activities, for instance being prepared to swear oaths with the formula 'by Earth, Sun and Zeus' (**85–6**).

It is, accordingly, not surprising that some of these pagan Hypsistarians became more closely acquainted with Jewish cult. Both Jewish and non-Jewish writers of the early imperial period inform us that many pagans were attracted to and attended Jewish synagogues, and adopted certain Jewish customs. 'The masses have long since shown a keen desire to adopt our religious observances; and there is not one city, Greek or barbarian, nor a single nation, to which our custom of abstaining from work on the seventh day has not spread, and where the fasts and the lighting of lamps, and many of our prohibitions in the matter of food, are not observed.'[82] Most scholars agree that these Jewish sympathisers included the σεβόμενοι or φοβούμενοι τὸν θεόν who appear in the Acts of the Apostles, the so-called 'God-fearers'.[83]

In my 1999 study, and in a separate article of 1998, I proposed the simple but radical equation that these God-fearers should be identified with the worshippers of Theos Hypsistos. The main reasons set out there for identifying the Hypsistarians and the God-fearers are the close similarities between the beliefs and activities of the two groups, as well as their very similar geographical and chronological distribution.[84] Stein claims that the similarities are explicable simply in terms of the same milieu to which the two groups belonged, and that they are insufficiently specific to provide a definition of the same religious groups at different times and places.[85] The first point about the similar milieu concedes most of my argument – if two very similar religious groups occupy the same milieu they have every chance of being virtually indistinguishable; the second is simply false – the similarities are specific: Sabbath observation, dietary regulations, and rituals involving fire and lamplight.

In an early notice of this 'provocative thesis', Harry Pleket observed that 'even if it could be shown that the *theosebeis* called their god *Theos Hypsistos*, this does not entail the conclusion that all worshippers of *Theos Hypsistos* were *theosebeis*'.[86] This observation is just, as far as it goes. It is evident, at least, that the worshippers of Theos Hypsistos included full Jews, who are clearly distinguished from *theosebeis* in the documentation, above all in the famous Aphrodisias inscription (*IJO* II, no. 14). Moreover, in the documentation with which we are concerned the term *theosebes* (or

---

[82] Josephus, *Contra Apionem* 2.39, 282. For the attractions of Judaism to gentiles see Liebeschuetz (2001).

[83] The documentation is collected in Wander (1998) and discussed in Schürer (varying dates) III.1, 150–76 and Ameling, *IJO* II, 16–21.

[84] Mitchell (1998) and (1999), 115–21.   [85] Stein (2001), 125.   [86] *SEG* 46 (1996), 1617.

its equivalent, *sebomenos ton theon*) only occurs very infrequently outside demonstrably Jewish contexts.

In the polytheistic and permissive religious environment of the early Roman Empire it was much rarer for pagans than for Christians or Jews to identify themselves as adherents of a particular religion.[87] Those who called themselves *theosebeis* are an exception to this rule. It is reasonable to ask under what circumstances they chose to do so. A partial answer is that they did so whenever they were associated with a synagogue and needed to distinguish themselves from full members of the Jewish community. This is clear with the usage of the terminology in the New Testament and by Josephus. The same situation can be observed in the attestations of God-fearers at Aphrodisias, Sardis, Philadelphia and Tralles,[88] all of which refer to the presence of *theosebeis* in the midst of the Jewish community, if not precisely in the synagogue itself, and also in at least four cases in late Roman Italy, where the texts belong in an explicitly Jewish context.[89] On the other hand, several persons are simply called *theosebeis* on gravestones with insufficient contextual information to tell us whether they were presenting themselves as part of the broader Jewish community or not.[90] One of these, the gravestone from Prusa in Bithynia for Ἐπιθέρσῃ τῷ θεοσεβῆ καὶ Θεοκτίστῳ, depicts a funerary banquet scene with a reclining male figure beside a small altar with a flame. Ameling plausibly interprets this as a visual allusion to the use of fire in the rituals of the Theos Hypsistos cult.[91] This may be a rare example of an individual Theos Hypsistos worshipper being identified as a God-fearer outside a Jewish context.

In general, worshippers of Theos Hypsistos had no cause to identify themselves as such except in two contexts. One was on the occasions that they offered votives to their god. The other was when they needed to distinguish themselves from the Jews, and it is in the latter cases that they identify themselves, or are identified by others, as God-fearers.[92] However, the remarkable similarity of the beliefs of the two groups provides strong grounds for the conclusion that if an enquirer asked a pagan worshipper of

---

[87] This essential point forms a central part of John North's contribution to this volume. Groups sometimes called themselves *Sarapiastai* or similar, but this was usually used to show that they were members of a local religious association that worshipped Sarapis, and was not a claim to be part of an empire-wide community.

[88] *IJO* II, nos. 27 and 49.

[89] *JIWE* I, nos. 9 (Pola), 12 (Lorium), 113 (in the Jewish catacomb at Venosa); II, no. 392 (Rome).

[90] *JIWE* II, no. 627 (Rome); *IJO* II, no. 6 (Cos); *IG* XII.1, 893 (Rhodes, not included in *IJO* II); *JIWE* II, no. 207 (Rome).

[91] T. Corsten, *I.Prusa* I, no. 115 with Ameling (1999).

[92] See the comment of Ameling, *IJO* II, 20 n. 105: 'Da sich Verehrer des *Theos Hypsistos* nur auf wenigen Inschriften bezeichnen, ist Mitchells Ausdruck vielleicht etwas stark.'

Theos Hypsistos whether he was a *theosebes* or not, the answer would have generally been affirmative.

Glen Bowersock has challenged the equation with a different line of argument, maintaining that the *theosebeis* simply never constituted a unified category. 'As always we must attend to local conditions.... There is no justification for generalizing the use of the term throughout the Graeco-Roman world.'[93] Specifically, Bowersock rejects the view that the formal distinction found in the Aphrodisias inscription between the categories of Jews (Ἰουδαῖοι) and God-fearers (θεοσεβεῖς) (to say nothing of the third category of proselytes), and the apparently similar distinction to be found in the texts from the Sardis synagogue, applies to the remaining evidence. In other words, the significance of the term *theosebeis* varies from case to case. He has picked on two controversial items from the dossier to support his argument. Both are extremely precarious.

The first item comes from an important series of first-century manumission inscriptions from Panticapaeum and Phanagoria, recently republished by Noy, Panayotov and Bloedhorn in the Eastern Europe corpus of inscriptions from the Jewish East.[94] The manumission procedure can be recognised in the regular format of the inscriptions, although they differ in minor details from one another. First came a reference to the ruling king and a date. The owner then made a formal proclamation in the prayer house (*proseuche*) that the slave would henceforth be free from any obligation to the owner or his/her heirs, and free to go anywhere, save for an obligation to show reverence and provide service to the prayer house. This declaration was witnessed by the community in the synagogue. The two parts of the epigraphic formula relevant for our purposes are the statements that related to the freed slave's obligations to the prayer house, and the witness borne by the synagogue community, which agreed to act as guarantor or guardian of the ex-slave's new status. In two of the texts from Panticapaeum (BS 5 and BS 6) these take the form χωρὶς εἰς τὴν προσευχὴν θωπείας τε καὶ προσκαρτερήσεως, followed by συνεπιτροπευούσης δὲ καὶ τῆς συναγώγης τῶν Ἰουδαίων. BS 9 also ends with the same formula for the synagogue community. BS 17 from Phanagoria ends with two broken lines that have been tentatively restored to read τῆς θωπεί[ας ἕνεκα καὶ] προσκαρ[τερ]ήσεως. BS 18 has formulae identical with the first two Panticapaeum texts except that the first phrase reverses the terms to read χωρὶς εἰς τὴν προσευχὴν προσκαρτερήσεως τε καὶ θωπείας and this is

[93] Bowersock (2007), 251.
[94] Noy, Panayotov and Bloedhorn, *IJO* I, BS nos. 5–9 and BS nos. 17–18. These new editions were not yet available to Bowersock.

separated from the guarantor clause by the imperative καὶ ἔσταν ἄφετοι. The meanings of the unusual terms *thopeia* and *proskarteresis*, which are unparalleled in any other documents of this nature, are reasonably clear from the context. The former meant not flattery, in a pejorative sense, but reverence or devotion, while the latter has the sense of constant or sustained attendance to the place of prayer.[95] BS 7 from Panticapaeum now needs discussion. This released a *threptos*, probably identified by the female name Elpis,[96] ὅπως ἐστὶν ἀπαρενόχλητος καὶ ἀνεπίληπτος ἀπὸ παντὸς κληρονόμου χωρὶς τοῦ προσκαρτερεῖν τῇ προσευχῇ, ἐπιτροπευούσης τῆς συναγώγης τῶν Ἰουδαίων καὶ θεὸν σέβων. The last word or words have been the cause of all the trouble. One interpretation, favoured by Nadel, Levinskaya and Bowersock, is to treat them as supplying the sense of the term *thopeia*, which has been omitted from the preceding formula. This not only defies normal syntax, by requiring us to understand a major anacolouthon and a change of construction from the infinitive προσκαρτερεῖν to a participle θεὸν σέβων, but also involves the editorial coinage of an unattested active verbal form σέβω to replace the regular middle form σέβομαι.[97] Bowersock further suggests that 'the replacement of *thopeia* with θεὸν σέβων not only confirms the rare meaning of *thopeia* but also maintains the structure of the local legal formula for new freedmen'.[98] In fact the structure of the inscriptions clearly reflects the sequence of events during the manumission. The declaration of the manumitted slave's obligations was followed by the witness statement of the assembled synagogue community. It would be wholly anomalous to add a further asseveration of the slave's piety as an afterthought to the procedure. Each of these factors alone would render the proposed interpretation extremely dubious. Collectively they rule it out of court definitively. The alternative solution to the difficulty is to understand the final phrase as the genitive plural noun θεοσεβῶν, into which the engraver had inserted a redundant nu, thereby inadvertently creating

---

[95] See Bowersock (2007) for the meaning of *thopeia*, endorsed independently by the editors of *IJO* I, BS no. 5, who provide additional helpful discussion of *proskarteresis*.

[96] Bowersock and Levinskaya's interpretation of the text requires that we restore the slave's name at the beginning of the inscription not as the common female form Elpis, but as the rarer masculine Elpias, in order to avoid the grammatical error of joining a feminine subject to a supposed masculine participial form. The textual problem is not easy to resolve, as is clear from the discussion in *IJO* I, 281–2, whose editors opt for Elpis. In any case, Bowersock's preference for Elpias requires him to reconstruct the line as Ἐλπια<ν> [ἐμ]α[υ]τῆς θρεπτ[όν], thus committing him to a methodological procedure (supplying a letter omitted by the stone mason) equivalent to the one that he charges me with, in supposing that the mason inserted a redundant nu in θεοσεβῶν (see below).

[97] Levinskaya (1996), 74–6 and 232–4.   [98] Bowersock (2007), 252–3.

the common word θεόν at the line end.[99] This simply conveys the meaning that the community in question included both Jews and *theosebeis*, as attested by the inscriptions at Aphrodisias and Sardis.

The second text cited by Bowersock is one of eight inscriptions which designated the seating positions of groups in the theatre at Miletus. The full collection of these texts was published for the first time in 1998 by Peter Herrmann. Four were for the *aurarii*, in the lower rows near the right-hand edge of the cavea,[100] one was for the *neoteroi*, close to the top right of the cavea, and three were for the Jewish community and their associates.[101] The first inscription of this final group, five rows up and four seating blocks from the right edge of the cavea, reads τόπος Είουδέων τῶν καὶ Θεο<σ>εβίον (the sigma of the last word has been mistakenly carved as an epsilon) (940f); this text is carved three rows above the inscription for ΘΕΟ[.]ΕΒΙΟΝ, restored as Θεο[σ]εβίον (940g), which is two rows up and on the fifth seating block, and two rows above the inscription for Βενέτων ΕΙΟ[.]ΕΩΝ, restored as either Είο[υδ]έων or Είο[δ]έων (940h), which is in the third row up and extends across the sixth and fifth seating blocks from the right. Bowersock follows Deissmann, the first editor, Louis Robert and others in the view that 940f should be interpreted at face value: this was the place of 'the Jews also known as the Theosebioi'. This is impeccable as a construction of the Greek,[102] but poses a problem of interpretation, for it implies that at Miletus the two terms referred to the same group, in contrast to the differentiation which is attested at Aphrodisias and Sardis. One way to avoid this contradiction is to suppose that the late antique form θεοσέβιοι was not equivalent to and did not have the technical meaning of θεοσεβεῖς, but was simply an additional designation of the local Jews who, at Miletus, were 'also called God-reverers'.[103] Alternatively, and this is Bowersock's view, we must conclude that the designation θεοσεβής/θεοσέβιος was simply being used in a different sense to that encountered at Aphrodisias, despite

---

[99] Precisely this error, at the same point where the name breaks across a line, occurs in a Jewish epitaph of late antiquity: κοιμητήριον | Εὐτυχίας τῆς | μητρὸς Ἀθη|νέου κὲ Θεο{ν}|κτίστου (*IJO* I, Ach no. 28, Athens). A less plausible explanation of the Panticapaeum text is that the engraver intended the participial phrase θεὸν σεβομένων, which would reproduce a formula found in the Theos Hypsistos inscriptions of Tanais (**96, 98, 100, 101**), but omitted the letters -ομεν- from the middle of the word.

[100] See Roueché (1995).

[101] See P. Herrmann, *Inschriften von Milet* VI.2 (Berlin 1998), no. 940 (a) – (h). All the new texts clearly date to late antiquity and contradict the suggestion of earlier commentators that the main Jewish text, 940 (f), may date to the second or third century AD.

[102] Bowersock (2002), 356; (2007), 253. For a full account of earlier readings and interpretations see Ameling, *IJO* II, no. 37.

[103] So Ameling, *IJO* II, 170, following Robert (1964), 47.

the obvious confusion that this might cause between 'the Jews also called God-reverers' at Miletus, and the separate categories of Jews and God-fearers encountered elsewhere. I continue to find the explanation that the engraver simply swapped the positions of τῶν and καί, thereby producing a very common, but in this case erroneous, double name formula, to be the simplest resolution of the dilemma. A new factor has been introduced to the old argument by Herrmann's publication of the two other relevant texts from the Miletus theatre, which clearly distinguished the θεοσέβιοι and the Εἰουδέοι, who were supporters of the blues, from one another. This strongly favours the view that the inscription which names them both in one phrase also intended to distinguish them as separate groups.[104]

The interpretation of the Miletus inscription remains in the balance, but it is important to observe the axiom that hard cases make bad law. This is the only possible instance to be found in the inscriptions where a strong argument can be made for identifying the God-fearers as full Jews. Literary sources indeed sometimes refer to Jews as θεοσεβεῖς, God-fearing,[105] but do not use this, as the Miletus inscription purportedly does, as an alternative title or designation of the category to which the Jews belonged. Elsewhere the God-fearers are either certainly or probably to be distinguished from the Jews in the full sense, and as such can be equated with the Jewish sympathisers named in the Acts of the Apostles and by Josephus as σεβόμενοι or φοβούμενοι τὸν θεόν, who are similarly distinguished from full Jews and Jewish proselytes.

Two of our sources provide a direct terminological link between the category of the σεβόμενοι τὸν θεόν and θεοσεβεῖς and the cult of Theos Hypsistos. Four third-century inscriptions from Tanais identify the local cult association as οἱ εἰσποιητοὶ ἀδελφοὶ σεβόμενοι θεὸν ὕψιστον (**96, 98, 100, 101**), and Cyril of Alexandria in the early fifth century reported that Palestinian and Phoenician worshippers of Theos Hypsistos called themselves *theosebeis*.[106] Bowersock regards it as a weakness of my hypothesis that these attestations are widely separated in space and time.[107] It would be legitimate to make precisely the opposite inference, that this wide

---

[104] The most recent treatment of the problem is by Baker (2005), who accepts my identification of the God-fearers with the worshippers of Theos Hypsistos and argues for translating the inscription as 'the place of the Jews [real Jews], who are called [part of] the group of *theosebioi* [followers of the Most High God]'. However, this entails subsuming the Jews into a secondary position, part of the wider category of God-fearers, a situation and a form of self-representation for which there are no parallels, and which also requires a forced interpretation of the phrase τῶν καί, to mean 'part of'.

[105] See Ameling, *IJO* II, 17, citing IV Macc. and Strabo 16.2.37, 761, as well as some usage in Josephus.

[106] *PG* 68, 281c.   [107] Bowersock (2002).

separation supports the argument that both the *theosebeis* and the worshippers of Theos Hypsistos can and should be identified as widespread
and enduring participants in the religious landscape of the eastern Roman
empire, as is suggested by the portrayal of their beliefs in authors as disparate
as Josephus, Juvenal and Gregory of Nazianzus.[108] Here too the space/time
divide argues strongly against the interpretation of either phenomenon in
a purely local sense, and for the conclusion that the worshippers of Theos
Hypsistos and the *theosebeis*, if not formally identical, were very closely
related to one another.

USING ALL THE EVIDENCE

Belayche and Stein have suggested that it is methodologically improper
to have started my study with the evidence of the patristic writers, which
has then distorted the interpretation of the earlier documents.[109] In this
response I have deliberately reversed the order of my approach. However,
the charge in any case has little substance. As even Stein concedes, the
patristic writers provide four largely similar accounts of the worship of
Theos Hypsistos in the fourth and fifth centuries AD.[110] Certainly they
are written from an orthodox viewpoint and are designed to contrast
the cult unfavourably with Christianity, but they provide information
about its followers, the locations where they were to be found, and their
practices, which are both specific and for the most part directly verified
by the documents. Gregory of Nazianzus knew that his own father had
been one of a hypsistarian group which rejected idols and sacrifice, but
worshipped fire and lights; its members respected the Sabbath and Jewish
dietary regulations, but were not circumcised, and they were called (by
others) Hypsistarians.[111] Gregory of Nyssa, who doubtless also had direct
acquaintance with the cult in Cappadocia, saw them as being very close
to Christians, revering their god as *hypsistos* and *pantokrator*, but denying
him the name of the Father (and thus being indifferent to the essential
doctrine of the incarnation).[112] An inscription from Nacolea (**A50**) provides
contemporary Anatolian evidence for 'the people of the Highest God,
known for their spiritual writings and Homeric verses', who appear to be a

[108] Mitchell (1999), 120.   [109] Belayche (2005a), 36 n. 12; Stein (2001), 124 (*Überinterpretation*).
[110] Stein (2001), 124: 'die in wesentlichen Pünkten übereinstimmenden, zum teil sich ergänzenden Berichte'.
[111] Gregory of Nazianzus, *Oratio* 18.5 (*PG* 35, 990).
[112] Gregory of Nyssa, *Refutatio Confessionis Eunomii* 38 (II, 327 Jaeger; *PG* 45, 482).

similar group in Phrygia. Another text from Asia Minor, long-known but overlooked in the debate until recently, reveals that a priest of Hypsistos was one of the small property owners of the Ionian city of Magnesia on the Maeander in the early fourth century AD.[113] This reference also supports the conclusion that Hypsistos was conceived as a god in his own right, not as a way of representing a god more familiar by another designation. Cyril of Alexandria reported that persons in Palestine and Phoenicia worshipped *hypsistos theos*, acknowledged the reality of other gods, including the sun, moon and stars, earth and heaven, and called themselves *theosebeis*.[114] Epiphanius of Salamis referred to the Messalians or Euphemitai, names which derive from Semitic or Greek words to mean 'those who pray'. The practices that he ascribes to them, at greater length than the other authors, leave little doubt that these too were Hypsistos worshippers, and Epiphanius alluded to specific groups in Samaria and Phoenicia.[115] The geographical distribution of these groups itself refutes Bowersock's contention that the patristic authors reflected only a localised Cappadocian cult.[116]

The fourth- and fifth-century writers indicate a consistency of beliefs and cult practices over a geographical area that extended across Palestine, Phoenicia and central Anatolia. This is consistent with the evidence of the inscriptions, taken in its entirety, which provides a coherent picture of a unified religious phenomenon, manifested with significant local and circumstantial variations, across the east Mediterranean and Black Sea basins, as well as in Egypt and the Near East. The worshippers of Theos Hypsistos were already widespread and well-rooted in the first and second centuries AD. Many of these groups established close links to the Diaspora Jewish communities. They can be considered, at least from our historical perspective, as a serious competitor with early Christianity. Hypsistarians remained prominent and identifiable at least until the fifth century AD.

We cannot call the cult monotheistic in the strictly exclusive sense that is applied to ancient Judaism and Christianity, but it involved a series of coherent and explicit rituals and practices which were based on belief in a unique, transcendent god, who could not be represented in human form. Many of the followers of Theos Hypsistos clearly worshipped him

---

[113] **A42**, observed by Thonemann (2007) 438 n. 12.
[114] Cyril of Alexandria, *De adoratione in Spiritu et Veritate* 3.92 (*PG* 68, 281c).
[115] Epiphanius, *Panarion* 80.1–2.   [116] Bowersock (2002).

alone. They called themselves 'worshippers of god'. In essence and in spirit, if not in the narrowest definition, this was a form of monotheistic religion.

ADDITIONAL CATALOGUE OF HYPSISTOS INSCRIPTIONS

There are useful, but not exhaustive, collections of the epigraphic material in Colpe and Löw (1993), Levinskaya (1996) and Wischmeyer (2005). For convenience and speed of consultation I have generally avoided 'Harvard-style' references in the following catalogue.

Achaea

A1. Athens. *IG* ii.2, 4056; S. Lambert, *ABSA* 95 (2000), 505–6; *SEG* 50 (2000) 201. Cylindrical altar of Pentelic marble with garlanded bucranion below inscription. i–ii AD? [–? ὑψ]ίστῳ ὑπὲρ Ζωπύρας | [καὶ ᾿Ανθ]εστηρίου

A2. Athens. B. D. Merritt, *Hesperia* 17 (1948), 43 no. 74. Top of small columnar altar. ii–iii AD. Διὶ ὑψίσ[τωι] | [– –]ν[–]

A3. Athens. B. D. Merritt, *Hesperia* 23 (1954), 256 no. 40. Small cylindrical altar of Pentelic marble. i AD. Ὑψίστ[ῳ ἀνέθη]|κε Δα[– –] | εὐχήν

A4. Athens. A. Lajtar, *ZPE* 70 (1987), 165. [Δι]ὶ ὑψίστῳ Δαφνὶς | [εὐ]χὴν ἀνέθηκε

A5. H. Thompson, *Hesperia* 5 (1936), 155 (a). Small marble plaque depicting a breast. i–ii AD. Ὑψίστῳ Γαμικὴ εὐχήν

A6. H. Thompson, *Hesperia* 5 (1936), 155 (c). Top left corner of small marble plaque. i–ii AD. Ὑψ[ίστῳ –]

A7. *IG* ii², 4843. Top of plaque of Pentelic marble. i–iii AD. [–]α Διὶ ὑψ|ίστῳ εὐχ]ήν

Thessaly

A8. Azoros Elassonas. A. Tziafalias, *AD* 46 B1 (1991 [1996]), 226; *SEG* 46 (1996), 640. Stele with relief of an eagle. i AD. Ἑρμοκλῆς Ὑψίστῳ | εὐξάμενος δῶρον

A9. Phthiotic Thebes. P. Chrysostomou, *AD* 44–6 *Melet.* (1989–91 [1996]), 60 no. 2; *SEG* 46 (1996), 659. Marble column. ii AD. ᾿Αγέαρ-χος | Τείμωνος | Διὶ ὑψίστῳ | εὐξάμενος

A10. Evangelismos. A. Tziafalias, *AD* 48 B1 (1993 [1998]), 258 no. 58; *SEG* 47 (1997), 730. Column fragment. I–II AD. Ὑψίστῳ | Τρόφιμος καὶ | Λεύκιος | δῶρον ὑπὲρ ἀγαθῶν

Macedonia

See Chrysostomou (1996) for a valuable synopsis and catalogue of documents for the cult of Zeus in Thessaly and Macedonia; Pilhofer (1995), 182–8 for Theos Hypsistos and Hypsistos cults in Macedonia and Thrace; and Pandermalis (2005) for important information about the sanctuary of Zeus Hypsistos at Dion (*SEG* 53 (2003), 596).

A11. Amphipolis. C. Bakirtzis, *PAAH* 151 (1996 [1998]), 233; *AE* 1997, 1361; *SEG* 47 (1997), 878. I–II AD. Λεύκιος Αἰφίκιος | καὶ Πῶλλα Ἐλουία | Διὶ ὑψίστωι χαριστήριον

A12. Anthemous. D. M. Robinson, *TAPA* 69 (1938), 72 no. 30; *SEG* 42 (1992), 562. II AD. Ἀσκληπιόδωρος | Ἱέρωνος | Διὶ | ὑψίστῳ

A13. Antigoneia. Chrysostomou (1996), 57–8 no. 2; *SEG* 46 (1996), 726; *AE* 1995, 1390. Statue base. I–II AD. Κόϊντος Μάρκιος | Νουμήνιος Διὶ | ὑψίστῳ

A14. Belbendos. Chrysostomou (1996), 50; *SEG* 46 (1996), 728. Marble stele showing Zeus holding a sceptre and a phiale, an altar and a vase. I–III AD. Διὶ ὑψίστῳ | . . . Λ . . . Ι . . .

A15. Beroia. Gounaropoulou and Hatzopoulos (1998), 130–3 no. 27; Chrysostomou (1996), 36–9 no. 4; *SEG* 46 (1996), 737; *AE* 1995, 1382. Marble stele with relief of an eagle above a bucranion and a garland of oak leaves. The iconography and find-spot indicate that this was a dedication to Zeus Hypsistos. The inscription contains the names of members of a cult association, some with patronymics and indications of their professions. Late II–early III AD.

A16. Dion. *SEG* 53 (2003), 596. Marble plaque referring to monthly banquets (δοχαί) of Zeus Hypsistos. AD 251/2.

A17. Dion. *SEG* 53 (2003), 596. Document relating to estates of Zeus Hypsistos followed by a list of *threskeutai*. Roman imperial period.

A18. Dion. Pandermalis (2005), 417 (ph); *SEG* 53 (2003) 597; *AE* 2003, 1579. Ionic capital supporting a marble eagle. I–II AD. Διὶ ὑψίστῳ | Λ. Τρέβιος | Λέων | εὐξάμενος

A19. Dion. Pandermalis (2005), 417 (ph); *SEG* 53 (2003), 598; *AE* 2003, 1580. Marble pediment. Eagle between two ears, with a wreath above. I–II AD. Διὶ ὑψίστῳ εὐχὴν Γ. Ὀλύμπιος Παῦλος ἱερη[τεύσας]

200 STEPHEN MITCHELL

A20. Dion. Pandermalis (2005), 417 (ph); *SEG* 53 (2003), 599. Marble basin. I–II AD. Διὶ ὑψίστῳ Δημήτριος εὐχήν

A21. Dion. Pandermalis (2005), 418; *SEG* 53 (2003), 600; *AE* 2003, 1582b. Small column. Dedication to Zeus Hypsistos by Αὖλος Μαίκιος Σπόριος and Νεικοπολίς. Roman imperial period.

A22. Edessa. Chrysostomou (1996), 31–2 no. 3; *SEG* 46 (1996), 744. Marble stele with relief of an eagle in an oak-leaf garland. AD 51. Διὶ ὑψίστῳ | ὑπὲρ τῆς σωτηρίας | Μ. Οὐιβίου Ἀμβούα | οἱ συνήθεις ἐπιμεληταὶ κτλ. [nine names follow, mostly Roman citizens, one female] ἔτους θηρ´ Περιτίου ἱερητεύοντος Μ. Ἀττίου Λόγγου· ΡΥΣ ἐποίει

A23. Between Edessa and Kyrrhos (near Anydron). A. Panayotou and P. Chrysostomou, *BCH* 117 (1993), 370–2 no. 6. Rectangular cippus. AD 132 or 135. ἔτους | δξρ´ | Δείου λ´ | Εὔλαιος | Λαοίτα | πολειτα|ρχήσας | Δι|ὶ ὑψίστ|ῳ

A24. Heracleia Lyncestis. S. Düll, *Die Götterkulte Nordmakedoniens in römischer Zeit* (Munich 1977), 357–8 no. 167; Chrysostomou (1996), 55 no. 1; *SEG* 46 (1996), 750. Lower part of a stele showing Zeus Hypsistos offering a libation, with an eagle below. AD 209/10. Μ. Αἴλιος ὁ καθυδρεύσα[ς] ἔτους ντ´

A25. Kyrrhos (Bottiaia). Chrysostomou (1996), 40–1; *SEG* 46 (1996), 760. Fragment of a Doric capital. Late II–early III AD. [Δ]ιὶ ὑψίστῳ | [Δ]όλιχος

A26. Pella. Chrysostomou (1996), 43 no. 3; *SEG* 46 (1996), 785. Lamp depicting eagle and bucranion, with inscription on base. II–III AD. Ὑψίστου

A27. Stobi (Drenovo). S. Düll, *Die Götterkulte Nordmakedoniens in römischer Zeit* (Munich 1977), 356 no. 164; Chrysostomou (1996), 56 no. 1; *SEG* 46 (1996), 743. C. AD 200–50. Δ[ι]ὶ ὑψίστῳ | Π. Αἴλιος Που|βλανὸς κατ᾽ εὐ|χὴν ἀνέθηκεν

A28. Thessalonica. V. Misailidou-Despotidou, Επιγραφὲς Αρχαίας Μακεδονίας από τὴ συλλογὴ τῆς ΙΣΤ´ Εφορείας (Thessalonica 1999) 47 no. 37; *SEG* 47 (1997), 963; *Bull. Ep.* 1998, 255 (Hatzopoulos). Marble plaque with a dedication to θεὸς ὕψιστος and the συμποσιασταὶ θεοί set up by Ἀμύντας Ζωίλου. I–II AD.

NB In addition to **55–8** in my original catalogue (= *IG* x.2, 67–8 and 71–2), the inscriptions *IG* x.2, 69–70, although they do not mention Theos Hypsistos, clearly belong to the same series as **55** and **56**, being columns from a building associated with the cult.

A29. Unknown provenance, but transported from Thessalonica to Chalkidike. I. A. Papangelos, *Tekmeria* 7 (2002), 163–5; *SEG* 52 (2002),

650. Marble plaque. II–III AD. Διὶ ὑψίστῳ τὸν ναὸν ἐκ θεμε|λίων κατεσκεύασαν ἐκ τῶν ἰδί|ων Ζωΐλος Μένωνος τοῦ Με|νάνδρου τοῦ Διονυσίου Ἀν|τιοχιδεὺς καὶ Κρατιστὼ Μέ|νωνος τοῦ Σωσιβίου Ἀντιο|χιδεῖτις ἡ γυνὴ αὐτοῦ

Thrace

A30. Abdera. A. D. Loukoupoulou, *Epigraphes tes Thrakes tou Aigaiou* (Athens 2005), 219 E.19. Thymiaterion. III AD. Ξ | Σαβ(β)αὶς · | Δειὶ ὑψίστῳ | εὐχήν

A31. Bizye (near Ajtos). *IGBulg*. v, 5647. Small marble altar. II AD? [ἀ]γαθῇ τύχῃ | [θ]εῷ ὑψίστῳ | Χρῆσμος | Ἑρμογένου | ὑπὲρ τῶν | ἰδίων | εὐχαριστῶ

A32. Byzantium. A. Lajtar, *I.Byzantion* 24. Small white marble altar. II AD? [θεῷ ὑ]ψίστῳ | [Μακ]εδώνι[ς | κα]ὶ Ἀρωμάτιν | [μετ]ὰ τῶν τέ|[κνων καὶ τῶν | [ἰδίων π]άντων
[Perinthos. Mitchell **64** is now published by M. H. Sayar, *I.Perinthos* 302; *SEG* 48 (1998), 922. [– –] Ε̣Ι̣Ω̣Ν̣ | [– –]ωνις | [θ]εῷ ὑψί[στῳ] εὐχαρ|ιστήριον]

A33. Philippopolis (Dinkata). *IGBulg*. v, 5472. Bronze *tabula ansata*. II AD. Διὶ ὑψί(σ)τῳ | Γ. Μαίλιος Ἀγαθό|πους ὑπὲρ τῆς | τῶν πατρώνων | Γ. Μαιλίου Ἀκύλου κα(ὶ) | Φλαουίας Τιουτης | καὶ τῶν τέκνων αὐ|τῶν σωτηρίας καὶ ἑ|αυτοῦ χαριστήριν

North shore of the Black Sea

For recent discussion of the regional evidence see Ustinova (1999); Bowersock (2002) and (2007). Both argue for an interpretation of the evidence for Theos Hypsistos that is different from the one that I propose: Ustinova for a supreme masculine deity, ultimately of Scythian or Iranian origin, whose cult was dominant throughout the communities along the north shore of the Black sea and around the Sea of Azov; Bowersock for distinct and separate cults of the 'Highest God', not identifiable as a single deity, in the various north Black Sea communities: Tanais, Gorgippia, Panticapaeum.

Aegean Islands

A34. Cos. G. Pugliese Caratelli, *M. Segre, Iscrizioni di Cos* I and II (Rome 1993), EV no. 69; *SEG* 43 (1993), 549. Θεῷ ὑψ[ίστῳ]

202 STEPHEN MITCHELL

A35. Cos. G. Pugliese Caratelli, *M. Segre, Iscrizioni di Cos* I and II (Rome 1993), EV no. 27; *SEG* 43 (1993), 549. Διὶ ὑψίστῳ καὶ Ἥ[ρ]ᾳ Οὐρανίᾳ καὶ Ἀσκληπίῳ [καὶ Ὑ]γιείᾳ καὶ πᾶσι τοῖς θεοῖς ΣΙΕΙΕΩΙΤΑΙ

Crete

A36. Gortyn. A di Vita. *ASAA* 76–8 (1998–2000 [2001]), 428–34; *SEG* 50 (2000), 909; 54 (2004), 854. Small limestone altar. Late I–early II AD. θεῷ ὑψίστ[ῳ] | εὐχὴ[ν] | Τι. Κλαύδι[ος] | Κατάπλο[υς]

Italy

A37. Torre dell'Orso (Apulia, near Otranto). C. Pagliaro, Ἱστορίη: *Studi offerti dagli allievi a Giuseppe Nenci in occasione del suo settantesimo compleanno* (Lecce 1994), 345–58; *SEG* 45 (1995), 1482. Rock cut inscription at Grotta S. Cristoforo. A large superimposed cross postdates the inscription. II–III AD? Θεῷ ὑψίστῳ ἐπηκόῳ | Πούπλιος [Ἀνί]κιος Νικηφόρος Ἀνικίῳ [–]ις πατρώνῳ | καὶ Πο[–]ῳ πατρώνῳ

Spain

[Mitchell **126** from Valentia may be from Almeida in Portugal, see *SEG* 46 (1996), 1372.]

Tripolitania

A38. Lepcis Magna. G. Pugliese Caratelli, *Quaderni di archeologia della Libya* 18 (2003), 272–3 no. 2; *SEG* 53 (2003), 1169–70; *RICIS* II, 702/0108. Base found beside the entrance to the temple of Sarapis, dedicating a statue of Zeus Hypsistos. After AD 161. On top: (A) Αὐρήλ[ιος – –] (B) [–]ν″Υψ[ιστ –]; on the shaft there is a dedication by members of the family of Aurelius Dioskoros Δία ὕψιστον ἐπ' ἀγαθῷ

Ionia

A39. Miletus. P. Herrmann and others, *Inschriften von Milet. Teil 3* (*Milet* VI.3, Berlin 2006), 160 no. 1252. Slender marble altar. II–III AD. Διὸς | ὑψίστου | κατὰ | χρησμόν

A40. Miletus. P. Herrmann and others, *Inschriften von Milet. Teil 3*, 160 no. 1254. Top of small marble altar, poor late lettering. III AD. [? Διὸς] | [ὑ]ψίσ|του

A41. Miletus. P. Herrmann and others, *Inschriften von Milet. Teil 3*, 161 no. 1255. Small grey marble altar with rounded top. I–II AD. Ζήλω|τος | θεῷ | ὑψί|[στω]

[Mitchell **135–6**, the two inscriptions from Miletus for Ulpius Carpus, the priest and prophet of Theos Hypsistos, are published in *Inschriften von Milet. Teil 3*, 89–91 nos. 1138–9 and dated by W. Günther not *c.* AD 140 but to the second half of II AD on the basis of letter forms. **134** for Zeus Hypsistos, republished as *Inschriften von Milet. Teil 3*, 160 no. 1253, is not Hellenistic but belongs to II–III AD.]

A42. Magnesia on the Maeander. A ἱερεὺς Ὑψίστου is mentioned as owning a small property on the tax registers of the early fourth century, *c.* AD 310. *I.Magnesia* 122 d.13; cf. Thonemann (2007), 438 n. 12.

Caria

A43. Pisye. A. Bresson and others, *Les hautes terres de la Carie* (Bordeaux 2001), 131 no. 28; *SEG* 51 (2001), 1549. Marble altar. II–III AD. Ὑψίστου

Lydia

A44. Collyda. H. Malay, *Researches in Lydia, Mysia and Aiolis*, Ergänzungsheft zu den *TAM* (Vienna 1999), 137 no. 150; *SEG* 49 (1999), 1588. Bottom of marble stele with figure of a man praying. II–III AD. Θ[ε]ᾷ ὑψίστη ΚΛΑ | . . . . . τῶν προκαθημένη

A45. Medar (Ovaköy). H. Malay, *Researches in Lydia*, 42 no. 26; *SEG* 49 (1999), 1708. Rectangular altar. II AD. Ἰουλιανὸς | βαφεὺς θεῶι | [ὑ]ψίστω εὐχα|ριστήριον ὑ|πὲρ τῆς αὐτοῦ | σωτηρίας

A46. Medar (Ovaköy). H. Malay, *Researches in Lydia*, 42–3 no. 27; *SEG* 49 (1999), 1709. Marble altar with acroteria. II AD. Μοῦσα Μηνοφίλου θεῷ ὑψίστω | εὐχὴν ἀνέθη|κεν

A47. Philadelphia (territory?). G. Petzl, *TAM* v.3, 1634. Plain gabled stele with a circle and two ivy leaves in the pediment. AD 184/5. ἔτους σξθ´ μη. Αὐδναίου ι´ Φλα|βία θεῷ ὑψίστω | εὐχήν

A48. Philadelphia (territory, Manisa Museum). H. Malay, *I.Manisa Museum* (1994), 181; G. Petzl, *TAM* v.33, 1637. II AD. Θεῷ Ὁσίω καὶ Δικαίω

| Μελτίνη εὐξαμένη ὑπ|ὲρ Γλαύκου τοῦ συνβίου | εὐχαριστοῦσα ἀπέδ-ωκα | τὴν εὐχήν. ἔτους τκζ΄ | μηνὸς Ξανδίκου η΄. Under the letters ΟΣΙΩ in line 2 the engraver originally carved ΥΨΙΣ, evidently expecting to cut ὑψίστῳ.

Pontus

A49. Amaseia (Yassıçal). D. French, *EA* 26 (1996), 94 no. 19; *SEG* 46 (1996), 1617. Inscription from a building, perhaps an architrave. I–II AD. Θεῷ ὑψίστῳ εὐχὴν Στρατόνικος | Μητροδώρου σωθεὶς ἐκ μεγάλων | κινδύνων

A50. Sinope (Germa). L. Ruscu, *EA* 38 (2005), 125–6; *SEG* 52 (2002), 1240. Marble altar. II AD? θεῷ ὑψίστῳ | Οὐαλερία | Μαρκιανή

Paphlagonia

A51. Amastris. C. Marek, *EA* 32 (2000), 135–7; *SGO* II, 10/03/01; *SEG* 50 (2000), 1225. Slender altar. II–III AD. Θεῷ ὑψίστῳ | ὀμφῇ ἀκερ|σεκόμου βῶ|μον θεοῦ ὑψίσ|τοιο, ὃς κατὰ πάντων ἔστι καὶ οὐ βλέπε|ται, εἰσορᾷ δὲ | δείμαθ᾽ ὅπως | ἀπαλάλκηται | βροτολοιγέ|α θνητῶν

Galatia

A52. Pessinus. J. Devreker, *EA* 24 (1995), 73 no. 1; *SEG* 45 (1995), 1703; *AE* 1995, 1532; *I.Pessinus* 23. Small marble altar. I–II AD. Πρεῖμα Πρ[εί]|μου μεγά|λῳ θεῷ ὑψ[ί]|στῷ εὐχ[ήν]

Phrygia

A53. Amorium/Docimium (Kurudere). T. Drew-Bear, C. M. Thomas, M. Yıldızturan, *Phrygian Votive Steles* (Ankara 1999), no. 163. Elegiac distych. *c.* AD 170. Ζηνὶ πανυψίστῳ | Χαρίτων Δοκιμε[ὺς] | ἀνέθηκεν εὐξά|μενος στήλην | ἀγλαΐσας παλά|μαις

A54. Dorylaeum (Aşağı Çavlan Köy). M. Ricl, *ZA* 44 (1994), 169 no. 25; *SEG* 44 (1994), 1058. Small limestone altar with ear of corn and acroteria in pediment. II AD. Νεῖλος | Δημοσ|θένου | [θ]εῷ ὑψί[σ]τῳ εὐχ|ήν

A55. Nacolea (Yapıldak). C. H. E. Haspels, *The Highlands of Phrygia* (Princeton 1971), 313–14 no. 40; *SEG* 43 (1993), 945. Verse epigram. III–IV AD. Ζώσιμος Πατρικίου καὶ Δόμνης γέ|νος ἐσθλόν, πάτρης ἔντειμος ἐῆς καὶ ἐκ | λαοῦ ὑψίστοιο, πνευματικαῖς γραφαῖς καὶ | Ὁμηρίοις [ἐ]πέεσσιν κτλ.

Pamphylia

A56. Perge. S. Şahin, *I.Perge* 230. Bottom of block of coarse stone. III AD? – – – | [–] θεῷ [ὑ]ψίστῳ εὐχήν

A57. Perge. S. Şahin, *I.Perge* 231. Bottom of small limestone altar. II AD? – – | !ỌEI!! [–] | Συντύ[χης θεῷ] | ὑψίστ[ῳ] | εὐχήν

Lycia-Cibyratis

A58. Cibyra (Sorkun). *I.Kibyra* I, 92; N. Milner, *RECAM* III, 27 no. 58; *SEG* 48 (1998), 1595; 52 (2002), 1431. Round altar. II–III AD. θεῷ ὑψίστῳ

A59. Oinoanda. Dr Nicholas Milner reports the discovery in 2008 of votive texts for Hypsistos, Artemis and Leto carved into the city wall at a point close to the Clarian oracle (**233**) and the dedication by Chromatis (**234**), which have hitherto served to identify the sanctuary of Theos Hypsistos. See the brief report at: www.dainst.org/index_8097_en. html.

Lycaonia

A60. Konya Museum (unknown provenance). B. H. Maclean, *RECAM* IV, 39; *SEG* 52 (2002), 1458. Small reddish limestone altar. Roman imperial period. θεῷ ὑψ|ίστῳ | εὐχήν

Cyprus

A61. Amathous. I. Nicolaou, *RDAC* 1994, 191 no. 45. Cylindrical sandstone cippus. I–II AD. θεῷ ὑψίσ[τῳ] | Πασικράτης

A62. Amathous. I. Nicolaou, *RDAC* 1993, 223–4 no. 1; *SEG* 53 (1993), 1003. Cylindrical cippus. I–II AD. [θεῷ] ὑψίστῳ | Πάτρων Ἀρίστωνος | εὐχήν

A63. Golgoi. O. Masson, *BCH* 95 (1971), 331 no. 12; *SEG* 52 (2002), 1491. Rectangular marble plaque with two painted eyes and suspension holes. I–II AD. θεῷ ὑψίστῳ εὐξάμενος | Χαρίτων ἀπέδωκεν

A64. Golgoi. O. Masson, *BCH* 95 (1971), 331 no. 12 bis; *SEG* 52 (2002), 1492. Rectangular marble plaque with two painted eyes and suspension

holes. Painted inscription. I–II AD. θεῷ ὑψίστῳ ἀνέθηκεν εὐξάμενος |
Μᾶρκος [–]ς

A65. Golgoi. O. Masson, *BCH* 95 (1971), 331 no. 13; *SEG* 52 (2002),
1493. Rectangular marble plaque, with painting of a nose (?). I–II AD. θεῷ
ὑψ[ίστῳ] | Ἀφροδεί|σις | ἀνέθηκεν | εὐξάμενος

A66. Limassol. I. Nicolaou, *RDAC* 2000, 299 no. 1; *SEG* 50 (2000), 1373.
Limestone cippus. I–II AD. κυρίωι ὑψίστωι | Ζωΐλος Διδύμου | ἀνέθηκε

A67. Limassol. I. Nicolaou, *RDAC* 2001, 299–300 no. 2; *SEG* 50 (2000),
1374. Limestone cippus. I–II AD. κυρίῳ ὑψίστῳ | Δίδυμος Ὀνησίμου |
ἀνέθηκε

A68. Limassol. I. Nicolaou, *RDAC* 2001, 291 no. 1; *SEG* 50 (2000),
1375. Limestone cippus. I–II AD. θεῷ ὑψίστωι ὑπὲρ τέκν[ου] | Μάρους
εὐχήν

A69. Limassol. I. Nicolaou, *RDAC* 2001, 291–2 no. 2; *SEG* 50 (2000),
1376. Limestone cippus. I–II AD. θεῷ ὑψίστῳ Δημήτρ[ιος?] | εὐχήν
ΚΓΖΗ

Syria

A70. Dmeir. *SEG* 43 (1993), 1028. After AD 245. Line 21 of this official
Roman protocol refers to events κατὰ τὴν κείνησιν τοῦ ὑψίστου Διὸς
τὰς θύρας ἀνυγείσας ὀφθῆναι.

A71. Dura-Europos. J. F. Gilliam, *The Excavations at Dura Europos:
Preliminary report of the ninth season of work 1935–6. Part III. The palace of the
Dux Ripae and the Dolichenum* (Yale 1951), 114. AD 211–20. Διὶ Ἡλίῳ Μίθρᾳ
ἁγίῳ ὑψίστῳ ἐπηκόῳ Το[υρ]μασγάδη . . . Ἰουλιανὸς στρα. [λε]γ. ιϛ
Φ. Φ. Ἀ.

A72. Palmyra. M. Gawlikowski and K. Aṣ'ad, *Studi Palmyreńske* 10
(1977), 27–8 no. 7; *SEG* 47 (1997), 1938. II AD? [Δι]ὶ ὑψίστ[ῳ | κ]αὶ
ἐπηκό[ῳ] | Ἡρώδ[η]|ς Μαλί[χ]|ου Νασ|ούμο[υ] | – –

A73. Palmyra. *SEG* 38 (1988), 1575; 47 (1997), 1939. Early III AD.
[Δι]ὶ ὑψίστῳ καὶ ἐπ|ηκόῳ Μάλι[χος] Μουκιαν|[οῦ] – Ἀνανίδος |
[εὐ]ξά[μ]ενος | [καὶ]ι ἀκουσθεὶς ἀ|[νέ]θηκεν ἔτους | [. .] μηνὸς
Δύσ|[τρ]ου

A74. Palmyra. *SEG* 45 (1995), 1910. Limestone block. AD 302. Διὶ ὑψίστῳ
καὶ | ἐπηκόῳ Ἀουεῖτος | ὀπτίων πρίνκιψ | εὐχὴ[ν | ἀ]νέθηκεν ἔτους γιχ´
Γο[ρπ]ιαίου εκ´

Mitchell 273. Palmyra. *OGI* 634; republished by D. Piacentini, *Aevum*
13/14 (2001/2), 525–34; *SEG* 52 (2002), 1581. Bilingual Aramaic–Greek

inscription. 162/3 AD. Διὶ ὑψίστῳ μεγίστῳ καὶ ἐπηκόῳ ['Lord of eternity' in Aramaic].

Arabia

A75. Rasun. N. Atallah, *ZPE* 121 (1998), 145–8; *SEG* 48 (1998), 1923. Altar with acroteria. II–III AD. θεῷ ὑψίστῳ | Λιτανος | τῆς κώμης | Ρησους ἐν|θάδε ἀνέ|θηκεν

Mitchell **282** Petra. F. Zayadine, *Le Qasr al-Bint de Pétra: l'architecture, le décor, la chronologie et les dieux* (Paris 2003); *SEG* 36 (1986), 1386; *IGLS* XXI.4, 25; *SEG* 53 (2003), 1904. Marble statue base. Late II AD. [–]ς Ὑψ[ιστ –]ια.

Egypt

A76. Unknown provenance. D. R. Jordan and R. D. Kotansky, in M. Gronewald and others, *Kölner Papyri* VIII, 53–69; *SEG* 47 (1997), 2152. Silver exorcism tablet now in Köln. III–IV AD. ἐσκορκίζω πᾶν πνεῦμα πο|νηρὸν καὶ κακόν, κατὰ τοῦ μεγάλου | ὑψίστου θεοῦ τοῦ κτίσαντον τὸν οὐ|ρανὸν καὶ τὴμ γῆν καὶ τὰς θαλάσ|σας καὶ πάντα τὰ ἐν αὐτοῖς, ἐξελθεῖν ἀπὸ Ἀλλοῦτος, ἣν ἔτεκεν Ἄννις, τῆς ἐχούσης τὴν σφραγῖδα τοῦ Σολομῶνος...

Cyrenaica

A77. Cyrene. Fraser (1962), 25–7 II; *Bull. ép.* 1964, 561. Small dedicatory altar. Roman imperial period. πατρὶ θεῶι Σαμοθρᾶκι ἀθανάτωι ὑψίσ[τωι]

Unknown provenance

Franken (2002), (see *SEG* 52 (2002), 1858) publishes seven bronze objects of unknown provenance with suspension holes, inscribed or blank *tabulae ansatae*, and dolphin fittings, which he demonstrates were elaborate hangers for the dedication of bronze lamps. Five have inscriptions and three are dedications to Theos Hypsistos (including Mitchell **290**). The other inscribed examples are his no. 5 = *IGBulg.* V, 5261 from Sofia: Πρισκείνιος | Βάλης τεσ(σεράριος) λε|γι. πρώτης Ἰτ|αλικῆς θεῷ Διὶ|εὶ ὑπὸ σωτη|ρίας εὐχὴν ἀ|νέθηκα (*legio I Italica* was stationed at Novae on the Danube), and no. 7: συνβιώσεως | ξυστοπλα|τειτῶν τα|μιεύοντος | Στεφάνου. This, like **A79** below, probably came from one of the cities of Asia, where associations such as the *symbiosis* of the *Xystoplateia* (the street of the gymnasium) are well attested.

A78. Franken (2002), 370 no. 1; *SEG* 52 (2002), 1858. Bronze *tabula ansata*. II–III AD. Ἀετὶς | θεῷ | ὑψίστῳ | εὐχήν

A79. (doubtless Lydia). Franken (2002), 371 no. 4; *SEG* 52 (2002), 1859. Bronze *tabula ansata*. Λαυδί|κη Ὑπαιπη|νὴ θεῷ ὑψίστ|ῳ ἀνέθη|κεν

A80. L. J. Delaporte, *Catalogue des cylindres, cachets et pierres gravées de style orientale* (Paris, Musée du Louvre) II (1923), 219 A1270 and pl. 108 figs. 17a and b (cited from Belayche 2005a, 37 n. 21). Entaglio engraved *heis* Theos Hypsistos with a figure of Hekate.

A81. Campbell Bonner, *Studies in Magical Amulets, Chiefly Graeco-Egyptian* (Michigan 1950), 177; (*Bull. ép.* 1953, 205). Cornelian gemstone. III–IV AD. Μέγα τὸ ὄνομα· | τὸν θεόν σοι τὸν ὕψιστον, | μή με ἀδικήσεις

Addenda

A82. *Pisidia*, Termessos. B. Iplikçioğlu, G. Çelgin, A. Vedat Çelgin, *Epigraphische Forschungen in Termessos und sein Territorium* IV (Vienna 2007), 58–62 no. 6. Altar, ht.1.06. Mid II AD. Πρ(οβούλου) T. K. Οὐάρου | υἱοῦ Μαρκέλλου | Ὑψίστῳ βωμὸν | ἀστυνόμος Στέ|φανος ὑπὲρ δήμου

A83. *Lycaonia* (Konya Museum). M. Metcalfe, *AS* 59 (2009), 78 no. 2. Small altar. Θεῷ ὑ|ψίστῳ | εὐχή

Bibliography

Ahn, G. (1993) '"Monotheismus" – "Polytheismus": Grenzen und Möglichkeiten einer Klassifikation von Gottesvorstellungen', in *Mesopotamia – Ugaritica – Biblica: Festschrift für K. Bergerhof*, ed. M. Dietrich and O. Loretz. Neukirchen and Vluyn: 1–24.

Albert, K. (1980) *Griechische Religion und platonische Philosophie.* Hamburg.

Alföldy, G. (1997) 'Die Mysterien von Panóias (Vila Real, Portugal)', *Madrider Mitteilungen* 38: 197–246.

Ameling, W. (1999) 'Ein Verehrer des θεὸς ὕψιστος in Prusa ad Olympum (IK 39, 115)', *EA* 31: 105–8.

(2004) *Inscriptiones Judaicae Orientis* II. *Kleinasien.* Tübingen.

Ando, C. (2003) Introduction to Part IV, in *Roman Religion*, ed. C. Ando. Edinburgh: 141–6.

(2005) 'Interpretatio Romana', *CPh* 100: 41–51.

(2008) *The Matter of the Gods.* Berkeley.

Andresen, C. (1955) *Logos und Nomos: Die Polemik des Celsus wider das Christentum.* Berlin.

Asad, T. (1993) *Genealogies of Religion: Discipline and reasons of power in Christianity and Islam.* Baltimore and London.

Assmann, J. (1997) *Moses the Egyptian: The memory of Egypt in western monotheism.* Cambridge, Mass.

(1998) *Moses der Ägypter: Entzifferung einer Gedächtnisspur.* Munich and Vienna; Frankfurt a.M.

(1999) 'Monothéisme et mémoire: le Moïse de Freud et la tradition biblique', *Annales* 54: 1011–26, reprinted in Assmann (2000), 62–80.

(2000) *Religion und kulturelles Gedächtnis: Zehn Studien.* Munich. English translation *Religion and Cultural Memory*, trans. R. Livingstone, Stanford 2005.

(2003) *Die mosaische Unterscheidung oder der Preis des Monotheismus*, Munich and Vienna.

(2004) 'Monotheism and Polytheism', in *Religions of the Ancient World: A guide*, ed. S. I. Johnston. Cambridge, Mass. and London: 17–31.

Athanassiadi, P. (1999) 'The Chaldaean oracles: theology and theurgy', in Athanas-
    siadi and Frede (1999), 149–83.
    (forthcoming) 'The gods are God: polytheistic cult and monotheistic theology
    in the world of late antiquity', *Collection Eranos* 14.
Athanassiadi, P. and Frede, M. (eds.) (1999, corrected reprint 2002) *Pagan Monothe-
    ism in Late Antiquity*. Oxford.
Aubriot, D. (2005) 'L'invocation au(x) dieu(x) dans la prière grecque: contrainte,
    persuasion ou théologie?', in Belayche and others (2005), 473–90.
Auffarth, C. (1993) 'Henotheismus/Monolatrie', in *Handbuch religionswissensch-
    aftlicher Grundbegriffe* III, ed. H. Cancik and others. Stuttgart, Berlin and
    Cologne: 104–5.
Avagianou, A. (2002) 'Physiology and mysticism at Pherai: the funerary epigram
    for Lykophron', *Kernos* 15: 75–89.
Avi Yonah, M. (1944) 'Greek inscriptions from Ascalon, Jerusalem, Beisan and
    Hebron', *QDAP* 10: 160–9.
Baker, M. (2005) 'Who was sitting in the theatre at Miletos: an epigraphical
    application of a novel theory', *Journal for the Study of Judaism* 36: 397–416.
Battifol, P. (1929) *La paix constantinienne et le catholicisme*. Paris.
Baumeister, Th. (1978) 'Gottesglaube und Staatsauffassung – ihre Interdependenz
    bei Celsus und Origenes', *Theologie und Philosophie* 53: 161–78.
Beard, M., North, J. and Price, S. (1998) *Religions of Rome*, 2 vols. Cambridge.
Beck, R. (2004) 'Four men, two sticks and a whip: image and doctrine in a Mithraic
    ritual', in *Theorizing Religions Past: Archaeology, history and cognition*, ed. H.
    Whitehouse and L. H. Martin. Walnut Creek, Calif.: 87–103.
    (2006) *The Religion of the Mithras Cult in the Roman Empire*. Oxford.
Belayche, N. (2001) Iudaea Palaestina: *The pagan cults in Roman Palestine (second
    to fourth century)*. Tübingen.
    (2003) 'En quête de marqueurs des communautés "religieuses" gréco-romaines',
    in *Les communautés religieuses dans le monde gréco-romain: essais de définition*,
    ed. N. Belayche and S. C. Mimouni. Turnhout: 9–20.
    (2005a) '*Hypsistos*: une voie de l'exaltation des dieux dans le polythéisme gréco-
    romain', *Archiv für Religionsgeschichte* 7: 34–55.
    (2005b) 'De la polysémie des épiclèses: Hypsistos dans le monde gréco-romain',
    in Belayche and others (2005), 427–42.
    (2005c) '"Au(x) dieu(x) qui règne(nt) sur . . . ": *basileia* divine et fonctionnement
    du polythéisme dans l'Anatolie impériale', in *Pouvoir et religion dans le monde
    romain: en hommage à Jean-Pierre Martin*, ed. A. Vigourt and others. Paris:
    257–69.
    (2006a) 'Quel regard sur les paganismes d'époque impériale?', *Anabases* 3:
    11–26.
    (2006b) 'Les stèles dites de confession: une religiosité originale dans l'Anatolie
    impériale?', in *The Impact of Imperial Rome on Religions, Ritual, and Religious
    Life in the Roman Empire*, ed. L. de Blois, P. Funke and J. Hahn. Leiden and
    Boston: 73–81.

(2007a) 'Les dieux "nomothètes": Oracles et prescriptions religieuses à l'époque romaine impériale', *RHR* 224: 171–91.

(2007b) 'Rites et "croyances" dans l'épigraphie religieuse de l'Anatolie impériale', in *Rites et croyances dans le monde romain*, ed. J. Scheid (Entretiens Fondation Hardt 53). Geneva-Vandoeuvres: 73–115.

(2008) 'Du texte à l'image: les reliefs des stèles "de confession" d'Anatolie', in *Image et religion*, ed. S. Estienne, C. Pousadoux and others (CEFR). Rome and Naples: 181–94.

Belayche, N. and others (eds.) (2005) *Nommer les dieux: théonymes, épithètes, épiclèses dans l'Antiquité*. Rennes.

Bell, C. (1992) *Ritual Theory, Ritual Practice*. New York and Oxford.

Bendlin, A. (2000) 'Looking beyond the civic compromise: religious pluralism in late republican Rome', in *Religion in Archaic and Republican Rome: Evidence and experience*, ed. E. Bispham and C. Smith. Edinburgh: 115–35.

(2001) 'Rituals or beliefs? Religion and the religious life of Rome', *SCI* 20: 191–208.

(2006a) 'Vom Nutzen und Nachteil der Mantik: Orakel im Medium von Handlung und Literatur in der Zeit der Zweiten Sophistik', in *Texte als Medium und Reflexion von Religion im römischen Reich*, ed. D. Elm von der Osten, J. Rüpke and K. Waldner. Stuttgart: 159–207.

(2006b) 'Nicht der Eine, nicht die Vielen: zur Pragmatik religiösen Verhaltens in einer polytheistischen Gesellschaft am Beispiel Roms', in Spieckermann and Kratz (2006), 279–311.

Bernand, E. (1969) *Inscriptions métriques de l'Egypte gréco-romaine*. Paris.

Berns, C. (2006) 'Konkurrierende Zentren: Überlegungen zur religiösen Repräsentation in Ephesos und den Städten der Provinz Asia in der Kaiserzeit', in *Zentralität und Religion*, ed. H. Cancik and others. Tübingen: 273–308.

Berrens, S. (2004) *Sonnenkult und Kaisertum von den Severern bis zu Constantin I (193–337 n. Chr.)*. Stuttgart.

Bianchi, U. and Vermaseren, M. (eds.) (1981) *La soteriologia dei culti orientali nell'impero Romano*. Leiden.

Birley, E. (1974) '*Cohors I Tungrorum* and the oracle of the Clarian Apollo', *Chiron* 4: 511–13.

Bloch, R. (2000) 'Monotheism', in *Der Neue Pauly* VIII: 375–8.

Bonner, C. (1950) *Studies in Magical Amulets Chiefly Graeco-Egyptian*. Ann Arbor, Mich.

Bonner, C. and Nock, A. D. (1948) 'Neotera', *HThR* 41: 213–15.

Bonnet, C. and Motte, A. (eds.) (1997) *Les syncrétismes religieux dans le monde méditerranéen antique: Actes du colloque international en l'honneur de Franz Cumont à l'occasion du cinquantième anniversaire de sa mort*. Rome.

Borgeaud, P. (2003) *Aux origines de l'histoire des religions*. Paris.

Boudon-Millot, V. and Pietrobelli, A. (2005) 'Galien resuscité: édition *princeps* du texte grec du *De propriis placitis*', *REG* 118: 165–213.

Boulogne, J. (1997) 'Hénothéisme et polythéisme sous les Antonins: l'imaginaire religieux de Plutarque', *Euphrosyne*: 281–93.

Bousset, W. (1926) *Die Religion des Judentums im späthellenistischen Zeitalter*, 3rd edn. Tübingen.

Bowen, J. R. (2002) *Religions in Practice: An approach to the anthropology of religion*. Boston.

Bowersock, G. (2002) 'The highest god with particular reference to North-Pontus', *Hyperboreus* 8: 353–63.

(2007) '*CIRB* no. 71 and recent debates', in *Une koinè pontique: cités grecques, sociétés indigènes et empires mondiaux sur le littoral nord de la Mer Noire*, ed. A. Bresson and others. Bordeaux: 251–4.

Boys-Stones, G. R. (2001) *Post-Hellenistic Philosophy*. Oxford.

Bradbury, S. (1995) 'Julian's pagan revival and the decline of blood sacrifice', *Phoenix* 49: 331–56.

Bremmer, J. N. (1995) 'The family and other centres of religious learning in antiquity', in *Centres of Learning*, ed. J. W. Drijvers and A. A. MacDonald. Leiden: 29–38.

(2002a) *The Rise and Fall of the Afterlife*. London and New York.

(2002b) 'How old is the ideal of holiness (of mind) in the Epidaurian temple inscription and the Hippocratic oath?', *ZPE* 141: 106–8.

Bricault, L. (2005a) *Recueil des inscriptions concernant les cultes isiaques* (*RICIS*) i–ii. *Corpus*; iii. *Planches* (Mémoires de l'Académie des Inscriptions et Belles-Lettres xxxi). Paris.

(2005b) 'Zeus Hélios Mégas Sarapis', in *La langue dans tous ses états: Michel Malaise in honorem*, ed. C. Cannuyer (Acta Orientalia Belgica 18). Brussels: 243–54.

Brisson, L. (1990) 'Orphée et l'orphisme à l'époque impériale: témoignages et interprétations philosophiques de Plutarque à Jamblique', in *ANRW* ii.36.4: 2867–931.

Brixhe, C. and Hodot, R. (1988) *L'Asie Mineure du nord au sud*. Nancy.

Brown, P. (1963) 'Saint Augustine', in *Trends in Medieval Political Thought*, ed. B. Smalley. Oxford: 1–21, reprinted in Brown (1972), 22–45.

(1972) *Religion and Society in the Age of Saint Augustine*. London.

Brox, N. (1982) 'Mehr als Gerechtigkeit: die außenseiterischen Eschatologien des Markion und Origenes', *Kairos* 24: 1–16, reprinted in Brox (2000), 385–403.

(2000) *Das Frühchristentum: Schriften zur historischen Theologie*, ed. F. Dünzl, A. Fürst and F. R. Prostmeier. Freiburg, Basle and Vienna.

Brünnow, R.-E. and Domaszewski, A. von (1909) *Die Provincia Arabia auf Grund zweier in den Jahren 1897 und 1898 unternommenen Reisen und Berichte* iii. Strasbourg.

Burkert, W. (1977) *Griechische Religion der archaischen und klassischen Epoche* (Religionen der Menschheit 15). Stuttgart etc.

Busine, A. (2005) *Paroles d'Apollon: pratiques et traditions oraculaires dans l'Antiquité tardive (iie–vie siècle)*. Leiden.

Cadotte, A. (2002–3) '*Pantheus et dii deaeque omnes*: les formules de synthèses divines en Afrique du Nord', *Antiquités africaines* 38–9: 55–72.

Cassirer, E. (1946) *Language and Myth*. London. (German original: Leipzig, 1925.)

Cerutti, M. V. (2009) '"Pagan Monotheism"? Towards a historical typology', in Mitchell and Van Nuffelen (2009), 15–32.

Chadwick, H. (1953) *Origen*. Contra Celsum. Cambridge.

(1965) *Origen*: Contra Celsum. Translation, with introduction and notes, 2nd edn. Cambridge.

Chaniotis, A. (1997) 'Reinheit des Körpers – Reinheit der Seele in den griechischen Kultgesetzen', in *Schuld, Gewissen und Person*, ed. J. Assmann and T. Sundermeier. Gütersloh: 142–79.

(1998) 'Willkommene Erdbeben', in *Stuttgarter Kolloquium zur historischen Geographie des Altertums 6: Naturkatastrophen in der antiken Welt*, ed. E. Olshausen and H. Sonnabend. Stuttgart: 404–16.

(2000) 'Das Jenseits – eine Gegenwelt?', in *Gegenwelten zu den Kulturen der Griechen und der Römer in der Antike*, ed. T. Hölscher. Munich and Leipzig: 159–81.

(2002a) 'The Jews of Aphrodisias: new evidence and old problems', *SCI* 21: 209–42.

(2002b) 'Zwischen Konfrontation und Interaktion: Christen, Juden und Heiden im spätantiken Aphrodisias', in *Patchwork: Dimensionen multikultureller Gesellschaften*, ed. C. Ackermann and K. E. Müller. Bielefeld: 83–128.

(2002c) 'Old wine in a new skin: tradition and innovation in the cult foundation of Alexander of Abonouteichos', in *Tradition and Innovation in the Ancient World*, ed. E. Dabrowa. Krakow: 67–85.

(2003) 'Negotiating religion in the cities of the eastern Roman empire', *Kernos* 16: 177–90.

(2004a) 'Under the watchful eyes of the gods: aspects of divine justice in hellenistic and Roman Asia Minor', in *The Greco-Roman East: Politics, culture, society*, ed. S. Colvin. Cambridge: 1–43.

(2004b) 'New inscriptions from Aphrodisias (1995–2001)', *AJA* 108: 377–416.

(2006) 'Rituals between norms and emotions: rituals as shared experience and memory', in *Rituals and Communication in the Graeco-Roman World*, ed. E. Stavrianopoulou. Liège: 211–38.

(2007) 'Religion und Mythos in der hellenistischen Welt', in *Kulturgeschichte des Hellenismus*, ed. G. Weber. Stuttgart: 139–57 and 448–54.

(2008a) 'Konkurrenz von Kultgemeinden im Fest', in *Festrituale: Diffusion und Wandel im römischen Reich*, ed. J. Rüpke. Tübingen: 67–87.

(2008b) 'Acclamations as a form of religious communication', in *Die Religion des Imperium Romanum: Koine und Konfrontationen*, ed. H. Cancik and J. Rüpke. Tübingen: 199–218.

(2009) 'Ritual performances of divine justice: the epigraphy of confession, atonement, and exaltation in Roman Asia Minor', in *From Hellenism to Islam: Cultural and linguistic change in the Roman Near East*, ed. H. Cotton and others. Cambridge: 115–53.

(2010) 'The ithyphallic hymn for Demetrios Poliorcetes and Hellenistic religious mentality', in *Royal Cult and Imperial Worship from Classical to Late Antiquity*, ed. P. P. Iossif and A. S. Chankowski (Acts of the International Conference Organized by the Belgian School at Athens (1–2 November 2007)). Leuven.

(forthcoming) 'Listening to stones: orality and emotion in ancient inscriptions', in *Proceedings of the 13th International Congress of Greek and Latin Epigraphy*, ed. J. K. Davies and J. J. Wilkes. Oxford.

Chaniotis, A. and Chiai, G. F. (2007) 'Die Sprache der religiösen Kommunikation im römischen Osten: Konvergenz und Differenzierung', in *Antike Religionsgeschichte in räumlicher Perspektive*, ed. J. Rüpke. Tübingen: 117–24.

Chrysostomou, P. (1991) 'Δυτικομακεδονικὰ εὐχαριστήρια στὸ Δία "Ὕψιστο', *To Archaiologiko Ergo sten Makedonia kai Thrake* (Thessalonica) 5: 91–9.

(1996) 'Ἡ λατρεία του Δία ως καιρινού θεού στη Θεσσαλία και τη Μακεδονία', *Archaiologikon Deltion* 44–6 (1989–91, published 1996): 21–72.

Cobb, W. F. (1895) *Origines Judaicae*. London.

Cohen, H. (1915) *Der Begriff der Religion im System der Philosophie*. Giessen.

Cole, S. (2001) 'The dynamics of deification in Horace's *Odes* 1–3', in *Between Magic and Religion: Interdisciplinary studies in ancient Mediterranean religion and society*, ed. S. R. Asirvatham, C. O. Pache and J. Watrous. Lanham, Md. and Oxford: 67–91.

Colin, J. (1965) *Les villes libres de l'Orient gréco-romain et l'envoi au supplice par acclamations populaires*. (Collection Latomus 154) Brussels.

Collas-Heddeland, E. (1995) 'Le culte impérial dans la compétition des titres sous le Haut-Empire: une lettre d'Antonin aux Ephésiens', *REG* 108: 410–29.

Colpe, C. and Löw, A. (1993) 'Hypsistos (theos)', in *Reallexicon zum Antiken Christentum* XVI: 1035–55.

Corbin, H. (1981) *Le paradoxe du monothéisme*. Paris.

Crowfoot, J. W., Crowfoot, G. M. and Kenyon, K. M. (1954) *Samaria-Sebaste: Reports of the work of the joint expedition in 1931–1933 and of the British Expedition in 1935* III. *The Objects at Samaria*. London.

Cudworth, R. (1678) *The True Intellectual System of the Universe: The first part; wherein, all the REASON and PHILOSOPHY of ATHEISM is confuted; AND its IMPOSSIBILITY demonstrated*. London (reprinted Stuttgart 1964).

Cumont, F. (1924) *Les religions orientales dans le paganisme romain*, 4th edn. Paris.

Davies, J. P. (2004) *Rome's Religious History*. Cambridge.

de Hoz, M. Paz (1991) 'Theos Hypsistos in Hierokaisareia', *EA* 18: 75–7.

(1997) 'Henoteísmo y magia en una inscripción de Hispania', *ZPE* 118: 227–30.

(1999) *Die lydischen Kulte im Lichte der griechischen Inschriften* (Asia Minor Studien 36). Bonn.

(2002) 'Men, un dios lunar, con corona de rayos', *Mene* 2: 189–201.

Decharme, P. (1966) *La critique des traditions religieuses chez les Grecs*. Paris.

Decourt, J.-C. (2004) *Inscriptions grecques de la France*. Lyon.

Delaporte, L. (1923) *Catalogue des cylindres orientaux du Musée du Louvre* II. Paris.

Delling, G. (1964/5) 'Die Altarinschrift eines Gottesfürchtigen in Pergamon', *Novum Testamentum* 7: 73–80.

Di Segni, L. (1990) 'The Church of Mary Theotokos on Mount Gerizim: the inscriptions', in *Christian Archeology in the Holy Land: New discoveries*, ed. G. C. Bottini, L. Di Segni and E. Alliata. Jerusalem: 343–50.

(1994) 'ΕΙΣ ΘΕΟΣ in Palestinian inscriptions', *SCI* 13: 94–115.

(1998) 'The Samaritans in Roman-Byzantine Palestine: some misapprehensions', in *Religious and Ethnic Communities in Later Roman Palestine*, ed. H. Lapin. Bethesda, Md.: 51–66.

Dillon, J. (1999) 'Monotheism in the gnostic tradition,' in Athanassiadi and Frede (1999), 69–79.

Dörrie, H. (1967) 'Die platonische Theologie des Celsus in ihrer Auseinandersetzung mit der christlichen Theologie, auf Grund von Origenes, c. Celsum 7.42ff.', *Nachrichten der Akademie der Wissenschaften in Göttingen, Phil.-hist. Klasse* 2: 19–55, reprinted in Dörrie (1976): 229–62.

(1976) *Platonica minora*. Munich.

Dräger, M. (1993) *Die Städte der Provinz Asia in der Flavierzeit*. Frankfurt.

Drew-Bear, T., Thomas, C. M. and Yildizturan, M. (1999) *Phrygian Votive Steles*. Ankara.

Droge, A. J. (2006) 'Self-definition vis-à-vis the Graeco-Roman world', in *The Cambridge History of Christianity* i. *Origins to Constantine*. Cambridge: 230–44.

Dumézil, G. (1970) *Archaic Roman Religion*. Chicago and London.

Durand, J.-L. and Scheid, J. (1994) '"Rites" et "religion": remarques sur certains préjugés des historiens de la religion des Grecs et des Romains', *Archives de Sciences Sociales des Religions* 82: 23–43.

Edwards, M. (2000) Review of Athanassiadi and Frede (1999), *JThS* 51: 339–42.

(2004) 'Pagan and Christian monotheism in the age of Constantine', in *Approaching Late Antiquity: The transformation from early to late empire*, ed. S. Swain and M. Edwards. Oxford: 211–34.

Ehrenberg, V. (1965) 'Athenischer Hymnus auf Demetrios Poliorketes', in *Polis und Imperium*. Zurich and Stuttgart: 503–19.

Engelmann, H. (2001) 'Inschriften und Heiligtum', in *Der Kosmos der Artemis von Ephesos*, ed. U. Muss. Vienna: 33–44.

Engster, D. (2003) *Konkurrenz oder Nebeneinander: Mysterienkulte in der hohen römischen Kaiserzeit*. Munich.

Erbse, H. (1995) *Theosophorum Graecorum fragmenta*. Stuttgart and Leipzig.

Fédou, M. (1988) *Christianisme et religions païennes dans le* Contre Celse *d'Origène*. Paris.

Feeney, D. (1998) *Literature and Religion at Rome: Cultures, contexts, and beliefs*. Cambridge.

Feldman, L. H. (1993) *Jew and Gentile in the Ancient World: Attitudes and interactions from Alexander to Justinian*. Princeton.

Flusser, D. (1975) 'The great goddess of Samaria', *IEJ* 25: 13–20.

Foschia, L. (2005) 'Θεὸς γεννήτωρ πάντων: divinité païenne et/ou chrétienne?', in Belayche and others (2005), 453–66.

Fowden, G. (1991) 'Constantine's porphyry column: the earliest literary allusion', *JRS* 81: 119–31.

(1993) *From Empire to Commonwealth: The consequences of monotheism in late antiquity*. Princeton.

Fowler, W. Warde (1912) *The Religious Experience of the Roman People*. London.

François, G. (1957) *Le polythéisme et l'emploi au singulier des mots THEOS, DAIMÔN dans la littérature grecque d'Homère à Platon*. Paris.

Franken, R. (2002) 'Lampen für die Götter: Beobachtungen zur Funktion der sogenannten Vexillumaufsätze', *MDAI(I)* 52: 369–81.

Frankfurter, D. (1998) *Religion in Roman Egypt: Assimilation and resistance*. Princeton.

Fraser, P. M. (1962) 'Two inscriptions from Cyrenaica', *Annals of the British School at Athens* 57: 25–7.

Frede, M. (1997) 'Celsus' attack on the Christians', in *Philosophia Togata* II. *Plato and Aristotle at Rome*, ed. J. Barnes and M. Griffin. Oxford: 218–40.

(1999) 'Monotheism and pagan philosophy in later antiquity', in Athanassiadi and Frede (1999), 41–68.

Frede, M. and Athanassiadi, P. (1999) 'Introduction', in Athanassadi and Frede (1999), 7–20.

Fuhrer, Th. (1997) 'Die Platoniker und die civitas dei', in *Augustinus*: De civitate dei (Klassiker auslegen II), ed. C. Horn. Berlin: 87–108.

Fürst, A. (2000) 'Laßt uns erwachsen werden! Ethische Aspekte der Eschatologie des Origenes', *Theologie und Philosophie* 75: 321–38.

(2004a) '"Wer das glaubt, weiß gar nichts": eine spätantike Debatte über den Universalanspruch des christlichen Monotheismus', *Orientierung* 68: 138–41.

(2004b) 'Monotheismus und Gewalt: Fragen an die Frühzeit des Christentums', *Stimmen der Zeit* 222: 521–31.

(2006a) 'Christentum im Trend: monotheistische Tendenzen in der späten Antike', *Zeitschrift für antikes Christentum* 9: 496–523.

(2006b) 'Seneca – ein Monotheist? Ein neuer Blick auf eine alte Debatte', in *Der apokryphe Briefwechsel zwischen Seneca und Paulus* (SAPERE II), ed. A. Fürst and others. Tübingen: 85–107.

(2007) 'Wahrer Gott – wahre Gerechtigkeit: politische Implikationen des Monotheismus in der Spätantike', in Palmer (2007), 251–82.

Gallini, C. (1970) *Protesta e integrazione nella Roma antica*. Bari.

Gerson, L. (1990) *God and Greek Philosophy: Studies in the early history of natural theology*. London.

Girone, M. (2003) 'Una particolare offerta die chiome', *EA* 35: 21–42.

Gladigow, B. (1993) 'Polytheismus', in *Handbuch religionswissenschaftlicher Grundbegriffe* IV, ed. H. Cancik and others. Stuttgart, Berlin and Cologne: 321–30.

Gnuse, R. K. (1997) *No Other Gods: Emergent monotheism in Israel*. Sheffield.

(1999) 'The emergence of monotheism in ancient Israel: a survey of recent scholarship', *Religion* 29: 315–36.

Gödde, S. (2003) 'Emotionale Verschiebungen: zur Bedeutung der *euphemia* im griechischen Ritual', in *Die emotionale Dimension antiker Religiosität*, ed. A. Kneppe and D. Metzler. Münster: 21–46.

Goldhill, S. (2006) 'Religion, Wissenschaftlichkeit und griechische Identität im römischen Kaiserreich,' in *Texte als Medium und Reflexion von Religion im römischen Reich*, ed. D. Elm von der Osten, J. Rüpke and K. Waldner. Stuttgart: 125–40.

Goodman, M. (1994) *Mission and Conversion: Proselytizing in the religious history of the Roman Empire*. Oxford.

(2003) 'The Jewish image of God in late antiquity', in *Jewish Culture and Society under the Christian Roman Empire*, ed. R. Kalmin and S. Schwartz. Leuven: 133–45, reprinted in Goodman (2007), 205–17.

(2007) *Judaism in the Roman World: Collected essays*. Leiden and Boston.

Gordon, R. (2001) 'Ritual and hierarchy in the mysteries of Mithras', *Antigüedad: Religiones y Sociedades* 4: 245–73.

(2003) (with J. M. Reynolds) 'Roman inscriptions 1995–2000', *JRS* 93: 212–94.

Goukowsky, P. (2002) 'Sur une épigramme de Thespies', in *L'Épigramme de l'Antiquité au XVIIe siècle ou Du ciseau à la pointe*, ed. J. Dion. Nancy: 217–46.

Gounaropoulou, L. and Hatzopoulos, M. (1998) *Epigraphes kato Makedonias* I. *Epigraphes Beroias* (= *I. Beroea*). Athens.

Graf, F. (1985) *Nordionische Kulte: Religionsgeschichtliche und epigraphische Untersuchungen zu den Kulten von Chios, Erythrai, Klazomenai und Phokaia*. Rome.

(1996) *Gottesnähe und Schadenzauber: Die Magie in der griechisch-römischen Antike*. Munich.

Graf, F. and Johnston, S. I. (2007) *Ritual Texts for the Afterlife: Orpheus and the Bacchic gold tablets*. London and New York.

Gragg, D. L. (2004) 'Old and new in Roman religion: a cognitive account', in *Theorizing Religions Past: Archaeology, history and cognition*, ed. H. Whitehouse and L. H. Martin. Walnut Creek, Calif: 69–86.

Grandjean, Y. (1975) *Une nouvelle arétalogie d'Isis à Maronée* (EPRO 49). Leiden.

Gruen, E. (1990) 'The Bacchanalian affair', in *Studies in Greek Culture and Roman Policy*. Leiden: 34–78.

Habicht, C. (1969) *Altertümer von Pergamon Band* VIII.3. *Die Inschriften des Asklepieions*. Berlin.

Hall, A. S. (1977) 'A sanctuary of Leto at Oenoanda', *AS* 27: 193–7.

(1978) 'The Klarian oracle at Oenoanda', *ZPE* 32: 263–8.

Harland, P. A. (2003) *Associations, Synagogues and Congregations: Claiming a place in Mediterranean society*. Minneapolis.

Harrison, S. J. (2000) *Apuleius: A Latin sophist*. Oxford.

Hartung, J. A. (1836) *Die Religion der Römer*. Erlangen.

Hawthorn, G. (1991) *Plausible Worlds: Possibility and understanding in history and the social sciences*. Cambridge.

Hayman, P. (1991) 'Monotheism – a misused word in Jewish studies?', *JJS* 41: 1–15.

Heller, A. (2006) *'Les bêtises des Grecs': conflits et rivalités entre cités d'Asie et de Bithynie à l'époque romaine (129 a.C.–235 p.C.)* (Ausonius, Scripta Antiqua 17). Bordeaux.

Henig, M. and McGregor, A. (2004) *Catalogue of the Engraved Gems and Finger-Rings in the Ashmolean Museum* II. *Roman* (BAR International Series 1332). Oxford.

Herrero de Jáuregui, M. (2009) 'Orphic god(s): theogonies and hymns as vehicles for monotheism', in Mitchell and Van Nuffelen (2009), 77–99.

Herrmann, P. (1978) 'Men, Herr von Axiotta', in *Studien zur Religion und Kultur Kleinasiens* (EPRO 66/2). Leiden: 415–23.

(1998) *Inschriften von Milet* VI.2. Berlin.

Herrmann, P. and Malay, H. (2007) *New Documents from Lydia*. Vienna.

Herrmann, P. and Polatkan, K. Z. (1969) *Das Testament des Epikrates und andere neue Inschriften aus dem Museum von Manisa*. Vienna.

Heyking, J. von (1999) 'A headless body politic? Augustine's understanding of a populus and its representation', *History of Political Thought* 20: 549–74.

Hirsch-Luipold, R. (2005) 'Der eine Gott bei Philon von Alexandrien und Plutarch', in *Gott und die Götter bei Plutarch*, ed. R. Hirsch-Luipold (RVV 54). Berlin and New York.

Hirschmann, V.-E. (2005) *Horrenda secta: Untersuchungen zum frühchristlichen Montanismus und seinen Verbindungen zur paganen Religion Phrygiens* (Historia Einzelschriften 179). Stuttgart.

Hornung, E. (1986) *Les dieux de l'Égypte: l'un et le multiple*. Paris. (First published in 1971.)

Horsley, G. H. R. (1992) 'The inscriptions of Ephesos and the New Testament', *Novum Testamentum* 34: 105–68.

Hübner, S. (2003) 'Spiegel und soziale Gestaltungskraft alltäglicher Lebenswelt: der Kult des Men in Lydien und Phrygien', in *Religion und Region: Götter und Kulte aus dem östlichen Mittelmeerraum*, ed. E. Schwertheim and E. Winter. Bonn: 179–200.

Hume, D. (1956) *The Natural History of Religion*, ed. H. E. Root. Stanford, Calif.

Hurtado, L. W. (2003) *One God, One Lord: Early Christian devotion and ancient Jewish monotheism*, 2nd edn. London.

Jaeger, W. (1934) *Paideia: Die Formung des griechischen Menschen*. Leipzig and Berlin.

Janko, R. (2002–3) 'God, science and Socrates', *BICS* 46: 1–18.

Jarry, J. (1988) 'Datierungsprobleme in Nordsyrien', *Tyche* 3: 129–34.

Johnston, S. I. (1992) 'Riders in the sky: cavalier gods and theurgic salvation in the second century AD', *CP* 87: 303–21.

Jones, C. P. (2005) 'Ten dedications "to the gods and goddesses" and the Antonine plague', *JRA* 18: 293–301.

(2006) 'Cosa and the Antonine plague', *JRA* 19: 368–9.

Jordan, D. R. (2004) 'Magia nilotica sulle rive del Tevere', *Mediterraneo Antico* 7: 693–710.

Kahlos, M. (2002) *Vettius Agorius Praetextatus: A senatorial life in between* (Acta Instituti Romani Finlandiae 26). Rome.

Kaizer, T. (2006) 'In search of oriental cults', *Historia* 55: 26–47.

Kayser, F. (1994) *Recueil des inscriptions grecques et latines (non funéraires) d'Alexandrie impériale (1er–111e s. apr. J.-C.)*. Cairo.

Keel, O. (ed.) (1980) *Monotheismus im Alten Israel und seiner Umwelt*. Fribourg.

Kelly, J. N. D. (1972) *Early Christian Creeds*, 3rd edn. Harlow.

Kenney, J. P. (1986) 'Monotheistic and polytheistic elements in classical Mediterranean spirituality', in *Classical Mediterranean Spirituality: Egyptian, Greek, Roman*, ed. A. H. Armstrong. New York: 269–92.

(1991) *Mystical Monotheism: A study in ancient Platonic theology*. London.

King, C. (2003) 'The organization of Roman religious beliefs', *Classical Antiquity* 22: 275–312.

Kirk, G., Raven, J. and Schofield, M. (1983) *The Presocratic Philosophers: A critical history with a selection of texts*. Cambridge.

Knibbe, D. (2002) 'Private evergetism in the service of the city-goddess: the most wealthy Ephesian family of the 2nd century CE supports Artemis in her struggle against the decline of her cult after the meteorological catastrophe of 186 CE', *Mediterraneo Antico* 5: 49–62.

Kobusch, Th. (1983) 'Das Christentum als die Religion der Wahrheit: Überlegungen zu Augustins Begriff des Kultus', *Revue des Études Augustiniennes* 29: 97–128.

Koch, K. (1994) 'Monotheismus und Angelologie', in *Ein Gott allein? JHWH-Verehrung und biblischer Monotheismus im Kontext der israelitischen und altorientalischen Religionsgeschichte*, ed. W. Dietrich and M. A. Klopfenstein. Fribourg: 565–81.

(1999) 'Monotheismus als Sündenbock?', *Theologische Zeitschrift* 124: 873–84, reprinted in Assmann (2003), 221–38.

Krämer, J. (2004) 'Lateinisch-griechisches Glossar: Celtis' Abschrift aus einem Papyruskodex', in *Paramone: Editionen und Aufsätze von Mitgliedern des Heidelberger Instituts für Papyrologie zwischen 1982 und 2004*, ed. J. M. S. Cowey and B. Kramer. Leipzig: 43–62.

Krebernik, M. and Van Oorschot, J. (eds.) (2002) *Polytheismus und Monotheismus in den Religionen des Vorderen Orients* (Alter Orient und Altes Testament 298). Münster.

Labarre, G. and Taşlıalan, M. (2002) 'La dévotion au dieu Men: les reliefs rupestres de la Voie Sacrée', in *Actes du 1er Congrès International sur Antioche de Pisidie*, ed. T. Drew-Bear and others. Lyon: 257–312.

Laks, A. (ed.) (2002) *Traditions of Theology: Studies in Hellenistic theology, its background and aftermath*. Leiden.

Lancellotti, M. G. (2000) *The Naassenes: A gnostic identity among Judaism, Christianity, classical and ancient near eastern traditions*. Leiden.

Lane, E. N. (1975) *Corpus Monumentorum Religionis Dei Menis* II. *The Coins and Gems.* Leiden.

(1976) *Corpus Monumentorum Religionis Dei Menis* III. *Interpretations and Testimonia.* Leiden.

Lane Fox, R. (1986) *Pagans and Christians in the Mediterranean World from the Second Century AD to the Conversion of Constantine.* Harmondsworth.

Lang, B. (1993) 'Monotheismus', in *Handbuch der religionswissenschaftlicher Grundbegriffe* III, ed. H. Cancik and others. Stuttgart, Berlin and Cologne: 148–65.

Latte, K. (1960) *Römische Religionsgeschichte.* Munich.

Le Bris, A. (2001) *La mort et les conceptions de l'au-delà en Grèce ancienne à travers les épigrammes funéraires: étude d'épigrammes d'Asie Mineure de l'époque hellénistique et romaine.* Paris.

Le Dinahet, M.-T. (2002) 'Les inscriptions votives au dieu Men à Antioche: état des recherches', in *Actes du 1er Congrès International sur Antioche de Pisidie*, ed. T. Drew-Bear and others. Lyon: 201–12.

Leclercq, H. (1924) 'Anges', in *Dictionnaire d'Archéologie Chrétienne et de Liturgie* 1.2: 2080–2161.

Lehmann, Y. (1980) 'Polythéisme et monothéisme chez Varron', *REL* 58: 25–9.

Lehmler, C. and Wörrle, M. (2006) 'Neue Inschriften aus Aizanoi IV: Aizanitica Minora', *Chiron* 36: 45–111.

Levinskaya, I. (1996) *The Book of Acts in its Diaspora Setting.* Grand Rapids, Mich.

Liebeschuetz, J. H. W. G. (1979) *Continuity and Change in Roman Religion.* Oxford.

(1999) 'The significance of the speech of Praetextatus', in Athanassiadi and Frede (1999), 185–205.

(2001) 'The influence of Judaism among non-Jews in the imperial period', *Journal of Jewish Studies* 52: 234–52.

Lieu, J. (1998) 'The forging of Christian identity and the *Letter to Diognetus*', *Mediterranean Archaeology* 11: 71–82, reprinted in Lieu (2002), 171–89.

(2002) *Neither Jew nor Greek.* London and New York.

Livrea, E. (1998) 'Sull'iscrizione teosofica di Enonda', *ZPE* 122: 90–6.

Lona, H. E. (2005) *Die 'wahre Lehre' des Celsus, übersetzt und erklärt* (Kommentar zu den frühchristlichen Apologeten. Erg.-Bd. 1). Freiburg etc.

Luhmann, N. (2000) *Die Religion der Gesellschaft.* Frankfurt.

Maas, M. (2000) *Readings in Late Antiquity: A sourcebook.* London and New York.

MacDonald, N. (2004) 'The origin of "monotheism"', in *Early Jewish and Christian Monotheism*, ed. L. T. Stuckenbruck and W. E. S. North. London: 204–14.

MacGregor, G. (1968) *Introduction to Religious Philosophy.* London and Melbourne.

MacMullen, R. (1977) *Christianising the Roman Empire.* New Haven.

(1981) *Paganism in the Roman Empire.* New Haven and London.

Malaise, M. (2005) *Pour une terminologie et une analyse des cultes isiaques.* Brussels.

Malay, H. (1994) *Greek and Latin Inscriptions in the Manisa Museum.* (Ergänzungsbände zu den TAM 19). Vienna.

(2003) 'A praise on Men Artemidorou Axiottenos', *EA* 36: 13–18.

(2004) 'A dedicatory statuette of a mother goddess', *EA* 37: 181–2.

(2005) 'ΦΙΛΑΝΠΕΛΟΙ in Phrygia and Lydia', *EA* 38: 42–3.

Malouf, A. (1992) Préface to *De la Divination/Cicéron*, ed. G. Freyburger and J. Scheid. Paris.

Manemann, J. (ed.) (2002) *Monotheismus* (Jahrbuch Politische Theologie 4). Münster, Hamburg and London.

Manns, F. (1977) 'Nouvelles traces des cultes de Neotera, Sérapis et Poséidon en Palestine', *Liber Annus* 27: 229–38.

Marek, C. (1993) *Stadt, Ära und Territorium in Pontus-Bithynia und Nord-Galatia.* Tübingen.

(2000) 'Der höchste, beste, größte, allmächtige Gott: Inschriften aus Nord-kleinasien', *EA* 32: 129–46.

Markschies, C. (2001) 'Heis Theos? Religionsgeschichte und Christentum bei Erik Peterson', in *Vom Ende der Zeit: Geschichtstheologie und Eschatologie bei Erik Peterson* (Symposium Mainz. Religion-Geschichte-Gesellschaft Band 16), ed. B. Nichtweis. Münster: 38–74.

(2002) 'Heis Theos – Ein Gott ? Der Monotheismus und das antike Christentum', in *Polytheismus und Monotheismus in den Religionen des Vorderen Orients*, ed. M. Krebernik and J. van Oorschot (AOAT 298). Münster: 209–34.

(2006) 'Ist Monotheismus gefährlich? Einige Beobachtungen zu einer aktuellen Debatte aus der Spätantike', *Berichte und Abhandlungen der Berlin-Brandenburgischen Akademie der Wissenschaften* 10: 11–24.

(forthcoming) Revised new edition of Peterson (1926). Würzburg.

Markus, R. (1990) *The End of Ancient Christianity.* Cambridge.

Marquard, O. (ed.) (2000a) *Abschied vom Prinzipiellen: Philosophische Studien.* Stuttgart.

(2000b) 'Lob des Polytheismus', in Marquard (2000a): 91–116. (First published in 1981.)

Mastandrea, P. (1979) *Un neoplatonico latino: Cornelio Labeone.* Leiden.

Mauser, U. (1986) 'εἷς θεός and μόνος θεός in biblical theology', *JBTh* 1: 71–87.

Mawson, T. J. (2005) *Belief in God: An introduction to the philosophy of religion.* Oxford.

Meier, M. (2003) *Das andere Zeitalter Justinians: Kontingenzerfahrung und Kontingenzbewältigung im 6. Jahrhundert n. Chr.* Göttingen.

(2004) *Justinian: Herrschaft, Reich und Religion.* Munich.

Merkelbach, R. (2001) *Isis regina – Zeus Sarapis: Die griechisch-ägyptische Religion nach den Quellen dargestellt.* Munich and Leipzig.

Michel, S. (2001) *Die magischen Gemmen im Britischen Museum.* London.

Mikalson, J. D. (1998) *Religion in Hellenistic Athens.* Berkeley.

Mitchell, S. (1993), *Anatolia: Land, men, and gods in Asia Minor* II. *The rise of the Church.* Oxford.

(1998) 'Wer waren die Gottesfürchtigen?', *Chiron* 28: 55–64.

(1999) 'The cult of Theos Hypsistos between pagans, Jews, and Christians', in Athanassiadi and Frede (1999), 81–148.

(2003a) 'Inscriptions from Melli (Kocaaliler) in Pisidia', *AS* 53: 139–59.

(2003b) 'Rom und das Judentum in der frühen Kaiserzeit: Überlegungen zu den Grenzen zwischen Heiden, Juden und Christen', in *Leitbild Wissenschaft?* (Altertumswissenschaftliches Kolloquium 8), ed. J. Dummer and M. Vielberg. Stuttgart: 149–72.

(2005) 'An Apostle to Ankara from the New Jerusalem: Montanists and Jews in Late Roman Asia Minor', *SCI* 24: 207–23.

(2008) 'La comunicazione di ideologie religiose nell'impero romano', in *La comunicazione nella storia antica: fantasie e realtà*, ed. M. Angeli Bertinelli. Rome: 57–69.

(forthcoming) 'Ein Gott im Himmel: zur Problematik des heidnischen monotheismus in der Kaiserzeit und der Spätantike', *ZAC*.

Mitchell, S. and Van Nuffelen, P. (eds.) (2009) *Monotheism between Pagans and Christians in Late Antiquity*. Leuven.

Miura-Stange, A. (1926) *Celsus und Origenes: Das Gemeinsame ihrer Weltanschauung nach den acht Büchern des Origenes gegen Celsus. Eine Studie zur Religions- und Geistesgeschichte des 2. und 3. Jahrhunderts*. Gießen.

Moberly, R. W. L. (2004) 'How appropriate is "monotheism" as a category for Biblical interpretation', in *Early Jewish and Christian Monotheism*, ed. L. T. Stuckenbruck and W. E. S. North. London: 216–34.

Moltmann, J. (2002) 'Kein Monotheismus gleicht dem anderen: Destruktion eines untauglichen Begriffs', *Evangelische Theologie* 62: 112–222.

Momigliano, A. D. (1984) 'Religion in Athens, Rome and Jerusalem in the first century BC', *Annali della Scuola Normale di Pisa* 3rd ser., 14: 873–92, reprinted in Momigliano (1987), 74–91 [= *Ottavo contributo*, 279–96].

(1986) 'The disadvantages of monotheism for a universal state', *CPh* 81: 285–97.

(1987) *On Pagans, Jews and Christians*. Middletown, Conn.

Moreschini, C. (1983) 'Monoteismo cristiano e monoteismo platonico nella cultura latina dell'età imperiale', in *Platonismus und Christentum: Festschrift für Heinrich Dörrie (JbAC* Erg. Band 10), ed. H.-D. Blume and F. Mann. Münster: 133–61.

Most, G. W. (2003) 'Philosophy and religion', in *The Cambridge Companion to Greek and Roman Philosophy*, ed. D. Sedley. Cambridge: 300–22.

Mrozek, S. (1971) '*Primus omnium* sur les inscriptions des municipes italiens', *Epigraphica* 33: 60–9.

Mühlenkamp, C. (2008) '*Nicht wie die Heiden': Studien zur Grenze zwischen christlicher Gemeinde und paganer Gesellschaft in vorkonstantinischer Zeit (JbAC* Erg.-Bd. Kleine Reihe 3). Münster.

Müller, B. (1913) Μέγας θεός (Diss. Philologicae Halenses XXI). Halle.

Müller, F. M. (1882) *Lectures on the Origin and Growth of Religion, as Illustrated by the Religions of India*. London.

Niebuhr, H. R. (1943) *Radical Monotheism and Western Culture*. New York.

Nilsson, M. (1950) *Geschichte der griechischen Religion* II. *Die hellenistische und römische Zeit*. Munich.

(1963) 'The High God and the mediator', *HThR* 56: 101–20.

Nock, A. D. (1928) 'Oracles théologiques', *REA* 30: 280–90, reprinted in Nock (1972), 160–8.

(1933) *Conversion: The old and the new in religion from Alexander the Great to Augustine of Hippo.* Oxford.

(1940) 'Orphism or popular philosophy?', *HThR* 33: 301–15.

(1972) *Essays on Religion and the Ancient World,* ed. Z. Stewart. Oxford.

Nollé, J. (1993) 'Die feindlichen Schwestern: Betrachtungen zur Rivalität der pamphylischen Städte', in *Die epigraphische und altertumskundliche Erforschung Kleinasiens: Hundert Jahre Kleinasiatische Kommission der Österreichischen Akademie der Wissenschaften. Akten des Symposiums vom 23. bis 25. Oktober 1990,* ed. G. Dobesch and G. Rehrenböck. Vienna: 297–317.

(1996) *Side im Altertum: Geschichte und Zeugnisse* I. Bonn.

North, J. (1979) 'Religious toleration in republican Rome', *PCPS* 25: 85–103.

(1992) 'The development of religious pluralism', in *The Jews among Pagans and Christians,* ed. J. Lieu, J. North and T. Rajak. London: 174–93.

(2003) 'Réflexions autour des communautés religieuses du monde gréco-romain', in *Les communautés religieuses dans le monde gréco-romain: essais de définition,* ed. N. Belayche and S. C. Mimouni. Turnhout: 337–47.

(2005) 'Pagans, polytheists and the pendulum', in *The Spread of Christianity in the First Four Centuries: Studies in explanation,* ed. W. V. Harris. Leiden: 131–4.

(2007) 'Arnobius on sacrifice', in *Wolf Liebeschuetz Reflected,* ed. J. Drinkwater and B. Salway. London: 27–36.

O'Daly, G. (1999) *Augustine's City of God: A reader's guide.* Oxford.

Osborne, T. P. (2003) 'Le conflit des cultes dans l'Apocalypse de Jean', in *Dieux, fêtes, sacré dans la Grèce et la Rome antiques,* ed. A. Motte and C. M. Ternes. Turnhout: 236–54.

Palmer G. (ed.) (2007) *Fragen nach dem einen Gott: Die Monotheismusdebatte im Kontext* (Religion und Aufklärung 14). Tübingen.

Pandermalis, D. (2005) 'Ζεὺς Ὕψιστος καὶ ἄλλα', *To Archaiologiko Ergo sten Makedonia kai Thrake* (Thessalonica) 17 (2003, published 2005): 417–28.

Parker, R. (1998) 'Pleasing thighs: reciprocity in Greek religion', *Reciprocity in Ancient Greece,* ed. C. Gill, N. Postlethwaite and R. Seaford. Oxford: 105–25.

(2005) *Polytheism and Society at Athens.* Oxford.

Peek, W. (1930) *Der Isishymnus von Andros.* Berlin.

Peres, I. (2003) *Griechische Grabinschriften und neutestamentliche Eschatologie.* Tübingen.

Pernot, L. (2005) 'Le lieu du nom (ΤΟΠΟΣ ΑΠΟ ΤΟΥ ΟΝΟΜΑΤΟΣ) dans la rhétorique religieuse des Grecs', in Belayche and others (2005), 29–39.

Peterson, E. (1926) ΕΙΣ ΘΕΟΣ: *Epigraphische, formgeschichtliche und religionsgeschichtliche Untersuchungen* (Forschungen zur Religion und Literatur des Alten und Neuen Testaments 24). Göttingen.

(1951) 'Das Problem des Nationalismus im alten Christentum', *Theologische Zeitschrift* 7: 81–91.

Petrovic, I. and Petrovic, A. (2006) '"Look who is talking now!": speaker and communication in Greek metrical sacred regulations', in *Rituals and Communication in the Graeco-Roman World*, ed. E. Stavrianopoulou. Liège: 151–79.

Petzl, G. (1994) *Die Beichtinschriften Westkleinasiens* (Epigraphica Anatolica 22). Bonn.

(1998) *Die Beichtinschriften im römischen Kleinasien und der Fromme und Gerechte Gott* (Nordrhein-Westfälische Akademie der Wissenschaften, Vorträge G 355). Opladen.

(2003) 'Zum religiösen Leben im westlichen Kleinasien: Einflüsse und Wechselwirkungen', in *Religion und Region: Götter und Kulte aus dem östlichen Mittelmeerraum*, eds. E. Schwertheim and E. Winter. Bonn: 93–102.

Philipp, H. (1986) Mira et magica: *Gemmen im Ägyptischen Museum der Staatlichen Museen Preussischer Kulturbesitz, Berlin-Charlottenburg*. Mayence.

Phillips, C. R. (1986) 'The sociology of religious knowledge', in *ANRW* II.16.3: 2677–773.

Pichler, K. (1980) *Streit um das Christentum: Der Angriff des Celsus und die Antwort des Origenes*. Frankfurt a.M. and Berne.

Pilhofer, P. (1995) *Philippi* I. *Die erste christliche Gemeinde Europas*. Tübingen.

Pleket, H. W. (1981) 'Religious history as the history of mentality: the "believer" as servant of the deity in the Greek world', in *Faith, Hope and Worship: Aspects of religious mentality in the ancient world*, ed. H. S. Versnel. Leiden: 152–92.

Porter, B. N. (ed.) (2000) *One God or Many? Concepts of divinity in the ancient world*. Chebeague.

Posamentir, R. and Wörrle, M. (2006) 'Der Zeustempel von Aizanoi: ein Großbau flavischer Zeit', *MDAI(I)* 56: 227–46.

Potter, D. S. (1990) *Prophecy and History in the Crisis of the Roman Empire*. Oxford.

Preisendanz, K. (1928) *Papyri Graecae Magicae*. Leipzig and Berlin.

Price, S. R. F. (1984) *Rituals and Power: The Roman imperial cult in Asia Minor*. Cambridge.

(1999) *Religions of the Ancient Greeks* (Key Themes in Ancient History). Cambridge.

(2003) 'Homogénéité et diversité dans les religions à Rome', *ARG* 5: 180–97.

Queyrel, F. (1992) 'Les acclamations peintes du xyste', in *Delphes: centenaire de la grande fouille réalisée par l'EFA (1892–1903)* (Travaux du CERPOGA 12), ed. J.-F. Bommelaer. Strasbourg: 333–48.

(2001) 'Inscriptions et scènes figurées peintes sur le mur du fond du xyste de Delphes', *BCH* 125: 333–87.

Ramnoux, C. (1984) 'Sur un monothéisme grec', *RPhL* 82: 175–98.

Ramsay, W. M. (1883) 'Unedited inscriptions of Asia Minor', *BCH* 7: 297–327.

(1889) 'Artemis-Leto and Apollo Lairbenos', *JHS* 10: 216–30.

Rappaport, R. (1999) *Ritual and Religion in the Making of Humanity*. Cambridge.

Ratzinger, J. (1971) *Die Einheit der Nationen: Eine Vision der Kirchenväter*. Salzburg and Munich.

Richter, G. M. A. (1956) *Catalogue of Engraved Gems: Greek, Etruscan and Roman, Metropolitan Museum of Art, New York*. Rome.

Ricl, M. (1991–2) 'Hosios kai Dikaios', *EA* 18: 1–70 and 19: 71–103.

Ritti, T. (2002–3) 'Antonino Pio, "padrone della terra e del mare": una nuova iscrizione onoraria da Hierapolis di Frigia', *Annali di archeologia e di storia antica* 9/10: 271–82.

Rives, J. (1999) 'The decree of Decius and the religion of Empire', *JRS* 89: 135–54.

(2007) *Religion in the Roman Empire*. Maldon, Mass., Oxford and Carlton.

Robert, J. and Robert, L. (1948) *Hellenica* VI. *Inscriptions grecques de Lydie*. Paris.

Robert, L. (1937) *Études anatoliennes*. Paris.

(1938) *Études épigraphiques et philologiques*. Paris.

(1955) *Hellenica* X. Paris.

(1958) 'Reliefs et cultes votifs d'Anatolie', *Anatolia* 3: 103–36. (= Robert, *OMS* 1: 402–35).

(1964) *Nouvelles inscriptions de Sardes*. Paris.

(1968) 'Trois oracles de la *Théosophie* et un prophète d'Apollon', *CRAI* 1968: 568–99 (= Robert, *OMS* V: 584–615).

(1969) 'Les épigrammes satiriques de Lucilius sur les athlètes: parodies et réalités', in *L'épigramme grecque* (Entretiens Fondation Hardt 14). Geneva-Vandoeuvres: 179–295 (= Robert, *OMS* VI: 317–431; *Choix d'écrits*, ed. D. Rousset, Paris 2007: 175–246).

(1971) 'Un oracle gravé à Oinoanda', *CRAI* 1971: 597–619 (= Robert, *OMS* V, 617–39).

(1983) 'Reliefs d'Asie Mineure', *BCH* 107: 583 (= *Documents d'Asie Mineure*, Paris 1987: 427).

Roberts, C., Skeat, T. C. and Nock, A. D. (1936) 'The guild of Zeus Hypsistos', *HThR* 29: 39–87, reprinted in Nock (1972), 414–43.

Rose, H. J. and others (1954) *La notion du divin depuis Homère jusqu'à Platon* (Fondation Hardt, Entretiens sur l'Antiquité classique 1). Geneva-Vandoeuvres.

Rothaus, R. M. (1996) 'Christianization and de-paganization: the late antique creation of a conceptual frontier', in *Shifting Frontiers in Late Antiquity*, ed. R. Mathisen and H. J. Sivan. Aldershot: 299–308.

Roueché, C. (1984) 'Acclamations in the later Roman empire: new evidence from Aphrodisias', *JRS* 74: 181–99.

(1989a) *Aphrodisias in Late Antiquity*. London.

(1989b) 'Floreat Perge', in *Images of Authority: Papers presented to Joyce Reynolds on the occasion of her seventieth birthday*, ed. M. M. Mackenzie and C. Roueché. Cambridge: 206–28.

(1995) 'Aurarii in the auditoria', *ZPE* 105: 37–50.

Rougemont, G. (2004) 'Dédicace d'Héliodotos à Hestia pour le salut d'Euthydème et de Démétrios', *Journal des Savants* 2004: 333–7.

Roussel, P. (1931) 'Le miracle de Zeus Panamaros', *BCH* 55: 70–116.

Rudhardt, J. (1966) 'Considérations sur le polythéisme', *Revue de Théologie et de Philologie* 99: 353–64.

Rüpke, J. (2001) *Die Religion der Römer*. Munich.

(2004) 'Acta aut agenda: relations of script and performance', in *Rituals in Ink*, ed. A. Barchiesi. Stuttgart: 23–44.

(2005) *Fasti sacerdotum: Die Mitglieder der Priesterschaften und das sakrale Funktionspersonal römischer, griechischer, orientalischer und judisch-christlicher Kulte in der Stadt Rom von 300 v. Chr. bis 499 n. Chr.* Stuttgart.

(2006) 'Literarische Darstellungen römischer Religion in christlicher Apologetik: Universal- und Lokalreligion bei Tertullian und Minucius Felix', in *Texte als Medium und Reflexion von Religion im römischen Reich,* ed. D. E. von der Osten, J. Rüpke and K. Waldner. Stuttgart: 209–23.

Rutgers, L. (1995) *The Jews in Late Ancient Rome: Evidence of cultural interaction in the Roman diaspora.* Leiden.

(1998) *The Hidden Heritage of Diaspora Judaism.* Leuven.

Rutherford, I. (2000) 'The reader's voice in a horoscope from Abydos', *ZPE* 130: 149–50.

Şahin, M. Ç. (2002) 'New inscriptions from Lagina, Stratonikeia and Panamara', *EA* 34: 1–21.

Sanzi, E. (2002) 'Magi e culti orientali', in *Gemme gnostiche e cultura ellenistica,* ed. A. Mastrocinque. Bologna: 207–24.

Scheid, J. (1988) 'L'impossible polythéisme: les raisons d'un vide dans l'histoire de la religion romaine', in *L'impensable polythéisme,* ed. F. Schmidt. Paris.

(1998a) *Commentarii Fratrum Arvalium qui supersunt: les copies épigraphiques des protocoles annuels de la confrérie arvale.* Rome.

(1998b) *La religion des romains.* Paris.

(1999) 'Hiérarchie et structure dans le polythéisme romain: façons romaines de penser l'action', *ARG* 1: 184–203.

(2005) *Quand croire, c'est faire: les rites sacrificiels des Romains.* Paris.

(ed.) (2007) *Rites et croyances dans le monde romain* (Entretiens Fondation Hardt 53). Geneva-Vandoeuvres.

Schelling, F. W. J. (1985) *Philosophie der Mythologie.* Frankfurt. (First published in 1842.)

Schleiermacher, F. (1828) *Der christliche Glaube.* Berlin.

(1960) *Der christliche Glaube nach den Grundsätzen der evangelischen Kirche im Zusammenhang dargestellt: Auf Grund der 2. Auflage und kritischen Prüfung des Textes neu herausgegeben von Martin Redeker.* Berlin.

Schmidt, F. (ed.) (1988) *L'impensable polythéisme.* Paris.

Schneider, A. M. (1949/51) 'Römische und byzantinische Bauten auf dem Garizim', *ZDPV* 68: 211–34, reprinted in Schneider (1998), 187–204.

(1998) *Reticulum: Ausgewählte Aufsätze und Katalog seiner Sammlungen.* Münster.

Schröder, H. O. (1986) *Heilige Berichte. Einleitung, deutsche Übersetzung und Kommentar.* Heidelberg.

Schürer, E. (1897) 'Die Juden im bosporanischen Reich und die Genossenschaft der σεβόμενοι θεὸν ὕψιστον ebendaselbst', *Sitzungberichte der preussischen Akademie der Wissenschaften zu Berlin* 1897: 200–25.

(varying dates) *The History of the Jewish People in the Age of Jesus Christ,* revised edition by G. Vermes, F. Millar and others, I–III.2. Edinburgh.

Schwabe, M. (1951) 'A Jewish inscription from Ed-Dumèr near Damsacus', *PAAJR* 20: 265–77.

Schwöbel, C. (1994) 'Monotheismus iv. Systematisch-Theologisch', in *TRE* 23: 256–26.

Sérandour, A. (2004) 'De l'apparition d'un monothéisme en Israël', *Diogène* 205: 28–51.

Sfameni Gasparro, G. (1986) *Soteriology and Mystic Aspects in the Cult of Cybele and Attis*. Leiden.

(1996) 'Alessandro di Abonutico, lo "pseudo-profeta" ovvero come construirsi un'identità religiosa i. Il profeta, "eroe" e "uomo divino"', *Studi e Materiali di Storia delle Religioni* 62: 565–90.

(1999) 'Alessandro di Abonutico, lo "pseudo-profeta" ovvero come construirsi un'identità religiosa ii. L'oracolo e i misteri', in *Les syncrétismes religieux dans le monde méditerranéen antique: Actes du colloque international en l'honneur de Franz Cumont*, ed. C. Bonnet and A. Motte. Brussels and Rome: 275–305.

(2003) 'Monoteismo pagano nella Tarda Antichità: una questione di tipologia storico-religiosa', *Annali di Scienze Religiose* 8: 97–127.

(2006) 'Strategie di salvezza nel mondo hellenistico-romano: per una tassonomia storico-religiosa', in *Pagani e Cristiani alla ricerca della salvezza (secoli i–iii): xxxiv Incontro di studiosi dell'antichità cristiana, Roma, 5–7 maggio 2005* (Studia Ephemeridis Augustinianum 96). Rome: 21–53.

Simon, M. (1973) 'Early Christianity and pagan thought: confluences and conflicts', *Religious Studies* 9: 385–99.

Skarsaune, O. (1997) 'Is Christianity monotheistic? Patristic perspectives on a Jewish/Christian debate', *Studia Patristica* 29: 340–63.

Smith, J. Z. (1990) *Drudgery Divine: On the comparison of early Christianities and the religions of late antiquity*. London.

(2002) 'Great Scott! Thought and action one more time', in *Magic and Ritual in the Ancient World*, ed. P. Mirecki and M. Meyer. Leiden: 73–91.

(2004) *Relating Religion: Essays in the study of religion*. Chicago and London.

Speigl, J. (1970) *Der römische Staat und die Christen: Staat und Kirche von Domitian bis Commodus*. Amsterdam.

Spieckermann, H. and Kratz, R. G. (eds.) (2006) *Götterbilder – Gottesbilder – Weltbilder: Polytheismus und Monotheismus in der Welt der Antike 1/2* (Forschungen zum Alten Testament 2. Reihe 17/8). Tübingen.

Spier, J. (1992) *Ancient Gems and Finger Rings: Catalogue of the collections of the J. Paul Getty Museum*. Malibu, Calif.

Stark, R. (1996) *The Rise of Christianity: A sociologist reconsiders history*. Princeton, NJ.

(2001) *One True God: Historical consequences of monotheism*. Princeton.

Stark, R. and Bainbridge, W. S. (1987) *A Theory of Religion*. New Brunswick, NJ.

Stehle, E. (2004) 'Choral prayer in Greek tragedy: euphemia or aischrologia?', in *Music and the Muses: The culture of mousike in the classical Athenian city*, ed. P. Murray and P. Wilson. Oxford: 121–55.

(2005) 'Prayer and curse in Aeschylus' *Seven Against Thebes*', *CP* 100: 101–22.

Stein, M. (2001) 'Die Verehrung des Theos Hypsistos: ein allumfassender pagan-jüdischer Synkretismus?', *EA* 33: 119–26.

Stemberger, G. (1987) *Juden und Christen im Heilige Land: Palästina unter Konstantin und Theodosius*. Munich.

Stolz, F. (1996) *Einführung in den biblischen Monotheismus*. Darmstadt.

Stroumsa, G. G. (2005) *La fin du sacrifice: les mutations religieuses de l'Antiquité tardive*. Paris.

Strubbe, J. (1997) Ἀραὶ ἐπιτύμβιοι: *Imprecations against desecrators of the grave in the Greek epitaphs of Asia Minor. A catalogue*. Bonn.

Suarez de la Torre, E. (2003) 'Apollo, teologo cristiano', *Annali di Scienze Religiose* 8: 129–52.

Taeuber, H. (2003) 'Graffiti als Hilfsmittel zur Datierung der Wandmalereien in Hanghaus 2', in *Das Hanghaus 2 von Ephesos: Studien zu Baugeschichte und Chronologie*, ed. F. Krinzinger. Vienna: 93–9.

Teixidor, J. (1977) *The Pagan God: Pagan religion in the Graeco-Roman Near East*. Princeton.

Theissen, G. (1985) *Biblical Faith: An evolutionary approach*. Philadelphia.

Thom, J. C. (2005) *Cleanthes' Hymn to Zeus*. Tübingen.

Thonemann, P. (2007) 'Estates and the land in late Roman Asia Minor', *Chiron* 37: 435–78.

Tod, M. N. (1949) 'Greek record-keeping and record-breaking', *CQ* 43: 105–12.

Totti, M. (1985) *Ausgewählte Texte der Isis- und Sarapis-Religion*. Hildesheim, Zurich and New York.

Trebilco, P. (2002) 'The Christian and Jewish Eumeneia formula', *Mediterraneo Antico* 5: 63–97.

Tremlin, T. (2006) *Minds and Gods: The cognitive foundations of religion*. Oxford.

Trombley, F. R. (1993–4) *Hellenic Religion and Christianisation* (Religions in the Graeco-Roman World 115), 2 vols. Leiden and New York.

Turcan, R. (1989) *Les cultes orientaux dans le monde romain*. Paris.

(1998) *Rome et ses dieux*. Paris.

(1999) 'Conclusions', in *Les syncrétismes religieux dans le monde méditerranéen antique: Actes du Colloque F. Cumont, septembre 1997*, ed. C. Bonnet and A. Motte. Rome: 385–400.

(2000a) *Mitra et le Mithracisme*, 2nd edn. Paris.

(2000b) *The Gods of Ancient Rome* (English translation of Turcan 1998). Edinburgh.

Tybout, R. A. (2003) 'Naar een andere wereld: verkenningen van het Griekse grafepigram op steen', *Lampas* 36: 329–77.

Ustinova, Y. (1991) 'The *thiasoi* of Theos Hypsistos in Tanais', *History of Religions* 31: 150–80.

(1999) *The Supreme Gods of the Bosporan Kingdom: Celestial Aphrodite and the Most High God* (Religions in the Graeco-Roman World 135). Leiden, Boston and Köln.

Van den Bosch, L. P. (2002) *Friedrich Max Müller: A life devoted to the humanities.* Leiden.

Van den Broek, R. and others (eds.) (1988) *Knowledge of God in the Graeco-Roman World.* Leiden.

van der Horst, P. W. (1992) 'A new altar of a god-fearer?', *JJS* 43: 32–7, reprinted in van der Horst (1998), 65–70.

(1998) *Hellenism – Judaism – Christianity.* Leuven.

Van Nuffelen, P. (forthcoming a) 'Varro's *Antiquitates rerum divinarum*: Roman religion as an image of truth', *Classical Philology.*

(forthcoming b) *Philosophical Readings of Religion in the Post-Hellenistic Period.*

Van Selms, A. (1973) 'Temporary henotheism', in *Symbolae biblicae et Mesopotamicae Francisco Mario Theodoro de Liagre Böhl dedicatae*, ed. M. A. Beek and others. Leiden: 341–8.

Vanderlip, V. F. (1972) *The Four Greek Hymns of Isidorus and the Cult of Isis.* Toronto.

Vermaseren, M. J. and Van Essen, C. C. (1965) *The Excavations in the Mithraeum of the Church of Santa Prisca in Rome.* Leiden.

Vernant, J-P. (1985) *Mythe et pensée chez les Grecs*, 2nd edn. Paris.

Versnel, H. S. (ed.) (1981a) *Faith, Hope and Worship: Aspects of religious mentality in the ancient world.* Leiden.

(1981b) 'Religious mentality in ancient prayer', in Versnel (1981a) 1–64.

(1990) *Inconsistencies in Greek and Roman Religion* I. *Ter unus. Isis, Dionysos, Hermes: Three studies in henotheism.* Leiden.

(2000) 'Thrice one: three Greek experiments in oneness', in *One God or Many? Concepts of divinity in the ancient world*, ed. B. N. Porter. Chebeague: 79–163.

Veyne, P. (1986) 'Une évolution du paganisme gréco-romain: injustice ou piété des dieux, leurs ordres et "oracles"', *Latomus* 45: 259–83, reprinted in Veyne (1991), 281–310.

(1990) 'Images de divinités tenant une phiale ou patère: la libation comme "rite de passage" et non pas offrande', *Metis* 5: 17–28.

(1991) *La société romaine.* Paris.

(2005) *L'Empire gréco-romain.* Paris.

Victor, U. (1997) *Lukian von Samosata, Alexander oder Der Lügenprophet. Eingeleitet, herausgegeben, übersetzt und erklärt.* Leiden, New York and Cologne.

Vinzent, M. (1998) 'Das "heidnische" Ägypten im 5. Jahrhundert', in *Heiden und Christen im 5. Jahrhundert*, ed. J. van Oort and D. Wyrwa. Leuven: 32–65.

Waldner, K. (2007) 'Les martyrs comme prophètes: divination et martyre dans le discours chrétien des Ier et IIe siècles', *RHR* 224: 193–209.

Wallraff, M. (2002) *Christus verus sol.* Münster.

(2003) 'Pagan monotheism in late antiquity: remarks on a recent publication', *Mediterraneo Antico* 6: 531–6.

Wander, B. (1998) *Gottesfürchtige und Sympathisanten.* Tübingen.

Warde Fowler, W. (1912) *The Religious Experience of the Roman People.* London.

Weichlein, S. (2003) Review of Jürgen Manemann (ed.), *Monotheismus* (Münster 2002), *Humanities and Social Sciences* 2003, available at: http://www.h-net. org/reviews/showrev.php?id=17616.

Welles, C. B. (1938) 'The inscriptions', in *Gerasa*, ed. C. H. Kraeling. New Haven: 355–494.

West, M. (1999) 'Towards monotheism', in Athanassiadi and Frede (1999), 21–40.

Whitehouse, H. (2004) *Modes of Religiosity: A cognitive theory of religious transmission*. Walnut Creek, Calif.

Wiemer, H.-U. (2004) 'Akklamationen im spätrömischen Reich. Zur Typologie und Funktion eines Kommunikationrituals', *Archiv für Kulturgeschichte* 86: 27–73.

Wifstrand, A. (1942) 'Die wahre Lehre des Celsus', *Bulletin de la Société Royale des Lettres de Lund* 1941–2: 391–431 (in separate pagination: 1–41).

Williams, B. (1963) 'Hume on religion', in *David Hume: A Symposium*, ed. D. F. Pears. London: 77–88, reprinted in Williams (2006), 267–73.

(2006) *The Sense of the Past*, ed. M. Burnyeat. Princeton and Oxford.

Wischmeyer, W. (2005) 'ΘΕΟΣ ΥΨΙΣΤΟΣ: neues zu einer alten Debatte', *ZAC* 9: 149–68.

Wissowa, G. (1912) *Religion und Kultus der Römer*, 2nd edn. Munich.

Zeller, E. (1862) *Die Entwicklung des Monotheismus bei den Griechen*. Stuttgart.

(1875) *Vorträge und Abhandlungen geschichtlichen Inhalts* 1, 2nd edn. Leipzig.

General index

acclamations 122–3, 135, 140, 142, 145–6, 156, 164, 165–6
'acclamatory hyperbole' 130–1
Christian 155, 159
at Delphi 126–8, 155
political tool 159–62
Alexander of Abonuteichos (Abonou Teichos) 113, 115, 120, 140
angels 110, 117, 139, 158, 184
anthropology, and religion 22
Artemis, at Ephesus 114–15, 150–1
Asclepius 162–3
in Galen 76–8, 80
at Pergamum 75, 80, 128
at Rome 123
authority, religious 8–9

Bacchic worship 50
belief (religious), pagan 22, 35, 43

Christianity
defined 32
as form of monotheism 53–4, 56–7, 85–6, 98, 110
in fourth century AD 6
language of 170
and pagan monotheism 31
and pagan worship 87
and utopianism 45
competition, religious 6, 11, 12, 36, 113–15, 128, 137–8, 140
concepts of divinity 13, 22, 26, 28, 39, 83, 94, 97, 112, 132, 185–6
Christian 56, 58–9, 61
Roman 41, 45–7
cults (pagan)
Augustine on 85–7
in Celsus 92, 96
Egyptian 10
Imperial 88
Oriental 10, 22–3, 30–1
spread in Roman Empire 169–70

demiurge 72, 78, 80–1

eagles, and Hypsistos cults 170–1
emotions, religious 12
epiphany 134
eulogia 156
euphemia 123 n. 47
exaltation of divinity 24, 32, 125, 166, 171
experience, personal religious 12, 40, 113, 115, 124, 129, 133, 138

fire 79, 139, 146–7, 191
in Stoicism 71
fundamentalism, religious 2, 9

Gerizim, Mount 107
Gnostics 31
Godfearers 31, 189–96

henotheism 7, 18–19, 25, 113 n. 2, 180
hierarchy, divine 121–2, 141, 149, 182

identity, religious 8, 10, 37, 43–4, 49, 108
intolerance, religious 2, 4
Isis 50
aretalogies 122, 132, 151–2, 172

Jews, Judaism 12, 30, 31
in 5th-cent. Syria 104–5
in Galen 75
and Hypsistos 144, 185–9
at Miletus 194
and the Mosaic distinction 103
in Numenius 60
and pagan monotheism 31, 185–9
at Phanagoria and Panticapaeum 192–3
Julian (emperor) 117
and the Jewish God 145
and the 'one god' formula 108

lamps 176

magic, magical texts 133
Manichaeism 45
megatheism 12, 112, 132–8, 140
Mes (Men) 122–5, 140
Mithras, Mithraism 10, 30, 50–1, 149,
    173
monotheism
  compared with polytheism 38–9, 74–5,
    109–11, 145
  cultic 6, 10, 11–12, 24, 25
  and Greek philosophy 3, 5, 8, 23, 28, 29,
    41–2, 67, 83, 87, 98, 143
  as heuristic tool 5, 17, 141–2, 144
  ideological issues 17–18, 20, 26, 142–3
  intellectual context 7, 11, 24, 101
  in modern world 2, 9, 101–4, 111
  non-exclusive 7, 20, 112, 179–80
  and politics 4, 9, 88–97
  in religious evolution 40, 42, 48–9, 54,
    60–1
  as religious phenomenon 4, 6, 14, 16–33
    passim
  shared ideas of Christians and pagans 84, 87,
    88, 97–8
  terminology 4–5, 7, 17–21, 59–60, 103–4,
    109, 111, 179–80
  trends towards 14–15, 24–5, 138–40
Montanism 31
Mosaic distinction 98 n. 58, 100–4, 105,
    109

Neoplatonism 26, 30
Nilsson, Martin 54–5, 67–70
nomos 94–5

'one god (*heis theos*)' inscriptions 10, 12,
    104–8, 119, 128, 131, 147–50
  in paganism 145, 151
oracles 11, 24, 29–30, 115–19, 147
  of Apollo Klarios 116–18, 132, 138–9,
    187
  Delphic 77
  at Didyma 119
  of Sarapis 116
  theological 147, 165
Orphism 116–17, 121–2, 132, 138 n. 129, 139,
    147
Ouranios 125, 139, 180

plague 117–18, 183
Platonism, Platonists 8, 9, 55, 67, 143, 152
  Augustine and 83–8
  Middle 26
  political order
    in Origen 90–1
polyonymy 132, 151, 164
polytheism, polytheists 1, 3, 10, 11, 14, 55, 144–5
  defined 8, 37, 53, 74
  pagan characteristic 40–1, 169
Presocratics 26, 28

relativism 93–4
ritual 21, 22, 36, 39, 41, 145
  and belief 43
  origins of 44–5

sacrifice, animal 47, 174
Samaritans 107–8
Sarapis 149–50, 151, 157–8, 162, 164
Socrates 62, 64
  on piety 56, 65, 77
stars (divine beings) 73
Stoics, Stoicism 26, 28–9, 66, 152
  as monotheists 70–1
Sun, cult of 25–6
  and Mithras 51
  and Theos Hypsistos 174

theology, pagan 22–3, 26, 125
Theos Hypsistos 12, 24, 31, 32, 131, 132, 140,
    167–208 *passim*
  characteristics of worship 187, 196–7
  and Clarian oracle 116, 117, 187
  cult associations 177
  gender of worshippers 178–9
  humility 178–9
  among Jews 144
  and polytheism 50, 120, 163–4, 168, 185
  Thea Hypsiste 120, 182
tolerance, religious 34
transformation of religion 4, 7–8, 13, 14, 25,
    27–9, 32–3, 36–7, 42–5, 47–8
  conditions for 51
truth, religious 4, 7, 26–7, 29, 93, 98, 100, 102,
    121, 137

Zeus Hypsistos 170–1

Index of authors, works and citations

Authors

Acta Alexandrinorum, pp. 20–1 (Musurillo)
  160 n. 114

Acta Pauli et Theclae 38   135 n. 96

Acts 17.23   163 n. 28, 176 n. 44
19.28   126 n. 56
19.34   126 n. 56, 142 n. 4, 151 n. 55, 159, 162

Acts of John 26.5   151 n. 55

Aelius Aristides   25
Hieroi logoi 2.7   123 n. 48, 135 n. 96
Hieroi logoi 4.50   128 n. 61, 162–3
Or. 42.4   80

Aeschylus, Suppl. 524   143 n. 8

Antiochus of Ascalon   29

Antisthenes, and pagan monotheism   62–70
frg. 39a–e Decleva Crizzi   62
frg. 40a–d Decleva Crizzi   62, 64

Apuleius
Apologia   43
De mundo 25   166 n. 144
Met. 11.5   50 n. 52
Met. 11.30   143 n. 9

Arion of Methymna, PMG 939 Page   173

Aristotle
Met. 1072b3, 1074a38ff.   68

[Aristotle]
Constitution of Athens 55.15–17   62
De mundo 397b23   79

Arnobius, Adversus nationes   37 n. 8, 46 n. 38

Athenagoras
Supplicatio 6.2 (PTS 31, 32)   83
Supplicatio 7.1 (PTS 31, 34)   83

Augustine   8, 56
De civ. D. 4.11–21, 6.8, 8.12   24 n. 32
De civ. D. 7   37 n. 8
De civ. D. 7.9 (citing Valerius Soranus)
  164 n. 136
De civ. D. 9.23 (I, 398 Dombart/Kalb)   85
De civ. D. 9.23 (I, 400 Dombart/Kalb)   86
De civ. D. 10.1 (I, 401 Dombart/Kalb)   85–6
De civ. D. 19.21 (II, 391 Dombart/Kalb)   96
De civ. D. 19.22 (II, 392 Dombart/Kalb)   84
Ep. 16 (Maximus of Madaura; PL 33.82)
  32 n. 54, 33

Callimachus, Hymn to Artemis 224–5
  134 n. 93

Cassius Dio 63.20.5   159 n. 105

Celsus   8–9, 29, 41 n. 18
  See also Origen, Contra Celsum

Chrysippus, and pagan monotheism   70–5

Cicero
Div. 2.4–7   39 n. 13
Div. 2.148–9   38
Nat. d.   147
Nat. d. 1.13.32   62
Nat. d. 2.27   46 n. 35, 152 n. 71

Cleanthes, Hymn to Zeus   68, 152 n. 63, 175

Clement of Alexandria
Protrep. 6.71.1   64, 65
Strom. 5.1.13.3   116 n. 15
Strom. 5.12.76   66
Strom. 5.14.108.4   64, 65

Cornelius Labeo, *On the Oracle of Clarian Apollo*
118

Cyril of Alexandria
De adoratione in Spiritu et Veritate 3.92 (*PG* 68,
281c) 195 n. 106
In Julianum 9.306B 110 n. 34

Demochares, *FGrH* 75 F 2 129 n. 69

Deuteronomy 6.4 105, 152
28 103 n. 14

Dio Chrysostom 29
Or. 31.11.8–10 113 n. 2

Diogenes Laertius
7.135–7 71–2
7.138 125 n. 53

Diogenes of Sinope, on cults 66

Dionysius of Halicarnassus 1.74 152 n. 69

Douris, *FGrH* 76 F 13 129 n. 69

Epiphanius, *Panarion* 80.1–2 197 n. 115

Eusebius
Praeparatio evangelica 3.15.3 137 n. 112
Praeparatio evangelica 13.13.35 64
Praeparatio evangelica 14.5 24 n. 32

Firmicus Maternus, *Mathesis* 5 *praef.* 166 n. 144

Galen, on pagan monotheism 75–81
De curandi ratione per venae sectionem 23
(11.314.18–315.7 Kuhn) 75
De libris propriis 2 (Scripta Minora 11, p. 99, 9–11
Müller) 75
De placitis Hippocratis et Platonis 9.7.12–14,
p. 588, 20–6 De Lacy 78
De propriis placitis 2 76, 78
De propriis placitis 14 79

Gregory of Nazianzus
Carmina (*PG* 37, 1571) 139 n. 120
Oratio 18.5 179 n. 52, 196 n. 131

Gregory of Nysa, *Refutatio Confessionis Eunomii*
38 (11, 327 Jaeger) 196 n. 112

Heraclitus 26
frg. B 52 165 n. 143

Herodotus
1.119 152 n. 69

Homer
Il. 4.397 152 n. 69
Od. 7.65 152 n. 69

Josephus
AJ 16.14 123 n. 47
Autobiography 244 160 n. 115

Julian
Contra Galilaeos, 72.20–1 110 n. 34
Ep. et leg. no. 89, 454a Bidez/Cumont 19,
145 n. 19
Ep. et leg. no. 134 Bidez/Cumont 161 n. 120
Or. 2 (*Basileus Helios*).10, 136A 157 n. 95
Or. 2 (*Basileus Helios*).16, 157A 158 n. 102

Justin, on pagan and Christian monotheism
84

[Justin]
Cohortatio ad Graecos 20.1 (*PTS* 32, 50), 22.1
(*PTS* 32, 55), 25.4 (*PTS* 32, 57)
87 n. 19

Lactantius
Div. inst. 1.5.18–19 62–3, 66
Div. inst. 1.7.1 116 n. 18
De ira Dei 11.14 62–3

Lucian
Alexander 24 115 n. 14
Icaromenippus 9 141

Macrobius
Sat. 1.17.1 163 n. 136
Sat. 1.17.7 152–3
Sat. 1.18.18–20 118 n. 28, 147 n. 30, 157 n. 95
Sat. 1.20.18 148 n. 36
Sat. 1.24.2 148
In somn. 1.2.20 148 n. 41

Marinus
Proclus 19, 20–6 143 n. 10
Proclus 19, 29–30 148 n. 42

Mark the Deacon, *Life of Porphyry* 31.2 155

Martyrium Pionii 19.10 156 n. 89

Menander Rhetor
2.381.10–14, 2.417.27–30 123 n. 47

Minucius Felix, *Octavius* 18.11 163 n. 128

Numenius 29
frg. 1b Des Places [Origen, *Contra Celsum* 1.15]
  60
frg. 11.13–14 Des Places 157 n. 95

Olympiodorus, Comm. on Plato, *Gorgias* 4.3
  (p. 32 Westerink) 83, 110 n. 40

Origen 8–9
Contra Celsum 41 n. 18
Contra Celsum 1.1 (*GCS* Orig. 1, 56) 89–90, 95
Contra Celsum 1.23 (*GCS* Orig. 1, 73) 91 n. 32
Contra Celsum 5.25 (*GCS* Orig. 2, 26) 91–2
Contra Celsum 5.28 (*GCS* Orig. 2, 28–9) 92–3
Contra Celsum 7.36 (*GCS* Orig. 2, 186) 89
Contra Celsum 7.68 (*GCS* Orig. 2, 217) 88 n. 20
Contra Celsum 7.69 (*GCS* Orig. 2, 218–19) 89
Contra Celsum 8.2 (*GCS* Orig. 2, 222) 88 n. 20,
  94
Contra Celsum 8.11 (*GCS* Orig. 2, 228) 94
Contra Celsum 8.72 (*GCS* Orig. 2, 288) 94–5
In Genesim homilia 14.3 (*GCS* Orig. 6.123–4) 84

Orphic hymns (Quandt, 2nd edn 1955)
2.1; 10.13; 11.10; 16.9; 27.4; 36.1; 40.1; 41.1; 42.2;
  45.2; 50.2; 52.1; 56.1; 59.2 132 n. 84
4.8; 8.1; 9.7; 34.8; 61.2; 62.1 135 n. 98
4.8; 8.17; 10.4; 12.6; 19.2; 61.6; 66.5 138 n. 119
8.3; 10.10; 12.9; 12.13 117 n. 20
10.4; 18.17; 29.10 137 n. 115
10.5; 15.1; 83.1 137 n. 112
12.4; 45.2 137 n. 115
16.7; 29.11; 68.1 131 n. 81

Orphicorum fragmenta (Kern)
239 113 n. 2
248.5 137 n. 112
248.9–10 117 n. 20

Ovid, *Fasti* 1.611–23 160 n. 109

Parmenides, *On true knowledge* 102

Pausanias 2.28, 5.15.5, 9.85 171 n. 15

Philo
De aeternitate mundi 49 74
De decalogo 61 (IV, 282 Cohn/Wendland)
  88 n. 20
De specialibus legibus 1.31 (V, 8 Cohn/Wendland)
  88 n. 20

Philodemus, *De pietate* 7 62

Plato
Euthyphron 26
Gorgias 83
Laws 72
Laws 10 59
Laws 10, 886a–b9, 886d3ff., 889e–890a3 63
Phaedo 74
Sophist 251b 64
Timaeus 72–3, 77, 85

Plautus, *Trin.* 823–4 146

Pliny (elder), *HN* 33.12.41 157 n. 99

Pliny (younger), *Ep.* 10.96 177 n. 48

Plotinus, *Enneads* 6.8 68

Plutarch 25, 29
Brut. 24.7 123 n. 47
De communibus notitiis 31–6, 1075b 71–2, 74
On the E at Delphi 393c 152
De stoicorum repugnantiis 1034b 66
De stoicorum repugnantiis 38–41 71–2, 74
De stoicorum repugnantiis 1051f–1052b 71

Poetae epici Graeci II.1 Bernabé
frg. 102 F 135 n. 98
frgs. 243, 377, 31 F 117 n. 20

Porphyry 84
Abst. 2.19.5 116 n. 15
Abst. 2.49 148 n. 42
Contra Christianos frg. 76 Harnack 32 n. 54

Servius, Comm. on Vergil, *G.* 1.5 143 n. 8

Simplicius, *De caelo* p. 485, 19–22 = frg. 49 Rose
  68

Stobaeus, *Ecl.* 2.1.33, p. 15, 6–10 Wachsmuth 65

Stoicorum veterum fragmenta I, 264 (Zeno,
  Politeia) 66

Strabo
12.5.2, 567 163 n. 132, 173 n. 30
16.2.37, 761 195 n. 105

Synesius of Cyrene 53

Tacitus, *Ann.* 3.61.1 114

Tertullian 56
Adversus Praxean 7 57
De spect. 25.5 159 n. 105

Theodoret, *Graecorum affectionum curatio* 1.75
64

Theosophia Tubingensis
13.105–8 (*Theosophorum Graecorum fragmenta*
pp. 8–9 Erbse) 116 n. 18
21 (*Theosophorum Graecorum fragmenta* p. 15
Erbse) 139 n. 120
22 (*Theosophorum Graecorum fragmenta* p. 15
Erbse) 135 n. 98
27 (*Theosophorum Graecorum fragmenta* p. 19
Erbse) 137 n. 115, 138 n. 119
35 (*Theosophorum Graecorum fragmenta* p. 23
Erbse) 147 n. 30
38 (*Theosophorum Graecorum fragmenta* p. 25
Erbse) 147 n. 30
39 (*Theosophorum Graecorum fragmenta* p. 26
Erbse) 113, 147 n. 30, 149 n. 43
42 (*Theosophorum Graecorum fragmenta* p. 27
Erbse) 139 n. 120, 147 n. 30, 151 n. 58
48 (*Theosophorum Graecorum fragmenta* p. 31
Erbse) 139 n. 20

Varro 84
Antiquitates 29
Antiquitates 1.3 (Augustine, *De civ. D.* 4.22)
149 n. 44

Xenophon 26, 39
Memorabilia 1.4 65
Memorabilia 4.3 56, 65, 66, 77

Inscriptions (arranged geographically as in *SEG*;
see also the list of Hypsistos inscriptions at
pp. 198–208)

Achaea
Akraephia: *IG* VII 2712 128,
160 n. 115
Athens: *IG* II², 4514 129, 138 n. 117
IJO I, Ach no. 28 194 n. 99
Delphi: *F.Delphes* III.4, 304 12 n. 41
Queyrel (2001), 350 no. 5 (*SEG* 51 (2001), 617)
156 n. 88
Queyrel (2001), 357–8 no. 10 (*SEG* 51 (2001),
622) 159 n. 107
Queyrel (2001), 357–8 no. 11 (*SEG* 51 (2001),
623) 155 n. 82
Queyrel (2001), 364 no. 14 (*SEG* 51 (2001), 626)
156 n. 88
SEG 51 (2001) 613–31 126–7
Epidaurus: *IG* XIV, 966 163 n. 127
Kerkyra: *IG* XI² 1, 1024 121
Megalopolis: *SEG* 28 (1978), 421
163 n. 126

Nemea: Museum inv. ST 783 163 n. 127
Sparta: *SEG* 31 (1981), 361 125 n. 53
Thespiae: *IG* VII, 1828 140 n. 125

Thessaly
Methone: *IG* IX.2, 1201 137 n. 115
Pherae: *SEG* 28 (1978), 528 121 n. 40
Thessalonica: *IG* X.2, 69 and 70 174 n. 32,
178 n. 50, 181 n. 63, 184

Thrace
Maronea: *RICIS* I, 114/020 (Grandjean (1975))
131 n. 81, 151
SEG 53 (2003), 659A 122 n. 41

North Shore of Black Sea
Chersonesos: *IOSPE* I², 352 134 n. 92
SEG 38 (1988), 748 172 n. 22
Gorgippia: *IJO* I, BS nos. 20 and 22
181 n. 61
Panticapaeum: *IJO* I, BS nos. 5–9 192 n. 94
IJO I, BS no. 7 193–4
Phanagorea: *IJO* I, BS nos. 17–18 192 n. 94

Aegean Islands
Andros: *IG* XII.5, 739 122 n. 42, 139 n. 121,
172 n. 21
Cos: *IJO* II, no. 6 191 n. 90
Crete: *SEG* 33 (1983), 736 137 n. 115
Delos: *RICIS* I, 202/0101 162 n. 123
Lindos: *LSCG Suppl.* 108 116 n. 15
Rheneia: *IJO* I, Ach no. 70 133 n. 89
Rhodes: *IG* XII.1, 893 191 n. 90
Thasos: *IG* XII.8, 613 155 n. 79

Italy
Calabria: Degrassi, *ILLRP* 511 (*SC de
Bacchanalibus*) 50 n. 56
Lorium: *JIWE* I, no. 12 191 n. 89
Pola: *JIWE* I, no. 9 191 n. 89
Rome: *CIL* VI, 532 156
CIMRM I, 463 149–50
IGUR 94–7 118 n. 27
IGUR 105 138 n. 118
IGUR 129 (*CIL* VI, 50) 173 n. 26
IGUR 136 173 n. 27
IGUR 148 (*SIG*³ 1173) 123 n. 48
IGUR 194 138 n. 118
JIWE II, no. 207 191 n. 90
JIWE II, no. 392 191 n. 89
JIWE II, no. 627 191 n. 90
Vermaseren and Van Essen (1965), 187
149 n. 41
Signia (Latium): *AE* 1996, 370 140 n. 126
Venosa: *JIWE* I, no. 113 191 n. 89

Gaul
Vasio Vocontiorum: *IG* xiv, 2482   115

Hispania
Panoias: *RICIS* ii, 602/0501   172 n. 19

Britannia
Deva: *SEG* 37 (1987), 840   138 n. 117

Asia Minor?
Graf (1985), 70–3   125 n. 53

Caria
Aphrodisias: *IJO* ii, no. 14   190
MAMA viii, 471, 477   130 n. 77
Roueché (1989a), 126 no. 83 i   128 n. 65
SEG 54 (2004), 1020   130 n. 77
Mylasa: *I.Mylasa* i, 306   129 n. 70
Stratonicea: *I.Stratonikaia* 10   135 n. 95
I.Stratonikaia 197, 224, 291, 527, 1101   137 n. 116
I.Stratonikaia 509, 1111, 1115, 1116   155 n. 78
I.Stratonikaia 513, 523, 527, 1101   134 n. 9
Şahin (2002), 17 no. 38 (*SEG* 52 (2002), 1106)   155 n. 78
SEG 38 (1998), 1087   125 n. 1087

Ionia
Didyma: *I.Didyma* 217   136 n. 102
SGO i, 84–5 no. 01/19/06   119
Ephesus: *I.Ephesos* 24 (*LSAM* 31)   114 n. 9
I.Ephesos 27   134 n. 94, 137 n. 116
I.Ephesos 599   130 n. 74
I.Ephesos 1391   123 n. 47
I.Ephesos 3100   135 n. 97, 136 n. 105, 155 n. 79
SEG 43 (1993), 756   115 n. 10
Miletus: *Milet* vi.2, 699   137 n. 111
Milet vi.2, no. 940 (f)   194
Milet vi.2, no. 940 (g)   194
Milet vi.2, no. 940 (h)   194
OGI ii, 755 and 756   163 n. 133
SEG 45 (1995), 1612   139 n. 120
Tralles: *IJO* ii, no. 49   191 n. 88

Lydia
North-East Lydia: Herrmann and Malay (2007), 110–13 no. 84   114 n. 6
Herrmann and Malay (2007), 113–16 no. 85   125–6, 136 n. 102
Malay (2003) (*SEG* 53 (2003), 1344)   156
Malay (2004) (*SEG* 54 (2004), 1776)   125 n. 51
Petzl (1994), 5–6 no. 4   137 n. 114
Petzl (1994), 7–11 no. 5   126 n. 35
Petzl (1994), 58–9 no. 50   159 n. 106
Petzl (1994), 68–9 no. 57   136 n. 105
Petzl (1994), 73–6 no. 59   160 n. 111

Petzl (1994), 122–5 no. 106   134 n. 90
Petzl (1994), 140–1 no. 122   135 n. 99, 166 n. 145
Robert and Robert (1948), 24 n. 2   125 n. 52
SEG 39 (1989), 1275   125 n. 51
SEG 39 (1989), 1278   125 nn. 51 and 53
SEG 42 (1992), 1280   122 n. 53
SEG 48 (1998), 1427   153 n. 77
SEG 49 (1999), 1588   120 n. 37
SEG 53 (2003), 1344   122–3
Strubbe (1997), 46 no. 51 (*SEG* 29 (1979), 1179)   124 n. 59
TAM v.1, 75   135 n. 97, 140 n. 129, 156
TAM v.1, 246   131, 153, 154Fig.1
TAM v.1, 247   153 n. 6
TAM v.1, 359   120 n. 36
TAM v.1, 450   125 n. 52
TAM v.1, 453   136 n. 101
TAM v.1, 575   125 n. 52
TAM v..2, 1306   125 n. 31
Philadelphia: *IJO* ii, no. 27   191 n. 88

Aiolis
Kyme: *I.Kyme* 41   122 n. 42

Mysia
Kyzikos: *SIG³* 798   122 n. 41
Pergamon: Habicht (1969), 128 no. 113b   134 n. 94
SEG 54 (2004), 1243 bis   176 n. 40

Bithynia
Calchedon: *SEG* 37 (1987), 1036   135 n. 98
Iuliopolis: *SEG* 50 (2000), 1222   129, 134 n. 94, 136 n. 104
Kios: *I.Kios* 21   138 n. 118
Nicaea: *I.Iznik* 1121, 1512   137 n. 115
I.Iznik 1141–2   130 n. 78
Prusa: *I.Prusa* i, no. 115   191 n. 91

Paphlagonia
Amastris: *SEG* 50 (2000), 1225   117 n. 22
Caesarea: Marek (1993), 193 no. 19   134 n. 93
Marek (1993), 194 no. 24   137 n. 112
Neoclaudiopolis: *SEG* 50 (2000), 1233   133

Galatia
Ancyra territory: *RECAM* ii no. 209b   163 n. 132, 187 n. 78
Tavium: *RECAM* ii no. 418   163 n. 132

Phrygia
Aizanoi: Lehmler and Wörrle (2006), 76–8   124 n. 50
SEG 40 (1990), 1227   163 n. 131
SEG 42 (1992), 1192   140 n. 130

Alsenos sanctuary: Drew-Bear, Thomas and
    Yildizturan (1999), 236 no. 364   138 n. 119
Drew-Bear, Thomas and Yildizturan (1999), 335
    no. 541   121 n. 39
Appia: *MAMA* x, 158   134 n. 98, 138 n. 118
Hosios kai Dikaios sanctuary: Malay (2005)
    (*SEG* 55 (2005), 1418)   182 n. 66
Lairbenos sanctuary: Ramsay (1889), 223 no. 11
    173 n. 28
SEG 50 (2000), 1244, 1256, 1270   137 n. 116
Nakoleia: *MAMA* v, 186 and 211   163 n. 131
SEG 51 (2001), 1801   133 n. 85, 137 n. 115
Neapolis: *I.Sultan Dağı* 509   125 n. 53
Philomelion: *I.Sultan Dağı* 44   133 n. 85
Sağır (Pisidian Antioch): *SEG* 6, 550   136 n. 100
Tiberiopolis: *MAMA* x, 261   163 n. 131

Pisidia
Andeda: CMRDM I, 129   163 n. 130, 180
Cibyratis: *SEG* 47 (1997), 1810–11   176 n. 41
Melli: *SEG* 53 (2003), 1587   117 n. 23, 178 n. 51,
    183

Pamphylia
Aspendos: *SEG* 38 (1988), 1335 (*IJO* II, no. 218)
    137 n. 109, 176 n. 42
Perge: *I.Perge* 331   130 n. 76
Side: *I.Side* 377   137 n. 116

Lycia
Oinoanda: *SEG* 27 (1977), 933   116 n. 17, 139,
    175, 183
Nysa: *TAM* II.2, 737   164 n. 135, 181–3
Xanthos; *SEG* 46 (1996), 1726   133 n. 89

Lycaonia
Iconium: *MAMA* VIII, 298   163 n. 131

Cappadocia
Ramsay (1883), 322 no. 52   140 n. 129

Cyprus
Peterson (1926), 281–2   138 n. 119

Babylonia
Susa: *SGO* III no. 12/03/1   129 n. 70, 130 n. 76,
    132 n. 84, 135 n. 98
SEG 7, 12–13   137 n. 135

Bactria
Kuliab?: *SEG* 54 (2004), 1569   130

Syria
Ainkania: *SEG* 37 (1987), 1145   160 n. 110
Berytos: *SEG* 45 (1995), 1897   137 n. 115

El-Dumeir: *IJO* III, 63–5 Syr. 41 (*CIJ* II 848)   105
Gebel Bariha: *IGLS* II, 536   106
IGLS II, 537, 543, 544   106
Palmyra: *CIG* 4502   138 n. 18

Palaestina
Ascalon: Di Segni (1994), 104 no. 31 (*SEG* 41
    (1991), 1544)   108, 161 n. 118
Caesarea Maritima: *SEG* 49 (1999), 2054
    128 n. 65
Jerusalem: Di Segni (1994), no. 28   157 n. 97
Samaria: Crowfoot, Crowfoot and Kenyon
    (1954), 36 no. 9   156 n. 84
Crowfoot, Crowfoot and Kenyon (1954), 37 no.
    14   156 n. 84
Flusser (1975)   155

Arabia
Bostra: Welles (1938), nos. 345–8   161 n. 121
Petra: *SEG* 51 (2001), 2074   130 n. 79

Egypt
Abydos: *SEG* 47 (1997), 2098   137 n. 109
Alexandria: Kayser (1994), 198–9 no. 59
    137 n. 115
SEG 48 (1998), 1961–2, 1964–5   130 n. 75
Medinet-Madi: Bernand (1969), 632–3 no. 175
    132 n. 84, 152, 164, 172 n. 22
Ptolemais: Peterson (1926), 238   148 n. 37
Talmis: Bernand (1969), 573–6 no. 165   119 n. 31

Cyrenaica
Cyrene: Fraser (1962), 25–7   137 n. 112, 173
RICIS II, 701/0103   152, 172 n. 20

Papyri
Derveni Papyrus   39, 54
PGM I, 262; II, 83 and 98; IV, 1924, 2037, 2098;
    VII, 330; XIV, 11   133 n. 89
PGM I, 296–327   165 n. 140
PGM IV, 1169–70   149 n. 48
PGM IV, 1708–15   158 n. 101
P.Gur. 1   128 n. 61, 157 n. 96
P.Oxy I, 235 no. 1382   150 n. 50
P.Oxy XI, 1380   139 n. 121
P.Oxy XI, 1382   135 n. 96

Gems, rings and amulets
Bonner and Nock (1948)   148 n. 37, 155–6 n. 83
CMRDM II, 174 no. A8   125 n. 51
Henig and McGregor (2004), no. 13.29
    162 n. 125
Michel (2001), no. 24   152 n. 6
Michel (2001), no. 31   150 n. 53
Michel (2001), no. 37   161 n. 116

Michel (2001), nos. 334 and 338   165 n. 142

Michel (2001), no. 484   157 n. 92

Michel (2001), no. 543   149 n. 46

Nock (1940), 313   108 n. 30

Peterson (1926), 190   151

Peterson (1926), 209   155 n. 79

Peterson (1926), 237   151 n. 57

Philipp (1986), no. 55   157 n. 94

Richter (1956), no. 253   157 n. 94

Richter (1956), no. 346   148

Sanzi (2002), 219 Fig. 6   158 n. 100

Spier (1992), no. 359   158 n. 100

Made in the USA
Columbia, SC
04 September 2024

41645286R00137